Y0-BTB-762

Founded in 1972, the Institute for Research on Public Policy is an independent, national, non-profit organization.

IRPP seeks to improve public policy in Canada by generating research, providing insight and sparking debate that will contribute to the public policy decision-making process and strengthen the quality of the public decisions made by Canadian governments, citizens, institutions and organizations.

IRPP's independence is assured by an endowment fund, to which federal and provincial governments and the private sector have contributed.

Institute for Research on Public Policy

Institut de recherche en politiques publiques

Fondé en 1972, l'Institut de recherche en politiques publiques (IRPP) est un organisme canadien, indépedent et sans but lucratif.

L'IRPP cherche à améliorer les politiques publiques canadiennes en encourageant la recherche, en menant de l'acance de nouvelles perspectives et en suscitant des débats qui contribueront au processus décisionnel en matière de politques publiques et qui rehausseront la qualité des décisions que prennent les gouvernements les citoyens. les institutions et les organismes canadiens.

L'indépendance de l'IRPP est assurée par les revenus d'un fonds de dotation auquel ont souscrit les gouvernements fédéral et provinciaux, ainsi que le secteur privé.

29

SIMON FRASER UNIVERSITY
W.A.C. BENNETT LIBRARY

HJ 8513 I8 2004

editors | **Christopher Ragan & William Watson**

is the debt war over?

DISPATCHES FROM CANADA'S FISCAL FRONTLINE

Copyright © The Institute for Research on Public Policy (IRPP) 2004
All rights reserved

Printed in Canada
Dépôt légal 2004

Bibliothèque nationale du Québec

National Library of Canada
Cataloguing in Publication Data

Is the debt war over?
edited by Christopher Ragan, William Watson.

Includes bibliographical references.
ISBN 0-88645-206-6

1. Debts, Public—Canada. 2. Fiscal policy—Canada.
3. Expenditures, Public—Canada.
I. Ragan, Christopher II. Watson, William G.
III. Institute for Research on Public Policy. IV. Title.

HJ8513.I8 2004   336.3'4'0971   C2004-900387-9

Suzanne Ostiguy McIntyre
Project Coordinator

Copy Editing and Proofreading
Marilyn Banting

Design and Production
Studio Duotone inc.

Cover Illustration
Studio Duotone Inc.

Published by
The Institute for Research on Public Policy (IRPP)
L'Institut de recherche en politiques publiques
1470 Peel Street, Suite 200
Montreal, Quebec H3A 1T1
Tel: 514 985 2461   Fax: 514 985 2559
email: irpp@irpp.org www.irpp.org

contents

acknowledgements

Some debts – though not public debt, alas – can be discharged partly by acknowledging them. Our greatest debt in the preparation of this volume is to Gerald MacGarvie of the Harold Crabtree Foundation. Three years ago, Gerald called Bill Watson to ask whether something could be done to focus public attention on the still serious problem of the country's public debts, which seemed to have been forgotten in the euphoria over the fact that, for the first time in a generation, most Canadian governments had finally eliminated their deficits. Our response was a hopelessly conventional one for academics. We proposed to commission a set of papers by several of the country's leading economists, to invite them to a conference and to publish the conference proceedings. Although we suspect Gerald may have been hoping for something more dramatic, the Crabtree Foundation undertook to sponsor the enterprise and, in addition to a very generous financial contribution, provided unstinting moral and practical support throughout. We hope Gerald and his colleagues at the Foundation will not be displeased by what has been produced, which we believe represents the best thinking on this issue currently available in Canadian economics.

Our second greatest debt is to Hugh Segal, president of the Institute for Research on Public Policy, and to all his colleagues at the Institute. The IRPP very kindly supplemented the Crabtree Foundation's grant and shepherded the project through the original conference all the way to the publication of this book. We are very grateful to Suzanne Ostiguy McIntyre, Institute vice-president, operations, who managed the project, to Suzanne Lambert, who ran the conference

i

with her usual mixture of charm and efficiency, to Marilyn Banting, who provided patient and perspicacious copy editing, to Francesca Worrall and Chantal Letourneau, who tied up all the loose ends, and to Studio Duotone who laid out the book's pages and provided our cover design.

We are also grateful to our home institution, McGill University, which hosted the conference, and to our colleagues in McGill's Department of Economics for their co-operation.

Finally, we thank the 20 paper-writers and discussants who accepted the challenge we set them and with great patience and professionalism responded to our many and sometimes variable requests for elaborations and modifications of their work both in substance and style. We naturally are prejudiced but it seems to us that in view of the care, knowledge and wisdom they bring to the analysis of the question whether conquering the deficit is enough or whether the nation's finances need further attention, all Canadians may eventually be in their debt.

Christopher Ragan
William Watson

is the debt war over? introduction and summary

Christopher Ragan and William Watson

In the mid-1990s, Canadian governments declared war on deficits. In a famous sound bite in his budget update of October 1994, then-federal Finance Minister Paul Martin declared that his government would hit its fiscal targets, which did not yet include a balanced budget, "come hell or high water." In 1997, ahead of the schedule outlined in his party's election manifesto, the federal government produced its first balanced budget in a generation, and the first in a series of a half dozen so far, with no end in sight. Provincial governments have not all been as successful as Ottawa in eliminating their deficits, but both public and professional opinion of deficits is now so thoroughly disapproving that it seems reasonable to talk in terms of the war against the deficit as having been won, convincingly.

As often happens in war, victory creates new problems. As deficits were vanquished in the late 1990s, the country faced the dilemma of "what to do with the surplus?" Leaving aside the logical difficulty that a surplus that is spent or used for tax reduction is no longer a surplus, there were three broad options. First, should the current excess of government revenues over government expenditures be spent on new programs? Second, should it be devoted to tax cuts? Or third, should it be devoted to a new fiscal war, this one aimed at reducing the country's debt, which, as this book goes to press in the winter of 2004, stands at $527 billion for the federal government and $786 billion for all levels of government (federal, provincial-territorial and municipal).[1]

Confronted with this three-pronged choice between tax cuts, new spending and debt reduction, Canadian governments, and especially the one in Ottawa, have answered, resoundingly, "yes!" At the federal level, the government has explicitly budgeted tax cuts and new spending and has treated debt reduction as a residual: if a special "contingency fund" is not needed in a year, then it will be devoted to debt reduction. In some years, all funds not explicitly budgeted have been used for debt reduction, of which there has been some $62 billion since 1997.

The question posed by this book and by the October 2002 conference on which it is based is, in effect, is that enough? Is the current rather modest pace of debt reduction – at the federal level a 10.5-percent decline from the peak in 1997, in the provinces just 3.8 percent from the peak in 1999 – enough? Or does more have to be done? To put things more dramatically, is the debt war over?

In answering this question, a number of subsidiary questions present themselves: How big is the debt? Where did it come from? (that is, what caused it?). What, if anything did we get for the debt? What are the costs of continuing to run such a large debt, and therefore what would be the benefits of reducing it? Can economics say anything about the optimal size of the debt? Is zero best? Or is some continuing debt desirable? And if we are to continue to have at least some government debt, what is the best way of managing it? Finally, do we need legislated "fiscal rules" in order to control either budget deficits or the level of debt? Although this seemed to us to be more than enough questions, you will see that one of our conference commentators (Jack Mintz of the C. D. Howe Institute) wished we had asked at least one more.

To answer each of the major questions we did pose, we brought together two distinguished Canadian economists, one to present a paper and one to provide a critique of the paper. The purpose of this introduction is to summarize the papers and commentaries and then to provide our own summary view on what this book says about whether the debt war either is or should be over.

How Big Is the Debt?

A first step in all this is to try to determine just how much Canadian governments owe. Of course, if a government's net liabilities are offset by equally large expected receipts then even a very large debt might not warrant a continued war. So what we are really interested in is the government's *net worth*: how much it owes, how much is it owed and whether the difference between the two is manageable.

To address this problem, we called on *William Robson*, senior vice-president at the C. D. Howe Institute in Toronto, who for some time has been interested in the problems posed by government debt. His paper is an impressively comprehensive discussion of how best, when estimating governments' net worth, to count the many different kinds of activities in which modern governments are involved.

Robson begins by asking the basic question why we might be concerned about the government's net worth. He proposes three answers and then goes on to provide an estimate of Canadian governments' net worth customized to answer each question.

Government net worth is an indicator of short-term liquidity. A government might fail to make its debt payments in full or on time and such a liquidity crisis could lead to financial instability. This was a clear possibility in some Canadian capitals during the Mexican peso crisis in 1994.

Government net worth is an indicator of longer-term solvency. A government may be in good financial shape today but, if no existing policy is changed, it may face a serious deterioration in its financial position in future. This concern comes from the government's failure to take proper account of the longer-term sustainability of its spending and tax polices. It points toward a calculation of net worth that tries to include as many future spending obligations and sources of revenue as possible, even if some such obligations are moral and implicit rather than legal and explicit.

Government net worth affects private sector behaviour. Changes in the government's balance sheet may affect behaviour outside the public sector and then feed back onto the public finances. These feedback effects should be reflected in any calculation of the government's net worth. (In the end, Robson does not attempt the very difficult task of producing a separate balance sheet incorporating such considerations but instead confines himself to describing possible feedback effects that would have to be taken into account if such an exercise were attempted.)

Viewed from these three perspectives, how do Canada's public debts stack up? On the first criterion, the possibility that our governments will default at any early date, the answer is: not at all badly. Before coming to this conclusion, Robson makes a number of small adjustments from valuation methods used in the official public accounts. These involve: foreign-exchange reserves, holdings of equity in Crown corporations, the carrying value of loans and securities, the net financial assets of workers' compensation boards and deposit-insurance corporations, federal pre-bookings of spending programs, the valuation of physical assets, coins, marketable debt, and, finally, deferred compensation. On balance, these changes actually make Canadian government's financial position look better than it appears in the official accounts. As of March 2000, the latest date for which complete data were available when our conference was held, Robson estimates, "net government obligations that matter for near-term liquidity amounted to some $760 billion ... about $70 billion less than the total reported" in the government's own Financial Management System. Although "this is still a sizeable amount, equal to 71 percent of 2000 GDP ... historical valuations along these lines would have yielded a pronounced decline in this ratio from its position four years earlier, and an update to 31 March 2002 would show it around 10 percentage points lower yet." Robson concludes that "from the point of view of credit-market participants, this was a decisive improvement in Canada's liquidity situation," an improvement reflected in the credit agencies' decision to return Canada to triple-A status. How big a deterioration in this position would be required to raise concerns of the sort that were common in the mid-1990s? Robson argues that as of October 2002 a 25-percentage-point increase in the debt-to-GDP ratio would probably cause problems, but "with GDP of about $1.2 trillion, this would amount to an increase in net liquidity-oriented obligations of some $420 billion – not a possibility that, given the current fiscal stance of Canadian governments, is likely to concern credit-market participants."

Turning to his longer-term analysis, Robson notes that many government obligations that loom large over the next few decades are more moral than legal. Unless the courts extend their discretion over social policy even further than they have to date, it is within the power of Parliament and the provincial legislatures to alter the terms under which they deliver education, health care and other social services. Still, many Canadians assume their governments are committed to continue to provide public services at least as good as today's and may make their personal plans on that basis. So it is useful to try to estimate the financial implications of running public services at a given level of quality into the future. Of course, part of this implicit contract with government is that Canadians expect to continue to pay taxes in order to finance these public services, so any reasonable estimate also needs to take into account the future inflow of revenues. The approach Robson adopts is to assume that Canadians expect to pay the same share of their income in taxes as they currently do. He therefore counts as an unfunded liability (i.e., government debt) any expenditure that would require taxes to rise as a share of GDP. This does not mean such expenditures would remain literally unfunded: governments may eventually decide to raise taxes in order to fund them. But as things currently stand, with the amount of GDP growth that it is reasonable to expect and with taxes held constant as a share of GDP, there would not be enough money to fund them.

Among the spending programs whose future funding requirements Robson estimates are: the Child Tax Benefit; primary, secondary and postsecondary education; medicare; the Canada and Quebec Pension Plans; deposit insurance; workers' compensation; and the Old Age Security/Guaranteed Income Supplement program. On the asset side, governments can expect to pick up more revenue in future as taxes which for the moment have been deferred – in Registered Retirement Savings Plans, for instance – come due. In each case, he looks out 50 years, figures out the unfunded liability (or asset) in each future year, and then computes its present (or "capitalized") value using a discount rate of 6 percent.

Robson's long-term assessment of Canadian governments' net worth is not as encouraging as his short-term assessment. Canada's governments have large unfunded liabilities. The current capital value of their total unfunded liabilities, both long term and short, is $1.1 trillion, or 107 percent of 2000 GDP. If economic growth does not proceed more quickly than the 3.9 percent Robson assumes, taxes will have to rise as a share of GDP to keep spending programs at their current per capita levels.

Robson makes a clear distinction between the federal and provincial governments. As he explains, "Ottawa can look forward to large amounts of deferred taxes, while the projected reductions in the share of GDP required to finance the Child Benefit and Ottawa's relatively modest support for postsecondary students largely offset its exposure to the OAS/GIS system. The bottom line – a net liability of about $355 billion – is better than that shown by conventional measures." In other words, Robson's calculation of the federal government's total debt is actually *less* than the numbers we usually see. Things are not as promising for the provincial governments, however. As a group, they too can look forward to the payment of deferred taxes and they can expect sizeable inflows from their nonfinancial assets, as well as a demographic bonus as the number of school-age Canadians declines. But all this is swamped by health-care expenditures, which skyrocket as the population continues to age. In sum, total unfunded provincial liabilities are $360 billion, about 40 percent higher than the numbers we usually see. Adding the municipalities' very substantial physical assets to the provincial balance – the municipalities are "creatures of the provinces," after all – does not alter the now-common view that the federation is suffering a fiscal imbalance.

Robson argues that because of this imbalance Ottawa should not spend its current surpluses, as it obviously is tempted to do, but neither should it hand them over to the provinces in transfers: that would create tens more billions of dollars of public spending for which accountability was unclear. Rather, Ottawa should consider ceding tax room to the provinces, lowering federal tax rates and thereby enabling provinces to raise theirs.

Robson's third balance sheet, which in fact he does not calculate, is what he calls the "nongovernmental-behaviour-oriented" balance sheet. Here he is concerned with the effects that unfunded liabilities and the policy changes they may eventually lead to will have on the evolution of the Canadian economy. What he seems to be seeking is nothing less than a comprehensive cost-benefit calculus for the entire public sector. Some public assets that are currently unfunded may lead to increased private-sector incomes, and thus higher tax revenues, so that the assets will end up being self-funding. On the other hand, the higher taxes that may eventually be required to fund other assets may lead households and firms to change their behaviour in order to avoid the taxes, thus reducing government tax revenues. As David Johnson shows in a later paper, there has been some work on how the existence of public debt does or does not change private sector behaviour, but to our knowledge no study has yet used Robson's second balance sheet in assessing these affects, let alone his third.

In closing, Robson argues that the effects of our governments' unfunded liabilities on Canada's international competitiveness need to be examined carefully. Research from the Organisation for Economic Co-operation and Development (OECD) shows that Canada is not alone in having significant unfunded liabilities in its social programs. On the other hand, "Canada's position is relatively poor by comparison to several countries that might be considered our close competitors for migration and investment: the United States, Australia, and the United Kingdom." This leads Robson to conclude, in answer to the question that defines the conference, that "the debt war must continue if Canada hopes to maintain or improve its attractiveness as a place to work and invest."

In his comments on Robson's paper, *Stephen Ambler* of the Université du Québec à Montréal says that although he would have preferred to see more "sensitivity analysis" of the expenditure and revenue projections, that is, more simulations using different assumptions about discount and growth rates, he essentially agrees with Robson's conclusions, both about the short-term unlikelihood of a cash crisis and about the more serious nature of our long-term predicament. Robson's bottom line is that as of October 2002 combined Canadian government (federal plus provincial plus municipal) liabilities were $308 billion higher than conventional measures suggest. Applying a discount rate of 2.1 percent (Robson's rate of 6 percent minus expected nominal GDP growth of 3.9 percent) gives an annual debt service cost of $6.47 billion, or 0.59 percent of 2001 GDP. Although that is a large number in absolute dollars it is not so big in relation to GDP.

Ambler provides two reasons why we should not be complacent about this number, however. First, it is not the same across all Canadian jurisdictions: "some provinces would have to raise much more then 0.59 percent of their gross provincial product in order to meet their implicit future liabilities." Second, "for the problem to remain small it must be faced immediately." Robson's calculations assume there will be no new spending beyond 2001 levels. By contrast, Ambler argues that politicians wanting to leave legacies seem intent on driving down the surplus, in which case their real legacy may be "higher taxes for our children."

Where Did the Debt Come From?

Santayana wasn't necessarily right: knowing history does not necessarily mean not repeating it. Even people who have taken the time to learn about the past can fall captive to syndromes with an ancient ancestry: consider the Middle East or Northern Ireland. Exactly where Canada's debt came from is a more innocuous question but it is interesting in and of itself and there is at least the possibility that studying it may illuminate pitfalls that can be avoided in future. To take on this retrospection, we asked *Ronald Kneebone,* professor of economics at the University of Calgary, and *Jennifer Chung,* a University of Calgary graduate student in economics, to extend work they have been involved in for some time.

At first blush, "Where did the debt come from?" may seem a simple-minded question. Surely the debt came from Canada's governments running deficits: over the years they spent more than they taxed. That much is definitional. But behind the definitions what sorts of forces were at work? A political scientist might talk about changes in public opinion, institutional influences on how governments make budgetary decisions, and so on. Kneebone and Chung are economists and instead focus on three forces that can be quantified, and to which they aim to attach hard numbers. The three components that explain changes in the debt-to-GDP ratio are:

The structural component. Changes in the debt-to-GDP ratio caused by the government's decision to change its level of spending or taxation (not including interest payments on the debt).

The cyclical component. Changes in the debt-to-GDP ratio caused by the effect that changes in the level of economic activity have on the government's spending and tax revenues

The rate component. Changes in the debt-to-GDP ratio caused by changes in the interest rate that must be paid to service the existing stock of government debt, relative to the rate of growth of GDP.

Let's take these three components one at a time. On the first, the structural component, as government consciously decides to spend or tax more or less there will be an obvious effect on its budget deficit and thus on the path of the debt-to-GDP ratio. An increase in spending or a reduction in taxes will tend to increase the deficit; a reduction in spending or an increase in taxes will tend to reduce it. The structural component excludes interest payments, thus allowing a focus on that part of government expenditures over which the government really does have discretion. Excluding interest payments gives us the government's *primary balance*. And because this discretionary component is calculated as any change in the government's primary balance as it would be if the economy were operating at capacity, we therefore refer to the *structural primary balance*. Changes in the discretionary component are thus completely removed from swings in economic activity and are therefore the "purest" possible measure of changes in the stance of fiscal policy.

By contrast, the cyclical component is beyond the control of current government policy. Even if the government makes no changes in its spending or taxation plans, fluctuations in the level of economic activity will alter both its deficit and the debt-to-GDP ratio. An increase in activity will normally cause the deficit to decline: less has to be spent on employment insurance and similar items while income taxes on corporations and individuals bring in more revenue. An economic slowdown will automatically increase spending on the unemployed and reduce tax revenues, so the deficit and debt-to-GDP ratio will rise. Algebraically, this second component is equal to the difference between the *actual* primary balance and the *structural* primary balance, and it emerges only when the level of economic activity deviates from the economy's capacity.

The third component of the budgetary balance, the "rate effect," is also outside government's short-term discretion: neither market interest rates nor GDP growth rates are within the control of the fiscal authority. If the government is already in debt, any rise in interest rates will tend to increase the interest cost of servicing this debt, especially the part of government debt that is short term and so gets rolled over frequently. Thus, a rise in the interest rate tends to increase the debt-to-GDP ratio. In contrast, an increase in the growth rate of GDP means that the denominator of the debt-to-GDP ratio is growing faster, and thus the ratio itself tends to fall.

It is tempting to think of the second and third components as somehow not being the government's fault, because they are not discretionary. But in the longer run everything is discretionary. Over time, a government can respond to the effects of economic fluctuations on its revenues and spending by altering the fiscal rules. Or it can offset the unfavourable effects of higher interest rates on its existing debt by reducing the amount of debt it is carrying. Where short periods are concerned, however, it may be useful to think of the first component as discretionary and the second and third as being, for want of a better term, "automatic."

In their paper, Kneebone and Chung estimate these three separate components in the evolution of federal and provincial government debt for every year dating back to 1970, just before the start of the big debt buildup in the mid-1970s. Calculating the effect of interest rate changes on the existing debt is straightforward enough, but trying to estimate the structural deficit or surplus – what the budgetary balance would have been had the economy been at capacity instead of where it actually was – is trickier. "Capacity output," which is sometimes called "potential output" or "full-employment output," cannot be observed directly and so must be estimated. But this makes it controversial, especially since it very likely changes over time as demographic patterns and government policies change. In the end, the statistical methods that Kneebone and Chung use provide estimates of the economy's capacity that fall within the bounds normally used by the profession.

Armed with estimates of capacity output in each year, Kneebone and Chung then calculate how different spending programs and taxes respond to changes in output and use these estimates to calculate the structural primary balance, what the deficit would have been at capacity output. That in turn allows them to figure out how much of the actual deficit is a result of deficient economic output and how much a result of discretionary spending and tax decisions.

A crucial aspect of the analysis, it turns out, is that these three components of debt accumulation – the structural, cyclical and rate components – can be offsetting. Although a government may be increasing its structural deficit this may not show up in the public accounts either because the economy is at the top of a business cycle (so that tax revenues are buoyant and employment insurance expenditures declining) or because interest rates have been falling or GDP growth rates rising. In fact, Kneebone and Chung argue that this is precisely what happened to the federal government in the 1970s. In the early years of that decade, Ottawa undertook large-scale public expenditures in an ultimately misguided attempt to fight stagflation. It then compounded its problems mid-decade by indexing the personal income-tax system against inflation and introducing a number of new tax expenditures. The combined effect of higher structural spending and lower structural tax revenues was a higher structural deficit that should have set off alarm bells. But in fact the actual deficit and debt increased only modestly, at least as a share of GDP. The reason was that real interest rates were low in comparison to the relatively high rate of economic growth. The rate effect outweighed the structural effect.

Kneebone and Chung conclude that the structural deficits Ottawa incurred in the early and mid-1970s proved to be very expensive. Fooled by the offsetting decline in the rate component, policy makers seemed to conclude from the decade's experience that even very unfavourable economic circumstances – two OPEC shocks and a flirtation with out-of-control inflation – could not create a long-run budgetary problem. It was only in the early 1980s, after a sharp interest rate spike and a consequent recession turned both the cyclical and rate components unfavourable that the true seriousness of the structural problem became evident. Following its election in 1984, the Mulroney government began to reduce what by then had become a large structural deficit. This it did both by raising taxes and by holding structural spending constant as a share of GDP, thus allowing the growth of GDP to reduce the debt-to-GDP ratio. Although the recorded deficit remained stubbornly high, the primary deficit was eliminated by 1990: for the first time since the 1970s tax revenues now covered program (i.e., non-interest) spending.

Just as the primary deficit disappeared, however, the cyclical and rate components produced very large deficit numbers – $45 billion is the commonly quoted figure – that finally created the political consensus which allowed a new government to begin to move toward a balanced budget, which Jean Chrétien's Liberals did, very rapidly, from 1994 on. As of 2001, when Kneebone and Chung's analysis ends, the rate component had stopped contributing to increases in the debt ratio, which means that recent declines in the federal government's debt-to-GDP ratio have been due solely to the large structural surpluses Ottawa has been running.

What is the bottom line of this analysis? According to Kneebone and Chung, between 1970 and 1997 Ottawa accumulated $564 billion of new debt, fully three-quarters of the new debt built up by Canada's governments. Of this amount, $432 billion (or 77 percent) was accumulated as a result of a mismatch between structural expenditures and structural revenues; $12 billion (2 percent) was the result of the business cycle and $120 billion (21 percent) was due to the difference between the interest rate and the economy's growth rate. Although the structural component was clearly dominant, the rate component played a crucial role in the 1970s, when it camouflaged the emergence of a large structural deficit. After 1975, policy makers took almost 15 years to close the structural deficit that had been incurred fighting post-1970 stagflation and then another seven years in the 1990s to create a structural surplus large enough to offset interest payments, bring the recorded budget into balance, and pay down at least some federal debt.

Canada's provincial governments also contributed to the accumulation of public debt in the period 1970–97, though not nearly as much as Ottawa. As we have seen, the federal government was responsible for 75 percent of the increase in public debt over this period. Another 11 percent was due to Ontario, 9 percent to Quebec, and just 4 percent to the eight other provinces combined. To a certain extent, Ontario and Quebec suffered the same syndrome as Ottawa. In the 1970s, low interest rates and relatively high rates of economic growth obscured structural deficits. When the rate component turned sour (in 1982 for Quebec, though only in 1990 for Ontario) actual deficits began to rise. Ontario took action against its problem early on and in fact by 1980 had substantially reduced its structural deficit. Over the next decade it gradually eliminated its structural deficit but then in the *annus horribilis* of fiscal year 1991 all three components turned unfavourable. Even so, the structural deficit had been eliminated by the time the Harris government took office in 1995 and subsequent spending and tax cuts kept the primary budget in balance. In Quebec, by contrast, spending cuts did not begin in a serious way until the mid-1990s. Even so, the province was able to achieve a structural surplus by 1996.

In his comments on Ron Kneebone and Jennifer Chung's paper, Université Laval economist *Marc Van Audenrode* congratulates them on their development of a methodology that allows a breakdown of the various sources of the debt. But then he takes them to task, albeit gently, for not going the extra step and being more explicit about which particular policies created such a large debt problem for Canadian governments after the 1970s. Unfortunately, he argues, the technique they use is not well suited to this task. There are two main problems with it. The first is that the analysis depends on making a clear distinction between what is structural and what is cyclical, and this is much easier after the fact than before. For example, in hindsight, it seems clear that policy makers in the 1970s did let the structural deficit get out of hand. At the time, however, it was widely thought that the economic slowdown known as stagflation was temporary and that the deficits of the day were therefore mainly cyclical in nature. We now know they were not. But should we really blame the policy makers of that time for not recognizing that fact quickly enough?

Van Audenrode argues that the second main problem with Kneebone and Chung's technique is that it is essentially an accounting exercise. As such, it does not attempt to model the interaction between cyclical and structural deficits, on the one hand, and the level of interest rates and the rate of growth of the economy, on the other. "Yes," he says, "the very lax fiscal policies of the early 1970s helped create a large structural deficit. But they also clearly helped sustain economic activity, which most likely made the cyclical component of the deficit much more favourable." His conclusion is that although Kneebone and Chung are very good on the mechanics of the debt's evolution, "more work is needed if we are to understand the links between these mechanics and policies."

What Do We Get for the Public Debt?

Debt is not necessarily bad. When private firms borrow they use the money to acquire assets. Unless they are Enron or Worldcom, the debit side of their balance sheet will be offset by physical or other assets. It is only natural to apply the same thinking to the public sector. Canada's governments may be very indebted, but if they have gone into debt to acquire genuinely useful assets, then maybe their decision to incur debt was a wise one.

To answer this question of "What do we get for the public debt?" we called on Queen's University's *Robin Boadway*, one of the world's leading experts in public finance and someone known for not being unsympathetic to government efforts to solve social and economic problems. Boadway immediately rewrote the rules on us and changed his assignment. He wanted to answer the slightly different question "What do we get for public indebtedness?" What's the difference? Let's follow his line of thought.

Public debt, as we have seen, is the contracted debt of the public sector. Boadway begins his paper by arguing that some kinds of public debt probably do not cause anyone much concern. For instance, if a government's revenues jump around from month to month or quarter to quarter, as they normally will, it does not make sense for it either to move its tax rates up and down to steady the inflow or to vary its public expenditures to match the fluctuations in its revenues. What it can do instead is borrow in periods when tax revenues are less than spending and pay back these loans when revenues exceed spending. The reason this sort of borrowing is ethically unobjectionable to most observers is that the people who benefit from the borrowing when there is a deficit are pretty much the same people who pay the loans back when there is a surplus. The same is true of borrowing and payback that balances over the slightly longer period of a business cycle. If the cycle is short enough, the same people pay back the loan as benefited from it.

Where borrowing may be more dubious ethically is when it involves an "intergenerational transfer." This occurs when most of the people who did the borrowing are *not* around to pay back the loan. In such cases, later generations are left holding the bag for earlier generations' spending. Boadway argues that this is a principal difference between public debt and private debt. In the private sector, as mentioned above, firms acquire assets in exchange for their debt. They get buildings or machines or know-how or goodwill. In the public sector, borrowing may lead to the accumulation of assets, some tangible, some not. But borrowing is also likely to involve an intergenerational transfer: the current generation will use the proceeds of the loan to buy now, while a future generation will be asked to repay the loan. Much of the current concern about government debt arises out of fear that today's taxpayers may be leaving an unfair fiscal legacy to their children.

Boadway's central point is that although the public sector debt that shows up in the public or national accounts may involve this sort of intergenerational transfer, incurring official public debt is not the only way the current generation can impose a cost on future generations. In fact, there are many ways it can do so.

One is by running a pay-as-you-go pension plan, like the Canada Pension Plan, in which the pensions of today's (old) retirees are paid by taxes on the earnings of (young) workers. It is true that today's retirees may have paid taxes to finance the pensions of the last generation's retirees, and perhaps turnabout is fair play, but that does not alter the fact that what is currently taking place is a transfer of purchasing power from today's younger generation to today's older generation. And it is usually the case that the first generation to retire after such a pension plan is established benefits by substantially more than it contributes to the plan. Indeed, as Boadway suggests, that may have been the very purpose of many such public pension plans, which were introduced at a time when many retirees had lost their savings to the Great Depression and to service in World War II.

Because many public policies can give rise to this kind of intergenerational transfer of resources focusing only on the transfer effected by formal government debt is misleading. Other things being equal, a long-lasting increase in public debt will shift the burden of financing public activities from today's taxpayers ("the old") to future taxpayers ("the young"). But other things may not be equal. If other public policies are hitting "the old" more than they are hitting "the young," then strong action to reduce the debt may in fact place an unfair burden on today's taxpayers.

Use of the word "unfair" makes clear that we have now entered the realm of ethics, or, as economists prefer to call it, "normative economics." That is inevitable as soon as we start talking about taking from one generation (or individual) and giving to another. How do we go about deciding whether a given array of public policies, including debt policy, is "fair"? First, Boadway argues, we need a lot of factual information, not just about public debt, but about "public indebtedness," a term he uses to indicate just how much the entire spectrum of public policies transfers tax obligations from the current to future generations. In particular, we need to know how both the tax burden and the benefits of public expenditures break down by age group. The professional term for gathering such information is "generational accounting," and a good deal of it has been done in the last 15 years.

Boadway argues that although existing Canadian studies suffer from a number of conceptually important deficiencies their results are intriguing nevertheless. One key finding is that the average tax rate over the lifetime of those age cohorts currently alive has evolved relatively smoothly over time. This suggests that, in the face of the very significant shocks, including the Great Depression and World War II, experienced by many of those still living, governments must have been smoothing the tax burden across generations. This work also places the importance of the current debate about what to do with the surplus into stark relief. As Boadway says when summarizing this body of work: "When budget surpluses are used to reduce the debt, the lifetime net tax rate for future generations is virtually the same as for the current young, about 38 percent. This is despite the coming demographic shock in which the proportion of the population over 65 is projected to increase dramatically. On the other hand, if the budget surpluses were used to increase government expenditures, the lifetime net tax rate for future generations would rise to 55 percent, substantially higher than that of the current young." Thus Boadway appears to support current debt repayment on the grounds of intergenerational equity.

When we have figured out the impact of the current fiscal stance on all future generations, which is itself no mean feat, we then have to decide whether the distribution of burdens and benefits that would result from changing that stance would be fair. To that end, we need some ethical precepts. Boadway offers up a few, drawn from standard economic theory. Among them are:

The Pareto principle. If a change makes no one worse off and at least one person better off, it is a good thing;

Inequality aversion. Other things being equal, people prefer less inequality in the income distribution than more;

Compensation and responsibility. People should be compensated only for misfortunes that are not their own doing; and

Social insurance. When individuals or generations cannot insure themselves against certain kinds of shocks, the state may decide to step in and provide the insurance in question.

What sorts of policies follow from these general precepts? If we do favour equality, then we may approve policies that take resources from richer generations and transfer them to poorer ones. If the march of technological progress means that later generations usually are richer than earlier generations, then, within limits, policies that take from later generations, as public indebtedness certainly does, may be unobjectionable. If a particular generation suffers a serious setback to its earnings for reasons beyond its control, then policies that move money to it may also be unobjectionable. Of course, an obvious practical difficulty with this idea is that although it is easier to decide whether a generation is deserving of help using the benefit of hindsight, policy decisions have to be made before the fact, while the generation is young or middle-aged.

At our urging, Robin Boadway agreed to extend an earlier draft of his paper by adding what he calls "speculative" comments to try to assess how the public debt policy of the last 30 years might fit into such an ethical framework. Have the debts accumulated over the last three decades created an unfair burden for future generations of Canadian taxpayers? Boadway's view is "maybe not." The debt buildup of the 1970s and 1980s may not have been unfair, given the circumstances of the time, while the rapid reduction of the debt beginning in the mid-1990s may well have placed too much of the burden on contemporary taxpayers. If anything, future taxpayers should be paying more taxes than they are. We are sure that Boadway himself would be the first to stress that without all the missing information he inventories in his article any such judgement can only be preliminary. Still, we are grateful to him for putting such a judgement on the table to be debated.

In his comments, the Department of Finance's *Jeremy Rudin* argues that the logic of Boadway's analytical framework is "inescapable." However much we might prefer otherwise, we cannot assess the fairness of one kind of policy-mandated intergenerational transfer without knowing about all the other policy-mandated intergenerational transfers currently taking place. The different transfers underway all net out and what is relevant for ethical judgements is this net transfer from one generation to another. Until all the information is in, information about the transfer implied by the growth or reduction of formal government debt is not that useful.

Does that mean nothing can be said until full-blown generational accounting is commonplace – a decision that would make life very difficult for people like Rudin and his colleagues at the Department of Finance, who have to make policy? Rudin argues that there may be special cases in which it is possible to make reasonably strong conclusions about fairness. There may be times – the Mexican peso crisis in the fall of 1994, for instance – when intergenerational transfers will pay off for *all* generations. Foreign holders of Canadian government bonds were not overly concerned with the intricacies of intergenerational fairness as they watched the collapse of the peso and worried about a possible collapse of the Canadian dollar. Their concerns caused them to demand a risk premium from Canadian borrowers, both public and private, that, had nothing been done, would have imposed significant economic costs on current Canadian taxpayers. Avoiding these costs, Rudin suggests, may well have been a good deal even for those who had to assume the burden of immediate tax increases and spending cuts to ensure that the federal deficit and debt were brought under control.

That point addresses the second of Robin Boadway's speculative conclusions, namely, that the debt reduction of the second half of the 1990s was too rapid. But what about his first conclusion, that the debt buildup from the mid-1970s to the mid-1990s may not have been unreasonable? That depends on questions like: How bad *were* the recessions of 1980–82 and 1990–91? How severe *was* the dislocation from the FTA and NAFTA? To what extent *should* successor generations be asked to pay for disappointed expectations about productivity growth? And what sorts of legacy were taxpayers of 1975–95 leaving in the other policy areas where intergenerational transfers are likely? If they were also despoiling the environment, running the Canada Pension Plan into unsustainability, eating up natural resources and shifting the tax structure away from themselves, it would have been a bit much for them to ask successor generations to assume the additional burden of helping them through what were in fact relatively mild economic shocks compared to the worldwide depression and war through which their parents lived. And just how well off are these successor generations likely to be? They may reasonably expect to enjoy more-rapid productivity growth and therefore a faster-growing standard of living than their immediate predecessors. On the other hand, they now have to live with the scourge of terrorism. Rudin's warning that the analysis of "well-being is fraught with difficulty" is obviously well taken. Moreover, we doubt Robin Boadway would disagree with any of these points. But he almost certainly would argue that they are the kind of thing that must be taken into consideration in deciding whether a given intergenerational transfer is fair.

Does Government Debt Matter?

Having seen how big the debt is and having spent some time on the questions of where it came from and what we got for it, a natural next question is "What does the debt cost us?" That implies it does cost something, as most people probably would expect. But in fact a logically prior question is whether the debt matters at all.

A question so existential might not occur to politicians, policy makers or taxpayers. How could the accumulation of almost a trillion dollars of Canadian government debt over the last quarter of the twentieth century not have mattered? But it is a question economists have been arguing about for almost two centuries. The idea that the debt might *not* matter even has its own name, *Ricardian equivalence*, after the great English economist, David Ricardo (1772–1823), who argued during the Napoleonic Wars that whether governments financed their spending by taxes or by borrowing might not actually make much difference. Governments might *wish* to make a difference by choosing one method of finance over the other, but people could respond to the state's decision by changing their behaviour in ways that frustrated its intentions. If the offset were perfect, the size of government would still matter, but how it had gone about financing itself, whether with taxes or debt, would not.

Ricardian equivalence, or RE for short, has been hotly debated in economics since an influential article by Harvard University's Robert Barro brought it back into the intellectual spotlight in 1974, at just about the time Canadian government debt was beginning its long, late-century rise. Although some economists regard RE as an interesting intellectual curiosum, with little relevance to the real world, others see it as having considerable practical importance. To try to tell us whether Canadian governments should worry about the tax-or-borrow choice, we called on *David Johnson* of Wilfrid Laurier University, who has been thinking and writing about this issue for several years. His paper explains Ricardian equivalence and assesses the current evidence on whether or not it applies in Canada.

Johnson begins by explaining how Ricardian equivalence might hold in a closed economy, that is, an economy that neither trades with, borrows from, nor lends to other countries. No economy in the world, not even North Korea's, is truly closed, but in economic theory the case of a closed economy is a useful benchmark. Later, Johnson opens up his model economy to see how RE operates when trade and capital flows are permitted, as they obviously are in Canada.

In a closed economy, the total amount of goods and services produced in any year, the nation's GDP, can be used in one of three ways. Output can be *consumed* for current purposes, and economists usually think of "households" as doing this consumption. It can be used for *investment* in capital equipment, an act economists usually ascribe to firms. Or, finally, output can be used by *government* to provide goods and services for citizens. In a closed economy there is no other use for a nation's output. This gives rise to one of the first accounting identities undergraduate students in economics see:

$$Y = C + I + G$$

where Y is the value of GDP, C the value of consumption expenditure, I the value of investment in physical capital, and G the value of government purchases of goods and services. This equation makes clear that, for any given level of GDP, if one of the components increases, at least one of the other two must decrease. For example, if consumption increases while the level of government spending is held constant, there must be a decline in the level of investment.

Ricardian equivalence is the idea that the method of government finance, taxes or debt, does not matter for the economy. That raises the Clintonesque question, what does "matter" mean? Economists agree that in this case "matter" means altering the combination of consumption, investment and/or government expenditure from what otherwise would have been observed.

How could the government's decision to run a bigger deficit *not* affect households' consumption? If taxes are lower, won't households spend at least some of the increase in their after-tax income? Maybe they will, maybe they won't. Economists like to believe people think about the future when they make decisions. After all, families save for their retirement and for their children's education, while firms often make investments that will pay off only in the distant future. Most people probably have at least a rough idea of how much income they will make in their working lives and how much they should therefore consume from year to year. Such forward-looking firms and households ought to recognize that today's tax reduction must somehow be matched by a future increase in taxes: if a government issues new debt today, sometime in the future it is going to have to raise taxes in order to pay the debt back. But if government borrowing merely means that people's current taxes fall and their future taxes rise, then their *lifetime* disposable income does not really change. So why should people change their consumption? In this case, forward-looking households and firms may gladly buy the new government bonds, but they will not alter their pattern of consumption and investment. In effect, they will save the entire tax cut implied by the government's decision to finance its spending by borrowing. This is the case in which RE holds completely and the government's method of financing has no impact on the economy. Government debt simply does not matter.

It is possible, however, that some households may not respond in this way but will instead spend at least part of the tax cut. They may not recognize the future tax obligation that the government's current borrowing implies. Or they may recognize it but not really care, maybe because they think the higher taxes will arrive only after they are gone. Or perhaps they believe that today's tax reductions will be matched by future reductions in government spending so that taxes really need not rise in the future. Or, finally, they may be "liquidity-constrained": they may wish to be consuming much more than their current income permits them to, but they are not able to borrow against their (much larger) future income. Many students are probably in this situation.

If for any or all of these reasons households do not fully recognize the future tax obligations that government borrowing implies, tax reductions will make them feel as if their lifetime income *has* gone up, and they may therefore increase their consumption. But if in our basic equation C goes up while G is constant, then I must fall. How would the reduction in investment actually come about? As the government enters the capital market to increase its borrowing, its demand for financial capital drives up interest rates, and the higher cost of capital then reduces the amount of investment firms are prepared to undertake. Thus, when Ricardian equivalence does *not* hold the government deficit "crowds out" private investment. The cost for the economy is a slower rate of capital accumulation and thus a lower rate of income growth in the future. By contrast, when RE *does* hold the increase in government borrowing does not increase interest rates. Why not? Because for every dollar of new government debt there is a new dollar of household saving. The increase in the demand for loans is perfectly offset by an increase in their supply.

That brings Johnson to the payoff question: "Does Ricardian equivalence actually hold?" Testing economic propositions with real-world data is always tricky. In a theoretical model, one variable can be changed at a time. In the real world, lots of things are changing all the time, and governments seldom, if ever, make the simple taxes-to-bonds switch envisioned in theory. Rather, they increase or decrease government spending at the same time as they make a financing choice to cover the change. Johnson reports that the various ways in which RE has been tested give rise to different and often conflicting results. On balance, however, he concludes that the more carefully done studies have tended to refute RE. It seems that at least some people *do* increase their spending when faced with a tax cut. In general, between 30 and 50 percent of a tax cut is consumed so that government borrowing will indeed crowd out private investment. Johnson concludes that Ricardian equivalence does not hold and government debt therefore matters (and this book and the conference it was based on are saved from complete irrelevance!).

That is the closed economy story. How does the story change in the more realistic case in which a country can both trade with its neighbours and borrow and lend in world capital markets? In some ways, not very much. The worry is still that a reduction in taxes and an associated increase in government borrowing will lead to an increase in domestic consumption and an eventual reduction in the growth rate of income. But the mechanism through which this reduction occurs is different in an open economy.

In an open economy, especially one with very mobile financial capital, domestic interest rates move in tandem with those in the rest of the world. Given Canada's small size in the world economy, budget deficits by Canadian governments have a negligible effect on either world interest rates or, therefore, on domestic investment, which depends on the interest rate associated with financing it. If government debt does not change interest rates, it does not crowd out investment.

How then might budget deficits matter in an open economy? If Ricardian equivalence does *not* hold, then the government budget deficit will lead to an increase in domestic consumption. But with domestic households saving less, who finances the bigger government debt and the unchanged level of domestic investment? Foreigners do. The increase in government borrowing, which in a closed economy would drive up the domestic interest rate, now simply attracts foreign financial capital. In effect, the government deficit is financed by foreign lenders.

Because the government deficit has no effect on the level of investment it also has no effect on amount of output produced in Canada. But it does reduce the amount of made-in-Canada output that Canadians get to keep. Some of our output must now be sent abroad to service our now greater foreign debts. In an open economy the problem with government debt is not its effect on the value of gross *domestic* product – the amount of output produced within our borders – but rather on the value of gross *national* product – the amount of our output that we actually get to keep as income.

Johnson's central test of the Ricardian equivalence proposition for an open economy is to look at the relationship between government budget deficits and the country's net foreign borrowing, which is equal to the country's *current account deficit*. This is the "twin deficits" problem that was much discussed in the United States when the Reagan budget deficits of the early 1980s contributed to rising foreign debt in that country. Johnson presents compelling evidence that the run-up in Canadian government deficits in the 1970s, but especially in the 1980s, coincided with a rise in Canada's international indebtedness. Nor is it coincidental, he argues, that since our governments began reducing their deficits in the mid-1990s the country's net borrowing from abroad has noticeably declined.

If Johnson is right, if Ricardian equivalence does not hold and if the deficits incurred by Canadian governments between 1976 and 1995 did indeed erode Canada's international capital balance, how great was the damage? How large has been the reduction in future Canadian income resulting from the greater reliance on foreign borrowing? Making use of his earlier estimate that consumption increases by between 30 and 50 percent of the government deficit, Johnson argues that the cost will have been between 3 and 10 percent of GDP. That may not sound like much, but even a lower-end estimate translates into $3,600 of yearly income, each and every year into the future, for an average family of four, an amount that in his (and likely their) view is substantial.

In his comments on David Johnson's paper, University of Ottawa's *Serge Coulombe* is not quite so hard on Ricardian equivalence. He agrees with Johnson that RE does not hold completely; consumers do not fully offset the government's issue of debt. On the other hand, even the studies that Johnson himself cites suggested there may be some offset, with estimates of its strength ranging between 30 and 50 percent. And there is conflicting evidence in the macroeconomic data on the role played by offsetting behaviour. On the one hand, Johnson is right that as Canadian government debts rose through the 1970s and 1980s into the 1990s, Canada's net overseas deficit also increased. The emergence of these twin deficits suggests that private Canadian borrowers were being forced into foreign markets by the crowding-out effect of government debt. On the other hand, private savings rates are positively correlated with government deficits: as deficits rose during the 1970s and 1980s, private saving typically rose, too, while as deficits fell from the mid-1990s on, so did saving rates. In other words, as governments began to run surpluses and in effect save on their behalf, Canadians evidently decided to reduce their own saving, exactly as Ricardian theory would suggest. Coulombe closes his comments by relating how he himself, by explaining the idea behind Ricardian equivalence, unwittingly converted one Canadian consumer to Ricardian-style behaviour: having learned from her economist-husband that, via the surpluses of the last five years, the government was now saving on her behalf, Coulombe's wife decided to go shopping.

What Is the Cost of Government Debt?

In 1995, when the federal government had apparently hit the debt wall, it was spending almost $50 billion per year on interest payments on its debt. Add in the other levels of government and total government interest payments were $78 billion per year. In the short term, governments can borrow to pay interest. In the long term, however, borrowing to pay interest is not a sustainable policy. If government debt eventually leads to higher taxes because of the need to service that debt, how do these higher taxes affect the economy?

Laymen think of the cost of taxation as being the dollar amounts taken away from them. Economists regard that amount as a simple transfer of purchasing power from taxpayers to the beneficiaries of public spending. They see the cost of taxation as instead being the cost of the "distortions" it imposes on economic activity. Taxes are distortionary when they cause changes in the relative prices of specific goods or activities and, as a result, lead households or firms to change their behaviour. For example, excise taxes on gasoline make gasoline more expensive than other goods and cause consumers to substitute away from gasoline and toward alternatives, such as car-pooling, public transportation, or the use of more fuel-efficient vehicles. In this day of environmental concerns, such a "distortion" of behaviour may seem like a good thing, but many tax-caused distortions are potentially very costly for the economy. For example, one distortion caused by high income taxes is that the rate of return from saving is reduced when interest and dividends are taxed as ordinary income. If taxation does reduce the return to saving, people may save less, which may in turn reduce the overall rate of investment and therefore the rate of growth in the economy.

To address this potential link between government debt, interest payments, taxation and economic growth, we turned to *Bev Dahlby* of the University of Alberta, a specialist in public finance and Canada's leading expert on the "marginal cost of public funds." Dahlby begins by noting that for many years economists who thought about economic growth organized their thinking with theoretical models in which the economy's long-run growth rate was in fact "exogenous," that is, was taken as given, rather than being explained by the model itself. Not surprisingly, no one was satisfied with such non-explanations for why some countries grow faster than others. In recent years, however, economists have worked hard at digging deeper, trying to unearth the wellspring of economic growth. As a result, they now generally use "endogenous" growth models in which the economy's long-run growth rate is explained by elements within the model, such as tax rates, inflation, investment, education and so on.

In his paper, Bev Dahlby uses a very simple endogenous-growth model to think about the relationship between government debt, income taxes and the long-run rate of economic growth. Stacking the argument against a debt-growth effect, he builds a model in which Ricardian equivalence holds perfectly. Yet he finds that even in such an extreme behavioural setting government debt *does* impose a cost on the economy. The reason is that his model assumes, realistically, that taxes are distortionary and that the distortions they cause end up reducing the economy's growth rate.

Dahlby's model is built on the following three key elements. First, the nation's output is assumed to be proportional to its capital stock. (All of the interesting action in this model involves capital, rather than labour, so he simply assumes the amount of labour available is constant.) Since the capital stock only rises through the act of investment, the rate of growth of output ends up being proportional to the economy's rate of investment.

Second, the model is of a closed economy. Domestic investment is therefore necessarily equal to domestic saving: there is no other way of financing investment. Domestic saving comes in two kinds, public and private. If taxes are greater than public expenditure, the government runs a surplus that is then available to finance private investment. If private individuals do not consume all of their after-tax income, they too can make funds available to private investors. Overall domestic saving is the sum of private and public saving.

Third, the government taxes income, which is just the value of output, in a proportional manner. The resulting tax revenue is used to finance government expenditures, which throughout Dahlby's analysis are held at a constant share of GDP.

Imagine what happens in this simple setting if the government chooses to finance more of its expenditures with debt. The greater stock of debt must be serviced and this requires taxes to be raised to make the necessary interest payments. Even though households are purely Ricardian in Dalhby's model, so that they end up increasing their saving by exactly enough to offset the decline in government saving, there is an additional effect on the economy coming from the distortionary effect of the higher income taxes required to pay the now-higher interest costs. As income taxes rise, the rate of return from saving declines. Households naturally choose to save less and consume more and the result is a decline in the economy's rate of investment, because in this closed economy investment can only be financed by domestic saving. As the rate of investment declines, so does the economy's long-run growth rate.

How large is this tax-distortion effect? Dahlby calibrates his model by choosing the tax rate, the level of government spending, and the debt-to-GDP ratio so that his "base case" resembles some of the key aspects of the current Canadian fiscal position. He then imagines an experiment in which the government reduces the debt-to-GDP ratio from 100 percent to 50 percent. Those numbers are not chosen by accident: in 1995 the combined (federal plus provincial) debt was approximately 100 percent of Canada's GDP and it is currently about 70 percent. Thus, if the actual debt-to-GDP ratio continues on what appears to be its likely path for the next few years, Dahlby's experiment gives us some sense of the changes we might expect in the economy's growth rate.

Dalhby finds that the 50-percentage-point decline in the debt-to-GDP ratio leads to an increase in the growth rate of GDP of 0.1 percentage points. On the face of it, this seems like a very small effect, but keep in mind that annual growth rates in real (inflation-adjusted) per capita terms are often in the range of 1.0 to 1.5 per-cent, so a change of 0.1 points is not to be dismissed quite so lightly. Moreover, the magic of compounding means that even small changes in annual growth rates can, if sustained over many years, have important effects on living standards.

Another way to think about the importance of a change in the annual growth rate of GDP is to express it in terms of present value. Dahlby computes the present value of the 0.1 percentage-point change in the annual growth rate of GDP to be approximately $15 billion. That is, a higher growth rate of 0.1 per-cent per year into the infinite future is equivalent to having higher GDP today of $15 billion, or roughly 1.3 percent of 2002 GDP.

Dahlby offers still another way to think about the cost of government debt, this one based on the concept of the "marginal cost of public debt," that is, the cost of increasing the debt by $1. This cost depends on how responsive people are to taxation and therefore on how great the economic distortions are from taxation. It also depends on the value of government-provided goods and serv-ices. If, as Dahlby's model assumes, government expenditures are a constant proportion of GDP, then a tax-induced slowdown of economic growth will cause the public sector to provide fewer goods and services than it otherwise would, and, as he writes, that is "an important aspect of the marginal social loss from a higher public debt."

Again using mid-1990s Canadian values for his calculations, Dahlby finds that the marginal cost of public debt is between $1.06 and $1.27 per dollar borrowed by Canadian governments, depending on what assumption is made about the responsiveness of saving to tax rates. The mid-range value of $1.15 implies that, if a public expenditure is financed by borrowing, it needs to bring a social benefit of $1.15 in order to be considered worthwhile. Another way to look at it is that public projects should have a rate of return of 15 percent in order to be accepted. This does not actually have to be a cash return but should be the cash-equivalent of any non-cash benefits public spending may bring, assuming they can be at least guesstimated. Dahlby concludes his paper by wondering whether many public projects currently proposed by supporters of new government spending can reasonably claim a 15 percent rate of return. Of course, one public project *would* bring such a return. If raising a dollar of public debt costs $1.15 after the economic inefficiency it induces is taken into account, lowering the public debt by a dollar would avoid $1.15 of cost, which suggests that reducing debt would itself clear the "hurdle" rate of return of 15 percent.

We asked *Tiff Macklem*, Chief of the Research Department at the Bank of Canada, to comment on Dahlby's paper. Since the late 1980s, Macklem has spent much time thinking about the interaction of government debt and monetary policy and especially about how public debt might affect both the level and the growth rate of GDP. He notes that, despite the simplicity of Dahlby's model, it is successful not only in illustrating one of the key mechanisms by which government debt affects the economy but also in giving us a reasonable sense of the magnitude of the effect.

But Macklem argues that the real world contains other mechanisms that we should not ignore and that, if included in Dahlby's model, would increase the predicted cost of government debt. First, as Johnson's paper emphasizes, Ricardian equivalence probably does not hold and so private saving will fall by more in response to government deficits than it does in Dahlby's model. The result will be a larger decline in investment and therefore in the economy's growth rate. Second, high income-tax rates also tend to discourage work effort in the real world, whereas in Dahlby's model, with the labour supply constant, this effect is absent. This reduction in work effort will decrease the level of GDP and, depending on one's view of the growth process, may have a negative effect on the economy's growth rate. Third, Dahlby's model contains only one type of tax and no uncertainty. In the real world, however, governments that need to increase their tax revenue may increase an entire range of taxes, and they will generally not be transparent about when the various changes will take place. Furthermore, there is sometimes uncertainty about whether the government will make good on its debt, the alternative being either the extreme step of outright repudiation or, less drastically, partial repudiation achieved by inflating away the debt via excessive monetary expansions. Macklem argues that these uncertainties add risk premiums to both government and private debt, and that these must also be viewed as a cost of government debt.

What Is the Optimal Debt-to-GDP Ratio?

Now we get to the $64,000, or perhaps that should be $786 billion, question: What is the "right" amount of government debt? *Is* the debt war over? Do Canadian governments need to reduce their debts more than they have already? Or have they already proceeded too far down the path of deficit and debt reduction? One Canadian economist, who has worked on this question extensively, and, together with a series of co-authors, has taken a firm stand on it, is *William Scarth* of McMaster University. We asked him to address this bottom-line question directly.

Economists typically analyze public debt from three perspectives: efficiency, macroeconomic stability and equity (or fairness). Scarth is no exception. His conclusion, somewhat surprisingly, is that analyses that focus on efficiency and macroeconomic stability do not lead to very precise recommendations regarding the optimal size of the public debt. By contrast, analyses based on equity do, though the precise recommendations depend on which definition of fairness is adopted. Economists will find this conclusion more than a little discomfiting, for if we have a true professional expertise, it is in the analysis of efficiency, which is the bedrock of positivist microeconomic analysis. And in macroeconomics we have contributed a great deal of knowledge and maybe even a little wisdom on the related questions of what makes the economy cycle and how its cycles may be dampened. But economists are the first to admit that we have no special remit for making policy recommendations based on questions of fairness. So if, as Scarth argues, fairness is the real reason for worrying about the debt, economists may not be better placed than anyone else to tell society what to do.

Let us begin with Scarth's review of efficiency, in particular, the efficiency of taxation that is required to service any government debt. We have already seen the meaning of distortionary taxation in our discussion of Bev Dahlby's paper. In economics, the concepts of "efficiency" and "distortions" are related. In fact, the most efficient tax an economist can imagine is one that is entirely non-distortionary, one that leads to no changes in relative prices, and therefore does not skew households' or firms' decisions regarding which specific activities to conduct. An example is a so-called lump-sum tax, a tax unrelated to people's income, consumption, saving, wealth or any other decision they make. Because the lump-sum tax does not alter the "rate of return" from any activity it does not skew people's behaviour. Unfortunately, such lump-sum taxes are a thing of textbooks only. They are widely viewed as unfair, a "fair" tax being one that *does* depend on the level of a person's income, wealth, or consumption. Margaret

Thatcher tried to introduce a lump-sum tax (she called it a poll tax) in the early 1990s and lost her job as a result.

Because real-world, non-lump-sum taxes are distortionary, perhaps it would be better if governments found other ways to finance their spending needs. Enter debt policy. One study Scarth quotes suggests that instead of being debtors (i.e., borrowers) governments should become creditors (i.e., lenders) and live off the interest payments their assets would generate. This way they could avoid having to levy inefficient taxes in order to service their debt. The same study concluded that in the United States the optimal debt-to-GDP ratio is *negative* 300 percent, that is, governments should build up assets equal to three times the economy's GDP and then pay their current expenditures out of the interest these assets would generate. If the same rule held in Canada, this would have required our governments (in 2002) to hold financial assets of roughly $3.6 trillion dollars. Of course, in 2002 Canada's governments actually owed about $786 billion, so pursuing this policy would have required them to start running very large surpluses for many years to come, a policy that, to put it mildly, does not seem to be in the cards politically.

The study Scarth cites assumes there are no benefits from governments running debts: the only efficiency consideration is avoiding taxes. But that may not be the case. As we saw in David Johnson's paper, government borrowing can help "liquidity-constrained" people by allowing them to smooth out their lifetime consumption. In economic models that assume, probably realistically, that significant numbers of people are liquidity-constrained in this way, government debt involves a trade-off. More debt helps those who are liquidity-constrained. But more debt also means more taxes (since the debt has to be serviced) and that, as we have seen, means inefficiency. Scarth notes that modifying the simple model already cited to take into account this added virtue of public debt produces an optimal debt-to-GDP ratio of 66 percent, news that is much more encouraging to Canadian governments, with their total combined debts of about 70 percent of GDP in 2002.

Unfortunately for those who would like to pin down an optimal level of the public debt and point government policy toward attaining it, the same study suggests there are only small costs from departing from the optimal public debt. The reason is that there are both costs and benefits to accumulating debt. The cost is that more debt requires more taxation. The benefit is that more debt means liquidity-constrained consumers are better able to borrow through the government. In the models Scarth reports on, it turns out that over a wide range of possible debt levels the costs and benefits may be more or less offsetting.

Scarth concludes from all this that efficiency analysis is not very helpful in determining the optimal level of government debt. The optimal debt-to-GDP ratio can change significantly according to the assumptions of the particular model used. And there may not be a large social cost to departures from the optimum. If the target is very sensitive to the assumptions economists make about the way the world works, and if missing the target does not really matter much, policy makers are likely to conclude that the debt war probably is over, since there does not seem to be much point in engaging in further battles.

If efficiency considerations provide little guidance to policy makers, how about concerns about macroeconomic stability? Since the Keynesian revolution of the 1940s and 1950s mainstream economics has held that governments can use deficit spending to help offset cyclical fluctuations in the economy. In the early postwar years there was great optimism about the possibilities for counter-cyclical fiscal policy. As the decades passed, however, and the difficulties of both anticipating downturns and implementing tax cuts or spending projects in a timely manner became clear, optimism faded. But the standard view among economists is still that balancing the budget on an annual basis is destabilizing, that it is far better policy to aim for balance over the longer period of the business cycle. The argument against balancing the budget every year is that, when the economy is hit by a shock that slows growth and maybe even causes a recession, budget balance will require some combination of an increase in taxes and a reduction in government spending. But these changes will only make the downturn worse, thus making the economy less stable. The standard view is that by allowing the budget deficit to rise during slowdowns and fall during recoveries, stability of output and employment can be enhanced.

Scarth suggests, however, that a policy of annually balanced budgets may not be as unwise as most people think. He has two reasons for believing this. The first is that, unless the government is to abandon debt targeting altogether, raising the debt ratio to fight a recession requires lowering it later to get it back to the desired long-run ratio. As a result, while the recession may not be as deep as it might have been had the government not run a deficit, the fiscal retrenchment required to get the debt ratio back on track means the subsequent recovery will not be as robust as it would have been, either. Perhaps that trade-off is acceptable, but it should be recognized and its acceptability should be debated.

Scarth's second reason for thinking that annually balanced budgets may not be too harmful involves the interaction of fiscal and monetary policies. Even if fiscal policy does react to the business cycle in such a way as to keep the budget deficit constant, a monetary policy that is guided by an inflation target, as it currently is in Canada, will automatically work in the direction of keeping the economy stable. For example, if a negative shock hits the Canadian economy and slows the rate of growth of GDP, taxes may be increased and government spending may be cut to keep the budget deficit constant. Taken by themselves, these fiscal policy adjustments would add to the negative shock, further slow-ing the growth rate of GDP. But if monetary policy is geared to keeping infla-tion within a target band, the central bank will respond to this combination of negative shock and fiscal tightening by lowering interest rates, thus stimulating spending in the economy. If the central bank does its job correctly, the economy will be no less stable than in the case where deficits were allowed to rise in response to the negative shock. Indeed, in a series of simulations, Scarth found that "short-run output volatility is increased only to a very limited extent when a fairly rigid target for the annual budget deficit is adopted." Scarth's conclusion is that concerns about macroeconomic stability do not bring us to a policy rec-ommendation about the optimal size of the government debt.

For Scarth, like Robin Boadway before him, optimality is mainly a question of intergenerational fairness, and that gets economists into deep water, for what is fair? Boadway gave a qualitative answer to that question: if a generation suffers a significant cut in its standard of living for reasons, such as war or depression, that seem temporary and are not of its own doing, then it may be reasonable for it to borrow and force future generations to share some of the costs of its short-term difficulties. Scarth tries to put numbers onto this kind of analysis to see what sorts of intergenerational transfers it leads to, and he does so in a forward-looking way, trying to estimate the intergenerational implications of the next big change likely to hit the Canadian economy – the retirement of the baby boomers.

Scarth argues that the boomers' retirement will cause a decline in living stan-dards – not an absolute decline, but a decline from what they otherwise would have been. Why is that? As the boomers retire and leave the labour force, labour will become scarcer. The result will be an increase in wages, which will tend to increase the living standards of the younger generations still working. A factor operating in the opposite direction, tending to reduce living standards, is that as labour does become scarcer, capital will become relatively more abundant, so its rate of return (whether in the form of interest or dividends) will fall. However, as the boomers age, taxes on the young will have to increase in order to continue funding the public pension system, so the net effect on the younger generation is ambiguous. A third effect on overall living standards relates to the well-being of the boomers themselves. As labour becomes scarcer, capital will become relatively more abundant, so its rate of return (interest or divi-dends) will fall. Since the retired boomers will be living off the return from their accumulated capital, their living standards will decline. Summing together all three effects, it is unclear what happens to overall living standards. Scarth argues, however, that under realistic assumptions, the overall effect is a decline in average living standards, and that this result is robust to reasonable changes in his assumptions.

This predicted reduction in living standards as a result of the baby-boomers' retirement is Scarth's starting point. He then asks whether reducing government debt might be a way to offset the fall in living standards. If so, how much of a reduction would be necessary to fully offset the shock.

How might a reduction in government debt increase future living standards from what they otherwise would be? First, lower debt means lower debt service, which creates room in the annual government budget for either new spending or reduced taxes. This is the "fiscal dividend" we have all heard about, though it pays off only after a period of costly "investment" in deficit reduction. Second, as the government deficit turns into a surplus, and thus the amount of government dissaving falls, the amount of national saving (private plus public) increases. In an open economy like Canada's, such an increase in national saving leads to a reduction in foreign indebtedness and thus an increase in the resources that can be consumed domestically rather than used to make interest payments to foreigners.

Putting this all together, Scarth now has two effects to balance. The retirement of the baby boomers will reduce overall average living standards in the future (at least from what they otherwise would have been). But a reduction in government debt will have the opposite effect. The policy question therefore is: "How much of a reduction in government debt is needed to exactly offset the effect of the boomers' retirement?" Scarth's answer, after calibrating his model for the predicted change in the age structure of the Canadian population, is that the federal government's debt-to-GDP ratio must fall by approximately 50-55 percentage points from its high point in the mid-1990s. At that time it was about 75 percent, and it has since declined by a little over 30 points, so to reach the level necessary to achieve intergenerational equality it must fall by another 20-25 points.

Scarth naturally is wary about using a simple exogenous-growth model to make firm conclusions about policy, and he discusses the importance of thinking through the same policy question in a more complicated setting in which population aging and tax changes may influence the economy's long-run growth rate. If the aging of the population leads to a reduction in the rate of accumulation of human capital, that is, skills and knowledge that are typically acquired on the job or through formal training, the economy's growth rate may fall, which means still further debt reduction would be required if the effect of the boomers' retirement is to be fully offset. On the other hand, the effect of distortionary taxation works in the opposite direction. Following the initial debt reduction in Scarth's policy experiment, reduced taxation leads to an increase in the rate of return to saving and thus to an increase in total saving and capital accumulation, which would tend to increase the economy's future growth rate (for exactly the same reason as Bev Dahlby emphasized) and thus reduce the necessary amount of debt reduction required to offset the effects of population aging.

After reviewing these and still other effects likely to be found in more sophisticated endogenous-growth models, Scarth concludes that, at least as a first pass at the problem, there is good reason to think that many of these effects more or less offset each other. He therefore sticks to his policy recommendation that the federal debt-to-GDP ratio be reduced to 25 percent.

In his comments on Bill Scarth's paper, the Université de Montréal's *François Vaillancourt* makes a number of interesting points and then proposes his own optimal debt rule. Vaillancourt argues that public policies to rectify alleged market failures having to do with people's liquidity constraints should take into account whether or not these constraints are voluntary. If people are poor through no fault of their own, that is one thing, though governments' borrowing on their behalf may not be the best way to remedy their poverty. But if people are living from hand to mouth essentially because they were "born to shop," it is not clear why public policy need respond.

On the question of intergenerational equity, Vaillancourt agrees with Scarth and with Robin Boadway before him that when large shocks hit a generation it may be justified in using public debt to pass along some of the cost to subsequent generations. But he takes a harder line than Scarth on the economic difficulties experienced by the baby-boom generation, arguing that the hardships involved in the oil shocks of the 1970s do not compare with either World War II or the Great Depression. If politics were not a constraint, Vaillancourt would like to see Canada's net debt reduced by a policy of age-specific taxes or user charges aimed at boomers.

Vaillancourt agrees with Scarth that a *Treaty of Maastricht*-style "zero-deficit" rule need not impede the conduct of a counter-cyclical macroeconomic policy, so long as monetary policy can adjust accordingly. But his own preferred deficit rule is different from that. He would take what he calls a "balance-sheet approach" to public debt and allow governments to run deficits only when the proceeds were used to purchase real capital, by which he means tangible assets of one kind or another, whether buildings, roads, dams, harbours, national forests and so on. Debt is only one side of the balance sheet. A debt of 50 percent of GDP may be perfectly appropriate if it has been used to finance the acquisition of public assets. By contrast, a debt of 25 percent may be inappropriate if it has been used to finance current consumption.

A glance at the evolution of Canadian government balance sheets over the last 30 years suggests to Vaillancourt that in fact the debt problem lies mainly with the federal government. Provincial governments maintained their net worth up until 1981, after which it went slightly negative. Municipal governments and school boards actually increased their net worth from 1971 through 1995. Taken together, non-federal governments essentially followed Vaillancourt's rule of only incurring debt when they were acquiring assets. The federal government, by contrast, saw a major decline in its net worth as, between the mid-1970s and mid-1990s, it borrowed heavily without offsetting this borrowing by the acquisition of assets.

How Should We Manage the Debt?

Even if governments heed the message of some of the contributors to this volume and reduce their debt loads, they are unlikely to eliminate their debts entirely. While economics textbooks at all levels have much to say about fiscal policy and the problems of government debt, the issue of how public debt should best be managed usually is absent. In Canada, the Bank of Canada is the federal government's fiscal agent and thus is responsible for managing the government's debt. We therefore turned to two government economists, one of them formerly at the Bank, *David Bolder* and *Clifton Lee-Sing*, to explain the choices available to governments, though not necessarily, since they are both public employees, to choose among them.

Bolder and Lee-Sing begin by canvassing the mission statements of debt managers in a number of countries, an exercise that leads them to a generic version of the modern debt manager's mission statement, namely: *to raise stable, low-cost funding for the government and to maintain a well-functioning market for government securities.* Bolder and Lee-Sing then structure their paper around an explanation of each of these attributes of good debt management.

There are many types of government debt instruments. Governments can issue treasury bills, coupon bonds, savings bonds, lottery bonds; it is almost true that the number of instruments is limited only by the issuer's imagination. And, of course, each instrument comes with a wide choice of time horizons. Debt can be contracted for as little as 30 days or as long as 30 years. And although most Canadian government debt is denominated in Canadian dollars it can also be issued in foreign currencies, usually US dollars. Finally, governments have recently introduced "real" or "indexed" bonds that specify not a nominal interest rate but rather a real (i.e., inflation-adjusted) rate of return.

How is a government to choose among this bewildering array of possibilities? To estimate the consequences of different economic scenarios for each of a large number of possible debt configurations most governments end up using computer models of their debt structure and the economic environment they operate in. Instead of guiding us through the dense technical thicket that these exercises involve, Bolder and Lee-Sing instead focus on two key principles that underlie all such analysis.

The first is the trade-off between cost and risk. In most countries, and at most times, short-term debt generally carries a lower interest rate than long-term debt. So why don't governments minimize their interest costs by issuing only short-term debt? Because the interest paid on short-term obligations tends to jump around more than that paid on long-term obligations, and the "yield curve" occasionally becomes inverted, that is, short rates sometimes exceed long rates. If a government does opt mainly for short-term debt, it may find that its interest costs rise to painfully high levels if it has to refinance its debt during a macroeconomic crunch. During the Asian crisis of the late 1990s many governments had to refinance at crisis-level interest rates.

This trade-off between risk and cost is well known to anyone who has ever had a mortgage. Should you keep your mortgage open to take advantage of low current interest rates or should you lock in for fear that rates will rise? It might be thought that governments, which seldom die or go bankrupt, should be indifferent to risk, but, as Bolder and Lee-Sing argue, unpleasant refinancing surprises can knock a hole in the most carefully planned budgets and may eventually cause governments to pay higher interest rates on all their debts.

As public employees, Bolder and Lee-Sing are not well placed to be critical of current debt-management policies in Canada. But they do note that since the mid-1990s the federal government has shifted its balance toward issuing more longer-term debt and less short-term treasury bills. Although short-term interest rates have remained very low by historical standards, the government's goal has been to avoid unpleasant refinancing surprises. Prudence was the official watchword of Paul Martin's term as finance minister and the move to lengthen the average maturity of government debt is simply one more example of that prudence. (Our conclusion, not Bolder and Lee-Sing's.)

The second key principle is that in order to maintain well-functioning markets for government securities, it is necessary to have at least some government securities in the market. If the drive to reduce government debt ultimately succeeded in eliminating the debt entirely, the market for government securities would cease to exist. Because the Bank of Canada transmits changes in interest rates to the markets by influencing the purchase and sale of government bonds, if the market for government bonds dried up that would make the conduct of monetary policy more complicated. Moreover, because government bonds are usually thought of as being risk-free, the interest rates they pay are a useful benchmark for participants in private credit markets. Without them, borrowers and lenders may not have a good idea of how much of any quoted interest rate is actually interest rate and how much is risk premium.

In sum, although the decline in Canadian governments' outstanding debts since the mid-1990s has almost certainly been a good thing for the country, it has complicated the job of maintaining well-functioning markets for government debt. On the other hand, things are not yet desperate in the debt markets. Governments have not got out of the debt game entirely. They still have large stocks of outstanding debt, substantial chunks of which are regularly coming due. Because government surpluses are not large enough to redeem all these debts at once, the debts have to be rolled over, that is, replaced with new debt, and this helps maintain the efficiency of the debt markets. In addition, as Bolder and Lee-Sing describe, government debt managers have come up with new ways of maintaining the gross flow of debt into the market even as the net flow has declined. This helps maintain the liquidity of the market, which they argue both provides Canadians with an important public good and also lowers governments' interest costs. It is also good for securities dealers, of course, though taxpayers may wonder whether what is good for Dominion Securities is necessarily good for the Dominion of Canada (again, our comment, not Bolder and Lee-Sing's). Those who argue that it is believe that keeping the market and its attendant expertise in place will save costs when and if governments go back to borrowing as frequently and as much as they used to.

In his comments on the Bolder and Lee-Sing chapter, Carleton University's *Huntley Schaller* focuses on an idea prompted by their discussion of the different types of financial instruments available to governments, but also firms. As noted already, an increase in Canadian government debt can cause no more than an infinitesimal rise in world interest rates: Canada is simply too small an economy to have more than that effect. As a result, most economists have assumed that greater government borrowing cannot affect the cost of capital Canadian firms face. Government borrowing may force them offshore to find funds, and that in turn may force Canadians to share more of their GDP with foreigners, but it will not affect the level of investment in Canada because interest rates will not change. But what if, with no change in the underlying world interest rate, foreign lenders know less about Canadian firms than Canadian lenders do and therefore charge them a higher risk premium, above and beyond the interest rate, than Canadian lenders would? If that is true, Canadian government borrowing still will not affect the world interest rate but because it will force Canadian firms to borrow from lenders who know less about them, it will raise the effective cost of their capital. And that may well cause the Canadian investment rate to decline. Schaller's own work on the interest rate/investment connection suggests that higher costs of capital can have quite substantial effects on the decision to invest. He concludes that "the crowding out caused by government deficits could be substantial even in the open-economy case."

Do We Need Rules for the Debt?

One approach to controlling government debt is to legislate against it. This may seem a deceptively simple approach, but in fact many governments around the world have asked their legislatures to impose self-denying ordinances on themselves. Fiscal rules come in many styles. To assess their usefulness, we asked *Don Drummond* to provide a paper. As senior vice-president and chief economist of the TD Bank, Drummond heads up one of the best applied policy shops in the country. Even more important for our purposes, he spent 23 years in the federal Department of Finance, ending up as associate deputy minister before moving on to the private sector.

Drummond is not opposed to the principle of having formal rules on budget deficits or government debt. Governments may have very good reasons for wanting to limit their ability to borrow money. Far-sighted politicians will understand that governments sometimes have trouble seeing beyond the next election or the passing of the current generation of voters. If future generations cannot vote their interests, then fiscal rules that prevent their exploitation, whether in the form of statutes or constitutional provisions, may serve as a useful substitute. Governments may also wish to reassure lenders who may be wary of being burned by profligate fiscal policies. Whether for these or other reasons, many jurisdictions around the world have decided to impose restraints on themselves. Most US states operate under borrowing restrictions while most Canadian provinces have fiscal rules of one kind or another, even if the majority were adopted only as recently as the 1990s.

Drummond's views on the practical value of fiscal rules seem to have been greatly influenced by the federal government's experience with them, which he lived through as an official in the Department of Finance. Conservative Finance Minister Michael Wilson introduced the *Spending Control Act*, which, as its name suggests, imposed legislative limits on the federal government's ability to spend money.

In Drummond's view, choosing exactly the right fiscal rules is a demanding art. Rules that are too rigid can put the government that must live by them in a fiscal straitjacket in times of economic or national emergency. Yet rules that are sufficiently flexible to deal with untoward economic events tend to be complex and thus quickly lose their transparency. The Mulroney government's rules exempted strongly cyclical spending programs such as unemployment insurance and also allowed the legislated spending limits to be exceeded so long as the excess was made good by undershooting the limits in the two succeeding years. In Drummond's view, these rules were too complicated and as a result failed the communications test: they could not easily be explained to ordinary Canadians, and therefore the government's success or failure in achieving the rules did not significantly affect its fiscal credibility.

Upon taking office in 1993, the Liberal government of Jean Chrétien decided to scrap fiscal rules in favour of a strong political commitment in favour of deficit reduction. Hence Paul Martin's declaration, already referred to, that his fiscal targets would be met "come hell or high water," a commitment that helped the Liberals achieve a balanced budget within five years of taking office. Drummond concludes that while fiscal rules may be useful in achieving fiscal targets, they clearly are not necessary. Some political commitments are every bit as good as formal rules (and some even better). The country now seems to have worked itself into a situation in which we have an informal but powerful rule that the federal budget must be balanced. After six years of surpluses, in both good and not-so-good economic times, the political cost to the finance minister who took the federal government back into the red would probably be very high.

Should we now move on to the federal debt and try to establish a fiscal rule concerning it? Drummond reports that in its early days, Paul Martin's Finance Department did consider establishing targets for the debt-to-GDP ratio but decided that these were not practical, mainly for reasons having to do with the denominator of the ratio, the GDP. GDP statistics are subject to frequent after-the-fact revision. The estimates that Statistics Canada publishes every quarter are normally revised a number of times, sometimes years later. A government that was running close to the statutory debt limit might find that every revision in the GDP required adjustments in its net debt, and therefore in its current budget balance. A second reason why targeting the debt-to-GDP ratio would be difficult is simply that, quite apart from problems of revisions, the government does not control the GDP. Granted, it may not control its debt (the ratio's numerator) all that closely either – changes in interest rates or economic conditions lead to changes in the current budget balance and therefore in the debt, as Kneebone and Chung demonstrate – but it has even less control over the GDP.

There is a further, even more important difficulty with targeting the debt-to-GDP ratio. In Drummond's view, what made the emergence of an informal deficit rule possible was widespread agreement both among economists and in the public at large that the deficit was badly out of control and in desperate need of reduction. As a couple of the other papers in this volume make clear, while there does seem to be a consensus that government debt is still too high in Canada, there is no agreement either inside or outside the economics profession about the optimal debt-to-GDP ratio. Drummond argues that until economists lay the intellectual groundwork for such an agreement, there is no point trying to devise a formal fiscal rule to govern the future evolution of government debt. He also argues that the deficit and debt are not the only fiscal variables of interest to policy makers. The path of public spending and the level and composition of taxation are also important and may be candidates for fiscal rules of one kind or another, although again Drummond implies that the economics profession is some distance from establishing exactly what the best policies in these areas are.

In his comments on Don Drummond's paper, the University of Alberta's *Paul Boothe*, a public finance economist with hands-on experience helping run fiscal policy in both Alberta and Saskatchewan, begins by underlining Drummond's conclusion that if rules are to work they must enjoy the support of both the government that has to live under them and the voters that put it in power. They should also be simple, strict, hard to amend and easy to communicate to both spending departments and the public. Moreover, adherence to fiscal rules should be easy to measure and the benchmark against which they are measured should be the actual objective – e.g., the realized budget balance – rather than forecast outcomes.

Boothe agrees with Drummond that governments can get their fiscal house in order without fiscal rules. Saskatchewan's NDP government, which Boothe worked for in the late 1990s, simply announced that it intended to balance its budget during its first mandate and then proceeded to do so. On the other hand, Ralph Klein's Conservative government of Alberta, which Boothe also worked for, used formal fiscal rules to guide its way to deficit and then debt reduction.

A common argument against budget-deficit rules is that they remove the government's ability to respond to economic shocks in a counter-cyclical and thus stabilizing, manner. Boothe does not see this as a major problem. He argues that the most effective counter-cyclical fiscal policy comes from the "automatic stabilizers" built into the tax-and-transfer system, and that much discretionary fiscal policy ends up being too late to be effective. Even worse, because of the lags involved in creating programs and planning the spending, such discretionary fiscal policy often ends up being destabilizing: its effects kick in only after the economy's natural adjustment process has begun to reverse the effects of the initial shock.

Drawing on his experience in Alberta and Saskatchewan, Boothe argues that fiscal rules have three main roles. First, they help political leaders resist demands for more spending, whether from around the cabinet table or from the general public. "Working in a finance department," he writes, "one quickly realizes that even after you eliminate spending requests of questionable value, there are always more worthy projects than there is money available to finance them." Second, setting and meeting formal rules or targets helps establish and then bolster the credibility of the fiscal authority. The main reason complex fiscal rules usually fail is that they are too complicated to allow the public to determine whether the government has been successful or not, thus leaving no way for it to establish its credibility.

A third role for fiscal rules is dealing appropriately with volatile revenues, which are especially important in a province dependent on its energy sector. Alberta's current fiscal rule stipulates that three-quarters of any windfall from the energy sector must be used for debt reduction, and a much smaller fraction (2.5 percent) as a cushion to prevent the budget from going into deficit. Thus the Alberta rule takes most of the revenue volatility out of the annual budget picture and helps focus public attention on longer-run averages for spending and revenues.

Boothe closes with a warning about the danger of moving to accrual accounting, as the federal and most provincial governments are doing. Under accrual accounting, only the current interest and depreciation expenses associated with a capital purchase show up in the annual budget. A jurisdiction that purchases a dollar's worth of new capital will increase its current budgeted expenses by only a small fraction of that dollar, say five cents. Such a change has significant implications for what the conventional measure of a budget deficit really means, and economists and policy makers will have to think carefully about what sensible fiscal rules might look like in such an environment. Moreover, allowing politicians to spend dollars that cost them only five cents in the budget may have dangerous implications for their behaviour. Boothe agrees with Drummond that the country needs to debate these issues, however arcane they may seem, if the fiscal achievements of the recent past are not to be squandered.

What Have We Learned?

After two days and eight papers, we needed a couple of "wise men" to try to put it all together and give us their assessment of what we had learned and what we had yet to learn. For this we turned to two outstanding Canadian economists who have long and distinguished records in analyzing many different problems in Canadian economic policy: *Lars Osberg* from Dalhousie University and *Jack Mintz*, President of the C.D. Howe Institute and an economics professor at the University of Toronto.

In his comments on the conference, *Lars Osberg* challenges what seemed to be a consensus among the paper-givers that the big question in any discussion of debt policy is intergenerational redistribution. In his view, what is more crucial is *intra*generational redistribution, an issue that arises because the debt debate is often a proxy for a more general and more ideological debate about the appropriate role and size of government.

Osberg observes that among economists there is quite a wide range of opinion about what level of debt would be optimal. An informal poll of attendees at this conference found that opinion ranged between 20 and 50 percent of GDP, which will strike most readers as a substantial variation – except that, as we have seen, within the literature on this question opinions range from –300 percent (a number that would require the government, as Osberg notes, to own just about all the capital in society) to +70 percent. A "fiscal anchor" whose size is so hard to pin down may be of dubious value.

But if so, what is all the fuss about in the debt debate? Osberg argues that in fact the debate is largely about how big the government should be. In principle, the questions of, on the one hand, of a government's optimal size and, on the other, how it should finance its spending, are separate. In practice, they are usually closely linked. As Osberg puts it, "expenditure cuts have been crucial in producing the recent surpluses of Canadian governments, and tax cuts have followed, so deficit elimination, debt repayment and a reduction of distributional equity and the role of government in Canadian society have coincided."

Use of the word "equity" requires some discussion of the question "equity for whom?" If more government spending is financed with bonds, then at some future date more potential consumption will be transferred from taxpayers to bondholders. Whether that is a good thing or not is a question of *intra*generational fairness. By contrast, a focus on *inter*generational equity, whose analysis usually regards all members of a given generation as identical, eliminates this problem by assumption. But government debt only comes into existence because people are different: some people are willing to postpone their consumption by purchasing the debt; others prefer to consume now and pay higher taxes later and they therefore urge the government to incur debt. That the members of a generation – best defined, in Osberg's view, as all the people alive at a certain time – differ in this respect is a key aspect of reality and should therefore be a key part of the analysis of government debt.

Another difficulty with emphasizing intergenerational rather than intragenerational equity is that doing so causes us to focus where the action isn't. Osberg argues that, except in very unusual times, the differences *between* generations in terms of income and consumption are quite small compared to differences *within* generations. It follows that if equity is to be seriously pursued as a social goal, there is a greater payoff from focusing on redistribution within rather than between generations.

That, says Osberg, is where the question of the size of government comes in. Although economists customarily argue that government interventions in the economy should aim at correcting "market failures," and therefore be efficiency-enhancing, in fact most of what Canadian governments do, whether in health care, education, or social welfare, aims at redistributing resources from those who have more to those who have less. Thus, if concern about debt reduction leads to a reduction in the size of government, the effect is likely to be a reduction in the amount of intragenerational redistribution in Canadian society.

Osberg argues that this is exactly what happened in the 1990s. The federal government's decision to eliminate its deficit led to an almost unprecedented reduction in the share of federal government spending in GDP. Although Ottawa characterizes this reduction as having brought federal spending to its lowest level in 50 years, Osberg notes that you have to go back 70 years, all the way to the 1930s, to see federal spending at such a low level over such a sustained period. The consequences for the distribution of income in Canada must have been as dramatic as the decline itself and the brunt of the change will have been borne by people lower down the income scale. Osberg concludes that "the real issue in the debt debate is the implication for equity, within generations, of how we choose to deal with debt." In his view, "it is misleading in the extreme to portray the debt issue as a conflict between generations."

In his commentary on the conference, *Jack Mintz* makes a number of points on various aspects of the debt debate and then focuses on whether the debt war is over.

On whether we should care about government debt, Mintz is emphatic: we definitely should. The Ricardian equivalence doctrine, under which private actions offset any effects of government debt in the capital markets, strikes him as "extreme." People are neither infinitely-lived nor so thoroughly altruistic that, confronted with new government debt, their reaction is to save in order to prepare for the consequent increase in the taxes of all members of all future generations. Mintz echoes both David Johnson and Bev Dahlby when he writes: "Debt therefore does matter, and it could well reduce economic growth."

That said, the question of what the optimal level of debt might be is not easy. The optimal rate need not be zero. Governments do at times make long-lived investments that will benefit future generations and it is not unreasonable to ask future generations to help finance them. On the other hand, if governments were as far-seeing as they should be, then Ricardian equivalence would probably hold, and the evidence suggests it does not. If governments *aren't* far-seeing, they will often be inclined to borrow whether or not the funds will be used to acquire long-lived public assets, and that may do considerable harm to future generations. A useful operating assumption therefore is that democratic governments may build up more than the optimal amount of debt.

On the practical question of what policy makers should do about the debt, Mintz argues that our conference, like others before it, has provided little help. In deciding whether to borrow in order to finance a specific public investment, policy makers will want to know whether and by how much the investment's rate of return exceeds the rate of interest on the debt incurred to finance it. Theory tells them that if the return is greater than the rate of interest, the use of debt is justified. Unfortunately, "we do not know very much about what aspects of public expenditure are truly investments rather than consumption. Nor do we know, except in limited cases, the actual rates of return on government investments." There is, to be sure, sketchy evidence on the rate of return to different kinds of education and to some forms of infrastructure investment. And cross-country studies suggest that too large a public sector may reduce the rate of economic growth. But in most cases we simply do not have the information we need in order to make an informed decision about whether debt finance is justified or not.

Mintz' final comment concerns what he regards as the coming fiscal crisis associated with the aging of the baby boomers. He accepts Robin Boadway's arguments about intergenerational fairness. If a generation is substantially poorer or faces substantially greater dangers than successor generations are likely to, then it may be justified in passing along tax burdens to future generations by financing many of its spending needs with debt. The generation that lived through the Great Depression and World War II may have been justified in spreading its burdens, but Mintz argues that "the buildup of Canada's debt since 1975 is less excusable. No war or special shocks can explain why Canada's indebtedness increased so much." Even so, the high rates of taxation resulting from the debt finance of the 1970s, 1980s and 1990s have imposed a heavy burden on the current generation of taxpayers.

In Mintz' view, the crucial question for the next few decades is how the aging and retirement of the baby boomers will impact on the tax rates of the generations that will be asked to finance the boomers' health care and retirement incomes. Bill Robson's paper goes some way in this direction, but the "missing paper" in this conference would have provided detailed estimates of the fiscal and economic consequences of the imminent rapid aging of Canada's population. In its absence, recent work from the OECD suggests that the demographic change the country is about to live through will erode its fiscal position – through increased expenditures and reduced taxes – by fully 8 percent of GDP. With taxes currently running around 43 percent of GDP, if the government sector as a whole continues to run balanced budgets, that means average tax rates may eventually have to rise to above 50 percent of GDP. The consequences for economic growth and for emigration from Canada would likely be very serious. On the other hand, Mintz emphasizes that there is still time to act. Reducing our combined (federal, provincial and municipal) government debt from its current roughly 75 percent of GDP to 25 percent would eventually save five percentage points of GDP in interest payments every year, savings that could be put toward public priorities. Although Jack Mintz' main message is that "real numbers are needed if we are, first, to understand current and future tax burdens and then to act on our understanding," his final comment is that "on balance, given recent analyses of demographic effects provided by the OECD and others, I believe the debt war is far from over."

What We Learned

Having summarized the eight papers and the discussants' comments, as well as the two rapporteurs' thoughts, we now lay out the main lessons we ourselves take from the collection of papers.

Total government debt is much larger than the formal government debt. William Robson's approach to calculating our governments' debts, which is to figure out how much the federal and provincial governments are likely to spend and earn in taxes over the next 50 years, is a daunting task laden with intellectual risks. Still, we are persuaded both by his basic message and approach and by his estimate of $1.1 trillion, at least as a ball-park value. The main difference between the basic debt figures of about $760 billion for the three levels of government for 2001, the year for which he undertook his study, and his estimate of $1.1 trillion comes from the unfunded liabilities that our governments have incurred by their implicit promise to maintain the current level of per capita spending on health care and other social programs. There is no reason to suppose the situation is greatly different today. If these commitments are to be honoured, either taxes will have to rise or governments will have to return to deficit financing. Alternatively, if taxes are to remain at their current per capita level and governments refuse to increase their borrowing, these commitments simply cannot be honoured. The conclusion we draw from Robson's paper is that the debt is still big and that a fiscal crunch is coming as the baby boomers begin to impose larger and larger burdens on the health-care and retirement income systems. The case for trying to get our governments' balance sheets in order before the crunch rather than during or after it is compelling.

The formal debt is not all that matters. We should also keep in mind the total amount of government indebtedness. The main point of Robin Boadway's paper is that the amount of marketable government debt (i.e., outstanding bonds) is only part of the picture. The entire range of government activities, whether taxation, expenditure or regulation, can move resources from one generation to another. Canadian economists need to dig harder to find out exactly which way the money is flowing and Canadian politicians need to keep in mind all the flows between generations before changing any of them. Still, just because the formal debt is not the only way of effecting intergenerational transfers does not mean the formal debt does not count. We should not simply assume that our governments' non-debt activities fully offset the debt's transfer of resources from future generations to current taxpayers. If essentially the same political coalitions decide most policy, then all transfers may move in the same direction. To be blunt, if we baby boomers were able to tilt debt policy in our favour, we may have been able to tilt *all* intergenerational policies in our favour, though until all the data are in this can only be an hypothesis.

Although economic conditions can change quickly, policy is often slow to respond. In their paper, Ron Kneebone and Jennifer Chung argue that Canada's debt problems of the 1980s and 1990s were the result of a time bomb that was set ticking in the 1970s when growing structural deficits were camouflaged by the very low interest rates and relatively high economic growth rates of that era. The combination of the two meant that the debt-to-GDP ratio remained stable or declined even as cyclically-adjusted budget balances worsened. When in the early 1980s interest rates spiked and growth rates fell the fiscal turnaround was swift and brutal. Although at the federal level the Mulroney government eliminated the structural deficit by the early 1990s, it was not until the mid-1990s that the Chrétien Liberals finally ran a surplus. In recent years interest rates have been lower and growth rates higher than in the 1980s, but governments that remain heavily indebted must be constantly aware that they are vulnerable to changes in these key economic variables. Governments need to watch their structural balances very closely, and prevent them from getting out of control. In view of the last three decades' experience, prudence is best.

Government debt is costly and harms future generations. The papers by David Johnson and Bev Dahlby persuade us that government debt *does* matter. Johnson convinces us that Ricardian equivalence does not hold, and that government deficits in an open economy like Canada lead to a reduction in the share of domestically produced output that Canadians receive as income. Johnson estimates the cost of this effect at about $3,600 a year for a family of four. Dahlby's paper shows that even if Ricardian equivalence does hold, there may still be a decline in the rate of economic growth. The reason is that a higher debt means higher interest payments by governments. The higher taxation this requires imposes efficiency costs on the economy, including a lower rate of growth. Dahlby estimates the cost at about 15 percent of the amount borrowed, which means that any public project financed with borrowed funds should bring a return of 15 percent if it is to be worth the resources invested in it. Another way of looking at his calculation is that debt reduction brings a return in economic efficiency equal to 15 cents on the dollar. There may not be many more-productive investments open to governments. Moreover, 15 percent may understate the true cost of public borrowing. In Dahlby's model, higher taxes reduce the rate of economic growth by discouraging saving and reducing the future stock of capital. But in the real world they may also reduce the future stock of human capital by discouraging Canadians from investing in their own knowledge and skills.

The "optimal" level of government debt may have less to do with efficiency and macroeconomic stability than with intergenerational equity. Although he did not comment directly on David Johnson's and Bev Dahlby's calculations of the efficiency costs of public borrowing, William Scarth argues that considerations of fairness (or "equity") may be at least as important in any discussion of optimal debt policy. Scarth develops a simple model of economic growth in which the aging of the baby boomers reduces average future living standards, not in absolute terms but in comparison to where growth would take them had there been no boom, and he tries to calculate how large a reduction in government debt would be needed now to help share this burden between generations. Such calculations are always sensitive to the assumptions that lie behind them, but Scarth's bottom line that the federal debt-to-GDP ratio needs to be reduced to 20-25 percent of GDP seems plausible to us.

The recent move toward greater use of long-term debt instruments is a reasonable strategy for reducing the chances of unpleasant surprises in debt-servicing costs. This is one of the main points suggested by David Bolder and Clifton Lee-Sing's paper, and it seems right to us. Short-term interest rates can be volatile, and avoiding this volatility in the budget makes for easier fiscal planning. In an era of generally low interest rates it makes sense to lock in the benefits of such rates.

Formal rules are neither necessary nor sufficient for making significant headway on the deficit or debt. We agree completely with Don Drummond's main point that a credible political commitment is the fundamental requirement for deficit or debt reduction. The federal government's inability in the early 1990s to eliminate its deficit when it had fiscal rules and its subsequent balancing of its budget after these rules had been dropped show that rules are neither necessary nor sufficient. On the other hand, we agree with Paul Boothe that simple, well-crafted rules that are easy for the public to understand can be very useful to any government that wants to say "no" to interest groups seeking increased spending. What now seems to be the operative rule in Ottawa and several provincial capitals – "thou shalt always balance the budget" – is very easy to understand and does imply a rule for the debt ("so long as the economy grows the debt-to-GDP ratio will decline") but elaboration of a more precise rule for the debt, one that specified a target for either the debt-to-GDP ratio or the debt-per-person ratio, is made difficult, as Drummond says, by economists' inability to agree on what the best level for the debt would be.

The aging of Canada's population will put greater stress on the fiscal positions of Canadian governments. Continued debt reduction for the next several years will help ease this coming fiscal crisis. A fiscal crunch is coming in Canada. William Robson's calculations suggest that Canadian governments' unfunded liabilities amount to $300 billion, this on top of contracted debt of almost $800 billion. More-detailed calculations might well put the number higher. (They might also put it lower, of course, but upside risk is the main worry here.) In this case, an unfunded liability means an expenditure for which there is no corresponding tax revenue without an increase in tax rates. In his comments, Jack Mintz cites

OECD estimates that coming demographic changes will cause a deterioration in Canada's fiscal position of fully eight percentage points of GDP. With tax revenues currently running at about 43 percent of GDP, meeting those perceived expenditure obligations could take average tax rates above 50 percent of GDP, which would be bound to have harmful effects on investment, saving and economic growth. One way for governments to ease the fiscal squeeze would be to run budget surpluses over the next few years in order to reduce government interest payments and thus open up room for future expenditure needs. Another way would be to reduce current expenditures on all but truly essential public services so that current generations of taxpayers might also benefit from continuing tax reductions.

The baby-boom generation has some tough questions to ask itself as it enters the final few years of its working life. Believing as we do that public borrowing has important efficiency costs we were frankly surprised by how much of the discussion at the conference and in these papers had to do with fairness – something economists are by no means uniquely qualified to judge. There did seem to be widespread agreement that generations which through no fault of their own suffer grave misfortune should feel free to share their burden with future generations by financing at least part of their public expenditures by borrowing. The example of the generation that lived through the Great Depression and World War II – the generation that included the fathers and mothers of many people attending the conference – was mentioned in several papers and comments. Most commentators seemed to think that people in this generation had been entitled to share their burdens with their children and grandchildren by using debt finance more than governments normally should. But there was much less agreement about whether the generation that was politically decisive in the 1970s and 1980s should have felt itself entitled to share the burdens of stagflation and recession with its children and grandchildren. The recessions of 1980–82 and 1990–91 were unpleasant to live through, but in retrospect they were not nearly as severe as the Great Depression. By the same token the mental strain of the Cold War undoubtedly took its toll but hardly compares with the trauma of 1939–45. Moreover, now that the baby boomers are in their fifties, it becomes clear that despite the slower economic growth of the last third of the twentieth century compared to the first postwar decades, they have enjoyed a higher standard of living, by far, than all previous Canadian generations. Does this luckiest of generations want its legacy to its children to be severe indebtedness and high taxes, or does it wish to be fair to those who follow it and to leave them fiscal circumstances at least as favourable as it inherited?

Is the debt war over? No, it is not.

Note

1. The deficit is the difference between the government's revenues and its expenditures in a given year, while the debt is just the accumulated deficit. If a government runs a deficit, it adds to its debt. If it runs a surplus, it reduces its debt: the extra revenues can be used to retire bonds when they come due.

In fact, the numbers quoted are only approximately right. The numbers provided are the latest "consolidated government finance" data from Statistics Canada as of January 18, 2004. But the federal debt number ($527 billion) is as of March 31, 2003, the close of Ottawa's most recent complete fiscal year. Similarly, because it takes time for Statistics Canada to compile the relevant data the provincial-territorial number ($249 billion) is as of March 31, 2002, while the municipal government number ($10 billion) is as of Dec. 31, 2001.

Because the conference on which this book is based was held in October, 2002, any references to the "current value" of any fiscal figure are to values that were current at that time. This is particularly a problem for William Robson's paper, which attempts a detailed, customized tally of published values of government debt. Rather than ask Robson to update his remarkable accounting effort to take changing numbers into account, we have published his paper containing the numbers he presented at the conference. He and the other authors are absolved from any responsibility for publication delays, which are entirely the editors' fault.

1

how big is the debt?
three tallies for liquidity, sustainability
and competitiveness

William B. P. Robson

Introduction and Overview

Among the many deceptively simple questions one can ask, the one the editors of this volume posed to me for this paper deserves prominent mention. The implied analogy, that totting up government obligations is like, say, taking a tape measure to a plank, is misleading. Different concerns make different tallies relevant, and while clear concepts and readily available data sometimes coincide, they often do not. Anticipating this problem, the editors provided subsidiary questions about market versus carrying value, off-book liabilities, government employee and social-security pensions, and where governments should report such numbers. To be useful, however, those answers must follow an exploration of a more fundamental question: Why worry about government debt at all?

The first substantive section of this paper contains my attempt to say why we might care about government debt. I begin by noting an all-but-unbridgeable gap between views of the world in which debt is and should be a constraint on government action and views in which it is not and should not. Although rarely noted by economists, this non-meeting of minds strongly influences debates over the significance and measurement of government debt.

Moving into territory where differences in outlook are less stark, I distinguish three types of motives for caring about debt:

- concern about a specific event, for instance, a government failing to make payments in full or on time, and the financial instability that such a liquidity crisis would cause;

- concerns that government decision-making takes too little account of the medium and longer-term sustainability of existing spending and tax policies; and
- concerns about how changes in government balance sheets affect behaviour elsewhere in the economy.

While these concerns overlap, they draw attention to different types of assets and liabilities, and the tally most pertinent to one will not be to another.

The second substantive section looks at the liquidity-oriented balance sheet that is pertinent to concerns about cash payments. It begins with Statistics Canada's Financial Management System (FMS) presentation, which draws heavily on key public-accounts conventions, and follows traditional presentations of financial data in the government and nongovernment sectors, starting with the categories that shed most light on short-term cash flows. I make some adjustments to the usually reported figures, adjustments that reinforce the message from conventional balance sheets that Canadian governments are in no imminent danger of running short of cash.

The third substantive section of the paper uses the liquidity-oriented tally as a base on which to construct measures of net worth that bear on questions of longer-term sustainability and public-sector management. These adjustments add to both sides of the balance sheet – less to assets than to liabilities, however – and shed light on the scale of governments' commitments over time and the taxes Canadians must pay or the programs they must trim to prevent the first type of concerns, about liquidity, becoming acute at some future date. The overall impression left by this section is that large implicit liabilities associated with health-care spending are the most significant long-term challenge faced by Canadian governments, with the provinces bearing its brunt.

My foray into measures of government balance sheets that bear on nongovernmental sector behaviour in the final substantive section of the paper is far more tentative. Saying anything definite about the impact of the future taxes needed to cover government obligations would require a more detailed modelling of the tax and program changes implied by our existing liability structures than I can undertake here. Investigating the impact of government obligations on saving requires strong assumptions about how big and how certain nongovernmental actors think those obligations are, which this paper shows to be matters of some uncertainty. On a third question – how Canada's future mix of programs and taxes will affect its attractiveness to workers and investors – I present data on longer-term implicit liabilities and assets that show Canada in a less favourable light than the conventional measures suggest, thanks to the prospect of a move from a relatively young to an older population that is more dramatic than many other developed countries face.

Notwithstanding the uncertainties that forestall this third type of tally, the results of the first and second tallies of government net obligations do suggest answers to the overriding question posed by the editors: "Is the debt war over?" The liquidity-oriented balance sheet indicates that the battle against a possible cash crisis in the mid-1990s was indeed won. The longer-term balance sheet, however, indicates that the war against potentially unsustainable obligations will continue through our lifetimes, and such international comparisons as we can make show that Canada's relative attractiveness to migrants and investors may deteriorate if we do not wage it effectively.

Why Calculate Government Net Worth?

The appropriate tally of what Canadian governments owe – or, to use more general language, what their net worth is – depends on the normative and positive considerations that motivate the exercise.

The Great Divide: Constrained and Unconstrained Views

The outset of this paper and this volume is an apt place to note that normative considerations loom large in two philosophically and practically contradictory answers to the question "Is the debt war over?"

Many who take what Sowell (1987) calls "constrained" views of the world would find the question odd. They would point out that debt nearly always signifies that governments have spent beyond their means; likely represents an unconscionable redistribution of resources; and prefigures a painful adjustment. To them, debt is almost self-evidently bad: as long as governments owe, the war cannot and should not end.

Many who take an "unconstrained" view would find the question irritating. They would argue that governments have great capacity to improve well-being, and should command resources in proportion. To them, worrying about one financing method over another is a distraction or, worse, an attempt to hobble governments; the debt war was always misguided and cannot end too soon.

Most of us would deny taking such reflexive positions and insist that our concerns (or lack of them) are positive, grounded in evidence. My main focus below is on the middle ground where different concerns make different obligations significant. But experts share the constrained and unconstrained predilections of the general population, and these predilections will surface at times as we address possible reasons for caring about and counting different assets and liabilities.

Between the two extremes, I think we can discern three sets of motives for measuring and managing government net worth that are distinct enough to warrant separate treatment.

Concern About an Event: Liquidity, Default and Financial Instability

The sharpest-edged concern is fear of a government failing to make payment because it is short of cash and cannot raise it when required. For most of the past half-century, Canadians have seen this concern as remote, and observers of an unconstrained bent have tended to argue that it did not apply to us. Historically and elsewhere, however, fear of a liquidity crisis and the disruptions when the financial assets held by savers are devalued or cancelled have been the pre-eminent motive for watching government balance sheets.

Many governments in the developing world and the ex-communist countries defaulted on obligations in the 1980s and 1990s. Here in Canada, fear that some provinces might fail to re-fund in an orderly way helped spur the fiscal consolidation of the mid-1990s, and the Japanese government's inability to sell a bond issue sent tremors through world fixed-income and foreign-exchange markets in 2002.[1]

While decisions not to pay obviously rest with debtors, and decisions not to lend with potential creditors, these concerns can usefully be characterized as centring on an event. Financing crises can happen without governments deciding, under conditions of calm reflection, to default; market turbulence caused by unrelated events can impede what otherwise would be a normal refinancing. The actors proximately involved might fear the longer-term consequences of their actions but feel that circumstances force their hand. Concerns about liquidity motivate scrutiny of balance sheets to see if such circumstances threaten to arise.

Concern About Government Behaviour: Sustainability of Programs and Tax Rates

Concerns about the longer-term sustainability of fiscal policy overlap with concerns about cash, since one possible result of an unsustainable fiscal stance is default. The different time scales and decision making involved warrant a separate discussion, however.

The normal longer-term preoccupation is not ultimate failure to pay because of circumstances beyond the control of the parties involved: not until savers and others anticipate failure to pay acutely enough to affect actions today does the concern move from longer-term sustainability to short-term cash crisis. The central longer-term focus is whether governments are attentive enough to how revenue and spending will evolve over time. If formal and implicit obligations put spending on a faster growth path than revenue, avoiding a liquidity crisis will eventually require painful program cuts and/or tax hikes.

One subset of longer-term concerns focuses on public-sector assets, especially nonfinancial assets such as land, bridges, guns and monuments. Accurately recording depreciation on physical assets helps managers budget for their upkeep and replacement.[2] And nonfinancial assets that affect peoples' ability and willingness to pay taxes will affect the sustainability of programs.

Longer-term spending commitments raise more dramatic concerns. Informally, people who recognize constraints have speculated that longer-term commitments that outrun capacity to pay will undermine government programs, that rising taxes will undermine efficiency and competitiveness, and that future taxpayers, finding themselves on the wrong end of an intergenerational deal they did not sign, will force a renegotiation at the ballot box, disappear from the taxable economy, or emigrate. Others, perhaps reflecting more unconstrained views, have emphasized ways in which demographic change and other future developments may push government budgets toward surplus. More formal analysis has quantified the liabilities implied by explicit or implicit government promises, or produced "generational accounts" that show the changes in current programs and taxes needed to equalize the net fiscal benefits of the unborn with those of people currently alive.[3]

Again, the key concern is with decision making in the government sector itself. Legislators, officials and voters operating in ignorance of governments' explicit and implicit assets and liabilities may force awkward future changes in taxes and programs that more complete knowledge could prevent.

Concern About Nongovernmental Behaviour:
Distortions, Saving and International Competition

A third set of concerns centres on the influence of government balance sheets on the behaviour of outside actors.[4] Some of these concerns are implicit in the above discussions of default and longer-term sustainability, but at least three additional concerns warrant special note.

Citizens' claims against each other exercised through the institution of government differ from bilateral claims in that they must be serviced with taxes rather than private payments of interest and principal. Tax-finance changes relative prices and affects resource allocation. A government balance sheet that augmented its liabilities to reflect the distortions involved in servicing them, and augmented its assets to reflect their positive impacts, would shed useful light on governments' economic effects.

Claims exercised through government are also typically less transparent than private claims. If, for example, creditors feel one dollar richer for each dollar in claims they hold, but those who will be called on to service the claims do not feel poorer by the same amount, nongovernmental saving might be lower than otherwise.

Finally, people often compare fiscal positions in evaluating different jurisdictions as places to work or invest. However high or low Canadian government debt may look to a liquidity-oriented investor, a generational accountant, an economist calculating deadweight losses and positive externalities, or a saver, its level compared with that of governments elsewhere will influence flows of workers and capital across borders. Even if we conclude that Canada looks good by many measures, we might worry if other countries look better; conversely, if we conclude that Canada looks bad, we might draw comfort if others look worse.

Some Notes on Measurement and Valuation

Assembling numbers relevant to these different concerns presents several challenges. To reduce the footnotes and digressions later, I note some major measurement issues here. Readers more interested in the bottom lines than in the struggle to get to them can skip to the next section without loss of continuity.

Sources. My starting point for the overall government-sector balance sheet is Statistics Canada's Financial Management System (FMS). "General government" as defined in the FMS comprises all institutional units controlled and mainly financed by government, excluding government business enterprises, and for the most part corresponds to the definition of the public sector most readers would likely come up with on their own.[5] The "general government" tally also omits the balance sheets of health and social-service institutions, which is fine for my purposes: I consider these institutions along with other longer-term implicit obligations connected with the services they deliver.

The adjustments I make to the FMS data rely on official sources where possible, as when I use data from the Office of the Chief Actuary on the Canada Pension Plan (CPP) and the outlook for spending on Old Age Security and Guaranteed Income Supplement payments, or data from provincial workers' compensation funds on their assets and liabilities. For many other longer-term calculations, I use projections from a population-based model maintained at the C.D. Howe Institute that is adapted from the International Labour Organization Population Projection Model. Key assumptions in the projections are:

- provincial total fertility rates remain at their 2001 levels through the projection period;
- life expectancies at birth by sex improve at rates akin to those in Statistics Canada's "medium" assumption for improvement in life expectancy;
- net interprovincial migration for each age/sex category decreases linearly from the 2001 figure to zero over five years,[6] and
- net international migration for each age/sex category continues at the 1992–2001 average figure for the entire projection period.

I use the model to project expenditures on programs sensitive to demographic change, using assumptions about per-person constant-dollar spending and inflation that are detailed in each case. I also use the model to project future gross domestic product (GDP) by multiplying the projected working-age population by an index of per-person output growing at the rate that prevailed from 1980 to 2001 (1.7 percent). The key result is the projected change in spending under a particular program relative to GDP. I discuss the use of this number in augmenting standard measures of government balance sheets below.

Timing of observations. Ideally, all valuations in an all-government balance sheet would be "as at" a common, recent date; practically, this ideal is out of reach. The consolidated FMS data I use as my base represent the consolidated balance sheet of federal, provincial and local governments as at 31 March 2000. Many of the adjustments I make use official valuations from the end of the 2000 and 2001 calendar years, and from the end of the 2001/02 fiscal year. My projection-based valuations are implicitly dated from mid-year 2001.

The federal government has announced its intention to move shortly to full accrual accounting. Nonfinancial assets, for example, will be shown at something approaching their economic value, and the liability side will show several contingencies that do not now appear on the balance sheet. Postponed from its originally scheduled implementation with the release of Ottawa's financial statements for 2001/02, the move to accrual accounting means that I include some numbers in my balance sheets that may be superseded by new official estimates with the release of the 2002/03 numbers.

Valuations. Many of my valuations of government assets and liabilities use a benchmark rate of return/discount rate. Although there might be a case for using different benchmarks for different purposes, I think such an approach would add more complexity than enlightenment. Accordingly, I use one benchmark, 6 percent, in valuing several items, including income-yielding assets such as holdings in Crown corporations and natural-resource-bearing land, and implicit assets and liabilities represented by present values of future decreases and increases in spending. Six percent is roughly the average yield on federal and provincial long-term bonds over the five-year period, 1997–2001, and is also almost exactly equal to the yield on the federal real-return bond over that period turned into a nominal yield by multiplying by the Bank of Canada's 2-percent inflation target.[7]

Valuing assets always runs up against a conundrum: Is the amount they would fetch if sold under orderly conditions pertinent to a scenario where the sale may take place under pressure? I opt here for an ordinary-conditions, or "going-concern" approach. While assets will fetch less under "fire-sale" conditions, specifying those conditions precisely enough to speculate intelligently about what impact they might have on prices is impossible.

A final caveat: some official valuations I use assume rates of return and use discount rates other than 6 percent. The long-term returns assumed in the valuation of the CPP's actuarial liability, for example, are roughly 6.6 percent (OCA 2001). I make no attempt to reconcile these numbers but will simply note here that using a 6 percent rate of return in valuing the CPP would bump the CPP's liability up appreciably, while using 6.6 percent for all the other valuations in this paper would, on balance, reduce the net implicit liability of current spending programs.

Awkwardness and caveats noted, it is time for a closer look at the motives for calculating government assets and liabilities, and the numbers that different motives suggest are most relevant.

The Liquidity-Oriented Balance Sheet

When it comes to traditional liquidity concerns, the financial statements of governments themselves provide a good starting point.

Relevant Measures and Issues

The demands of lenders, the desire of parliaments and others to monitor the finances of the executive, and the established conventions of accounting make the financial statements of Canadian governments quite informative about many items affecting liquidity. Like their corporate and nonprofit counterparts, government balance sheets give pride of place to items most immediately affecting cash: receivables, payables, deposits, bank loans, and other short-term liquid assets and liabilities. Next come assets and obligations that will affect cash requirements later and less certainly: longer-term and less liquid financial assets on the credit side; longer-term debt securities and pension plan obligations on the debit side. Nearer the bottom of the ledger come obligations that may or may not affect cash: contingent liabilities such as loan guarantees and amounts at issue in lawsuits. The FMS provides a useful consolidation of figures drawn from public accounts on a consistent basis across different levels of government.

Even a relatively narrow focus on the short-term cash position does not, however, eliminate all ambiguities and uncertainties. To briefly anticipate some of the key issues:

- Financial assets may not be shown at market value. Equity holdings in Crown corporations and other loans, advances and investments may yield returns higher or lower than their value on the books would imply.[8] A cash-oriented valuation that neglected such discrepancies would omit important information.
- Some funds, such as those of workers' compensation agencies, are held against specific future commitments: I deduct these from the liquidity-oriented balance sheet and bring them back in under the discussion of the longer term.

- The valuation of physical assets will almost never correspond to market value, indeed the normal practice of Canada's federal and provincial governments, reflecting the traditional liquidity-oriented presentation of public accounts, is to accord them a nominal value of one dollar. The FMS compilations explicitly follow this reasoning (see Statistics Canada 2001a, 89). But many physical assets, such as natural-resource-bearing land, do produce income and could be sold or hypothecated to make at least part of their economic value available in cash.
- Balance sheets may, for legislative or other reasons, not record the same amounts for certain accrued liabilities, such as government-employee pensions and benefits, that actuaries and economists would recommend.
- Contractual commitments and contingent liabilities can affect short-term cash positions. Many would argue that contractual commitments belong in a liquidity-based analysis, but I omit them, since summing commitments over a period of years reveals little about the cost of terminating or renegotiating a contract. Contingent liabilities present a major challenge. Canadian governments have huge exposure to potential claims through enterprises that insure private-sector claims such as deposits, mortgages, trade financing and pensions, through direct debt guarantees, through international commitments, and through actual or potential lawsuits. These liabilities sometimes appear on balance sheets – as when provisions for losses on loans by Crown corporations reduce the value of financial assets – but many are shown separately or not at all. One approach to producing comprehensive tallies of government obligations involves adding to the normal financial-statement numbers all contingent liabilities to which governments have affixed a value, as Emes and Kreptul (1999, 10) do.[9] I prefer to accept governments' existing balance-sheet amounts for a liquidity analysis.[10]
- Formal and informal backstopping arrangements exist among governments and related entities. Some provinces borrow on behalf of Crown corporations, municipalities, school boards, and so on. During the 1990s, interest-rate spreads among Canada's provinces showed some fiscally weaker and smaller provinces in a remarkably favourable light, likely reflecting a perceived federal backstop. To some extent, the distortion that these guarantees may create in the balance sheet of an individual government will shrink in a consolidated presentation.
- A final problem worth a note at the outset is that the public accounts statements of a government may reflect deliberate deception. Limits of time and space make my response to this problem here a matter of drawing attention to it rather than trying to adjust financial statements to correct them. In one case, however, I remove a deliberate fudge.

Table 1

The Liquidity-Oriented Balance Sheet ($ billions)

	Federal	Provincial/ Territorial	Local	Consolidated FPL Total
FPL BALANCE SHEETS (FMS)				
Financial Assets				
Cash	18	5	9	31
Receivables	5	24	8	34
Advances	51	36	2	89
Securities	10	166	16	126
Other	2	2	4	8
Subtotal: Financial Assets	86	234	40	291
Nonfinancial Assets	0	0	0	0
Total Assets	86	234	40	291
Liabilities				
Bank Overdrafts & Loans	4	4	5	8
Payables & Advances	37	42	14	89
Coins	4	(0)	(0)	3
Marketable Debt	457	309	36	732
Deposits	11	49		60
Pension Liabilities	128	66		195
Other	10	21	3	34
Total Liabilities	651	490	52	1121
Balance	(565)	(256)	(12)	(931)
ADJUSTMENTS				
Financial Assets				
Market Value of Gold & Foreign Currency		5		5
Income-Based Value of Fin. Assets	6	(88)	(3)	(84)
Net Fin. Assets, Workers' Comp. Agencies		(29)		(29)
Net Fin. Assets, Deposit Ins. Agencies	(1)	(1)		(2)
Funds in Non-Arm's Length Organizations	7			7
Subtotal: Financial Assets	17	(118)	(3)	(104)
Nonfinancial Assets				
Income-Based Valuation of Land	4	196		200
Subtotal: Nonfinancial Assets	4	196	0	200
Total Adjustments to Assets	20	78	(3)	96
Liabilities				
Coins	(4)	0	0	(3)
Fair Market Value of Unmatured Debt	35			35
Over-Accrual of Pension Liabilities	(7)			(7)
Total Adjustments to Liabilities	24	0	0	25
Net Adjustments	(4)	78	(3)	71
LIQUIDITY-ORIENTED BALANCE SHEET				
Assets				
Financial Assets	103	116	37	187
Nonfinancial Assets	4	196	0	200
Total Assets	106	312	37	386
Liabilities	675	491	52	1146
Balance	(569)	(178)	(15)	(760)

Source: Author's calculations as described in the text.

The Tally

My starting point is the consolidated balance sheet of Canadian federal, provincial, and local governments as compiled in the FMS, shown in the top panel of table 1.[11]

The middle panel of table 1 shows a number of adjustments that I think produces a balance sheet that is more informative about governments' liquidity position.

Valuation of financial assets. I begin with an often-advocated adjustment to the federal government's foreign-exchange reserves (see, e.g., AG/GAO 1986, 91, 114). For historical reasons, Ottawa shows its holdings of gold at their official value of 35 Special Drawing Rights (roughly $70) per ounce. Along with other adjustments to the foreign-exchange account to more realistically value foreign-currency holdings, this change produces a $5 billion increase in this category of federal financial assets (Receiver General for Canada 2002, 1.19).

More important is my revaluation of holdings of equity in Crown corporations and the carrying value of loans and securities. A detailed examination of the individual holdings of various governments is beyond my capacity, but the key point is that actual investment income suggests that the market value of many of these assets differs from their carrying value. To obtain an income-based valuation of financial assets, I take "investment income" as shown in the FMS, and estimate the amount that arises from returns from Crown corporations, securities, and so on, on the one hand, and natural resource royalties, on the other.[12] For each type, I use my benchmark rate of return of 6 percent to get a valuation.[13] I then add to, or subtract from, the financial-asset tally the measure by which the amounts calculated in respect of investments in Crown corporations and securities exceed, or fall short of, their carrying value. For the federal government, this adjustment creates a small improvement in net worth; for the provinces, a much larger deterioration.

I note in passing that this treatment brings the federal government's ownership of the Bank of Canada into the picture. The Bank of Canada reimburses, as profit, most of the interest paid on the federal debt securities it holds as a counterpart to its liabilities of bank-notes, which effectively adds a financial asset to the federal balance sheet roughly equal to the Bank's holdings of debt. From a liquidity perspective, the Bank's money-creating power might appear more significant than this, indeed, because of their unique access to the printing press national governments typically get higher ratings from credit-rating agencies on their domestic-currency than on their foreign-currency debt. In some sense, the carrying value I ascribe understates the Bank of Canada's potential contribution to Ottawa's cash position.

Additions and subtractions of categories of assets. The next adjustment is to remove the net financial assets of workers' compensation agencies and deposit-insurance agencies from the tally. Although the FMS provides figures for CPP and QPP net financial assets, it does not include them in the consolidated balance sheet for federal, provincial/territorial and local governments. I concur with this omission, and think that, like the CPP and QPP, the funds held by these agencies belong, along with their actuarial liabilities, in the longer-term balance sheet.[14]

A final adjustment I make to financial assets is to remove the fudge referred to earlier and add $7 billion to the federal government's financial assets. The federal government has over the last few years "pre-booked" the transfer of large amounts of money to organizations that are not clearly at arm's-length, thus overstating spending and net debt. This practice has drawn criticism from outside observers (Robson 1999) and the federal Auditor General (Receiver General, 2002, 1.34-1.35), in some cases the spending was recorded before the institution that was to receive the funds existed or the authorizing legislation had been passed. By putting this money, barely any of which has been spent, into financial assets, I show it as still under federal control. The foundations involved would, in the event of wind-up, not return these funds to the government, but wind-up is unlikely and the funds they disburse will substitute for other program spending the government might undertake in their absence, so recording an asset on the balance sheet seems the best approach.

Valuation and inclusion of physical assets. As noted already, federal and provincial public accounts – and the FMS, which follows much of their logic – record essentially no value for physical assets (except for inventories, which I ignore). I accept this treatment with respect to reproducible assets for a liquidity-oriented tally and show them at zero in table 1, since items such as buildings, bridges, jails and military equipment are hard to liquidate. I do not, however, think it appropriate for land. Leases of land and royalties paid on natural-resource harvesting and extraction are a substantial source of revenue, especially for provincial governments.

To value land, I use the method already described: I take the actual flows of natural-resource royalties and apply the benchmark 6-percent rate. This approach yields a substantial asset value, around $200 billion, for provincial governments. (Some of the return on investments enjoyed by local governments is probably attributable to land. Absent any way of distinguishing the two types of flows, I show the entire adjustment as an entry under their financial assets.)

Coins. Like my adjustments to the credit side of the balance sheet, my adjustments to the debit side also start small. The FMS shows coins as a liability of the federal government. Since there is no servicing cost associated with coins, and the liability represented by bank-notes and other deposits at the Bank of Canada has already been balanced on the asset side by my income-based valuation, I take coins out of the federal balance sheet. (I adjust for the coins held by provincial and municipal governments by arbitrarily allocating each of them equal amounts – an adjustment that in any case disappears as rounding error.)

Valuation of marketable debt. While the market value of ordinary funded debt presents no major challenges in the liquidity-oriented framework, since cash-crisis scenarios do not contemplate redemption before term, dealings in financial derivatives may create gains or losses that are not disclosed on balance sheets. The information needed to make some of these adjustments appears in government financial statements themselves. The federal *Public Accounts* (Receiver General 2002, 1.20), for example, contain a table showing the difference between carrying and fair market value for a number of key items in the balance sheet. I use this table to adjust the value of federal unmatured debt upward by $35 billion.

Accrued deferred-compensation liabilities. Also significant are adjustments to the value at which governments report liabilities related to the pensions of their own employees. The FMS includes the assets and actuarial liabilities of government-employee pensions (Statistics Canada 2001a, 92). In accepting the federal government's reported figures for its superannuation plans, however, the FMS uses an overstated number: the legislation that governed these plans while they were completely unfunded specified accrual formulas different from what actuarial valuations of the cost of entitlements earned would suggest. At the end of the 2001/02 fiscal year, Ottawa's over-accrual of its superannuation liabilities stood at slightly more than $7 billion. I deduct this amount from liabilities.

The Bottom Line

The net result of these adjustments, shown in the bottom panel of table 1, is a balance sheet that on the whole is more cheering than that provided by the familiar measures. The income-based valuation of provincial holdings of land accounts for the bulk of the improvement. Disregarding discrepancies arising from the timing of some valuations, net government obligations that matter for near-term liquidity amounted to some $760 billion at the end of March 2000, about $70 billion less than the total reported in the FMS. This is still a sizeable amount, equal to 71 percent of 2000 GDP. Like the more commonly reported measures, however, historical valuations along these lines would have yielded a pronounced decline in this ratio from its position four years earlier, and an update to 31 March 2002 would show it around 10 percentage points lower yet. From the point of view of credit market participants, this was a decisive improvement in Canada's liquidity situation, as indicated by Moody's adjustment of its rating on Canadian sovereign debt from Aa1 to Aaa in May 2002, and by a similar move by Standard & Poor's in July.

It is hard to say what level of net obligation calculated in this way would trigger fears of, or actual, failure to pay. If Canadian governments were indeed on the edge of refinancing difficulties in the mid-1990s, when the FMS debt-to-GDP ratio was some 20 percentage points higher than it was by March 2000, increasing the ratio by 25 percentage points, especially if much of the deterioration took place at the provincial level, might put Canada in a serious danger zone. In today's terms, with GDP of about $1.2 trillion, this would amount to an increase in net liquidity-oriented obligations of some $420 billion, not something that, given the current fiscal stance of Canadian governments, is likely to concern credit-market participants.

The Longer-Term-Oriented Balance Sheet

What about the longer term? Do the current structures of revenue and of spending, and other commitments governments have made that show up only in partial form, or not at all, on balance sheets promise that governments can maintain their current programs and tax rates indefinitely?

Relevant Measures and Issues

Although the liquidity-oriented balance sheet provides a good starting place for answering this question, putting together the relevant information requires going well beyond official sources, and involves some less familiar measures.

Addressing the concerns about proper budgeting for and use of physical assets that do not generate income requires some valuation of these assets. Again, different questions would suggest different measures. To adequately capture the contribution of these assets to prosperity and well-being, one would want the discounted value of the stream of benefits they will yield in the future. For practical purposes, however, the available measure is depreciated replacement cost, that is, purchase cost, minus depreciation, adjusted for inflation using the relevant investment price deflator.

Longer-term evaluations of fiscal positions also need to look at two categories of what might be termed "implicit assets": improvements in cash flow that we can reasonably expect if current tax rules and program structures remain in place. One such implicit asset is deferred tax revenue – taxes that would have been paid in the past but for provisions in the personal or business tax codes that permit taxpayers to pay them later. Key items in this category are taxes that will be payable on savings in employer-sponsored registered pension plans or registered retirement saving plans (RPP/RRSPs) when they are taken into personal income, as well as corporate income taxes that may become payable when deductions for tax purposes become less than deductions shown on income statements.[15]

A handful of assumptions permit a valuation of these assets that is comparable with that used for other financial liabilities and assets. For both pension savings and deferred corporate income taxes, I assume that the tax rate that will apply when the income in question becomes taxable is the same as the tax rate that applied when it was deferred. For pension savings it is convenient, and makes the calculations more transparent, to assume that the rate of return on investments in the plan is the same as the discount rate (as in Robbins and Veall 2002). I use my standard benchmark rate of 6 percent for both.

A second category of implicit asset involves more subtle considerations. Important spending programs will evolve with Canada's demographic structure. Some changes will move fiscal balances in a negative direction, and constitute an implicit liability; others will have the opposite effect. An overall valuation of governments' implicit obligations needs to take into account the present value of both reductions and increases in spending.[16]

Valuing these assets requires both a baseline against which to compare future spending and a time horizon over which to value the difference. My approach is to think about these programs, as well as their counterparts that foreshadow spending increases, as an implicit promise that governments have made to Canadians currently alive. Specifically, governments have implicitly committed to provide transfers and public services of similar generosity and quality, and on substantially the same terms, in the future as they do today. This approach suggests useful candidates for both the baseline and the time horizon.

In defining a baseline, treating all future expenditures on education, old-age pensions, or whatever as obligations suitable for a present-value discounting, as though governments had promised to provide these things for nothing, is unreasonable.[17] Canadians are already paying taxes to fund these programs and do not expect to stop doing so. A more realistic view would see the implicit bargain as a promise to provide a certain type of program at a familiar price, say, the share of GDP in the most recently available year. The projected rise or fall in that price as demographic change affects the program is the pertinent amount. As for time horizon, infinity is clearly too long for the valuation: one cannot say anything sensible about what governments have promised to current voters' unborn children. An alternative would be to adopt horizons specific to the people to whom different promises apply, but this approach would founder on overwhelming practical obstacles, not only would data limitations overwhelm the calculation, but different time scales might apply to the expenditure and revenue sides of a program, rendering a single figure for both incoherent. My preference is to adopt a 50-year horizon for all programs, on the grounds that this is approximately the life expectancy of the average-age Canadian.

On this basis, the implicit asset or liability associated with a program has a ready interpretation. In the case of an asset, it is the amount of additional debt that, at the assumed rate of return, a government could service and still keep aggregate tax rates (total taxes as a share of GDP) stable over 50 years, as the falling costs of the program offset the cost of this imaginary amount. In the case of a liability, it is the fund that the government would need to hold to discharge the obligation in question without increasing the share of national income that it taxes.[18]

Turning to the debit side, perhaps the least controversial additions to the net liabilities of governments in Canada in any longer-term tally are the unfunded liabilities of the C/QPP and workers' compensation agencies.

The CPP and QPP resemble employer-sponsored defined-benefit pension plans in that participants earn their entitlement to benefits by participating in and contributing to the plans. This link between entitlement and participation allows actuaries to estimate the benefits that current and past participants have earned at a point in time, and, with assumptions about future demographic, earnings, and rate-of-return variables, to estimate how much money the plans would need to have on hand to pay those benefits if further benefit accruals and contributions were to cease. The difference between the obligations and the assets actually held in the plan is the unfunded liability. Although the actuarial projections of the QPP do not provide an estimate of the unfunded liability, the similarity of the QPP to the CPP allows a reasonable approximation.

Workers' compensation programs also loosely link entitlement to contributions, and past claim histories provide a basis for actuarial valuations based on assumptions about future payments. Again, calculating the difference between the amount of money that would be required to meet likely future claims and what is actually on hand provides a meaningful and publicly available measure of an unfunded liability.

Although the federal Employment Insurance (EI) program also levies contributions that resemble a dedicated payroll tax and pays benefits that are linked to work history, some of the program's expenditures were met out of the regular federal budget in the past, and a major part of EI revenue now funds programs that are not related to workforce participation. These facts justify consolidating EI with the rest of the federal budget, so I take no separate note of it.

As noted already in discussions of the credit side of the balance sheet, less explicit promises to provide transfers or goods and services may also lend themselves to discounted valuations. Canada's Chief Actuary produces long-term projections for Old Age Security and Guaranteed Income Supplement (OAS/GIS) payments, and Robson (2001 and 2002) has calculated the implications of demographic change for the share of GDP absorbed by future provincial health budgets.

As with valuing implicit assets, putting a discounted present value on these liabilities requires a baseline and a time horizon. My approach is the same for both sides of the balance sheet: I evaluate the dollar increase in the share of

GDP expected to flow through these programs over a 50-year period. The implicit liability calculated in that manner can be thought of as the fund that, at the assumed rate of return, would be needed to cover the program's incremental cost over 50 years, so that the government could meet the obligation over that time without increasing the share of national income that it taxes or eroding the primary surpluses needed to cover its funded obligations.

Although government balance sheets sometimes show liabilities that may arise as a result of a default by a creditor or a claim on a public insurance program, they usually do not, presumably reflecting a view that a given contingency is unlikely to affect cash requirements soon, if at all. While I follow the lead of government accountants in this respect in my liquidity-oriented balance sheet, the practice of only disclosing many contingent liabilities in notes to the financial statements, or not disclosing them at all, is less acceptable for a longer-term look. The problem – and an important reason why such liabilities often do not appear in public accounts balance sheets – is that their proper valuation is usually not obvious. For this reason, many of the figures I show are much more indicative than definitive.

The Tally
As a starting place for this longer-term tally, I use the liquidity-oriented balance sheet created earlier, a condensed version of which appears in the top panel of table 2. The middle panel details the augmentations I make.

Financial assets. The first step is to put workers' compensation agencies into the picture. I add the net financial assets deducted in the previous section back to the credit side for provincial governments, and I also add the funds' actuarial liabilities, some $39 billion, to the debit side. (I discuss the other small addition related to deposit insurance below.)

Another relatively straightforward addition is C/QPP assets and liabilities. Assets in the two plans were $44 billion and $18 billion respectively on 31 December 2000 (OCA 2001, 113; Québec 2001, 49), for a total of $62 billion. For the liability side, the Office of the Chief Actuary (OCA 2001) calculated a figure as of 31 December 2000 of $487 billion. I estimate the QPP liability by assuming that it is proportional to the ratio of Quebec's population age 15 and up to that of the rest of Canada, 32 percent, which yields a value of $156 billion. The sum of these two figures, $643 billion, appears as an addition to government liabilities in the middle panel of table 2.

Physical assets. To add reproducible assets to the financial investments and land accounted for already, I know no better source for a valuation than the *National Balance Sheet Accounts*, which calculate depreciated cost, updated for changing prices. The amounts they show for structures, machinery and equipment of

Table 2

The Longer-Term-Oriented Balance Sheet ($ billions)

	Federal	Provincial/ Territorial	Local	Consolidated FPL Total	C/QPP	Total
LIQUIDITY-ORIENTED BALANCE SHEET (FROM TABLE 1)						
Assets						
Financial Assets	103	116	37	187		187
Nonfinancial Assets	4	196	0	200		200
Total Assets	106	312	37	386		386
Liabilities	675	491	52	1146		1146
Balance	(569)	(178)	(15)	(760)		(760)
ADJUSTMENTS						
Financial Assets						
Net Fin. Assets, Workers' Comp. Agencies		29		29		29
Net C/QPP Fin. Assets					62	62
Net Fin. Assets, Dep. Ins. Agencies	1	1		2		2
Subtotal: Financial Assets	1	30		32	62	93
Nonfinancial Assets						
Reproducible Assets	47	145	169	361		361
Deferred Business Tax	16	8		24		24
Def. Tax, Pension Saving	204	102		306		306
Implicit Asset, Child Benefit	77			77		77
Impl. Asset, PSE (Fed)	9			9		9
Impl. Asset, E&S Ed (Prov)		166		166		166
Impl. Asset, PS Ed (Prov)		60		60		60
Subtotal: Nonfin. Assets	353	480	169	1002		1002
Total Adjustments, Assets	354	511	169	1034	62	1096
Liabilities						
Workers' Comp. Agencies		39		39		39
C/QPP					643	643
Impl. Liability, OAS/GIS etc.	129	1		130		130
Impl. Liability, Health Care		639		639		639
Liabilities, Dep. Ins. Agencies	1	1		2		2
Pension Benefit Guarantee (Ont)		1		1		1
Contingent Liabilities	10	10		20		20
Total Adjustments, Liabilities	140	691		831	643	1474
Net Adjustments	214	(180)	169	203	(581)	(379)
LONGER-TERM-ORIENTED BALANCE SHEET						
Assets						
Financial Assets	104	146	37	218	62	280
Nonfinancial Assets	357	676	169	1202	0	1202
Total Assets	461	823	206	1420	62	1482
Liabilities	815	1182	52	1977	643	2620
Balance	(355)	(359)	154	(557)	(581)	(1139)

Source: Author's calculations as described in the text.

federal, provincial and local governments appear next to the heading "repro-ducible assets" in the middle panel of table 2.[19]

Deferred taxes. The total amount of deferred corporate income taxes shown on the books of businesses in Canada as of June 2002 was $66 billion.[20] Some people mistakenly believe that this figure represents a pot of money that governments have allowed business not to pay and could collect at any time. The full amount of deferred taxes appearing on balance sheets, however, does not accurately reflect what business will actually pay. Carry-forwards of prior years' losses and investment tax credits can effectively eliminate some deferred-tax liabilities, and others may disappear from company books for a variety of reasons, such as bankruptcy. The deferred taxes that do become payable, moreover, may not do so for a long time.[21] I do not know any reliable method for estimating the present value of the deferred taxes that will become payable. I therefore enter a provisional figure based on the assumption that half this amount will become payable in equal amounts over ten years, and divide it between the federal and provincial/territorial governments on the basis of recent shares of corporate income tax (almost exactly two-thirds/one-third).

The revenue that will come in through the personal income tax when exist-ing assets in registered pension plans and retirement saving plans (RPP/RRSPs) become subject to taxation is larger and somewhat easier to estimate with con-fidence. Robbins and Veall (2002) provide estimates of these amounts at the end of 1999. As long as the discount rate is equal to the rate of return in the funds, the present value of tax-deferred pension savings to governments is equal to the amount saved times the pertinent tax rate. I follow Robbins and Veall in showing a little over $200 billion for the federal government in this category, and half the federal amount for the provinces.[22]

Implicit assets. Along with revenues that current tax structures should bring in over time, we need to consider reductions in spending that current program struc-tures will trigger in the future. Fewer young people will mean smaller federal expenditures on child benefits and postsecondary education, and smaller provin-cial expenditures on education at all levels. These amounts are not easy to estimate with confidence, however. The number of future children is a matter of conjecture: except for the very near term, the relevant people have not been born yet.

Notwithstanding the uncertainties, it makes sense to reflect these prospects in a longer-term-oriented balance sheet. Accordingly, I make a number of entries in table 2.

I show an implicit asset for the federal government of $77 billion to reflect shrinking payments on the Child Benefit, and another of $9 billion to reflect shrinking payments under the Canadian Education Saving Grant and other pay-ments in support of postsecondary students.[23] Although the federal government also provides financial support for elementary and secondary education, mainly for Aboriginals, and funds postsecondary institutions directly, the links between these programs and broader population numbers are too weak to allow even a tentative appraisal, so I make no entry to reflect increases or decreases in these amounts.

Provincial governments can also look forward to substantial decreases in spending as the young population gets relatively smaller. I enter an implicit asset of $166 billion to represent declining expenditures on elementary and secondary education, and another of $60 billion to represent declining expenditures on postsecondary education.[24]

The debit side also has substantial implicit amounts. The Office of the Chief Actuary produces estimates of future spending under the federal government's Old Age Security and Guaranteed Income Supplement programs (OCA 2002). Valued over the 50-year time horizon discussed earlier and discounted at 6 percent, the net increase in the cost of these programs over their current share of GDP comes to some $129 billion. This is a major implicit liability for the federal government. Several provinces also provide transfers to seniors, but these transfers amount to only about 1 percent of the federal amount, so I show a token amount for the provinces in this category.

Publicly funded health programs are also sensitive to demographic change. Because older people tend to absorb more health-related goods and services than younger people, unchanged patterns of expenditure by age and sex (and unchanged patterns of contributions to national income) will tend to increase health budgets as a share of GDP in the future (Robson 2001, 2002). Here, I treat the projected increase in health budgets as a share of GDP arising from demographic change as a liability of provincial governments of more than $640 billion, a huge addition to the debit side.[25]

To make the derivation of these amounts somewhat more transparent, I show in figure 1 the evolution of the key expenditures as shares of GDP over a 50-year period. The discounted value of the difference between each line and its starting value is the asset or liability shown in table 2.

Guarantees of private-sector claims. A further set of obligations worth noting are government guarantees of private-sector claims such as deposits in financial institutions and pension benefits. Like all situations involving a very small chance of a very large payout, these obligations are hard to value with confidence.

Some $460 billion in deposits at financial institutions were insured by various deposit-insurance bodies of Canadian governments in 2001: roughly $340 billion by the federal Canada Deposit Insurance Corporation (CDIC); and roughly $120 billion by various provincial agencies.[26] Reserves held against possible claims amounted to roughly $1 billion at the CDIC, and almost as much provincially. The CDIC has no formal target for funding relative to insured deposits, but its funds exceed its provision for losses by a considerable margin, and it has lowered its premiums to reflect a view that improved balance sheets of member institutions and tight monitoring have lessened the risk of failures over time. At the provincial level, the aggregate target for the various funds amounts to slightly more than 1 percent of insured deposits, or about $1.3 billion, which is the figure I show in table 2.[27]

The Government of Ontario guarantees a portion (up to $1,000 per month) of the benefits promised by employer-sponsored defined-benefit pension plans. Although no official figures are available, some two million workers in Ontario are covered by employer-sponsored plans. A rough estimate of the actuarial liability covered by the US Pension Benefit Guaranty Corporation (US PBGC 2001) would amount, in Canadian dollars, to a little less than $500 per worker. Multiplying this amount by the number of covered workers yields a figure that is too high for the Ontario fund, since its coverage of defined-benefit plans is less than complete and its guarantee is less generous than that of the American agency. In view of the sizeable aggregate under-funding that has recently developed in defined-benefit plans, I nevertheless think it appropriate to enter a token figure of $1 billion in table 2 as a reminder that a sizeable potential liability exists.

Other contingent liabilities. The final row of adjustments in the middle panel of table 2 is, as noted earlier, highly speculative. Governments in Canada have sizeable exposure to a number of contingencies. One notable example at the federal level is the exposure created by the Canada Mortgage and Housing Corporation's mortgage insurance and guarantees of mortgage-backed securities, the combined value of which stood at $246 billion at the end of 2001 (up from $179 billion five years earlier). Although impairments of the company's loan portfolio are reflected in its carrying value on the federal balance sheet (and indirectly in my income-based valuation of federal financial assets), it is hard to put a figure on the exposure these guarantees create. Similar uncertainties exist with regard to the activities of the Farm Credit Corporation, the Export Development Corporation, the Business Development Bank of Canada, and guarantees of loans to students. The $1 billion I add to federal obligations in the middle panel of table 2 is a token amount to recognize that such liabilities exist rather than a serious estimate of their size.

Because the federal government's accrual-based public accounts will contain new figures for a variety of other contingent liabilities, including those arising from environmental clean-up and litigation – the latter category including the somewhat open-ended exposure created by lawsuits on behalf of Aboriginal people – there is little point in attempting an independent valuation ahead of

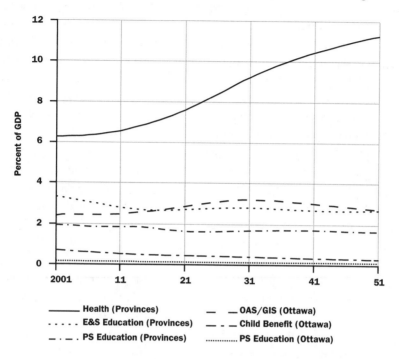

Figure 1

Projected Spending in Key Demographically Sensitive Programs

Legend:
——— Health (Provinces)
· · · · · E&S Education (Provinces)
— · — · PS Education (Provinces)
— — OAS/GIS (Ottawa)
— · · — Child Benefit (Ottawa)
············ PS Education (Ottawa)

that release. I add a relatively small amount ($10 billion) to table 2 in this category, recognizing that Ottawa faces a powerful incentive to recognize a small amount, since its own provisions in these areas will likely figure strongly in the plaintiffs' cases against them, and amounts recognized therefore become likelier to be lost. In even more impressionistic fashion, I add a similar amount to the provincial total, on the grounds that their somewhat larger total of program spending, and the extensive contingencies that may attach to their holdings of land, probably provide a similar range of targets for litigants.

The Bottom Line

The result of all these adjustments, the longer-term-oriented balance sheet, appears in the bottom panel of table 2. Unlike its liquidity-oriented counterpart, the longer-term tally is less cheering than the familiar public-accounts and FMS measures. At more than $1.1 trillion, or 107 percent of 2000 GDP, the bottom-line obligation represents a net addition of about half as much again to the net figure in the liquidity-oriented balance sheet.

A notable feature of this tally is its contrast with conventional measures and the liquidity-oriented tally when it comes to the distribution of net obligations among different levels of government. The federal government's situation looks relatively good. Ottawa can look forward to large amounts of deferred taxes, while the projected reductions in the share of GDP required to finance the Child Benefit and Ottawa's relatively modest support for postsecondary students largely offset its exposure to the OAS/GIS system. The bottom line – a net liability of about $355 billion – is better than that shown by conventional measures.

The provinces look less good. The longer-term balance sheet shows even larger additions to the credit side than it did for Ottawa. The provinces are relatively large holders of nonfinancial assets, have favourable exposure to deferred taxes, and can look forward to declining program costs related to young people. Their sizeable implicit liability related to future health spending, however, outweighs these assets, and leaves them with a net liability of around $360 billion, worse than the federal government's, and worse than conventional measures.

Adding local governments, with their substantial nonfinancial assets, yields a consolidated bottom line for federal, provincial and local governments that, at some $560 billion, is not as daunting as conventional measures or the liquidity-oriented tally. But adding the net unfunded liabilities of the C/QPP puts the overall figure much further into the red.

The longer-term-oriented tally confirms, in qualitative terms, the conclusions drawn by generational accounting exercises (Oreopoulos and Vaillancourt 1998): that the average future taxpayer will pay a price greater than the value of the government services and transfers he or she receives in return.[28] More than this, the longer-term tally shows that provincial governments likely face the toughest adjustment. It is commonplace that a dynamic vertical fiscal imbalance exists in Canada, with the federal government having access to revenue sources that are more robust over time, while provincial governments face the faster-growing obligations.[29] The longer-term tally calculated here does not suggest that Canadians can look forward to lower aggregate tax rates in the future. It does suggest, however, that, barring an effective transfer of much of the net provincial liability to Ottawa through an increase in federal-provincial transfers so large as to raise serious concerns about political accountability, Ottawa should not react to its relatively attractive situation by increasing spending, but should try to create tax room that the provinces are likely to need.

The Nongovernmental Behaviour-Oriented Balance Sheet

What do these obligations imply about nongovernmental behaviour? Readers who recognize constraints will incline to stress responses that will lead to liquidity crises more rapidly and make the adjustments in taxes and programs prefigured by the longer-term balance sheet more painful. Readers who do not will incline to stress responses, or lack of them, that make liquidity crises or painful adjustments less likely and less necessary.

The Relevant Measures

Unfortunately, and without prejudging the findings of later papers in this volume, making confident judgements about which of these views is likelier to be right, or what the truth is that may lie between them, requires more knowledge than we currently have about the impact of tax rates and public services on behaviour, about the way Canadians perceive and react to government obligations, and about the state of Canada's public sector relative to those in the rest of the world. The exploration of these topics in this section is necessarily very preliminary.

Tax distortions and positive externalities. To take stock of the overall significance of governments' net obligations for the future growth of income in Canada, the balance sheet relevant to longer-term sustainability would be a good starting point. Many of the adjustments involved in producing that balance sheet, such as the attempt to record a value for physical assets that comes closer to their economic worth, are pertinent for this exercise (AG/GAO 1986, 111), as is the production of present values of implicit obligations.

The key steps in producing a new balance sheet that would adjust the value of government assets and liabilities to reflect judgements about the present value of their net effects on future income would involve: augmenting the value accorded nonfinancial assets such as physical infrastructure that provide positive externalities, reducing the present value net cost of transfers and publicly-funded services that augment growth, and increasing the amount recorded for net obligations to reflect the distortions caused by the taxes that will service them.[30]

Those closer to the unconstrained end of the spectrum will emphasize the sizeable returns that past investments in physical and social assets have produced, and note that developed economies continue to grow under tax burdens that are far higher than would have appeared practical a generation ago. Those closer to the constrained end of the spectrum will note that marginal returns on public investments are likely to be lower, and marginal deadweight costs of taxes higher, than average returns and costs, and that calculations relevant to current incremental decisions should reflect that fact. My view, assuming that net tax increases in the future will take the form of increased rates on a mix of bases similar to today's, is that the bottom line of such a tally would show a negative number larger than that in the longer-term-oriented balance sheet.

Nongovernmental actor perceptions and reactions. Work on how nongovernmental actors perceive and react to net claims on each other and to foreigners through government encounters a problem to which this paper's existence directly attests: we do not know the appropriate measure of net worth for such an exercise. Past investigations of Ricardian offsets have tended to use measures that were readily available, such as net financial assets (Johnson 1994) or estimates of social-security liabilities.[31] Neither my liquidity-oriented balance sheet nor my longer-term-oriented balance sheet justifies these focuses, however, and many other tallies are possible: if I am the only Canadian who thinks the tally presented in this paper is appropriate, an econometric exercise that uses it to explain national saving will be badly mis-specified.

To take this work further, we will need two things. First, we need to know more about how Canadians actually perceive government obligations. If it is true, for example, that most Canadians do not believe the C/QPP will pay their promises in full, and that this scepticism is greater among younger people, perhaps a national balance sheet intended to test their responses to government debt should show an appropriate discount for the CPP's unfunded liability. Second, for time-series work, we will need some extension of the relevant tallies back for a number of years. This is a less demanding task conceptually, but a significant one nevertheless.

International competitiveness. The third set of concerns worth a comment in a discussion of nongovernmental behaviour is the influence of Canada's fiscal condition on its relative attractiveness as a place to work and invest. Greater attractiveness presumably will mean higher levels of output and employment in Canada than will otherwise occur and, especially if higher levels of investment boost productivity, incomes and consumption as well. People and businesses will locate in places that offer better combinations of public programs and taxes than the alternatives. So, even if the longer-term-oriented balance sheet of Canadian governments suggests some deterioration in this combination in the future, Canada might still fare all right if the deterioration in other jurisdictions is larger.

Since the longer-term-oriented balance sheet presented here is not one around which there is currently much consensus in Canada, let alone internationally, I am not in a position to present comparable figures for other jurisdictions. Some recent work at the OECD (Dang et al. 2001), however, estimates the overall impact of demographic change on a number of major programs – old-age pensions and retirement programs, health and long-term care, education, and child and family benefits – and summarizes its net effect on government budget balances in 15 OECD countries. Their estimates are in percentage points of GDP, which I convert to a present-value liability relative to current GDP using a net discount rate of 2.1 percent (my benchmark of 6 percent minus nominal GDP growth of 3.9 percent, which is the nominal growth rate I assume in my long-term projections for Canada).[32]

The resulting liabilities, expressed relative to 2000 GDP, are shown in table 3, along with OECD figures for the net funded debt of the countries concerned. This comparison shows that Canada is not alone in having overall liabilities considerably larger than conventional measures reveal. But it also shows that Canada's position is relatively poor by comparison to several countries that might be considered close competitors for migration and investment, namely, the United States, Australia and the United Kingdom. From this perspective, then, Canada's net obligations look like a threat to Canada's ability to compete for workers and capital.

The Bottom Line

Pending further investigation along these and possible other lines, my assessment is that modifications to the balance sheet of Canadian governments to capture things that might matter for nongovernmental behaviour, in particular, adjustments to allow for positive and negative impacts on growth from programs and taxes, as well as for Canada's relative position in the competition to attract labour and capital, would amplify the message from the longer-term-oriented tally: there are more battles to fight before the debt war will be won.

Conclusion

The figures presented here may not sway anyone who, in constrained fashion, deplores government debt and thinks that Canadian governments have blundered in building up so much of it. And they may not sway anyone who, in unconstrained fashion, thinks that attention to government debt is a distraction and ill-motivated obstacle to more active government. Between these two extremes, however, these numbers do allow a tentative answer to the overall question posed by this conference.

The liquidity-related tally tells a reassuring story. Some adjustments to conventional public-accounts figures reinforce the impression from recent budgetary outcomes: Canadian governments face no immediate danger of failing to make payment or rollover debt. Only a sustained return to large deficits would raise such concerns among actual and potential creditors. In this respect, a major battle in the debt war has been won.

The longer-term-oriented tally, by contrast, shows that Canadian governments are still far from a sustainable fiscal stance. The news is not all bad. Adding nonfinancial assets to the credit side reveals that Canadian governments bring more than just debt to the national balance sheet. Deferred taxes will boost revenue in the future. And some demographically driven decreases in spending are in prospect, which constitute a kind of implicit asset. The federal government in particular stands out as being in better longer-term shape than is sometimes supposed. Against this, however, several major items on the debit

Table 3

Net Liabilities of Age-Related Spending and Funded Debt for 15 OECD Countries (% of GDP)

	Age-Related Spending	Net Debt	Total
Australia	73	11	84
Austria	72	47	119
Belgium	70	99	169
Canada	113	53	166
Czech Republic	90	15	104
Denmark	132	23	155
Finland	110	(48)	63
Japan	39	59	97
Korea	134	(34)	100
Netherlands	159	42	201
New Zealand	109	20	129
Norway	215	(75)	140
Sweden	58	1	59
United Kingdom	12	31	43
United States	71	42	113

Source: Author's calculations based on Dang et al. (2001, 25); OECD (2002) for all countries except Czech Republic (IMF 2001).

side need noting, especially major pension obligations and the huge implicit liability of future health spending. Provincial governments in particular face a continuing fiscal squeeze in the years ahead, and Canadians are likely to see continued upward pressure on tax rates and downward pressure on the generosity of public programs as this part of the debt war continues.

When it comes to nongovernmental responses to government debt, we know much less. The one area where some tentative conclusions seem justified is Canada's ability to attract labour and capital. Canada's longer-term position is less favourable than that of many competitors and trading partners, suggesting that the debt war must continue if Canada hopes to maintain or improve its attractiveness as a place to work and invest.

Notes

I thank Pierre Lemieux, Jean-Claude Menard, Andy Poprawa, David Walker and the participants in the IRPP's conference, especially Steve Ambler, Chris Matier, Jack Mintz, Chris Ragan, and Bill Watson, for comments on an earlier draft of this paper. Yvan Guillemette provided valuable research assistance. I am responsible for remaining errors and omissions and, to balance the ledger, will happily take credit for the conclusions.

Readers should note that a number of new releases of government financial results have occurred between the time this paper was presented and its publication. In particular, the federal government has released its financial results on a full accrual basis of accounting. The new federal numbers superceded several of the adjustments made to the federal government's balance sheet in this paper. Because the principal thrusts – though by no means all the details – of the changes were in the directions anticipated, the overall conclusions still stand.

1. On the former point, see Robson (1994). *The Financial Post* describes recent Japanese events (Thorpe 2002).

2. AG/GAO (1986, 4-5, 11-12, 88, 111, 134) discusses the accounting issues surrounding management and accountability in the government sector, emphasizing the needs of legislative users of data and officials, as well as the discipline that proper accounting imposes on management.

3. The seminal reference for generational accounting is Auerbach et al. (1994). Oreopoulos and Vaillancourt (1998) provide calculations of net lifetime tax burdens for Canadians of different ages. See also the discussion by Robin Boadway in this volume.

4. I use the clumsy phrase "nongovernmental" rather than "private" because these actors can be outside the government in question or outside the government sector altogether.

5. The primary distinction between units assigned to general government and those assigned to government business enterprises is whether or not their principal activity is commercial (operating in the marketplace at prices that have a significant influence on the amounts the producers are willing to supply and on the amounts purchasers wish to buy). For discussion of FMS classifications, see Statistics Canada (2001a, 22-24).

6. This somewhat artificial assumption seems preferable to the alternative of projecting recent experience forward, since interprovincial migration is sensitive to economic and fiscal develop-

ments, and the policy responses to the trends predicted here are uncertain.

7. Using a benchmark return to value financial assets might be acceptable for a liquidity-oriented analysis, but it is less acceptable for an analysis focused more on the longer term. Governments might be squeezing unsustainable returns from some assets. Or, if governments are using market power to raise revenues above their competitive level – as with liquor monopolies, for example – divestiture might accompany changes in policy that would lower the value of the asset to a purchaser. I do not think the former problem is serious, and the latter is too speculative to cope with. Either way, my calculations involve no attempt to correct for such possibilities.

8. Some classification issues complicate the returns/assets comparison. The FMS treats remittances of profits of provincial liquor boards and lottery and gaming corporations as consumption taxes, since government-owned liquor boards and government-owned lottery and other gaming corporations operate as fiscal monopolies (Statistics Canada 2001a, 59, 66).

9. These amounts are substantial. The federal government reported contingent liabilities of $87 billion as of 31 March 2002 (Receiver General 2002, 10.18-10.19).

10. I also accept governments' write-downs of loans such as concessional loans to developing countries and international organizations (see Receiver General 2002, 1.24). The federal government has already stated that its move to accrual accounting will involve the recognition of new environmental and Aboriginal liabilities (Canada 2001).

11. Note that consolidation eliminates intergovernmental holdings of financial instruments, which means that the items in the federal, provincial/territorial and local columns do not necessarily sum to the "FPL" total.

12. The FMS shows this breakdown for the federal government, but not for provincial governments. My estimate, based on income and expenditure accounts data, is that natural resource royalties account for slightly more than half of provincial "investment income."

13. More precisely, in order to avoid a valuation that is over-sensitive to the latest figures, I take the average dollar returns over the past five years, apply the benchmark rate to that figure, and then make an inflation adjustment to bring the calculated value up to an amount that would apply in the final year.

14. Some other categories of funds held against long-term liabilities would ideally get the same treatment. The only such instance I deal with explicitly here, however – the Ontario Pension Benefit Guarantee Fund – has assets too small to register.

15. The major factor behind these deferred taxes is capital consumption allowances used in calculating taxable profits that are more generous than normal accounting conventions, which presumably more closely reflect economic depreciation, would suggest. When annual capital consumption allowance on a given asset falls below annual income-statement depreciation, the taxes deferred in respect of the difference may become payable.

16. Those who object to the presumption behind this definition of "asset" – that it treats current tax levels as a benchmark – might prefer to see a net figure for all such "assets" and "liabilities." I prefer the separate presentation; among other merits, it is easier to follow.

17. Emes and Kreptul (1999, 16) show amounts for OAS and medicare of $644 billion and $1,278 billion respectively in 1998, which must reflect calculations using a baseline considerably lower than the current cost of these programs.

18. Analysis of fiscal sustainability often describes an intertemporal budget constraint for governments in which current net debt equals the present value of future primary surpluses, with the latter – the excess of tax revenue over program spending – representing a wedge that debt drives between what citizens pay and the publicly financed consumption and transfers they receive in return. Adding implicit net liabilities extends this approach by bringing into the picture net tax increases implied by constant per-beneficiary program spending in the presence of demographic change. A further extension would be to look at the implicit asset or liability represented by the likely evolution of different tax yields in the face of demographic change. The current distribution of tax liabilities by age and sex suggests that the passage of time will erode most tax bases, with the payroll tax base being highly vulnerable, the personal income tax less so, and the base for consumption taxes less yet (Robson 2002).

19. Statistics Canada, CANSIM, Table 378-0004.

20. Statistics Canada, CANSIM, Table 187-0001.

21. At year-end 1993, total deferred taxes amounted to $34.3 billion. At that time, the stock of unused deductions arising from prior-year losses and other carry-forwards was $115.3 billion, and the stock of unused investment tax credits was $4.4 billion (Technical Committee on Business Taxation 1997, 4.12).

22. Robbins and Veall (2002) note that unrealized capital gains represent another type of deferred tax. Not having any data that would allow a calculation of this amount, I make no entry for it.

23. The population 0–18 drives the projections for the Child Benefit and the CESG, and the population 18–24 drives the projections for other federal PSE support. I assume that the per-person amounts paid under the Child Benefit rise with inflation, that the per-person amounts paid under the CESG remain constant in dollar terms, and that federal amounts in support of PSE students (other than that paid under the CESG) rise with inflation and with output per working-age person (the same assumption as in the health-care projections below).

24. The population 5–18 years drives the projections for the former and the population 18–24 years the latter. Per-person amounts are projected to rise with inflation and with output per working-age person. Formally, the FMS shows both provincial and local governments contributing to spending on elementary and secondary education. Since provincial governments have now assumed almost total control over education funding, I allocate this asset to provincial governments. In view of the fact that these assets have counterpart liabilities in the health-care field, one might object to the implied dollar-for-dollar offset on the grounds that it assumes costless conversion of schools into nursing homes and teachers into nurses. But the baseline spending levels in both already include a lot of such frictional costs.

25. Current utilization rate by age and sex and the entire population drive these projections. Health spending per person of a given age and sex rises with inflation and with output per working-age person.

26. CDIC figures are as of 30 April 2001; provincial figures are estimates based on DICO (2002, 25) for year-end 2001.

27. Using the legislated target for the US Federal Deposit Insurance Corporation – 1.25 percent of insured deposits – as a benchmark for the Canadian system would produce an estimate of an aggregate target of $5.6 billion: $4.1 billion of which would be federal and $1.5 billion provincial. The US is not a good benchmark for Canada and especially for the federal component, however, since the American system has been more prone to generating claims.

28. The alternative is to reach a state where liquidity-oriented fears come to the fore and are then realized.

29. Ruggieri (2002) has recently restated this thesis, although Norrie (2002) argues persuasively that the imbalance is more a reflection of federal and provincial choices with regard to taxation than a preordained fact.

30. Kneller, Bleaney and Gemmel (1999) provide a useful econometric investigation of the impacts of various types of programs and taxes on growth.

31. I do not know of any such study for Canada. Engen and Gale (1997) provide a useful review of some US literature.

32. Dang et al. (2001, 25) show values for 2000, the peak year, and 2050. I use linear interpolations to calculate the changes in the share of GDP absorbed by the programs. My own figure for net age-related spending in Canada, based on the numbers in table 2, comes to 98 percent of 2000 GDP. Dang et al. assume that pension benefits are indexed to wages, which overstates the impact of pension spending in countries, like Canada, where they are in fact indexed to prices.

Bibliography

Auerbach, A.H., J. Gokhale and L.J. Kotlikoff. 1994. "Generational Accounting: A Meaningful Way to Evaluate Fiscal Policy." *Journal of Economic Perspectives* 8:73-94.

Canada. 2001. "Implementation of Full Accrual Accounting in the Federal Government's Financial Statements." Backgrounder. Ottawa: Department of Finance, 10 August.

Dang, T.T., P. Antolin and H. Oxley. 2001. "Fiscal Implications of Ageing: Projections of Age-Related Spending." Economics Department Working Papers no. 305. Paris: Organization for Economic Co-operation and Development.

Deposit Insurance Corporation of Ontario (DICO). 2002. "Discussion Paper on the Deposit Insurance Reserve Fund." Toronto. October.

Dominion Bond Rating Service (DBRS). 2002. "DBRS Upgrades Gov't of Cda. L.T. Foreign Currency Debt to AAA." Toronto. 16 December.

Emes, J., and A. Kreptul. 1999. *Canadian Government Debt 1999: A Guide to the Indebtedness of Canada and the Provinces.* Critical Issues Bulletin. Vancouver: Fraser Institute.

Engen, E.M., and W.G. Gale. 1997. "Effects of Social Security Reform on Private and National Saving." *Social Security Reform Conference Proceedings: Links to Saving, Investment, and Growth,* ed. S. Sass and R. Triest. Boston: Federal Reserve Bank of Boston.

International Monetary Fund (IMF). 2001. *International Financial Statistics Yearbook, 2001.* Washington, DC: IMF.

Johnson, D. 1994. "Ricardian Equivalence: Assessing the Evidence for Canada." In *Deficit Reduction: What Pain? What Gain?* ed. W. Robson and W. Scarth. Toronto: C.D. Howe Institute.

Kneller, R., M. Bleaney and N. Gemmel. 1999. "Fiscal Policy and Growth: Evidence from OECD Countries." *Journal of Public Economics* 74, no. 2:171-90.

Office of the Auditor General of Canada and the United States General Accounting Office (AG/GAO). 1986. *Federal Government Reporting Study.* Gaithersburg and Ottawa: US General Accounting Office and Office of the Auditor General of Canada.

Office of the Chief Actuary (OCA). 2001. *Actuarial Report (18th) on the Canada Pension Plan, as at 31 December 2000.* Ottawa: Office of the Superintendent of Financial Institutions.

———. 2002. *Actuarial Report (5th) on the Old Age Security Program, as at 31 December 2000.* Ottawa: Office of the Superintendent of Financial Institutions.

Oreopoulos, P., and F. Vaillancourt. 1998. *Taxes, Transfers, and Generations in Canada: Who Gains and Who Loses from the Demographic Transition.* Commentary no. 107. Toronto: C.D. Howe Institute.

Organisation for Economic Co-operation and Development (OECD). 2002. *OECD Economic Outlook.* Paris: OECD.

Québec. 2001. *Analyse actuarielle de Regime des rentes du Québec.* Régie des Rentes.

Receiver General for Canada. 2001. *Public Accounts of Canada,* Volume 1, *Summary Report and Financial Statements.* Ottawa: Minister of Public Works and Government Services Canada.

———. 2002. *Public Accounts of Canada,* Volume 1: *Summary Report and Financial Statements.* Ottawa: Minister of Public Works and Government Services Canada.

Robbins, J., and M. Veall. 2002. *Registered Saving Plan Holdings as a Government Asset*. Backgrounder. Toronto: C.D. Howe Institute.

Robson, W. 1994. *Digging Holes and Hitting Walls: Canada's Fiscal Prospects in the Mid-1990s*. Toronto: C.D. Howe Institute.

———. 1999. *Hiding the Good News: Ottawa's Book-Cooking Is a Troubling Sign for the Future*. Backgrounder no. 31. Toronto: C.D. Howe Institute.

———. 2001. *Will the Baby Boomers Bust the Health Budget? Demographic Change and Health Care Financing Reform*. Commentary. Toronto: C.D. Howe Institute.

———. 2002. *Saving for Health: Prefunding Health Care for an Older Canada*. Commentary. Toronto: C.D. Howe Institute.

Rosen, H., B. Dahlby, R. Smith and P. Boothe. 2002. *Public Finance in Canada*, 2d ed. Canadian. Toronto: McGraw-Hill Ryerson.

Ruggieri, J. 2002. *Fiscal Imbalances and the Financing of National Programs*. Ottawa: Caledon Institute of Social Policy.

Sowell, T. 1987. *A Conflict of Visions: Ideological Origins of Political Struggles*. New York: William Morrow and Co.

Statistics Canada. 2001a. *Financial Management System*. Catalogue no. 68F0023XIB. Ottawa: Minister of Industry.

———. 2001b. *Public Sector Statistics: Financial Management System, 2000-2001*. Catalogue no. 68-213-XIB. Ottawa: Minister of Industry.

Technical Committee on Business Taxation (TCBT). 1997. *Report*. Ottawa: Department of Finance.

Thorpe, J. 2002. "Japan Panic Spreads as Bond Issue Falls Short." *Financial Post*, 21 September.

United States Pension Benefits Guaranty Corporation (US PBGC). 2001. *Annual Report 2001*. Washington, DC: GPO.

how big is the debt?

Steve Ambler

Introduction

Bill Robson's paper tries to correct conventional measures of government assets and liabilities to account for liquidity and for implicit assets and liabilities representing the future evolution of program spending and taxes. The goal is ambitious and the author generally succeeds. The most important corrections seem eminently sensible given a basic understanding of economic and demographic trends. They have to do with the unfunded liabilities of the Canada and Quebec Pension Plans (C/QPP) and the implicit liabilities arising from healthcare spending in the context of an aging population. The author offers two main conclusions. First, Canadian governments are very unlikely to be facing a liquidity crisis by failing to make payments or to roll over debt. Second, the long-term situation is less rosy. The author judges that "Canadian governments are still far from a sustainable fiscal stance."

My comments are organized as follows. First, I summarize the main arguments of the paper, commenting on some of its details as I go along. Then, I try to assess the importance of one of Robson's main results, that the longer-term position of governments is considerably less rosy than conventional measures indicate.

Structure of the Paper

The author motivates his recalculations of government balance sheets in a preliminary section that summarizes economic arguments about the costs of government debt. He contrasts two views of the importance of debt, which he calls the "constrained" and "unconstrained" views. The constrained view holds that debt is "almost self-evidently bad." The unconstrained view claims that issues of financing the debt are irrelevant. According to this view, "worrying about one financing method over another is a distraction or, worse, an attempt to hobble governments: the debt war was always misguided and cannot end too soon." I think the unconstrained view is almost a straw man. Believing that government programs are socially useful does not require believing that financing them via distortionary taxation is costless. I think very few economists would subscribe to the latter view. Most admit that having to finance payments on the debt through distortionary taxation imposes economic costs. However, they do differ concerning the potential benefits of government debt. There are several schools of thought on this issue.

First, there is the "representative agent optimal taxation" view, summarized by the work of Chari, Christiano and Kehoe (1995). Debt should be sufficiently negative in the long run to be able to finance all future expenditure from the returns on the government's assets. The main advantage of this policy is the possibility of eliminating all distortionary taxation. According to this view, the transition to this long run should be financed by higher rates of taxation in the short run, particularly on income from assets such as capital, which is inelastically supplied in the very short run. This view can be interpreted as mainly a theoretical curiosity derived within the restrictive framework of the neoclassical representative-agent growth model, but it has actually been taken seriously as a policy prescription (see Atkeson, Chari and Kehoe 1999). Since the analysis is conducted using a representative agent economy, issues of redistribution do not arise: the same agent is taxed more in the short run and less in the long run.

Second, there is the "intergenerational redistribution" view, best represented by the work of Auerbach and Kotlikoff (1987). This view focuses on the redistributional consequences of reducing the debt. Paying down the debt involves taxing more now and less later, which redistributes wealth away from the current generation in favour of future generations. The optimality of debt reduction depends on the initial intergenerational distribution of wealth and on the effect that a given debt-reduction plan will have. The optimal debt level in the long run balances the negative effects of distortionary taxation needed to finance interest payments on the debt and the effects on intergenerational redistribution. According to this view, debt is bad, but the costs of reducing it may very well outweigh the benefits.

Third, there is the "liquidity constrained" point of view, of which Aiyagari and McGrattan (1998) is the best example. Debt provides liquid assets to agents who otherwise do not have easy access to financial markets. These liquidity services are, of course, not costless, since interest payments on the debt must be financed by distortionary taxation. According to Aiyagari and McGrattan's calculations, the current debt-to-gross domestic product (GDP) ratios of countries like Canada and the US are approximately optimal.

The heart of Robson's paper consists of his explanations of the adjustments he has made to government balance sheets. Before presenting these results, he sets out some of his main methodological assumptions. These have to do with demographics, economic growth, and appropriate discount rates. For economic growth, the author takes projected labour force growth and assumes that per person output will continue to grow at the same rate that prevailed from 1980 to 2001, which is 1.7 per year. This would appear to neglect historical differences across provinces in the growth of per person output that may continue in the future. The nominal discount rate he uses to discount future revenue and expenditure is 6 percent. Because the results may be highly sensitive to both economic growth projections and to the discount rate, it would have been interesting to see some sensitivity analysis to changes in these assumptions.

We then get to the calculations themselves. For both the liquidity-based calculations and the long-run calculations, the main changes to governments' net asset positions come from a small number of large adjustments. For the liquidity-based calculation, the main correction is a $200 billion addition to assets to take account of the income generated by land. Most of this adjustment accrues to provincial governments. The results indicate that there are no foreseeable liquidity crunches on the horizon for Canadian governments. Standard measures of the debt-to-GDP ratio are 20 percentage points lower now than several years ago. The author judges that increasing this ratio by 30 percentage points "might put Canada back in the danger zone," but that this is not likely to happen.

For the long-run calculation, the two most substantial corrections are the unfunded liabilities of the CPP and QPP ($643 billion) and the implicit liability arising from publicly funded health care ($634 billion). There is also a positive adjustment from deferred taxes on pension saving ($306 billion) and from taking into account reproducible assets ($361 billion). When these four numbers are added to the $200 billion adjustment to the liquidity-based balance to account for land income, the adjustment to Canadian governments' net asset positions amounts to a reduction of $410 billion, which is very close to the overall adjustment of $379 billion, which includes all other categories. The relatively minor contribution of these categories makes this reader appreciate the effort that has gone into these adjustments. An adjustment of $1 billion can require as much data-gathering and number-crunching as an adjustment of several hundred billion dollars.

Robson summarizes the results from an Organisation for Economic Co-operation and Development (OECD) study which compares age-related spending obligations of different national governments. Canada looks worse in this table than the US, UK and Australia. The implication Robson suggests is that Canada may be viewed as not competitive by those thinking of investing or settling here. The figures require more explanation. Why does Japan have such a low number for age-related spending when it is projected to have one of the most rapidly aging populations? Presumably this is because the table reflects calculations of future marginal changes in age-related spending rather than current levels. Japan's figure is quite small since seniors already represent a high percentage of its total population.

Implications

The overall adjustment to long-term net balance compared to the conventional calculation is $308 billion (= $1,139 – $831 billion). Using the author's one-size-fits-all net discount rate of 2.1 percent, this gives an annual service cost of $6.47 billion.[1] We would have to raise this in taxes each year to service this extra debt in perpetuity without paying it off. GDP in 2001 was $1,092.3 billion, so the extra taxes represent 0.59 percent of 2001 GDP.

The absolute number is not small, but 0.59 percent of GDP seems not too large. Governments could immediately take another 0.59 percent chunk out of GDP and invest it in order to meet their future obligations. After this once and for all increase, there would be no further changes in tax rates. The Fraser Institute's Tax Freedom Day would be postponed by between one and two working days.

There are at least two reasons for not being complacent, however. First, the change in the long-term net balance is not evenly distributed across different jurisdictions. Some provinces may be required to raise taxes by fractions of their provincial GDP well in excess of 0.59 percent in order to meet their implicit future liabilities.

Second, for the problem to remain small it must be faced immediately. The extra liabilities arise from discounting spending that is projected to take place in the medium to long run. If we ignore the problem now, it could get a lot worse by the time we have to face it. In a context in which the federal government is running substantial surpluses in the short run, there may be a temptation to put off reducing the debt in favour of new spending programs, including "legacy projects'" such as the twinning of the Trans-Canada Highway around the north shore of Lake Superior. This paper is a potentially important contribution to the debate on the cost-benefit analysis of such projects.

Note

1. This is the nominal discount rate of 6 percent minus nominal GDP growth of 3.9 percent (see Robson paper).

Bibliography

Aiyagari, R., and E. McGrattan. 1998. "The Optimum Quantity of Debt." *Journal of Monetary Economics* 42:447-69.

Atkeson, A., V.V. Chari and P. Kehoe. 1999. "Taxing Capital Income: A Bad Idea." *Federal Reserve Bank of Minneapolis Quarterly Review* 23:3-17.

Auerbach, A., and L. Kotlikoff. 1987. *Dynamic Fiscal Policy.* Cambridge: Cambridge University Press.

Chari, V.V., L. J. Christiano and P. J. Kehoe. 1995. "Policy Analysis in Business Cycle Models." In *Frontiers of Business Cycle Research*, ed. T.F. Cooley. Princeton, NJ: Princeton University Press.

2

where did the debt come from?

Ronald Kneebone and Jennifer Chung

Introduction

In the early 1970s, following a long period during which the debts they had accumulated during World War II had been steadily reduced, Canada's federal and provincial governments changed direction and began to allow their debts to build up again. After two decades of this, in 1995, the federal government's debt was downgraded by a prominent credit-rating agency, prompting then-Finance Minister Paul Martin to make his famous declaration that he would eliminate the federal deficit "come hell or high water." In fact, most provincial governments had begun attacking their own deficits somewhat earlier, so by the mid-1990s, federal and provincial governments had changed direction again and had reverted to the more fiscally conservative policy of deficit avoidance that had been prevalent in the 1960s.

Government debts grow or decline as a result of government policy choices. Governments choose both tax rates and the sensitivity of spending programs to income. In doing so, they implicitly choose how much debt will be built up during recessions, how much will be paid down during expansions and how much will be either built up or paid down during "normal" economic conditions. By choosing how much debt to carry forward from one year to the next, governments choose their degree of exposure to the risks of higher interest rates. Of course, unforeseen events can make what may have seemed at the time to be sensible choices turn out badly. Once governments become aware of the budgetary implications of such events they must choose how quickly to try to reverse the implications for debt accumulation. The goal of this chapter is to try to identify which choices made by governments over the last three decades best explain why Canadian governments accumulated so much debt between 1970 and the mid-1990s.

Fortin (1998) has previously asked these kinds of questions using data describing the Canadian government sector in aggregate – federal, provincial and local governments, public hospitals, and public pension plans – for the period following 1982, when debt accumulation accelerated. His results suggest that what caused the buildup of debt was mainly governments' inability to react quickly and vigorously to the fiscal consequences of the Bank of Canada's tight monetary policy. In this chapter, we follow Fortin's basic approach, but we extend the period of analysis back to 1970. We also disaggregate the public sector so as to focus separately on the choices made by the federal government and each of the 10 provincial governments.[1] Both of these modifications turn out to be important.

The chapter proceeds as follows: the next section reviews the simple arithmetic of the government budget constraint. The following section shows how this simple arithmetic can be used to identify three separate sources of debt accumulation. The nuts and bolts of applying our method are discussed in the fourth section. A discussion of debt accumulation by the federal government is the subject of section five, while the sixth section focuses on the provinces in general and Ontario and Quebec in particular. Finally, in the last section, we offer a conclusion.

The Government's Budget Constraint

Like individuals, governments face a budget constraint: their "sources of funds" must equal their "uses of funds" over any period. What are a government's "uses of funds"? It can spend its funds on goods and services; it can transfer them to individuals or to other levels of government; or it can pay interest on its outstanding debts. Governments' non-interest spending is referred to as "program spending." What are a government's "sources of funds"? They consist of taxation, transfers received from other levels of government, returns on any investments it has made and borrowing. If a government spends more than it receives in taxes, in transfers from other levels of government and in returns on its investments, it is said to run a "deficit." A deficit requires it to either sell financial assets, if it has any, or borrow, thus adding to its direct liabilities. In either case, its net debt, defined as its direct liabilities less its financial assets, increases. By contrast, if a government brings in more in taxation, transfers from other levels of government and returns on investments than it spends, it is said to run a "surplus." A surplus enables it to retire liabilities or to add to its stock of financial assets. In either case, its net debt decreases.

Figure 1

Basic Accounting Concepts

Program spending ≡ spending on goods and services + transfers to individuals + transfers to other levels of government

---

Total expenditures ≡ program spending + debt charges

Deficit ≡ total expenditures − tax revenues − transfers from other levels of government − return on investment

---

Net interest payments ≡ debt charges − return on investment

Primary deficit ≡ deficit − net interest payments

Net interest rate ≡ net interest payments net ÷ debt from the previous year

---

Net debt ≡ direct liabilities − financial assets

Note: The identity sign (≡) indicates that the expression is a definition.

A government's "primary" surplus or deficit is calculated by looking, on the expenditure side, only at its program spending, that is, interest payments are excluded, and, on the revenue side, only at its tax revenues and transfers from other governments, that is, investment income is excluded. The primary deficit or surplus therefore shows what current spending and taxation choices would imply for debt accumulation if the government did not have any debt to begin with. The government budget constraint (GBC) just described is a simple accounting identity that can be represented by the following algebraic expression:

$$D_t - D_{t-1} = S_t - T_t + R_t D_{t-1} \quad (1)$$

Here D_t represents the value of the government's net debt at the end of period t while D_{t-1} is its net debt at the end of the previous period. The difference between the two is the change in the net debt over the period, which is equal to the budget deficit if it is a positive number, that is, the government's debt has grown over the period, or the budget surplus if it is a negative number, that is, debt has declined over the period. Program spending is given by S_t while T_t measures tax revenue and the value of transfers received from other levels of government. The difference $S_t - T_t$ defines the primary deficit ($PDEF_t$). R_t is the net interest rate owed on existing net debt during period t and the product $R_t D_{t-1}$ represents interest payments made in period t on the net debt inherited from period $t-1$. Appendix I defines all variables exactly and describes which data sources were used. Figure 1 above defines these concepts in words.

Judging whether a person's debts are large or small usually involves comparing them to his or her income. What is large for most of us might not be large for Conrad Black. In the same way, it is useful to evaluate the size of a government's debt by measuring it relative to gross domestic product, our collective national income. The same is true for tax revenues and government spending. Thus, it is useful to express all components of the government's budget constraint relative to national income. Some manipulation of (1) allows us to re-write the GBC as an expression describing the sources of change in the ratio of net debt to national income.

$$\frac{D_t}{Y_t} - \frac{D_{t-1}}{Y_{t-1}} = \frac{PDEF_t}{Y_t} + (R_t - G_t)\frac{D_{t-1}}{Y_t} \quad (2)$$

In this equation Y_t represents the level of national income at the end of period t, G_t the rate of growth in national income and D_t/Y_t the ratio of net debt to GDP (hereafter referred to as the "debt ratio").

The logic of these identities is straightforward. The expression on the left-hand side of the equation measures the change in the debt ratio during period t. On the right-hand side, $PDEF_t$ measures the net contribution to the deficit of choices made with respect to current spending, transfers from other levels of government and taxes. If program spending is equal to the sum of transfers from other levels of government and tax revenue, the primary deficit is zero and current fiscal policy choices have no effect on the debt, which neither rises nor falls. On the other hand, if $PDEF_t$ is positive, that means program spending exceeds tax and transfer revenue so that the government's current fiscal policy choices require it to borrow, while if $PDEF_t$ is negative, program spending is less than tax and transfer revenue, the government is in primary surplus and it can either retire debt or purchase new assets.

The second term on the right-hand side of both equations (1) and (2) shows, however, that even if the primary deficit is zero, the debt and debt ratio may increase simply because of the past accumulation of debt. Equation (1) shows that debt affects the current deficit because interest must be paid on it. The higher the interest rate, the more costly is this "debt service" and consequently the higher is the current deficit. Equation (2) shows that the effect of existing debt on the path taken by the debt ratio is determined by two factors; the rate of growth of output (G_t) and the interest rate (R_t). The interest rate appears because, as in equation (1), the government must pay interest on its debt. But equation (2) is concerned with the debt *ratio*, and the debt ratio can fall even if the government has an existing debt on which it must pay interest – so long as the rate of growth of the economy exceeds the interest rate on the debt. Thus, the faster national income grows, the smaller the debt will be when measured relative to it, and this will be true even if the debt is growing in absolute terms. A positive interest rate and a positive growth rate therefore have opposing influences on the change in the debt ratio. This is what the last term on the right-hand side of (2) shows.

In sum, the accounting identity described by equation (2) highlights three key sources of change in a government's debt ratio: the size of the primary deficit, the interest rate paid on previously accumulated debt and the rate of growth of output.

Debt Decomposition

A useful way of gaining insight into the sources of debt accumulation is to rewrite the GBC in the following way:

$$\frac{D_t}{Y_t} - \frac{D_{t-1}}{Y_{t-1}} = \frac{PDEF^*_t}{Y^*_t} + \left(\frac{PDEF_t}{Y_t} - \frac{PDEF^*_t}{Y^*_t} \right) + (R_t - G_t)\frac{D_{t-1}}{Y_t} \quad (3)$$

Here $PDEF_t^*$ and Y_t^* represent the "structural primary deficit" and the economy's "potential output" in year t, respectively. Potential output is the level of national income at which the economy is fully employed. More precisely, it measures the maximum sustainable level of output. In fact, maximum output is a tricky concept: for short periods, output may actually exceed this full-employment level although this requires that inputs be employed at greater-than-normal levels and is therefore not sustainable over the long run. For its part, the structural primary deficit measures what the primary deficit would be if actual output were equal to the maximum sustainable level of output.

The primary deficit changes with changes in the fiscal rules: with changes in tax rates, for example, or in the design of spending programs. But the primary deficit also changes with the level of output. This is so because some components of program spending (such as employment insurance payments) and tax revenue (such as income taxes) rise or fall as output rises and falls. In other words, the primary deficit is influenced both by the business cycle and by fiscal policy choices. The manipulation of the GBC presented in equation (3) separates out these two influences on the primary deficit.

In total, equation (3) allows us to identify three sources of change in the debt ratio. The first term on the right hand side, $PDEF^*/Y^*$, will be zero if the government has designed its tax rules and spending programs in such a way as to produce a zero primary deficit when the economy is operating at its maximum sustainable level of output. By contrast, it will be positive if the fiscal rules are set so that when the economy is at Y^* a primary deficit results. In this case, the design of spending and tax programs causes the debt ratio to increase even under favourable and sustainable economic conditions. Finally, $PDEF^*/Y^*$ will be negative if fiscal policy choices are such that at the maximum sustainable level of output tax revenues and transfers from other levels of government are more than sufficient to finance expenditures. In this case, fiscal policy choices will cause the debt ratio to fall.[2] Because debt changes caused by this variable being non-zero are due to a non-zero structural deficit, we will refer to the first term on the right-hand side of equation (3) as the *structural component*.

The second term we call the *cyclical component*. It measures the decrease (or increase) in the debt ratio that results from the economy operating at more (or less) than the maximum sustainable level of output. The cyclical component, then, measures the influence that the business cycle has on the amount of debt accumulated in the current period.

The third term on the right-hand side of (3) we will refer to as the *interest/growth component*. If the primary deficit were zero, the debt ratio would change only if the interest rate on net debt (R_t) were different from the rate of income growth (G_t). The debt ratio would rise if R_t were greater than G_t and fall if R_t were smaller than G_t. The interest/growth component measures the increase in the debt ratio that occurs because there is a gap between these two rates (and, of course, because the government has a net debt: if D_{t-1}/Y_t were zero, the entire term would be zero).

Our study of debt accumulation will try to evaluate these three separate components of the debt accumulation process, both for the federal government and for each of the 10 provincial governments. Doing so requires us to generate estimates of the maximum sustainable level of output for each province and for Canada as a whole and to generate estimates of the structural deficit for each of these 11 governments. The next section explains how we did this.

Measuring Potential Output and Structural Deficits

The measurement of potential output is critical for the decomposition of the debt into its structural and cyclical components. The Organisation for Economic Co-operation and Development (OECD), the International Monetary Fund (IMF) and the federal Department of Finance all generate values of potential output for national economies; but not for subnational economies. The approach used by these agencies creates problems for us because it requires the use of parameter estimates and data series not readily available at the provincial level. For this reason, we have resorted instead to a statistical technique called "the Hodrick-Prescott filter," which requires only data available at the provincial level. In appendix II we discuss issues involved in using the Hodrick-Prescott filter.

Recall that the structural primary deficit (*PDEF**) is the difference between what total program spending would be at potential output ("structural spending") and what the sum of tax revenue and transfers from other levels of government would be at potential output ("structural revenue"). *PDEF** is thus intended to measure the size of the primary deficit when the tax base and the expenditure base are at maximum sustainable levels. The first step in determining values of the structural primary deficit ($PDEF^*$) is to identify those elements of the primary balance that are cyclically sensitive. Candidates on the revenue side include personal and corporate income tax revenue and consumption tax revenue, while on the spending side federal expenditures on employment insurance and provincial spending on social assistance are usually identified. The next step is to form some judgement about the sensitivity of these expenditures and revenues to the business cycle and to use these assumed sensitivities to infer what total expenditures and revenues would be at potential output. Appendix II provides a more detailed discussion of how this is done. Here we simply record that our assumptions about the sensitivity of various tax and expenditure categories to the business cycle imply that a one-percentage point increase in observed relative to potential output has caused, on average, a 0.23 percentage point reduction in the federal government's deficit and a 0.11 percentage point reduction in the deficit of the aggregate provincial government sector. Thus, the federal budget is about twice as sensitive to the business cycle as are provincial budgets.[3]

Patterns of Debt Accumulation at the Federal Level

Because the federal government accumulated 75 percent of all federal-provincial government debt between 1970 and the mid-1990s, it seems appropriate to begin our story with it. Figure 2 shows the results of our decomposition of the federal deficit into structural, cyclical and interest/growth components. Although data on federal finances are available through 2001, our approach to producing an estimate of potential output gives us less confidence in the values of the structural and cyclical components for 1998-2001. We present the calculations for those four years both because they provide insight into what has been happening to government debt since it reached its peak and also because we feel the bias in these estimates, which is toward making the cyclical component smaller and the structural component larger in absolute value than might in fact have been true, is not so great as to change the essential message being delivered by the calculations. All calculations are based on data presented on a fiscal year basis ending 31 March of the identified year.

Panel A of figure 2 presents annual values for each component. Thus in the fiscal year ending 31 March 1971, the cycle added 0.76 percentage points of gross domestic product (GDP) to the federal net debt while the interest rate and structural components reduced the debt ratio by 0.71 and 0.62 percentage points of GDP, respectively. The sum of these three components, −0.57 percentage points of GDP, is the amount by which the federal net debt ratio decreased in 1971.

The lines in panel B show the *cumulative effects* of the cyclical, interest/growth and structural components on the net debt ratio since 1970, while the columns show the cumulative increase in the debt ratio since 1970.

Connecting the annual values of the cyclical component with a solid line confirms the expected wave pattern in which the economic cycle reduces the debt ratio during expansions and adds to the debt ratio during contractions. The cumulative cyclical component similarly rises and falls with contractions and expansions. Over the 32-year period of our sample, the cyclical component has contributed little to the growth in the federal debt ratio as the effects of expansions have more or less cancelled the effects of contractions. In panel A the positive areas between the solid line and the x-axis are roughly the same size as the negative areas between the line and the axis, while in panel B the line showing the cumulative cyclical effect seldom diverges from the x-axis.

Annual values of the interest/growth component show the effects on the federal budget of the difference between the output growth rate and the net interest rate on federal net debt. The early part of our sample period, from 1970 to 1982, was one of high growth rates and relatively low interest rates, with the result that the interest/growth component contributed to *reductions* in the debt ratio. By 1982 the interest/growth component had contributed to a 15-percentage point reduction in the federal debt ratio. After 1982, however, the relative sizes of the output growth rate and the net interest rate on federal net debt reversed so that now the interest/growth component was contributing to *increases* in the debt ratio. This turnaround can be attributed to the combined effects of the slowdown in the rate of growth of income experienced by most western economies in the mid- to late-1970s and to monetary policy choices of the US Federal Reserve and the Bank of Canada that pushed up interest rates in the early 1980s in an effort to fight inflation. When in 1989 the Bank of Canada again tightened monetary policy in an attempt to achieve price stability, the higher interest rates this caused, combined with slower rates of economic growth experienced at the time in Canada, the US and elsewhere, produced large, positive interest/growth components that boosted the debt ratio dramatically. By 1992 the cumulative effects of the interest/growth component had turned positive and in the nine years between 1989 and 1997 it added 20 percentage points to the debt ratio. Over the entire 32-year period from 1970 to 2001, the interest/growth component contributed 12 percentage points to the federal debt ratio.

Taken together, the cyclical and interest/growth components had between 1970 and 1997 added 11 percentage points to the federal debt ratio. The remaining 35 percentage points of increase were due to the structural component. The 18-percentage point *reduction* in the federal debt ratio between 1998 and 2001 was

Figure 2

Debt Accumulation by the Federal Government
Panel A: Annual Contributions to the Federal Debt Ratio

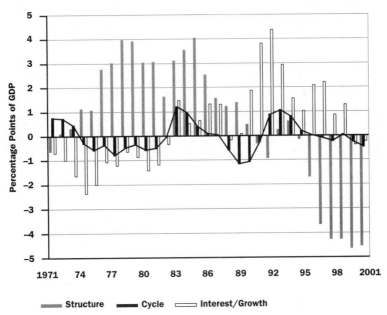

Panel B: Cumulative Contributions to the Federal Debt Ratio

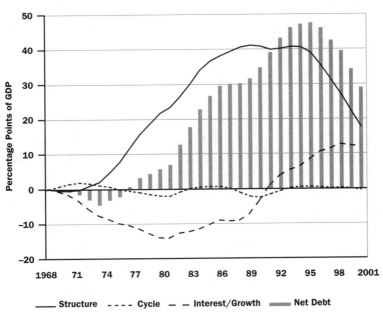

Figure 2

Panel C: Primary Expenditures and Revenues
as Percentage of Potential Output

——— Expenditure Ratio — — Revenue Ratio

almost wholly due to the structural component, although, as noted, we have some-what less confidence in the estimates of potential output underlying that conclusion.

Panel C of figure 2 presents ratios of structural spending and structural rev-enue to potential output, which we will refer to as the *expenditure ratio* and the *revenue ratio*, respectively. The difference between these values measures the struc-tural component of the debt presented in panel A. Panel C shows that the early period of structural debt accumulation had its beginning in a rapid increase in the expenditure ratio between 1971 and 1976. The effect of this surge on the deficit was exacerbated by a rapid decrease in the revenue ratio after 1975. Perry's (1989) description of the budget presentations of this period indicates that these changes were intended to be counter-cyclical stabilization policy. Budgets of the time expressed considerable concern about the new experience of rising unemploy-ment combined with higher inflation.[4] Tax cuts, accelerated depreciation allowances, investment tax credits, new spending on capital projects, and job-training programs highlighted the budgets of this period. This aggressive attack on unemployment from both sides of the budget (i.e., via both tax cuts and spending increases) moved the structural deficit from near zero to nearly 3 per-cent of potential output by 1976. Into this mix was thrown income tax indexa-tion beginning in January 1974, a reform that would prove very costly as the rate of inflation increased. Although the expenditure ratio began to be reduced after 1976 this was two years after the revenue ratio had already begun to fall; nor in the end did the expenditure ratio fall as far as the revenue ratio. As a result, by 1979 the structural deficit had widened to almost 4 percent of potential output; although, despite this large-scale experiment in discretionary fiscal policy, the unemployment rate (at 7.5 percent) was higher than it had been in 1972 (6.2 percent).

After 1980 the revenue ratio steadily increased. Tax reforms that closed a myriad of loopholes between 1982 and 1986 presumably helped in this regard, as did the partial de-indexing of personal income taxes that began in 1983. By 1986, indexation was restricted to a maximum of 3 percent so that for the rest of the decade, during which inflation averaged 4.2 percent per year, the federal government enjoyed a steady increase in personal income taxes even when real incomes were not rising. Unfortunately, after 1979 the expenditure ratio also reversed and rose more or less steadily to 1985. Important sources of this growth were renewed efforts at job creation via direct government expenditures. The rise can also be attributed to new spending on energy projects and transfers that resulted from negotiations with energy-producing provinces and the imposition of the National Energy Program (NEP). The NEP also provided a new influx of revenue, which can be seen in the jump in the revenue ratio in 1982. It is interesting that the only large category of federal expenditure showing declines to 1985 was transfers to the provinces for hospital and health insurance. Be that as it may, as a result of the post-1979 growth of the expenditure ratio, by 1985 the structural deficit had again grown to 4 percent of output.

The election of the Mulroney government toward the end of fiscal year 1985 coincided with a reversal in the rise of the expenditure ratio. Primary expenditures were reduced in the first complete year of the new government's mandate (fiscal year 1986), resulting in a large reduction in the expenditure ratio. Thereafter the decline in the expenditure ratio was slow but steady and resulted mainly from growth in potential output (i.e., expenditures were held more or less constant in real-dollar terms while the economy expanded). Substantial tax increases in the two following years (fiscal years 1987 and 1988) accelerated the rise in the revenue ratio even in the face of fast growth in potential output. By 1991 the structural deficit had been turned into Ottawa's first structural surplus since 1971. From that point forward improvements in the structural balance would be mainly due to reductions in the expenditure ratio.

In fiscal year 1994, a newly-elected government, a Liberal one this time, initiated a series of spending cuts that by 1997 had reduced the expenditure ratio by 3.8 percentage points from what it had been in 1993. By our calculations, 60 percent of this reduction was due to spending cuts while 40 percent was due to growth in potential output. Of the spending cuts, one-third came in the form of cuts to provincial transfers and just less than one-fifth in cuts to the generosity of the Employment Insurance (EI) program. Recognizing that cuts to federally-financed employment insurance often force former EI recipients onto provincially-financed welfare rolls, it is fair to say that one-third to one-half of federal efforts at expenditure reduction over the 1993–97 period came at the expense of provincial budgets. Put differently, of the 3.8-percentage-point reduction in the federal expenditure ratio between 1993 and 1997, 1.5 percentage points were due to growth in potential output, 0.8 percentage points to cuts to provincial transfers and 0.5 percentage points to cuts to EI. That leaves just one of the 3.8 percentage points as being due to cuts to other types of federal program spending, those not directly affecting provincial budgets. After 1997 there would be a further one-percentage-point reduction in the expenditure ratio. This came about despite some recovery in the size of provincial transfers and hence was solely due to growth in potential output.

What is striking about the calculations presented in figure 2 and described above is how persistent the gap between the expenditure and revenue ratios remained. For 19 years, 1972 to 1990 inclusive, the federal government produced budgets that would have yielded a deficit even at maximum sustainable levels of economic output. In our view, the mountain of federal debt accumulated between 1970 and 1997 is ultimately attributable to what proved to be a failed attempt at fiscal stabilization initiated in the mid-1970s. These actions created a persistent structural deficit that policy makers wrestled with for a full decade – unsuccessfully from 1980 to 1985, successfully from 1986 to 1990 – before finally closing it in 1991, by which time a structural debt equal to 40 percentage points of national income had been accumulated. Thus policies initiated in the 1970s can be seen as finally necessitating the aggressive deficit-cutting suffered 20 years later in the mid-1990s.

But why were the structural deficits so persistent and why did it take policy makers so long to eliminate them? It is interesting to speculate on the role played by the interest/growth component during the early part of the period, from 1970 to 1982. During this period the growth rate of the economy was high relative to the interest rate paid on federal debt. As a result, in those first 12 years, the interest/growth component contributed a 15-percentage point *reduction* in the debt ratio, the effect of which was to hide from view much of the 23-percentage point *increase* in debt caused by the structural component. The important role of the interest/growth component can be appreciated if we look only at the columns in panel B. These columns, which show the increase in the debt ratio since 1970, suggest that before the mid-1980s people might reasonably have concluded that there was little reason to be concerned about debt. After a decade of economic turmoil from oil price shocks, record rates of inflation and (to that point) unprecedented rates of unemployment, the debt ratio had risen by only seven percentage points. However, the columns only show the *net* result of the structural, interest/growth and cyclical components. Hidden from view was a rapid accumulation of structural debt that, should the interest/growth component ever stop contributing to an offsetting reduction in the debt ratio, would prove disastrous. No policy maker or voter who looked only at the debt ratio would have thought it necessary to take strong fiscal measures to curtail the accumulation of debt. In this way, then, the favourable interest/growth component may have delayed fiscal reform by slowing the increase in the debt ratio and so preventing the establishment of the political conditions required for governments to eliminate their structural deficits.

When the interest/growth component did turn around, in 1982, and began contributing to debt accumulation the debt ratio increased quickly: for the next eight years the structural and interest/growth components were both contributing to increases in the debt ratio, which as a result jumped 25 points. After 1990, just as the structural imbalance was brought under control, the interest/growth component became a serious contributor to debt accumulation. After that, the race was on: Could tax rates be increased and spending programs cut fast enough so as to produce structural surpluses large enough to offset the growth of the interest/growth component and so keep the debt ratio from rising still further? By 1996 the answer had proved to be "yes" but only at the cost of both persistently high tax rates and cuts to programs and provincial transfers. Of course, this race could be run at all only because the rapid increase in the debt ratio had established the political conditions that allowed it to be run: by the mid-1990s almost everyone in Canada was a fiscal hawk.

Our bottom line? Between 1970 and 1997 the federal government accumulated $564 billion of new net debt. Of this amount, $432 billion (or 77 percent of the total) was accumulated as a result of a mismatch between structural expenditures and structural revenues, $12 billion (2 percent) was the result of the business cycle and $120 billion (21 percent) was due to the difference between the interest rate paid on federal government debt and the economy's growth rate.

Patterns of Debt Accumulation at the Provincial Level

The provinces differ from the federal government in a number of ways. First, an important source of cyclical influence present in the federal budget, employment insurance, is not present in provincial budgets. Second, intergovernmental grants, an expenditure item for the federal government, are a revenue source for the provinces. Thus, cuts in intergovernmental transfers simultaneously aid federal but harm provincial efforts at deficit reduction, a process often referred to as "deficit off-loading." Third, the provinces are subject to far closer scrutiny by credit-rating agencies than the federal government, with the result that, despite having substantially lower levels of debt, they often pay significantly higher interest rates on their liabilities. Finally, the provinces have less-diversified tax bases than the federal government, which makes their primary deficits more sensitive to particular shocks.

Provincial governments also differ from one another. They do so in terms of their reliance on grants, the diversity of their tax bases, their size relative to the private sector, and their reliance on natural resource revenues. Ontario and Quebec have been the largest debt-generators amongst the provinces, contributing 11 percent and 9 percent, respectively, of all federal-provincial net debt accumulated over the period 1970–97. We consider them in turn and then provide a brief analysis of each of the other provinces, not because they are not important but because their combined contribution to the increase in public debt over this period was only four percentage points of GDP.

Ontario

Figure 3 presents our calculations for the Government of Ontario. Ontario added 22 percentage points to its debt ratio between 1970 and 1997, with most of the increase coming after 1990.

As was true of the federal government, the cyclical component has played an insignificant role in Ontario's debt accumulation. The periods 1981–85 and 1986–91 offer a nice example of the offsetting effects on the debt ratio of a cycle that took the economy first below and then above potential output. Movements in Ontario's interest/growth component contributed to debt reduction for longer than the federal government's did, all the way up to 1990. Although the interest/growth component then contributed a seven-percentage point increase in the debt ratio between 1990 and 1997 it nonetheless ended 1997 having contributed to a three-percentage point *reduction* in the ratio since 1970.

The rapid increase in structural expenditures as a fraction of output in the first few years of the 1970s is common to all the provinces. This reflects the impact of major federal-provincial cost-sharing programs established or expanded at that time which increased provincial responsibilities for social programs. The failure of revenues to keep up produced a series of structural deficits and an increase of 15 percentage points in the structural debt between 1970 and 1980. The interest/ growth component offset about half the increase in structural debt so that despite the structural deficits, the total net debt ratio rose by only seven percentage points to 1980. Despite this modest growth in the debt ratio, the Government of Ontario responded much sooner than the federal government and by 1980 had significantly reduced the size of the structural deficits it had run during the 1970s. Budgets in the mid- to late-1970s responded to the increase in debt by reducing the size of the civil service and imposing caps on employment growth. Maslove, Prince and Doern (1985) report that by 1984 the number of civil servants per 1,000 residents had fallen by 18 percent since 1975. That the Ontario government would respond so strongly to a relatively small increase in its debt ratio is consistent with what Maslove, Prince and Doern (ibid.) describe as a fairly constant priority of restraint and austerity expressed since the early 1960s.

During the 1980s the Ontario government ran a small but persistent structural deficit. Because the interest/growth component continued to reduce the debt ratio, the total debt ratio was kept under control. In fact, between 1986 and 1990 it actually fell, the result of favourable interest/growth and cyclical components offsetting a negative structural component. As had been true in Ottawa until the mid-1980s, because of these offsets the structural imbalance was largely hidden from view.

Fiscal year 1991 marked a turning point. Just as the persistent structural deficits of the 1980s were finally eliminated, spending took a sharp jump and structural deficits of about the same magnitude as those seen in the 1970s returned in 1992 and 1993. This time, however, the structural deficits were accompanied by an interest/growth component that contributed to, rather than

Figure 3

Debt Accumulation by the Ontario Government
Panel A: Annual Contributions to Ontario's Debt Ratio

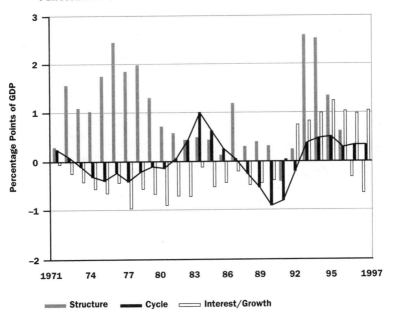

Figure 3

Panel B: Cumulative Contributions to Ontario's Debt Ratio

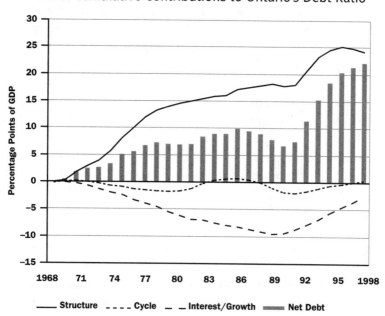

Panel C: Primary Expenditures and Revenues
as Percentage of Potential Output

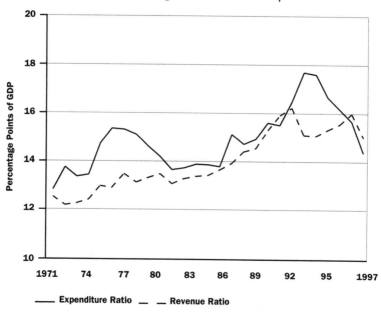

where did the debt come from?

offset, the accumulation of debt. The combination proved deadly and a sizable and rapid increase in the net debt ratio followed. The need to attack the structural deficit having thus been exposed to view, the policy response was vigorous. After initially making welfare even more generous and easier to get than the Peterson government had done, the Rae government set about cutting spending and raising revenues. The result was essentially a zero structural balance by 1995 when the Harris government came to power. Cuts to both spending and revenue, along with solid economic growth, would reduce the spending and revenue ratios still further while maintaining a zero structural balance, despite a $1.6-billion cut in federal transfers in 1997.

In sum, between 1970 and 1997 the Government of Ontario accumulated $85 billion in new net debt. On its own, the mismatch between structural expenditures and structural revenues actually caused an even bigger buildup than that, $93 billion (or 110 percent of the total), but over the period as a whole the interest/growth component offset this to the tune of $10 billion (12 percent of the total), while the cyclical contribution to the net debt was just $2 billion (2 percent of the total).

Quebec

Figure 4 presents our calculations for the Government of Quebec. Quebec added 27 percentage points to its debt ratio between 1970 and 1997. As in Ontario, much of the increase came about after 1990. The 1970s saw Quebec hold its debt ratio more or less constant. As we have seen now a few times, however, this stability in the debt ratio disguised a good deal of offsetting movement in the three debt components. In the early 1970s the province undertook a sustained level of capital expenditure in order to promote economic expansion and job creation (Maslove, Prince and Doern 1985). Revenues increased, though not so quickly as expenditures, with the result that the structural deficit grew. Programs to restrain spending and control public sector salaries in the late 1970s halted the growth in the expenditure ratio by 1981 but nonetheless left the provincial government with a structural deficit equal to 2.6 percent of potential output.

In the decade to 1981, a persistent structural deficit had resulted in the structural component adding 15 percentage points to the debt ratio while the cyclical and interest/growth components had reduced the debt ratio by an almost equal amount. Credit rating agencies that had upgraded Quebec's debt in 1974 and 1975 now downgraded it in 1982 (Kneebone 1998), thus increasing the interest rate the province had to pay on its financial liabilities.

In Quebec, the interest/growth component stopped contributing to a reduction in the debt ratio after 1982, eight years before this occurred in Ontario. This was due to a combination of slower growth and higher interest charges, either or both of which may have been influenced by the election of separatist governments in 1977 and 1981. The rapid increase in the debt ratio between 1981 and 1986 was due to all three of the debt components moving in the same direction. Then, beginning in 1990, Quebec suffered the consequences of the interest/growth component turning even more strongly positive. Between 1990 and 1997 it contributed over 12 percentage points to the debt ratio. In 1996 the cuts to spending that other provinces had started to introduce some years earlier also began in Quebec. These cuts proved large enough to produce structural surpluses in 1996 and, despite a $1.5 billion cut in federal transfers, in 1997.

In sum, between 1970 and 1997 the Government of Quebec accumulated $69 billion of new net debt. Of this amount, $63 billion (91 percent) was accumulated as a result of a mismatch between structural expenditures and structural revenues, $5 billion (7 percent) because of the difference between the interest rate and the economy's growth rate, and $1 billion (1 percent) because of the business cycle.

Brief Comments on the Other Provinces
The other eight provinces contributed a total of just 4 percent of all the federal-provincial net debt accumulated over the period 1970–97, which is why we do

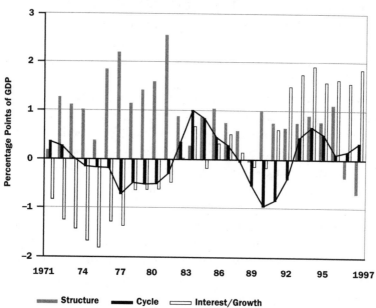

Figure 4
Debt Accumulation by the Quebec Government
Panel A: Annual Contributions to Quebec's Debt Ratio

where did the debt come from?

Figure 4

Panel B: Cumulative Contributions to Quebec's Debt Ratio

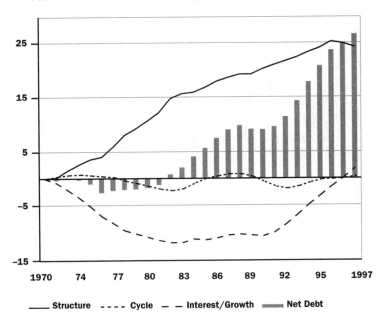

_____ Structure   - - - - Cycle   — — Interest/Growth   ▓▓▓ Net Debt

Panel C: Primary Expenditures and Revenues
as Percentage of Potential Output

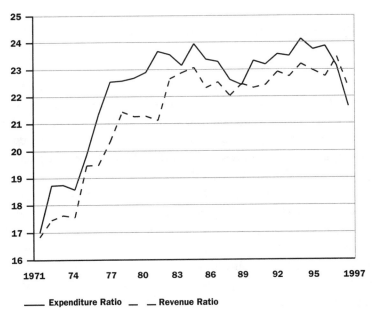

_____ Expenditure Ratio   — — Revenue Ratio

not spend as much time analyzing them. The annual values of the structural, interest/growth and cyclical components, along with their cumulative values, are presented in figure 5.

The province of Newfoundland is an interesting case, given its small size, high debt and consequent high exposure to interest rates. Although it took on little debt relative to income over our sample period – the debt ratio increased by just 11 percentage points of provincial GDP between 1970 and 1997 – this was despite large movements in the interest/growth and structural components making up changes in the debt ratio. The first decade was witness to a rapid accumulation of structural debt mirrored by an interest/growth component that moved the debt ratio in the opposite direction. The interest/growth component turned around in 1982 and over the next 15 years added 23 percentage points to the debt ratio, almost exactly the amount by which it had reduced the debt ratio between 1970 and 1981. Possibly because of an already high debt ratio and a very poor debt rating, the Government of Newfoundland preceded all others in successfully reducing its structural debt. The accumulated structural debt was reduced slowly but steadily from 1982 to 1993 and then quickly and steadily from 1993 to 1997. Virtually the entire increase in the debt ratio since 1970 was due to the structural component.

Prince Edward Island is interesting in that it substantially reduced its debt ratio during the 1970s and maintained that lower debt ratio thereafter. This was done by holding the structural deficit close to zero and allowing a favourable interest/growth component to pull the debt ratio down. Between 1977 and 1982 a structural deficit was maintained that prevented the debt ratio from falling further. After that point, a structural deficit was more or less offset by a favourable interest/growth component so the debt ratio remained constant.

Favourable interest/growth components allowed both Nova Scotia (slightly) and New Brunswick (slightly more) to reduce their debt ratios during the 1970s despite their maintaining positive structural deficits. New Brunswick reduced its structural deficit much earlier than Nova Scotia, however, with the result that despite the two provinces having similarly favourable interest/growth components, Nova Scotia's debt ratio increased by 20 percentage points of GDP over our sample period while New Brunswick's did not change.

The structural component in Manitoba describes an interesting saw-tooth pattern over the first 20 years of our sample. From fiscal years 1973 to 1978 the province's structural deficit was large and growing but it then fell almost to zero. The pattern is repeated with a large and growing structural component from 1980 to 1987 and then a dramatic fall to balance the following year. The fact that Manitoba changed governing parties on dates corresponding to these dramatic changes in the structural deficit suggests strongly that in this province at least

Figure 5

The Other Provinces
Newfoundland: Annual Contributions

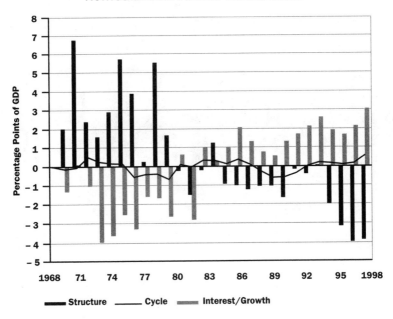

Newfoundland: Cumulative Contributions

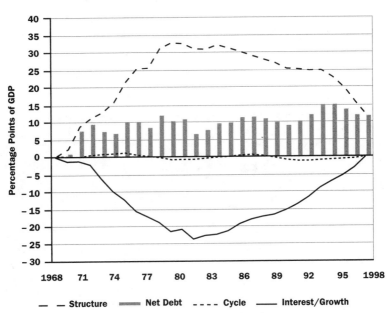

Figure 5

The Other Provinces
Prince Edward Island: Annual Contributions

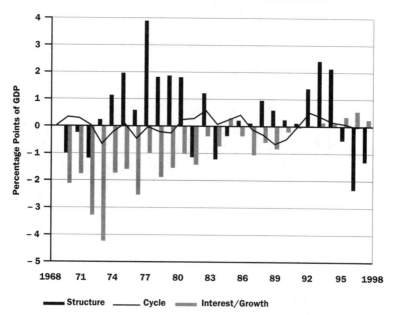

Prince Edward Island: Cumulative Contributions

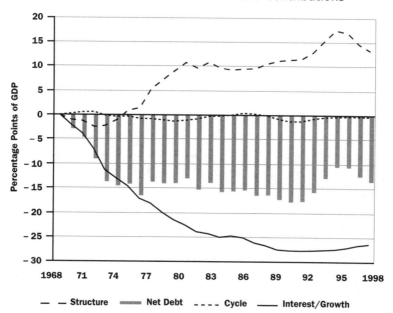

Figure 5
The Other Provinces
Nova Scotia: Annual Contributions

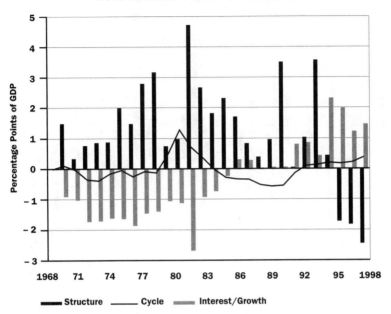

Nova Scotia: Cumulative Contributions

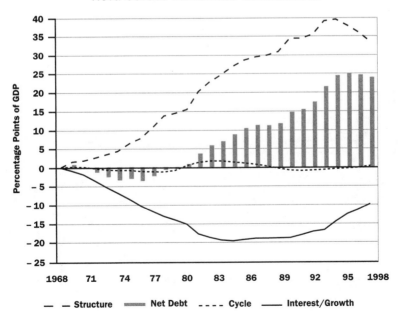

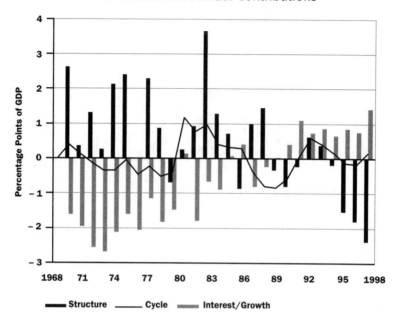

Figure 5

The Other Provinces

New Brunswick: Annual Contributions

New Brunswick: Cumulative Contributions

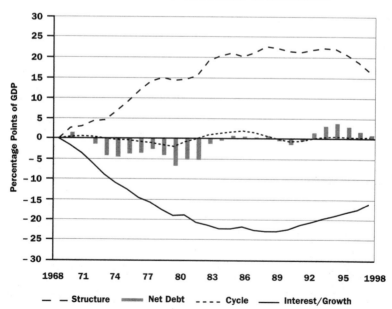

Figure 5

The Other Provinces
Manitoba: Annual Contributions

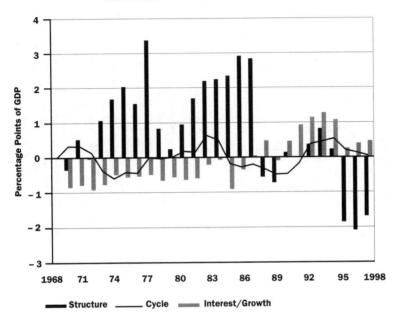

Manitoba: Cumulative Contributions

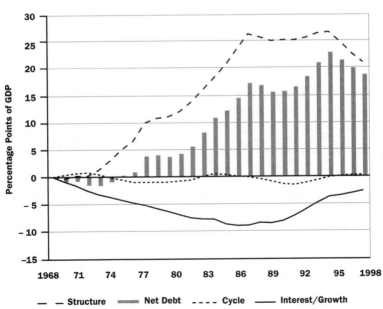

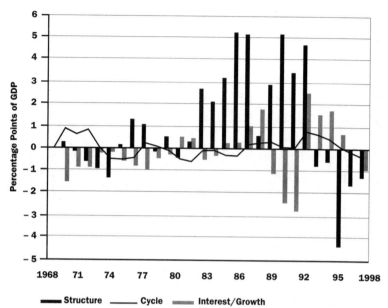

Figure 5

The Other Provinces

Saskatchewan: Annual Contributions

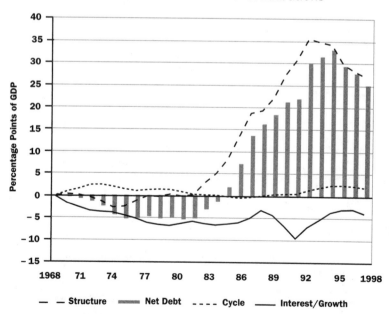

Saskatchewan: Cumulative Contributions

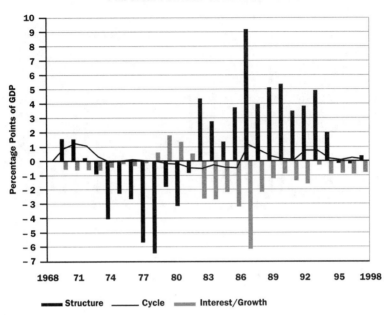

Figure 5

The Other Provinces

Alberta: Annual Contributions

Alberta: Cumulative Contributions

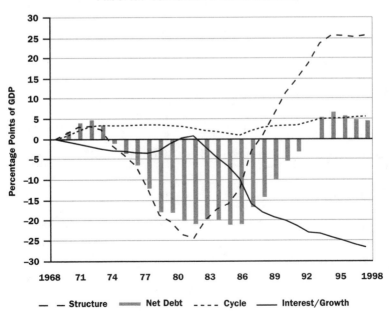

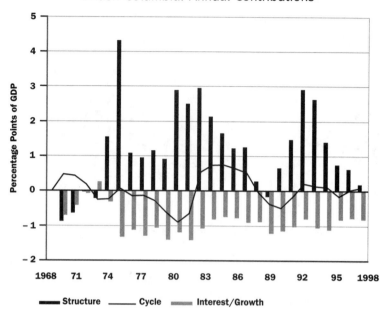

Figure 5

The Other Provinces

British Columbia: Annual Contributions

Legend: ■ Structure — Cycle ▮ Interest/Growth

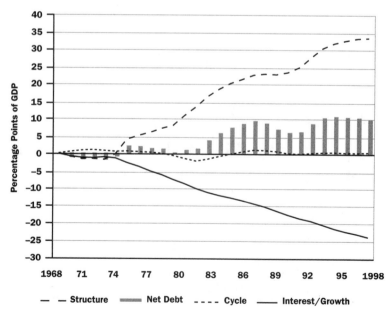

British Columbia: Cumulative Contributions

Legend: — Structure ▮ Net Debt - - - - Cycle — Interest/Growth

politics has a role in determining fiscal policy choices. In Manitoba politics, increases in the structural deficit in the 1970s and 1980s corresponded to periods of New Democratic Party (NDP) government while adjustments to smaller deficits and surpluses corresponded to a period of Conservative government.

Structural balances in Saskatchewan also suggest a political influence on fiscal policies but contrary to stereotype, with NDP governments cast in the role of fiscal conservatives. From 1970 to 1982 the structural component added nothing to accumulated debt. Net debt then exploded from zero to 35 percent of provincial GDP between 1983 and 1992, the only years of Conservative government in Saskatchewan's history. The role of energy prices needs to be taken into consideration, however. As we discuss in appendix II, because oil and natural gas royalties are driven by world demand and supply conditions rather than by provincial output, changes in natural resource revenues are reflected in changes in the structural, as opposed to the cyclical component. Thus, the large positive structural components after the fall in energy prices in 1986 partly reflect this influence. On the other hand, easily the largest influence on the structural component after 1986 was an increase in structural spending, not a fall in revenue.

The Government of Alberta entered our sample period in a small net asset position, built this into a large net asset position, saw this asset position disappear and become a small net debt before finally returning to a small net asset position in 1997. For obvious reasons, our calculations for Alberta are the most sensitive to our treatment of natural resource revenues. After the first Organization of Petroleum-Exporting Countries (OPEC) oil shock in 1973, the increase in oil and gas revenues produced large negative structural components that contributed to a rapid accumulation of net assets. The fall in energy prices in 1986 contributed to an equally rapid dissipation of net assets to 1994. The fact that the province was typically in a net asset position means that the interest/growth component contributed to decreases in the debt ratio during periods of high interest rates and low growth rates. Thus, unlike the experience of most other provinces, these conditions contributed to reducing Alberta's debt ratio (increasing its asset ratio).

British Columbia entered our sample period in a small net asset position and was left in 1997 in a small net debt position. This appearance of fiscal probity belies the steady accumulation of structural debt, however. Only a consistently negative interest/growth component offsetting the equally consistent positive structural component kept the net debt ratio from rising out of control. The consistently negative interest/growth component is due to the fact that British Columbia is a net recipient of interest income. Consequently, the effective net interest rate that the province of British Columbia pays on its net debt is negative and this in turn causes the rate component to be negative. An attentive reader might ask how a government with net debt (liabilities are greater than assets) can be a net recipient of interest income. This is possible if the interest rate paid on liabilities is greater than the interest rate received on assets. The difference in interest rates need not be large for this to be true if net debt is small. These conditions describe BC.

Conclusion

From the mid-1970s to the mid-1990s, Canadian governments accumulated large amounts of debt. A simple re-writing of the government budget constraint highlights the respective roles played in debt accumulation by fiscal policy choices, the business cycle, and interest rates and growth rates. We have employed a methodology suggested by Fortin (1998) that identifies the separate influences of these factors so as to better enable us to observe where the debt came from. Unlike Fortin, however, who examined the Canadian government sector in aggregate, we examine separately the sources of debt accumulation by the federal government and each of the 10 provinces. What's more, we extend the period of analysis backwards more than 10 years before the beginning of Fortin's analysis to the beginning of the 1970s. Both of these extensions prove to be important for understanding the sources of debt accumulation. The size and sources of debt accumulation differ by level of government and across provinces. Debt accumulation, caused by the interest rate paid on debt being greater than the growth rate of the economy, began for most governments in the early 1980s. Thus Fortin, who began his analysis at this point, could reasonably conclude that this was a key source of debt accumulation. Our calculations show, however, that this experience followed a period of a decade or more during which the growth rate of the economy was greater than the interest rate paid on debt. As a result, over the entire period of debt accumulation, from 1970 to 1997, the difference between interest and growth rates, while still significant, becomes less important as an explanation for debt accumulation. When we take this longer view, the mismatch between structural spending and structural revenue grows in importance. A closer examination of these measures, particularly during the early period of debt accumulation, suggests to us a different interpretation of the ultimate source of late-twentieth-century debt accumulation.

Over the period 1970–97, the federal government accounted for 75 percent of all the debt accumulated by federal and provincial governments. More than three-quarters of the increase in federal debt resulted from a mismatch between structural spending and structural revenue. If we are interested in understanding where the great majority of government debt in Canada has come from, we must therefore concentrate our attention on understanding where the federal government's structural debt came from.

We have argued that the years from 1971–76 were crucial to federal debt accumulation. This was a period of oil price shocks, high inflation and rising unemployment rates, presided over by minority governments and policy makers trained to believe in the efficacy of discretionary fiscal policy: in sum, a veritable witches' brew of ingredients designed to conjure up budget deficits! However, despite large structural deficits, the federal debt ratio ended the 1970s only three percentage points higher than it had been at the start of that decade. The reason was the favourable interest/growth component. As Robson (1996) notes, this was an historically unusual period in Canadian public finances; a period during which the economic growth rate exceeded the interest rate paid on government debt. An unfortunate by-product of this era was that the resulting favourable interest/growth component concealed a very large structural deficit. At the beginning of the 1980s the average voter could hardly have thought that the federal government was in serious financial difficulties. As a result, the political conditions required for an attack on structural deficits were not yet ripe. Yet if economic conditions changed to slower growth rates and/or higher interest rates, the federal budget was set to produce a rapidly growing debt ratio. At the end of the 1970s federal finances were in serious trouble even if this was not readily apparent from looking at the debt ratio.

Maslove, Prince and Doern (1985) describe how, reflecting changes in economic thinking, after 1978 federal budgets began to express less confidence in the power of discretionary fiscal policy to affect macroeconomic outcomes. Budgets now began to emphasize the strength of forces beyond the federal government's control as reasons why it could not affect, and could not be blamed for failing to affect, macroeconomic outcomes.[5] This retreat from activism was difficult and prolonged, however. As Maslove, Prince and Doern (1985) also note, the worst recession in 50 years was not the best time politically for the government to attempt to withdraw from activist fiscal policy. Thus, when in 1982 the interest/growth component changed from contributing to reductions in the debt ratio to contributing to increases in it, the structural component was slow to react. Now the observed debt ratio grew quickly as both the interest/growth and the structural components contributed to its growth. By 1990 the rapid accumulation of debt produced the political conditions required for an attack on structural deficits. Indeed, the steady rise in the debt ratio caused by the interest/growth component made it obvious that holding the structural deficit at zero would not be enough. By 1994 it had become obvious that structural surpluses were required to keep control of the debt ratio. Unfortunately, by 1994 the structural deficits of the early 1970s and the slow response that did not see them disappear until 1990 had caused the net debt ratio to increase by 41 percentage points. From this perspective, the economic pain and dislocation occasioned by the large spending cuts and tax increases that the federal government introduced after 1994 are in large part due to a failed attempt at discretionary stabilization policy 20 years earlier.

By contrast, the provinces have played a relatively minor role in debt accumulation. The major debt players amongst the provinces were the governments of Ontario and Quebec, which together accounted for 21 percent of all federal-provincial debt accumulated between 1970 and 1997. The remaining eight provinces were responsible for accumulating only 4 percent of this debt. In general, the accumulation of structural debt in the provinces followed a pattern similar to that experienced by the federal government. That is, for the first decade following 1970, the accumulation of structural debt was negatively correlated with the accumulation of debt due to the interest/growth component: as the debt ratio fell due to a favourable interest/growth component, the structural component filled the gap. When in the early 1980s the interest/growth component turned and began to contribute to increases in the debt ratio, reductions in the structural balance followed immediately or with a few years' lag.

Because of data limitations we stopped our analysis of the provinces at the end of fiscal year 1997. We were, however, able to extend our analysis of federal finances an extra four years to 2001. This extension showed that the interest/growth component has stopped contributing to increases in the debt ratio and that the steady fall in the federal debt ratio has been due solely to the structural component, which in turn is the result of a large structural surplus.

Is the debt war over? Given that the federal government has accumulated most of Canada's government debt, the question is more properly framed as: "Is Ottawa's debt war over?" The answer depends on the costs and benefits of further debt reduction and on what the optimal debt ratio might be, issues that are examined by Boadway, Dahlby and Scarth in this volume. To some extent, the answers to those questions depend on whether the current levels of interest rates and economic growth rates will be observed in the long term. At the moment, the interest/growth component is close to zero. The good news in this is that current structural balances are not being offset by the interest/growth component and are thus having a direct effect on reducing the debt ratio. The bad news is that over time the structural component has tended to be negatively correlated with the interest/growth component, which means that if the interest/growth component is no longer forcing politicians to maintain structural surpluses, the federal government may be tempted to relax the reins, thus beginning a new episode in the debt war.

appendix I

Data Sources and Definitions

Public accounts data on federal government expenditures, revenues, deficits and net debt were retrieved from the Fiscal Reference Tables published on the Department of Finance Web site (www.fin.gc.ca) in August 2002. These are fiscal-year data for the period ending 31 March. Data on provincial government expenditures, revenues and deficits are from CANSIM matrices 2781 through 2793. These are fiscal-year data on provincial "general government" and thus exclude the revenues and expenditures of universities, colleges, public hospitals and pension plans. The data in matrices 2781 through 2793 stop at 1997. Although provincial data taking us to 2001 were available from CANSIM matrices 3776 through 3788, those data include natural resource revenues with investment income, a treatment that makes it difficult to determine the effective rate of interest on financial net debt in those provinces, particularly Alberta, Saskatchewan and British Columbia, in which natural resource revenues are large. What's more, as explained in appendix II, our method for producing an estimate of potential output is such that we have confidence in our estimates only to 1997.

Provincial government budget data are measured according to the Financial Management System standardized accounting framework. The advantage of FMS data is comparability across governments. The disadvantage is that deficits defined by FMS data do not equal the change in debt indicated by public accounts data. Two approaches are available. Kneebone and Leach (2001) force the deficit as defined by the national accounts data to agree with the data on debt in public accounts by constructing a "reconciliation" series. In this chapter we have taken the alternative approach of constructing our own net debt series by adding to an initial value of net debt the cumulative sum of annual deficits and surpluses. Over our sample period, the difference between our constructed net debt series and that in the public accounts grows slowly. For example, by 1997 our constructed series produces a net debt for Ontario equal to 26.4 percent of GDP while the public accounts data produce a value equal to 29.3 percent of GDP. The advantage of our method is that our structural, cyclical and interest/growth components add up to exactly the size of the change in net debt. Initial values for provincial net debt (for 1970) were taken from CANSIM matrices 3202 through 3211. Net debt is defined as direct liabilities (net of liabilities of government employee pension plans) less financial assets.

Calendar year (CY) data on nominal GDP at market prices is from CANSIM matrices 2611 through 2619 (for years 1966–80) and from 9015 through 9024 (for years 1981–2001). These series were converted to fiscal year (FY) data according to the formula:

$$\text{GDP for FY}_t = 0.25^*(\text{GDP for CY}_t) + 0.75^*(\text{GDP for CY}_{t-1})$$

Our variable G measures the rate of growth of the fiscal year measure.

appendix II

Deriving Values of Y* and PDEF*

We generated values of provincial potential GDP (Y*) by applying the Hodrick-Prescott (HP) filter. Briefly, what it does is decompose data on GDP, Y, into trend and cycle components. It does so by calculating for each observation a moving average using data on either side of that observation. The moving average is interpreted as representing the level of potential output, Y*. Deviations of the moving average from the observed series are interpreted as the output cycle, Y-Y*. Experimentation with different values of the parameter in the generating process that determines the "smoothness" of the trend component relative to the cyclical component indicated that the choice yielding what is essentially a nine-part moving average, using four data points on either side of each observation, was preferred. The filter was applied to nominal GDP deflated by a fiscal-year consumer price index constructed from monthly data on the all-items CPI for major cities (CANSIM matrix 9953). The nominal value of Y* is recovered by multiplying by the CPI.

The attraction of the HP filter is that its application involves a minimum of judgement and requires a minimum of data. Further, the resulting smooth but nonlinear time series of potential output accords with most analysts' expectations of the evolution of that series. An important criticism of the HP filter is what is known as "end-sample bias." The HP filter draws upon past and future observations when calculating the value of potential output in any given year. At the beginning and end of the series of observations, past or future values, respectively, are missing, thus causing the estimate of potential output to gravitate toward the observed value. To minimize the importance of this problem we apply an HP filter to provincial and national output series covering the period from fiscal year 1967 to fiscal year 2001. As noted above, given our choice of value for the smoothing parameter the filter is essentially a nine-part moving average in which the four years before and after an observation significantly influence the calculation of potential output for that year. We use only the filtered values for fiscal years 1971–97. By omitting the first and last four filtered observations, we ensure that each estimated trend value was calculated using at least four years of data on either side.

In an effort to evaluate the "reasonableness" of our Y* estimates we identified those years when Y=Y* and observed whether the rate of unemployment in these years seemed like a reasonable estimate of the full employment (or natural) rate of unemployment. For the national value of Y*, for example, our estimate suggests a natural unemployment rate of 5.7 percent in 1974, 8.8 percent in 1982, 9.4 percent in 1987, and 8.9 percent in 1991. The rise and fall in the value of the natural rate described by these values tells a story often told: changes in graduation rates, demographics and the generosity of employment insurance have caused swings in the rate of full employment. Certainly, they fall within the confidence interval of estimates commonly cited.

In the federal government's budget, we identified as sensitive to the output cycle employment insurance benefits on the spending side and, on the revenue side, personal and corporate income taxes, indirect taxes and employee contributions to the employment insurance fund. In each provincial government budget, we adjusted spending on social services on the expenditure side, while on the revenue side we adjusted personal and corporate income taxes as well as consumption taxes. We investigated the possibility that federal transfer payments might be sensitive to the cycle but found little evidence of this. Our result in this regard is similar to the findings of Smart (2001), who provides some evidence that over the 1983–98 period a fall in provincial revenues yielded a small response from equalization payments but a smaller and statistically insignificant response from total federal transfers.

To define structural values of cycle-sensitive budget components we followed the method employed by the OECD. Each cyclically sensitive component of the budget was adjusted proportionately to the ratio of potential output to observed output, as determined by its elasticity with respect to nominal GDP growth. Thus,

$$T^*_{i,t} = T_{i,t}(Y^*_t / Y_t)^{\alpha_i} \quad \alpha_i > 0$$

$$S^*_{j,t} = S_{j,t}(Y^*_t / Y_t)^{\beta_j} \quad \beta_j < 0$$

where $T_{i,t}$ = observed revenue from revenue type i in year t, $S_{j,t}$ = observed expenditure on program j in year t, starred variables are values that would be observed at potential output, and α_i, β_j are elasticities measuring the sensitivity to output of revenue category i and program expenditure j, respectively. Once values $T^*_{i,t}$ and $S^*_{j,t}$ are calculated the remaining (nonadjusted) catgories are added in order to derive structural total revenues and expenditures. We investigated whether elasticities might differ across provinces but, finding little variation, chose to use the same values for all governments. See Chung (2002) for a discussion. Some experimentation shows that our results are not terribly sensitive to the choice of elasticity values, something that Giorno, Richardson, Roseveare and van den Noord (1995) also note with respect to calculations of the structural deficit of OECD countries.

Our treatment of natural resource revenues deserves comment. Natural resource revenues are particularly large in Alberta but are also significant in Saskatchewan and to a lesser extent British Columbia. Natural resource revenues differ from other sorts of tax revenue in that they are driven by the world commodity price cycle, not provincial GDP. For this reason we follow the approach of the OECD, the IMF and the Department of Finance in not adjusting natural resource revenues for the output cycle. The implication is that our estimates of the structural balance, $PDEF^*/Y^*$, will reflect discretionary policy choices *and* the effect on the budget of changes in world commodity prices. An alternative approach would be to identify a maximum sustainable level of the natural resource tax base in these provinces. Deviations from this value could then be identified as being due to the world commodity price cycle and be included as part of a more broadly defined cyclical influence, one showing the effect of output cycles and world commodity price cycles. See Kneebone (2002) and Chung (2002) for applications of this approach.

Notes

Although we are pleased to thank Annette Ryan, Chris Ragan, Marc Van Audenrode and conference participants for helpful discussions and comments we alone remain responsible for errors, omissions and opinions expressed in the paper. Kneebone acknowledges the support of the Social Sciences and Humanities Research Council.

1. Kneebone and Leach (2001) separated the federal and provincial government sectors from the rest of the public sector but continued to aggregate the provinces. Because provinces, municipalities and the federal government all face very different constraints in their budgeting, because provinces and municipalities can have wildly different budgetary experiences, and because public pension plans are a different kettle of fish altogether, it makes sense to consider each component of the Canadian public sector on its own.

2. It is tempting to make the value judgement that at full employment, when tax revenues are as high and income-sensitive expenditures as low as a policy maker can reasonably expect them to be, the primary balance ought to be zero. That is not necessarily so, however. Intergenerational fairness might require, for example, that spending on capital projects be debt financed even at full employment. Similarly, if debt levels are high it might be appropriate to realize a primary surplus at full employment until they are reduced.

3. A result also found by Kneebone and McKenzie (1997). Our estimate that a one-percentage point increase in observed relative to potential output causes the aggregate federal-provincial primary balance to fall by 0.34 percentage points is slightly smaller than the estimate of 0.41 percentage points reported by the OECD as the sensitivity of the entire Canadian government sector budget deficit to the business cycle (see van den Noord 2000).

4. Most analysts would agree that at least a few percentage points of the increase in the unemployment rate during the 1970s was due to unemployment insurance liberalization in 1971. To the extent this was not known to policy makers at the time some of the budgetary response to high unemployment may have thus been misdirected toward fighting structural, as opposed to cyclical, unemployment.

5. Feldstein (2002) reports a similar change of heart in the United States at the time. Research conducted during the Carter administration (1977–81) concluded that the timing of previous discretionary fiscal policies had been destabilizing and that monetary policy was the superior tool for stabilization purposes, a judgement that eventually became the standard professional view.

Bibliography

Chung, J. 2002. "Debt Accumulation by Canadian Provincial Governments." MA Thesis, University of Calgary, unpublished.

Feldstein, M. 2002. *The Role for Discretionary Fiscal Policy in a Low Interest Rate Environment.* NBER Working Paper no. 9203. Cambridge, MA: National Bureau for Economic Research.

Fortin, P. 1998. "The Canadian Fiscal Problem: The Macroeconomic Connection." In *Hard Money, Hard Times,* ed. L. Osberg and P. Fortin. Toronto: James Lorimer & Company.

Giorno, C., P. Richardson, D. Roseveare and P. van den Noord. 1995. *Potential Output, Output Gaps and Structural Balances.* OECD Economic Studies no. 24. Paris: OECD.

Kneebone, R. 1998. "Four Decades of Deficits and Debt." In *Hard Money, Hard Times,* ed. L. Osberg and P. Fortin. Toronto: James Lorimer & Company.

————. 2002. "Recent and Not So Recent Trends in Provincial Government Spending in Alberta." In *Alberta's Volatile Government Revenues: Policies for the Long Run,* ed. L.S. Wilson. Edmonton: Institute for Public Economics, University of Alberta.

Kneebone, R., and J. Leach. 2001. "The Accumulation of Public Debt in Canada." *Canadian Public Policy/Analyse de Politiques* 27, no. 3:297-312.

Kneebone, R., and K. McKenzie. 1997. "Stabilizing Features of Fiscal Policy in Canada." In *Fiscal Targets and Economic Growth,* ed. T.J. Courchene and J. Wilson. Kingston: John Deutsch Institute for the Study of Economic Policy, Queen's University.

Maslove, A., M. Prince and G. B. Doern. 1985. *Federal and Provincial Budgeting,* Volume 41 of the *Report of the Royal Commission on the Economic Union and Development Prospects for Canada.* Toronto: University of Toronto Press.

Perry, J. 1989. *A Fiscal History of Canada.* Canadian Tax Paper no. 85. Toronto: Canadian Tax Foundation.

Robson, W. 1996. *Putting Some Gold in the Golden Years: Fixing the Canada Pension Plan.* Commentary no. 76. Toronto: C.D. Howe Institute.

Smart, M. 2001. "Redistribution, Risk, and Incentives in Equalization: A Comparison of RTS and Macro Approaches." Working Paper Series. Kingston: Institute for Intergovernmental Relations, Queen's University.

van den Noord, P. 2000. "The Size and Role of Automatic Fiscal Stabilizers in the 1990s and Beyond." OECD Economics Department Working Paper no. 230. Paris: OECD.

where did the debt come from?

Marc Van Audenrode

The Paper

The paper by Ron Kneebone and Jennifer Chung is an impressive attempt at analyzing the sources of the Canadian public debt. They have succeeded, brilliantly, in my view, in developing and presenting a methodology that explains how Canadians managed to accumulate hundreds of billions in public debt in a little more than 25 years, and they do it without casting any blame.

Yet explaining without blaming proves difficult in this case. Debts do not grow on trees. Policies, and policies alone, ultimately cause public debts. It would be very informative if Kneebone and Chung's analysis allowed us to see more clearly what role these policies played. But such an exercise can hardly be performed without also providing the reader with a road map for casting blame; that's the price to pay for understanding how, one day, Canadians woke up and found themselves buried in debt. Unfortunately, the mathematical decomposition of the debt-to-gross domestic product (GDP) ratio that constitutes the cornerstone of Kneebone and Chung's analysis cannot easily be interpreted as illustrating the different policy failures to which our indebtedness can be traced.

Countries fall into financial trouble and accumulate unmanageable debts for three reasons.

Misconstrued policies. After the fact, many policies prove themselves to have been misconstrued. This is true in the case of the Canadian debt. A sharp ideological division exists, however, between those who are more prone to blame the incompetents of the early 1970s, who did not know anything about fiscal policies, and the incompetents of the early 1990s, who did not know anything about monetary policy. *Ex post* second-guessing of policies, however, is an easy game, and most economists would agree that there actually was gross overspending during the 1970s and 1980s and that the monetary policy of the early 1990s was way too tight. The fact that these policies proved to be wrong *ex post* does not prove however, that they were wrong *ex ante*. Given both the information available and the state of economic thinking at the time, they might actually have been the best possible choices.

Poor economic performance. Public finances rarely survive poor economic performance. Even when policies are well thought-out and adequately applied, deficits and debts can follow. Maybe in the last three decades of the twentieth century Canada just ran into a patch of bad economic luck.

The "Banana-Republic Syndrome." Obviously, Canada has not suffered at the hands of a "Banana Republic"-type dictator. Yet some of the overspending that has taken place in our recent history could be construed as a systematic looting of our public finances at the hand of a set of interest groups, or in fact at the hand of an entire generation, and systematic looting is one of the distinguishing characteristics of Banana Republics.

Kneebone and Chung's economic decomposition can be used to trace out a political or "policy-oriented" decomposition of the sources of the debt-to-GDP ratio. Poor fiscal policies (looting?) can be identified as the source of the structural deficit component they identify. Faulty monetary policy can be blamed as the source of the rate components. And the cyclical component can clearly be related to economic performance.

Such a tracing from the economic decomposition into the policy decomposition is what I believe we should ultimately care about. Unfortunately, although Kneebone and Chung's decomposition is an interesting and original way to look at the sources of our indebtedness, it suffers from two important drawbacks as a way of effecting the desired tracing.

First, the analysis depends heavily on the definition of the structural deficit. More precisely, how the deficit is split between its structural and cyclical component depends on how potential output is estimated.[1] As we now know, during the 1970s a sharp decline in potential growth occurred. This decline remained unrecognized for a long time. Because of that, the share of the accumulated debt attributed to the structural deficit might have been overestimated. If policy makers, like economists, failed to recognize this sharp decline in potential growth, they might well have thought that their fiscal policies were structurally balanced, while reality showed, *ex post*, at least, that they were not. It is hard to know how much to blame a policy generation for an error of this sort.

Second, many "endogeneity issues" are left unexplored by the Kneebone and Chung decomposition. Many of the key economic variables they are interested in are determined jointly, at the same time, or endogeneously, to use the technical term. Without taking account of these interconnections among variables, preferably in an explicit macroeconomic model, it is not easy to figure out what is causing what. Fiscal policy directly affects the structural component of the debt, of course. But fiscal policy also affects economic performance, and consequently the cyclical component, as well. Similarly, monetary policy directly affects the rate component, but through its impact on economic performance, it also affects the cyclical component.

In short, the mapping between the decomposition proposed here and policies is probably not as simple or clear-cut as it might seem at first sight. What Canada would have looked like *but for* these policies is hard to know. Yes, the very lax fiscal policies of the early 1970s helped crate a large structural deficit. But they also clearly helped sustain economic activity, which most likely made the cyclical component of the deficit much more favourable. These large structural deficits also helped sustain a high level of inflation, which contributed, at least in the short run, to lower real interest rates and a more favourable rate component.

Results

As in any bad movie, everybody knows how the story of Canadian indebtedness ended (at least for now), but many fewer people know how it started. The early 1990s explosion of our debt that gained Canada the reputation of being the Italy of America and was then followed by a dramatic and surprising flow of surpluses is still vivid in every memory. Yet the fact that this (we hope happy) ending had been set up long before is probably largely unknown. The decomposition of the evolution of our debt proposed by Kneebone and Chung gives us an insight into that aspect of our recent economic history.

Throughout the 1970s, a large structural deficit prevailed. However, because of the huge rate surplus that prevailed at the same time, no sizable debt was accumulated. The large rate surplus was caused both by low real interest rates and high growth rates. These twin disequilibria offset each other for most of the decade.

Things changed during the 1980s. Although the structural deficit shrank sizably, high interest rates reversed the impact of the rate component, which no longer provided a surplus but instead began contributing to debt accumulation. In other words, debt started to grow and to become noticeable at the very time when the federal government was taking the first steps to put its house in order.

During the 1990s, the Canadian debt exploded. Structural deficits were transformed into huge structural surpluses. But in the meantime, the Bank of

Canada engineered a large rate component deficit that eradicated the positive impacts of these changes in fiscal policy. Ironically, during the 1990s, the huge surplus in the structural component allowed the huge deficit in the rate component to survive unnoticed, exactly as the large rate surplus had allowed successive governments to run a huge structural deficit during the 1970s. Governments would clearly have been forced to revert to more reasonable fiscal policies much earlier, if the rate surplus had not existed in the 1970s. Similarly, the Bank of Canada would have been forced to revert to a more reasonable monetary policy much earlier if the large structural surplus had not existed in the 1990s.

Conclusion

As noted, the roots of any public indebtedness have to be found in policies. Kneebone and Chung offer us an interesting *ex post* decomposition of the sources of the mountain of debt Canadians accumulated during the last quarter of the twentieth century. The results of that decomposition provide us with a clear typology of the three decades over which the Canadian debt was accumulated.

Yet the link between this decomposition and policies is not straightforward. Although the analysis presented here is helpful in understanding the mechanics of Canadian debt accumulation, more work is needed if we are to understand the links between these mechanics and policies. Among the questions that remain to be answered are: Was the fiscal policy of the 1970s really misconstrued? To what extent, if any, did the huge structural deficit that prevailed during that decade also contribute to economic growth and therefore reduce the cyclical component of the debt? Was the monetary policy of the 1980s and 1990s misconstrued? Finally, was the combination of high structural deficit and large rate surplus that characterized the 1970s truly unsustainable in the long run? Most western countries did experience a large structural deficit similar to those that existed in Canada. Our experience of the early 1990s is, however, almost unique. The United States solved its fiscal problems through growth; most European countries solved them through slow and progressive readjustments in spending. Is it impossible to assume that Canada's fiscal problems are only due to our monetary policies of the early 1990s?

The Kneebone and Chung paper has two great merits: first, as good papers do, it raises more questions than it answers, which in itself is evidence that the right methodology was used. Second, it maps the direction in which future research in this area has to go.

Note

1. In their paper, Kneebone and Chung use the Hodrick and Prescott (HP) filter to estimate potential output. This technique has drawn some criticisms recently. (See Guay and St Amand 1996, for example). The HP filter has been found to imperfectly extract the cyclical component of macroeconomic series in some circumstances. It is therefore possible that the structural deficit estimated by the authors is too high.

Bibliography

Guay, A., and P. St-Amant. 1996. *Do Mechanical Filters Provide a Good Approximation of Business Cycles?* Technical Report no. 78. Ottawa: Bank of Canada.

3

what do we get for public indebtedness?

Robin Boadway

Introduction

The title of this paper has been surreptitiously, and perhaps provocatively, changed. The assigned title was: "What do we get for public debt?" On reflection, posing the question that way is potentially misleading, for two main reasons. First, the question suggests the wrong answer. It suggests that there is some "thing," like an asset, on the other side of the balance sheet that justifies the issuance of debt in the first place. This is based on what I shall argue is a false analogy with the role of debt in the private sector. Second, it suggests that debt transactions might some-how differ fundamentally from other government transactions, and that therefore they can be considered in isolation. This, I shall argue, ignores the fact that the basic economic features of debt, or of the government budget deficit, for that matter, can be mimicked by other policy instruments, and it would be mislead-ing not to take account of that in any evaluation of public debt.

The point of departure of this paper is that neither of those two potential implications is correct as regards either the effect that debt has on the economy or the part it plays in the overall policy stance of government. My substitution of the term "indebtedness" for debt, both in the title and throughout the paper, is intended to reduce the temptation to pursue those two lines of reasoning. Much of this paper is devoted to justifying this line of argument, and to drawing out its implications for what we should perceive to be the role of government debt and indebtedness.

The paper proceeds as follows. I begin in the next section with a consideration of the notion of public indebtedness, of which public debt is one component. I argue that the essential features of public debt are shared by other policies that involve intergenerational transfers, and that any discussion of the effects of public debt on the economy cannot ignore this equivalence. This is followed by a section in which public debt and assets are contrasted with their counterparts in the private sector. The one-to-one relationship that exists between assets and debt in the private sector simply does not carry over to the public sector, and this affects the way we might account for public indebtedness. The next section then discusses the principles that might be used to inform an evaluation of the level of public indebtedness. This requires taking a position on intergenerational welfare comparisons. I then consider suitable means of public indebtedness accounting. The new tool of generational accounting provides a device that potentially captures many of the features of public indebtedness that are relevant for evaluation purposes. Finally, I conclude with some tentative and speculative comments that explore the questions of whether the rapid buildup of the public debt in the latter part of the twentieth century could be justified, and whether the emphasis on reducing the relative size of the debt even more rapidly than it had been accumulated was reasonable.

Public Debt and Public Indebtedness

It is useful to begin with a discussion about the nature of public debt and its relationship to public indebtedness – a term whose meaning will become clearer as we proceed.

Suppose the government finances some of its expenditures by debt. The repayment of that debt ultimately comes from future taxes, and, unlike in the private sector, these are not necessarily related to the income generated by assets purchased with the debt. It is certainly possible that current government expenditures give rise to increased future tax collections, but this will be so no matter how the government spending is financed. A government's choice of debt financing therefore amounts to its deciding to finance its given expenditure obligations by future taxation rather than by current taxation. In that sense, we can think of debt as postponed taxation.

Now, if the debt is very short-term and is repaid when it matures, future taxpayers will be virtually the same as current taxpayers. In this case, the purpose of the debt might be mainly to smooth out the tax payments of existing taxpayers or to respond to the unpredictability of tax revenues. Presumably this is a less costly way of meeting purely temporary needs for cash than changing tax rates frequently, and is therefore simply prudent financial management. There is likely to be little concern about this very short-term use of debt finance, nor any call for public assets to set against the debt temporarily created. The existence of short-term debt used for financial management purposes is therefore not an issue with which we should be concerned.

The same might be said of debt used to smooth out the difference between tax liabilities and expenditure obligations over the business cycle, or even to pursue counter-cyclical fiscal policies, if policy makers feel justified in using them. In either case, this is a temporary function for debt financing, but one that in principle should be self-extinguishing over the cycle. Again, the length of the business cycle is typically such that there is relatively little change in the population of taxpayers over the period in which debt is accumulated and decumulated. What is involved is mainly a spreading out of the tax liabilities of given taxpayers relative to that which would occur if balanced budgets were fully adhered to. There is no question of the changes in debt being offset by asset holdings as debt rises and falls over the cycle. The issues that are presumably the source of contention with public debt are not relevant here.

Where they are relevant is with accumulations of debt over the medium and longer term, accumulations that span decades rather than months or business cycles, and these will be our main concern here. Such accumulations also represent postponed tax liabilities, but given the length of time for which repayment may be postponed, the taxpaying populations may well be substantially different: a significant proportion of the debt represents taxes that have been postponed from current cohorts or generations of taxpayers to future ones.[1] To some extent, therefore, the debt represents an involuntary intergenerational transfer. The longer the debt is held, the greater the amount of it that represents an intergenerational transfer. Now, assets may also be accumulated and transferred to future generations so that on balance the transfer is a wash. But it is useful for our initial purposes to separate the effects of intergenerational transfers on the financing side from those on the spending side.

Once we recognize the fact that the creation (and refinancing) of longer-term government debt is essentially an intergenerational transfer, the distinction between debt and other forms of government transactions becomes blurred. As pointed out by Kotlikoff (1984), there are other ways of effecting intergenerational transfers that have the same economic effect as government debt, but which do not appear as such according to standard public budgeting and accounting procedures. To see this, consider two important examples: unfunded public pensions and tax reforms.

Unfunded Public Pensions

An unfunded public pension is an ongoing transfer to the elderly financed by current taxes. Take the case where the current taxes are payroll taxes. Then, as long as it is in place, the unfunded pension is an intergenerational transfer from each current working generation to the corresponding retired generation. In other words, it is an intergenerational transfer from the young to the old. When such a system is introduced, those retired or partway through their working lives will obtain a windfall gain. Should the pension be extinguished at some future date, the elderly who had contributed during their working lives will be made worse off. In the intervening period, it can be shown that households are better off or worse off according to whether the rate of growth of the economy's wage bill exceeds the rate of return on investment. The former determines the implicit rate of return on the payroll tax and pension receipt over the household's life cycle, while the latter is the rate of return that could have been obtained if the household had been able to save their payroll contributions. The presumption is that the rate of return on saving exceeds the growth of the wage bill, implying that households are worse off than they would be if they had instead invested their payroll tax liabilities in the capital market. In effect, when a payroll tax is used to finance public pensions, taxpayers' savings fall since they no longer have to provide as much for themselves in retirement. The implicit rate of return that they obtain from their participation in the public pension scheme is less than the rate of return that their savings would have yielded in capital markets, and the economy is left with less capital stock.[2]

But this is the same pattern of intergenerational effects that occurs when new debt is issued as a result of running a budget deficit. In the year of issue, the existing taxpaying population obtains a windfall gain equal to the reduction in other tax liabilities. Subsequent generations each lose an amount equal to the cost of financing the interest on the debt as long as the debt remains outstanding. At the time the debt is extinguished, the working generations would see their tax liabilities rise. Thus, the debt financing effectively causes an intergenerational transfer of the same sort as the unfunded pension scheme.

The relevant point is that with respect to their effect on the sequence of cohorts, and presumably on the economy as well, the institution and maintenance of an unfunded public pension is equivalent to the issuance and holding of additional public debt. When the government borrows instead of taxing, it reduces tax liabilities for current taxpayers and increases them on taxpayers in the future. The problem is that conventional public sector budgeting treats these two conceptually similar actions quite differently: debt financing is reflected in a government budget deficit, while an increase in an unfunded public pension is not.

Of course, the implicit unfunded liability from Canadian public pensions can be, and has been, calculated. Indeed, the Canada Pension Plan's unfunded liability has been similar in size to the federal debt in recent years. And yet conventional public sector accounting has focused the most attention on the federal debt. This has been true even though, to the extent that the public pension system is unfunded, there are no assets associated with it, while the public debt may well have been issued to finance some assets. Leaving aside the discussion of assets, however, it is clear that we can conceptually separate out the financing role of public debt and the government expenditure that it may finance. If we hold the time stream of government expenditure fixed, changes in debt financing and the introduction of an unfunded public pension plan have essentially analogous effects on the real economy despite the fact that a financial asset is created in one case but not the other.

Tax Reform

The same applies for tax reforms that change the timing of tax liabilities over the life cycles of taxpayers. Consider a tax reform that substitutes a wage tax for a general sales tax on consumption and is revenue-neutral in the aggregate in each period. Such a reform leaves the government budget unchanged, yet has qualitatively the same effect as an increase in government debt from running a deficit. To see this, note that a consumption tax, such as the goods and services tax (GST), is spread over one's entire life cycle, while a wage tax is concentrated in the working years. If the consumption tax is reduced, tax liabilities in retirement as well as in working years are reduced, while if the wage tax is increased so that the same per-period revenue is raised, taxes in the working years are increased. Since the same revenues must be raised in each period, the net effect is that all taxpayers end up paying less tax in retirement and more in their working years. The result is an ongoing intergenerational transfer from the young to the old, just as with the unfunded pension. It too will have the same effect on the real economy as an increase in debt.

In fact, almost all tax reforms will have some intergenerational transfer component to them. A substitution of a wage tax for an income tax (i.e., a reduction in capital income taxation) will also entail an intergenerational transfer from the young to the old, simply because income tax liabilities tend to fall later in the life cycle than wage taxes. The sheltering of retirement savings by registered pension plans (RPPs) and registered retirement savings plans (RRSPs) financed from general revenues also transfers resources from the young to the old.

The point is that the essential feature of long-term debt financing is that it is essentially an intergenerational transfer. As such, it is not unique. Other changes in the structure of the government budget have similar effects. The implication is that actual measures of public debt lose their precision from the point of view of their economic effect. Or, to put it equivalently, public debt is but one component of the more general concept of public indebtedness, which incorporates the intergenerational impact of the government's long-term budgetary stance. That is why I prefer to use the term "public indebtedness" rather than "public debt," where public indebtedness refers to the obligations imposed on future generations by the various components of the government's long-term fiscal stance. A given amount of indebtedness can be associated with varying amounts of public debt. In a later section, I return to the issue of what this implies for how public sector indebtedness might meaningfully be measured.

While it is not the primary purpose of this paper, it might be worth briefly touching on the main effects that the various kinds of public indebtedness have on the economy. The fact that public indebtedness is essentially a reflection of intergenerational transfers implies that the main potential effect is a redistributive one. The primary effect of intergenerational transfers from the young to the old is to transfer income from future generations to current ones. The term "potential" is operative because, as is well known, in principle these publicly imposed transfers can be offset by equal and opposite private ones (i.e., bequests), an idea that economists refer to as the *Ricardo equivalence* proposition (Barro 1974). Ultimately, whether this equivalence result holds is an empirical question. But it is a difficult empirical question because any empirical evidence must take account of the fact that it is not just debt that is involved, but also other forms of intergenerational transfers such as those we have discussed. Moreover, the Ricardo equivalence proposition must overcome some formidable logical objections, especially the one raised by Bernheim and Bagwell (1988). As they have shown, if one takes the behavioural assumptions of Ricardo equivalence – altruism toward one's immediate heirs – and simply adds one realistic biological/sociological feature of society – that marriage and procreation are with a member of another family – the dynastic family underlying the proposition breaks down. As generations go by, each child born descends from an increasing number of current households. The benefits of one's bequests are then indirectly shared by many current households, and the incentive for intergenerational altruism to offset intergenerational transfers, as required by Ricardo equivalence, is strongly diluted. Voluntary intergenerational transfers disappear. Thus, even the theoretical case for Ricardo equivalence is not made.

In the absence of full Ricardo equivalence, policy-induced intergenerational transfers, apart from the purely redistributive effect that they have, will affect the amount of savings available for financing private investment. In effect, public indebtedness provides an implicit asset in the form of a future benefit that substitutes for private saving that would otherwise go to private asset accumulation (domestic investment or foreign assets). Contrary to what is sometimes thought, this reduction in investment is not in itself efficiency-reducing. Put differently, there is almost certainly no economic efficiency gain associated with increased saving and investment. The reason is that, although increases in capital accumulation can make persons better off in the future, to engineer the increased aggregate saving, older cohorts must be made worse off. This is an important point to make, and one that will come up again when we consider the role of public indebtedness below.

At the same time, public indebtedness is likely to have several secondary economic effects. Two potentially important ones are as follows. First, variations in public indebtedness may over the longer run be used to smooth tax rates, an effect emphasized by Barro (1974). Given that the efficiency costs of taxation increase more than proportionately with tax rates, this is said to reduce the total efficiency costs of taxation (although whether one can unambiguously say this in a world where intergenerational transfers are required to do the smoothing is a question to which we return). Second, and perhaps most important, to the extent that there are externalities associated with investment, such as the fact that innovations are embodied in new investments, or that human capital improvements can be obtained by experience working with new techniques, anything leading to a reduction in investment will reduce the benefits of those externalities.

Having presented the case that various forms of public indebtedness are interchangeable from the point of view of their real economic impact, I want to stress that some caveats are in order. For one thing, while all forms of indebtedness impose obligations on future taxpayers, the nature of and expectations concerning those obligations vary considerably. Public debt is an explicit contractual obligation that can be taken to be binding. Unfunded public pensions might be considered as an implicit obligation that gives rise to an entitlement that future generations might reasonably expect to receive. Tax reforms that transfer purchasing power from future to present generations might be considered a much weaker obligation, and might not even be regarded as an obligation by households in the economy (for example, because they do not understand the economics underlying it). These differences in perception might cause persons to react differently to the various forms of obligation, and so, of course, the real effects of these different forms of indebtedness would differ.

At the same time, it is not clear that in reality any one form of obligation is more binding than another, despite the differences in how explicit the obligation is. Governments can, and do, change their net liabilities to future generations at will, regardless of the form of the liability. Debt of any term can be paid off early, or it can be refinanced and extended. It can sometimes even be defaulted on. Tax reforms can change the implicit net liabilities imposed on future generations for financing a given path of expenditures. The path of expenditures itself can change, as well, quite apart from the method of financing. In other words, the government can, and does frequently, vary the overall pattern of intergenerational transfers simply by changing its policies. That poses a conceptually difficult social accounting problem, as we shall see later on.

These problems are made more complicated by the fact that different forms of intergenerational transfer can give rise to very different patterns of intragenerational transfers. Indeed, the choice of one form of public indebtedness over another normally will be affected by considerations of intragenerational redistribution, as will the overall mix of public indebtedness. For example, unfunded public pensions typically affect lower- relative to higher-income persons. Health care and other public services financed by current taxes both transfer resources between generations and confer higher benefits on less well-off persons. That is why they are provided through the public sector in the first place.

The distinctiveness of public debt may also be affected by political economy considerations. It might be possible to devise arguments based on public-choice considerations to explain why governments representing current voters might choose to burden future generations with obligations over which they have no say. And these arguments might well explain why the different forms of indebtedness might be chosen and in what relative amounts. More important, some might argue that the ability to use public debt itself leads to higher spending than would otherwise be the case. If so, reducing the debt would involve more than intergenerational transfers: it would involve reductions in the size of the public sector. However, verifying these public-choice arguments is conceptually difficult, and relatively little progress has been made in doing so. More success has been had in outlining the various normative arguments for intergenerational transfers, and using those as a basis for judging the fairness or otherwise of actual patterns of intergenerational transfers engaged in by the government. In a later section, I return to this issue of what are the potential roles of intergenerational transfers. These are necessarily normative in nature, and although economists have no monopoly on moral authority, some such basis for evaluation seems to be needed since the intertemporal policy stance of the government necessarily embodies some amount of public indebtedness.

Public Assets Versus Private Assets

In approaching the question of what we get for public indebtedness, it is natural to be influenced by the private sector analogy. There, owners of firms get income-earning assets for their indebtedness, and this is reflected on the balance sheet of the firm. Why not insist on a public sector balance sheet that sets public assets against public debt? In this section, I argue that the analogy is a false one. There are a number of reasons why the case for a public sector balance sheet cannot be based on the analogy with balance sheets routinely used in the private sector.

In the case of firms, assets are owned by a well-defined set of creditors: shareholders and bondholders. The value of the assets of the firm is in principle based on their future income-earning capacity, that is, the flow of interest and dividends that this income is expected to generate. This in turn determines the wealth of the firm and its division between shareholders and bondholders. The capital market establishes a share price that determines the value of the firm to shareholders, and that price presumably reflects the present value of future dividends suitably corrected for risk. There are certainly well-known problems associated with arriving at the correct values for the capital stock of firms, some of which have been prominent in recent accounting debacles, but the balance sheet remains a useful informational device for existing and potential creditors. There is in principle no ambiguity about the measuring device for evaluating private sector assets: it is simply their dollar value, unadjusted according to who happens to be the owner or by any considerations other than private profitability. A dollar is a dollar is a dollar, to use a maxim from cost-benefit analysis. And, of course, one can choose to become a creditor or to cease to be a creditor at will.

Public assets are fundamentally different from private assets in many respects, most of which have been hinted at already. For one thing, there is no analogue of the shareholder or of stock market valuation. Every member of society "owns" the public assets, and that ownership is passed on from one generation to the next as the membership of society changes. Indebtedness of private sector firms reflects an obligation of the current owners to repay the debt. Indebtedness in the public sector is involuntarily assumed by all members of society and can be passed on to future generations.

Second, most public sector assets do not generate income, so their values cannot be established in the same way that private sector assets are valued. Most public sector assets generate in-kind value. Thus, tanks and airplanes are inputs into the provision of defence services, which themselves are notoriously difficult to value. Schools are capital inputs into providing education services, hospitals into health services, and so on. We could potentially tote up the stream of future services attributable to each of these types of capital inputs, but valuing them is difficult. Since many of the services provided by government are redistributive in nature (e.g., health, education, social services), valuing them would involve using distributive weights according to how the benefits accrue to different classes of recipients. Unless we can put a dollar value on the services generated by these capital inputs, valuing them in a meaningful way is not possible. Of course, they could be valued by their resale value, which should reflect their value in alternative uses. But, apart from ignoring the distributive weight dimension, this alternative value is likely to be an underestimate of their value in their current uses. Hospitals, for example, cannot immediately be used for other purposes without incurring adjustment costs.

Third, and closely related to the previous point, some non-physical assets that are created by public spending are difficult to evaluate. The output of social spending of various sorts – on education and health, for instance – can be considered as adding to the human capital stock. If these could be valued, one would have a more general measure of the assets involved in these sectors. Past social spending leaves a stock of previously accumulated human capital, while the physical assets remaining in the sectors would be evaluated according to the future human capital they will create. Public spending on R&D and education should also increase the stock of knowledge in society, and this could in principle be evaluated. And, public spending could affect the stock of environmental capital. One might reasonably suppose that these accumulated intangible assets give rise to a stream of future benefits that could be set against any debt that was accumulated to finance them. But the task of first enumerating and then evaluating these benefits would be a mammoth one.

Next, even those assets that are physical and that could reasonably have a dollar value placed on them are difficult to evaluate from a social perspective. It is a precept of cost-benefit analysis that social values are different from private values, and this applies particularly to the types of physical assets acquired by the public sector. A good example concerns public transportation facilities. Conventional cost-benefit analyses of major transportation facilities, such as airports, bridges, roads and rail systems, typically find that the most important benefits are those that are not mainly reflected in revenues. Examples include time saved travelling by different types of travellers and reduced congestion on substitute modes of transport. Moreover, if their use affects resource allocation in distorted markets, the social cost of project inputs may differ significantly from their private costs. The evaluation of these assets would have to reflect these social benefits and costs rather than private benefits and costs. Again, this would not be a trivial exercise.

Finally, perhaps the main distinction between private and public approaches to balance sheet accounting concerns the very relationship between assets and liabilities. In the private sector, there is a natural connection between the two. Creditors who put money into a firm expect that money to be used to generate a future stream of revenue that is the source of the rates of return expected on the money. There is simply no need for that to be the case in the public sector where money is ultimately obtained coercively. Any requirement for a public sector balance sheet must be based on some other argument than the idea that taxpayers expect a rate of return to themselves on their tax payments. The next section considers this point in slightly more detail, but to anticipate that discussion, why should we not have a government balance sheet with public sector assets set against public sector indebtedness? If governments were somehow obliged to follow benefit taxation principles, that is, to tax citizens in proportion to the benefits they receive from public spending, then the balance-sheet approach might make sense. Assets that are accumulated now and provide lasting benefits to future taxpayers ought to be paid for by those who reap the benefits. In such a regime, there would be obvious measurement problems. On the asset side, account would have to be taken of the diverse number and types of assets that the public sector had a hand in creating. These would include not just physical assets like public sector capital and infrastructure. They would also include human capital accumulated through education, health care and various other public services, whether the human capital reflected higher earnings capacity or a greater ability to generate individual well-being through enhanced capabilities to participate fully in society, as stressed by Sen (1985). And, any benefits accruing to new knowledge created by the use of public funds could legitimately be charged to future beneficiaries. On the debit side, all of the forms of public sector indebtedness discussed earlier would have to be included since all reflect ways of postponing net tax liabilities to future generations.

Such social accounting would obviously be very difficult, but in principle it could be done, albeit imperfectly. But, unlike in the private sector, there is no compelling argument for applying the benefit principle across generations, just as there is none for applying it within generations. The benefit principle is but one of many potential principles that could be used for evaluating how resources should be distributed across generations. (There are further difficulties with it to which we turn in the next section.) That is not to say that some form of public sector capital budgeting cannot be an important management tool in the public sector. On the contrary, it can be indispensable for planning purposes and for projecting necessary operating and maintenance costs into the future. But computing a public sector balance sheet that is analogous to those used in the private sector would at best be misleading.

The Evaluation of Public Indebtedness

The fundamental feature of public indebtedness is its effect on the intergenerational distribution of welfare. Governments whose constituents are members of existing generations have the power to pass on the costs of present spending to future generations in the form of future net tax liabilities. In this section we discuss the principles that an economist might use for evaluating the public indebtedness that governments have chosen, leaving until the next section the question of how that public indebtedness might be measured. Because what is at stake is largely redistributive in nature, such evaluation obviously must be value-laden. The values implicit in one's views about the intergenerational policy stance that the government adopts cannot be definitive. Indeed, a similar problem applies with respect to the government's intragenerational policy stance. What we can do, however, is propose a set of principles that could potentially be used as the basis for evaluating the state of public indebtedness. Four different perspectives on the role of public indebtedness are presented, some of which are related and some of which contradict each other.

The Intergenerational Benefit Principle

The benefit principle, to which we have already alluded, would require that the costs of government programs be borne by the cohorts for whom benefits are created. Since some current government programs provide benefits for future generations, offsetting these by public indebtedness would be appropriate. As we have mentioned, there would be a myriad of such programs. Any public sector investment that creates lasting benefits provides some benefits to future generations. Such investments include: infrastructure investment; investment in human capital, which provides future benefits not only to the subset of current younger cohorts who receive it, but might also be passed on to their heirs in ways now emphasized by the economic growth literature; investments in human health and capabilities; and investment in knowledge creation.

While properly accounting for these benefits on a cohort-by-cohort basis would be a daunting task, other conceptual problems also need to be addressed if one is to take the benefit principle as one's criterion for the evaluation of public indebtedness. For one thing, while the principle's appeal might seem to be that it is value-free, or efficiency-based, in the sense that it incorporates no redistribution, that is a rather narrow interpretation of the principle's normative content. The benefit principle implicitly takes as given the existing set of property rights and treats them as preferable to other allocations with different property rights. While that may be a defensible position to take, few if any societies seem to have made the inviolability of property rights the cornerstone of their policies for intragenerational equity. Most violate property rights with at least some degree of regularity, and there is no particular reason why inviolability would have more appeal in the intergenerational context. Moreover, there is a further conceptual problem that the benefit principle does not resolve. Public programs presumably generate economic surpluses – that is, their total benefits exceed their total costs – and these may be of a significant size. This means that there is no natural way to apply the benefit principle to allocate costs among households without making some interpersonal judgement about how to allocate the surplus.

There is, however, an even more serious problem with applying the benefit principle to public sector capital operations. Some public assets, call them *natural assets*, are given to societies by nature. These include natural resources, both renewable and nonrenewable, as well as the natural environment. Government policies affect the stock of these natural assets, and therefore the amount that is passed on to future generations. Since these natural assets are "owned" by the society at large, property rights over them are not otherwise well defined. The intergenerational benefit principle cannot be applied without specifically assigning property rights to natural assets to different generations to determine which generations are entitled to which shares of the fruits of these natural assets. Such a problem does not arise with respect to private assets, including those that are obtained from nature, since their ownership is well defined. Moreover, it does not apply to government programs that are financed by taxes.

The fact that there is no natural way to assign property rights for natural assets across generations implies that the benefit principle in its usual form is in effect nonoperative. To apply it would involve implicitly assigning such property rights, and one cannot do that without invoking some intergenerational equity judgement. Since net public indebtedness in the comprehensive sense must take account of the amount of public assets passed on to future generations, some judgement must be made about intergenerational equity, if only implicitly.

Intergenerational Risk-Sharing/Social Insurance

A second principle that might be used to judge public indebtedness, or to justify its existence, arises from the fact that different generations are subject to various types of exogenous circumstances that affect their well-being. That is, generations can be born lucky or unlucky because of the circumstances that apply at their date of birth or over their lifetimes, and over which they have no control. These circumstances may be demographic: generations that are relatively large face a disadvantage relative to those that are relatively small. They enter a larger labour force, which tends to depress their wages, and their relatively large savings for retirement tend to depress the rate of return. The fact that they are large may also mean that they must share natural capital with more persons. And, preceding generations may not be willing to put as much resources into their education on a per capita basis when they are young, while succeeding generations may not be willing to put as much into their health care per capita when they are old. Although these demographic trends may be perfectly predictable, generations cannot avoid the consequences of bad demographic luck: people can neither choose their date of birth nor insure against an adverse date of birth.

The same applies for shocks that a given demographic cohort might face. If one is young during a major war, various sacrifices must be made. These include the requirement to fight the war, the resource costs of fighting the war (which may mainly benefit future generations), and the interruption of employment with the income and experience that it would have generated. As well as war, there may be natural catastrophes, such as earthquakes, floods, disease and droughts. And, there may be major economic shocks such as major depressions, structural adjustments to changing institutional settings (free trade), and productivity slowdowns.

In these circumstances, intergenerational transfers can provide a form of social insurance, effectively insuring cohorts who face adverse circumstances but are uninsurable using private insurance markets. Normative analysts sometimes pose this as an efficiency-type argument. If persons had the opportunity to purchase insurance before knowing if they are in a lucky or unlucky cohort, behind the "veil of ignorance" they would choose to do so.[3] All cohorts would be better off in the *ex ante* sense: their expected lifetime utility would increase. In reality, however, the redistribution is done *ex post*, after the lucky or unlucky cohorts have been born, so social insurance arguments of this sort are essentially intergenerational equity arguments.

The social insurance argument clearly has some validity in the real world. Governments do finance major wars and other shocks by increasing public indebtedness. Cohorts that are obviously unlucky are the recipients of major intergenerational transfers. Thus, major programs of public pensions have been introduced to provide retirement benefits for persons who, because of war and major economic depression, have been unable to accumulate sufficient savings to provide for themselves in retirement. It is important to note that public indebtedness incurred for social insurance reasons is by its nature temporary. Over the cycle of lucky and unlucky generations, the public budget should balance. There should be no permanent net public indebtedness on this account.

Tax Smoothing

A related argument, mentioned above, is that public indebtedness can be used to smooth tax rates over time. Since the economic efficiency cost of tax distortions rises more than proportionately with tax rates, a given amount of revenues obtained over time from tax rates that fluctuate will have a larger efficiency cost than if the tax rates were smooth. (The reason is that the increase in cost when tax rates are above average exceeds the fall in cost when they are below average.) This is related to the social insurance argument in the sense that the sources of fluctuating tax rates can be similar to those that lead to cohorts having better or worse fortunes. But the argument is posed purely in efficiency terms.

The problem is that in an intergenerational context, one cannot separate efficiency and equity arguments. Smoothing tax rates over time to reduce their overall distortion involves raising taxes for some cohorts and reducing them for others,[4] which therefore gives rise to a form of the usual equity-efficiency trade-off.[5] In this case, the equity side of the argument must rely on some intergenerational welfare comparison.

Intergenerational Equity

The previous discussion suggests that any evaluation of public indebtedness, whether to address temporary fluctuations in generational welfare or in tax rates, must involve an intergenerational comparison of welfare. This is even more apparent when there are systematic and persistent differences in well-being among different cohorts (and not just fluctuations in their fortunes). There are certain irreversible phenomena that might lead to ongoing increases in generational welfare as time passes, such as technical change, the acquisition of new knowledge and the invention of new products.[6] At the same time, running down the stock of renewable and nonrenewable resources and polluting the environment have the opposite effects. Public indebtedness might also be used for favouring present generations in a more permanent or systematic way.

Intergenerational welfare comparisons necessarily involve value judgements, and settling on interpersonal equity norms is a major and well-known problem in policy evaluation. In the end, there must be some social consensus, and the political process obviously plays an important part in forging, interpreting and applying that consensus. That does not imply that there is no role for normative analysis as a complement to the positive study of the political process. On the contrary, normative analysis and even normative advocacy are an indispensable role of economists and other policy advisors: the political system does not take the form of a political marketplace that yields a determinate outcome.[7] In the end, one simply cannot avoid making interpersonal welfare comparisons in policy advice and evaluation, and presumably the basis for the comparisons that one is using should be made explicit.

In fact, there is probably considerable consensus about some of the basic precepts of redistributive equity, whether applied within or between generations. At least, one infers as much from the kinds of policies governments institute in most Organisation for Economic Co-operation and Development (OECD) countries. After all, governments are engaged heavily in redistribution, and the forms and extent of that redistribution are very similar across countries. Moreover, they are quite different than one might predict if one were starting with a public-choice model based on purely self-interested voters. Some of these principles might include the following, the details of which are standard fare in the applied welfare economics literature.

- *The Pareto principle.* Policies that make some persons better off and no one worse off are preferred. This allows one to define the notion of society's utility possibilities frontier, which is conceptually useful in thinking of policy alternatives.
- *Aversion to inequality.* All other things being equal, society prefers outcomes in which welfare is more equally distributed to those in which it is less equally distributed. One's preferred degree of inequality aversion depends partly on ideology, and partly on the perceived severity of the equity efficiency trade-off. Nonetheless, the very acceptance of inequality aversion implies that redistribution from the better off to the worse off is condoned.
- *Equality of opportunity.* Not all sources of inequality might be judged relevant for redistributive correction. The "principle of compensation" suggests that persons ought to be compensated only for those adverse outcomes that are due to factors outside their control, such as their productive ability, their health and their date of birth. But, if persons are responsible for adverse outcomes (e.g., low incomes) because of the way they have freely chosen to behave, these differences ought not to be compensated: the "principle of responsibility." Taken together, the principles of compensation and responsibility lead to the idea of equality of opportunity as one of the guiding principles of redistribution: opportunities that households face, as reflected in, say, their budget possibilities, ought to be equalized.[8] This principle, which is enshrined in the Canadian constitution, complements the *ex post* notions of redistribution that are based on equalizing actual market outcomes. The principle of equality of opportunity gives rise to important policy instruments like education and health care alongside the tax-transfer system.
- *Social insurance.* A final principle, closely related to the notion of aversion to inequality, is that of social insurance. As argued above, households might be subject to unexpected shocks over which they have no control and against which they cannot fully insure. For example, insurance companies may not be willing to offer long-term health insurance, so that if an observable change in their health status occurs that makes them higher risk, they would become uninsurable.[9] Or, they may simply be uninsurable at birth. Private insurance might fail to address unemployment as well. These kinds of arguments constitute the major reason for the substantial programs of social insurance implemented by most OECD countries. While the examples given here refer mainly to intragenerational social

insurance, the same principle applies with respect to shocks that apply selectively to one generation rather than another.

While there obviously is not universal agreement on the details of application of these principles, there seems to be enough of a consensus about their relevance to take us a long way in judging in qualitative terms at least minimal standards of redistribution that should apply. And, although we may be less used to thinking of applying them with respect to intergenerational redistribution, there seems to be no particular reason why such an extension would not reflect societal consensus. For example, widely held concerns about the environment are based on notions of intergenerational equity.

We are left with an agnostic conclusion. What we get from public indebtedness is an intergenerational transfer. This can be set alongside the various other things that are passed on to future generations, including the stock of physical public capital, the human capital and capabilities that have been accumulated by public sector program spending, and the stock of natural public capital in the form of natural resources and the environment.[10] In assessing the sufficiency of what we are passing on to future generations on balance, some judgement must be made about whether, given this level of intergenerational transfers, we are satisfied with the resultant relative levels of well-being of future and current generations.

Some might argue that the normative principles of intergenerational economic justice enumerated above are hardly sufficient for evaluating the level of public indebtedness. Quite apart from the fact that there may be no clear consensus about the degree of aversion to inequality that should apply to intergenerational transfers, and the fact that the future is fraught with uncertainty, it might also be argued that governments might be overly short-sighted and will therefore discount the benefits of future generations who, after all, are not part of the voting constituency. What one makes of this argument depends on the view one takes of the political process in reflecting the public's preferences. If one takes the view that the political process is inherently inefficient, wasteful and captive of special interests, policy outcomes may well deviate from what the electorate truly wants, as is often suggested by analysts from the public-choice school. However, there is a strain of the public-choice literature that argues that political processes are efficient and that political competition does lead to outcomes that approximate the social consensus. In that case, if governments discount the welfare of future generations, it is because doing so reflects the social consensus among those currently alive. If one does not like the social consensus that has been formed, one can always try to persuade the public that it should adopt a different consensus. That, I would argue, is part of the role of normative analysis.

Accounting for Public Indebtedness

Whatever view one takes on the question of what the social consensus is or should be, translating one's view into practical policy advice and the evaluation of existing government policy stance is another matter. Just how much existing policies redistribute welfare among different cohorts is not easy to observe, and partial, if readily available, measures like the stock of public debt relative to the stock of public assets almost certainly will give a misleading impression. To make a very well-informed judgement about the appropriateness of the current level of public indebtedness, one would ideally need to have the following types of information:

- A comprehensive measure of the extent of public indebtedness, including all types of net tax obligations passed on to members of current and future generations that are implicit in existing tax policies;
- An account of the full benefits of government policies to existing and future generations, given some presumption about the path of government policies far enough into the future;
- An estimate of the allocation of the benefits of the stock of natural capital to existing and future generations, given the government policy stance;
- A measure of the relative levels of well-being of existing and future generations, given the policies that are in place.

These measures and estimates are obviously very difficult to obtain, both practically as well as conceptually. However, some recently-developed accounting procedures can go a significant way toward informing our judgements. These fall under the general rubric of *generational accounting*, which has been developed precisely to capture the full amount of intergenerational transfers that are implicit in public indebtedness.[11]

The idea of generational accounting is to assign to members of each currently alive and future (unborn) generation the net costs of financing existing fiscal policies projected into the future. It is basically an accounting exercise, with no account taken of behavioural responses to the fiscal policies (including any offsetting bequests in the spirit of Ricardo equivalence). The building block is a cohort's *generational account* under a given set of government policies projected into the future. Such an account is the present value of the net taxes that the representative household of a given age cohort is liable to pay either over their full lifetime, or over their remaining lifetime, depending on the context. Net taxes include tax liabilities of all forms attributed to the household, less transfers received and less whatever types of government expenditures can be attributed to the household. Thus, for example, in some applications (e.g., Oreopoulos and Vaillancourt 1998) health and education spending are assigned to each age cohort. Generational accounts can then be converted to generational *lifetime net tax rates* by dividing them by the present value of, say, lifetime income. Generational accounts or net tax rates can then be put to two sorts of uses.

First, comparing the lifetime net tax rates for various cohorts can give some indication of the intergenerational transfers implicit in a given policy stance. For example, in an innovative exercise, Oreopoulos and Vaillancourt (1998) calculate lifetime net tax rates for all age cohorts alive in 1995 under two alternative assumptions: that impending government surpluses go to debt reduction, and that they go to spending hikes. In the debt-reduction case, lifetime net tax rates gradually increase from 31.2 percent for cohorts born in 1910 to 38 percent for cohorts born in 1995. In the spending-hike case, lifetime net tax rates go from 31.2 percent to 34.1 percent: current generations are able to lower their lifetime net tax burdens by passing on greater debt to future generations. The change in net tax rates over time is virtually monotonic and gradual, reflecting the gradual increase in size of the public sector over the period: thus, those born in the immediate postwar period (baby boomers) have lifetime net tax rates of about 33–34 percent in both scenarios. These changes, which are surprisingly small, show no great cyclical variation despite the major wars and depression that occurred during the period. Apparently governments have smoothed the effects of these changes over cohorts reasonably well.

The second and much more common use to which generational accounts have been put is to calculate the burden that would be left for future generations from alternative government policies. The basis for this is the government's so-called *intertemporal budget constraint*, which requires that the government's future stream of net taxes must finance its existing net debt and its future stream of expenditures. In turn, the future stream of net taxes (again consisting of tax liabilities less transfers and government spending in areas like health and education) can be disaggregated into those attributable to currently alive and not-yet-born cohorts. For each currently alive cohort, a generational account is calculated consisting of the present value of net taxes owing from the current period to the predicted end of life. The present value of net taxes owed by all future generations is then the sum of current government net debt and the present value of future expenditure obligations less the sum of generational accounts for all those currently alive. Those obligations left for future generations are then typically assumed to be shared equally among all future cohorts to give an idea of the burden that on average is left for future generations. In effect, the net liabilities of the government as of today, its public indebtedness, are amortized over all future generations: they all share in paying the debt.

This methodology has been applied to the Canadian case, most recently by Oreopoulos and Vaillancourt (1998), and by Oreopoulos (1999), and the general findings are instructive. The pattern of generational accounts calculated by Oreopoulos using 1995 data takes the following general pattern. For households currently alive, the size of the generational account follows a hump-shaped profile with respect to age. Starting with the youngest, who have a positive generational account, it initially rises until about age 25, then declines, becoming negative between ages 55 and 60. The value is systematically higher for males than for females. These patterns are intuitively appealing once one thinks about the lifetime pattern of tax payments, benefits from health and education, and access to transfers. Perhaps as interesting is the comparison of the generational account for the newly born members of current generations with that for the representative member of future generations. In 1995 (in the wake of federal deficit reduction policies and reform of the Canada Pension Plan), the generational account for future generations is only slightly higher than for the current young (by 3.1 percent in the base-case calculation). This is true for both males and females. The orders of magnitude of the lifetime generational accounts for these cohorts are roughly $60,000: to be clear, this is the present value of future generations' lifetime net tax contributions to paying down the existing debt and financing future government spending, except for health and education.

In the above calculations, Oreopoulos assumed that future budget surpluses would go to pay down the debt. Oreopoulos and Vaillancourt (1998) calculate lifetime net tax rates for future generations under both the deficit-reduction scenario and the spending-hike scenario, and the results appear to be quite different. When budget surpluses are used to reduce the deficit, the lifetime net tax rate for future generations is virtually the same as for the current young: about 38 percent. This is despite the coming demographic shock in which the proportion of the population over 65 is projected to increase dramatically. On the other hand, if the budget surpluses were used to increase government expenditures, the lifetime net tax rate for future generations would rise to 55 percent, substantially higher than that of the current young.

These calculations are clearly very suggestive, and provide a useful tool for capturing at least some of the effects of public indebtedness. There can obviously be disputes about the various assumptions built into the calculations with respect to future policies, population, the assignment of taxes and transfers to various age cohorts and so on. For our purposes, a more interesting question is how generational accounts, assuming they could be measured accurately, would fare as a device for addressing all of the issues of intergenerational redistribution raised in our earlier discussion. We can identify a number of shortcomings of the current methodology of generational accounting as a complete measure of the intergenerational effects of a government's policy stance:[12]

- *Forward and backward looking generational accounts.* The standard generational accounting method is forward looking in the sense that the generational accounts for those currently alive include only the net tax liabilities for the remainder of their lives (Oreopoulos and Vaillancourt 1998 being a notable exception). This implies that one does not get a full picture of the intergenerational transfers that have applied to them. Since near-term future policies will undoubtedly affect them over the remainder of their lives, it is difficult to evaluate the pros and cons of different alternatives without knowing what such alternatives imply for the net benefits they have received over their full lifetimes. The same applies for unborn cohorts, although it is difficult to forecast their lifetime situation.
- *Public capital.* Neither the measure of government net debt nor the generational accounts takes account of the public capital stock and infrastructure that exists at the current time. In principle, that public capital stock yields services that are of benefit to current and future generations, and these should be included as an element of the benefits received. In practice, this would presumably be very difficult to do. It might be argued that an alternative would be to obtain a measure of public capital and include it as an asset component in government net debt. However, that would not be satisfactory. On the one hand, as we have mentioned, valuing the stock of public capital is problematic. Unlike private capital, whose value reflects future income streams, the public capital stock can only be valued by taking account of the future benefits it generates, and this gives rise to problems of distributive weighting and shadow pricing. For another, since these benefits accrue differentially to different cohorts it would be wrong to aggregate them into a single wealth measure.
- *Natural capital.* Natural resource wealth and environmental capital which are commonly owned are not included in generational accounts, despite the fact that they constitute a form of asset wealth that is shared among generations. Natural capital differs from the public capital stock in the sense that it has not been produced using public resources. Nonetheless, the benefit it provides to different cohorts depends on government policy. In principle, one could attribute to different generations the benefit that they obtain from natural capital, but that would be a heroic undertaking. In the Canadian case, this problem could not be avoided if provincial indebtedness were included in generational accounts. The benefit of natural resources is reflected in the resource tax revenues that the provinces collect.

One could not simply treat these as costs to the generations alive when the taxes are collected. For nonrenewable resources, such taxes represent a running down of an asset that becomes unavailable for future generations; for renewable resources, they represent the rent that continually accrues to each generation, and as such are not a cost to them.

- *Intangible public capital.* The most difficult assets to value are the invisible ones, such as accumulated knowledge, social capital or the society's institutions. Yet the passing on of intangible assets from one generation to the next represents an important form of intergenerational transfer.
- *Measures of generational well-being.* Finally, in order to make a judgement about the adequacy of intergenerational transfers, it would be useful to have measures of how well off future generations will be relative to current generations. There is a presumption in the generational accounting literature that the intergenerational balance is achieved when there is parity of generational accounts or of lifetime net tax rates among different generations. But that might only be the case if all generations are also equally well off. If they are not, unlucky cohorts should have lower lifetime net tax rates.

Having drawn attention to some drawbacks of generational accounts, I do want to affirm that the concept is the most suitable approach to evaluating public indebtedness, and one that serves as a basis for future development. Even if we as economists are not prepared to subscribe to a particular value judgement about intergenerational equity, we might still be interested in informing policy makers of the intergenerational outcomes that are implicit in their policies. The tool of generational accounting provides a promising approach since it focuses precisely on the relative financial burdens imposed on different cohorts, living and yet to be born, that will satisfy the government's intertemporal spending requirements.

Concluding and Speculative Comments

To return to the question that this session was meant to illuminate: What did we get for the substantial debt that was accumulated in the last quarter of the twentieth century? It seems clear that the answer is not bricks and mortar. Beyond that, there are various possibilities, most of which involve intergenerational transfers, if only implicitly:

Waste. It is conceivable that at least some of what we got for the debt was of no value. The debt may have caused excessive spending that produced nothing of value, perhaps because it was used up in bureaucratic inefficiency and caused economic inefficiencies due to the cost associated with the higher tax rates needed to service the debt in the future. Though these sources of waste are no doubt real, it might be hard to make the case that they constituted a substantial proportion of the consequences of accumulating the debt. It seems more likely that the debt financed something useful to someone, even if it was only pure consumption. The following categories take that to be the case.

Intergenerational risk-sharing. Suppose then that the debt and indebtedness is largely an intergenerational transfer rather than being a waste of resources or the financing of public-sector physical capital. The run-up and presumably subsequent run-down of indebtedness (as the generational accounts' numbers seem to suggest) may have been intergenerational risk-sharing in action, in the sense that it served in part to smooth out the adverse effects of high-unemployment years of stagflation and possibly the restructuring associated with the Free Trade Agreement and North American Free Trade Agreement. This smoothing would be reflected in relatively high transfers for unemployment insurance and social assistance financed in part by debt. This may not be an easy case to make, depending on the incidence of the costs of the economic downturn. For example, if older persons bore the brunt of the downturn, it might be reasonable to transfer the costs to the younger and future generations through an increase in indebtedness. On the other hand, if it was the young people whose lifetime outcomes were adversely affected, it is not so obvious that burdening them with future debt-servicing was fair.

Demographic smoothing. Related to the above, the indebtedness might to some extent reflect the changing demographics of the postwar period. To the extent that budget deficits were run to finance education and health expenditures of a relatively large cohort, the expenditures are benefiting a cohort whose income-earning and therefore tax-paying capacity comes sometime in the future. Postponing the financing of these expenditures through temporary indebtedness might make sense.

Intergenerational transfers. Finally, the increase in indebtedness might simply reflect unplanned, fortuitous or perverse intergenerational transfers from younger to older cohorts. These may or may not be warranted, depending on the relative levels of well-being of different cohorts and society's views of intergenerational aversion to inequality.

Presumably, the truth is that we have some of all of the above. To be more certain than that, it would be necessary to construct as comprehensive as possible a set of backward- and forward-looking generational accounts. From these, we could learn which generations among all those that are currently alive were net recipients of transfers over their entire lifetimes, and which were net donors. Then we would be in a better position to judge whether the run-up in debt was worth it. But even that would not be sufficient. We would also need to have some measuring rod of the well-being of each generation so as to judge what amount of intergenerational redistribution is justified, for as we have seen there is no reason why the generational accounts of all cohorts should be the same if some cohorts are otherwise significantly worse off over their lifetimes than others.

Failing that kind of detailed investigation, we can only speculate about the efficacy of past debt policies. Nonetheless, from an armchair perspective it is possible to give an account of some of the main forces that might allow us to judge whether (a) the buildup of debt (i.e., the large budget deficits) from the mid-1970s on and (b) the drastic deficit-cutting policies of the 1990s were warranted. Neither was inevitable, but can they be defended?

Let me begin with the debt buildup. One perspective to take is to ask whether the main population of taxpayers of that period was justified in postponing tax liabilities to future taxpayers, some of whom were younger cohorts and future generations. The taxpayers we are talking of are the generations that bracket the baby-boom generation. In fact, one can think of several reasons which, taken together, might have made it reasonable for these taxpayers to force later generations to share the cost of fiscal programs:

- Part of the extraordinary expenditures of the period were for items that went especially to benefit older generations who had not contributed to their financing. Examples are health insurance and transfers to the elderly, including Canada Pension Plan benefits. As well, the high debt levels incurred during the Second World War had largely been paid off, and in helping to pay them off taxpayers during this period had already shared some of the burden of the shocks felt by their parents.
- Other expenditures were for items that particularly benefited the following generations of taxpayers, again including the rapid expansion of health care, transfers to children and the growth in expenditures on postsecondary education (although the contribution of the federal government to this latter item was limited).
- RRSP and RPP contributions grew rapidly during this period. They essentially reflect postponed tax liabilities and were among the largest tax expenditures reported by the federal government. These postponed tax liabilities should be offset against the debt accumulation when reckoning the extent of intergenerational transfers: they represent a transfer of tax liabilities to later in the lives of the contributors rather than a transfer onto future generations.
- There was a substantial and seemingly long-lasting macroeconomic shock in this period. The recessions of 1981–82 and 1990–92 were the most severe since the Great Depression. The unemployment rate skyrocketed during the early 1980s to double-digit levels, producing higher transfer obligations and sluggish tax revenues. These changes in the budget deficit were

largely driven by automatic stabilizers rather than discretionary fiscal policy (although the early-1970s UI liberalization no doubt exacerbated matters). Actual GDP fell significantly below potential GDP during this period, and capacity utilization was very low. Moreover, many countries were experiencing similar phenomena so the slump cannot all be attributed to bad domestic policy. An insistence on more-balanced budgets would have placed an enormous burden on the taxpayers of the time.

- Inflation rates were also historically very high from 1975–85, thus requiring substantial debt-servicing charges. This was presumably an important factor contributing to the steady rise in the debt-to-GDP ratio from 1982–95 (when it reached the same level as in 1952). Although the debt-to-GDP ratio reached slightly higher levels than in other OECD countries, it did mainly reflect the international experience of a hitherto unheard-of combination of high inflation and high unemployment, both of which placed enormous pressure on budget deficits.

- The rate of growth of productivity was halved in the 1980s, and this was not fully expected.

Thus, the taxpayers of the period in question faced a combination of extraordinary shocks and a unique set of circumstances. Based on this bad luck, some sharing of the burden of these effects with subsequent generations may well have been reasonable. Against this it might be said that the taxpayers of the period had experienced a rapid rise in their own wages. And the rapid increase in participation rates made tax revenues much more buoyant without imposing any additional costs on the public sector. Moreover, it is possible to argue that younger cohorts will likely face unique hardships of their own. But, it would be hard to deny that some substantial run-up of budget deficits was reasonable in order to spread the burden of this barrage of adverse effects among cohorts.

If this view is accepted, it follows that in order to spread the burden across several generations, the debt should not have been reduced as rapidly as it was in the mid-1990s. Recall that generational accounting studies show in retrospect that fiscal balance between future generations and the current young had already been achieved by 1995, despite the predicted demographic changes in the offing.[13] As successful as debt reduction was from a purely financial perspective, from other perspectives it was a costly exercise. Much of the deficit reduction effort came from expenditure reductions, and relatively selective reductions at that. The cutback in cash transfers to the provinces was by far the larger component in proportionate terms. Apart from the undoubted animosity this caused in provincial capitals, it may have had long-term effects on the balance of our federal system that will permanently damage the economic and social union. Moreover, from a national point of view, the cuts in transfers may not even have reduced combined federal and provincial debt and public expenditures. The substantial downsizing of the federal public service that was also part of the cuts is alleged to have involved the loss of a large contingent of capable public sector managers who were hard to replace. Defence spending also took an obvious hit and left us with arguably too few resources to accomplish the tasks that were being set.

Different observers will disagree with the lasting magnitude of these costs. My own view is that they were a substantial price to pay to attempt to keep the burden of the sizeable shocks of the 1970s and 1980s from being shared among a larger number of cohorts.

Notes

I am grateful for the many comments provided by the discussant, Jeremy Rudin, the conference organizers, Chris Ragan and Bill Watson, the conference rapporteurs, Jack Mintz and Lars Osberg, as well as the conference participants. I have attempted to do justice to them in preparing the final version.

1. Note that "generation t" (or cohort t), refers to all those born at time t. By contrast, in his remarks at this conference Lars Osberg uses generation t to refer to all those alive at time t.

2. The fact that the capital stock falls when intergenerational transfers from the young to the old are made does not necessarily imply that there is any inefficiency caused by the transfer. That is, public indebtedness raises issues of intergenerational equity, not efficiency, as discussed in Boadway and Wildasin (1994).

3. A similar social insurance argument is also invoked to explain intragenerational redistribution (Rawls 1971). See Boadway and Keen (2000) for a general discussion of social insurance and other reasons for redistributive transfers.

4. The tax smoothing argument was devised by Barro (1974) in a context in which Barro-Ricardo equivalence applied so that intergenerational transfers arising from debt changes would be offset by bequests. Only in that context can one focus on the efficiency consequences of tax smoothing without worrying about intergenerational equity effects.

5. There may also be an equity-efficiency trade-off arising from the fact that as public indebtedness increases, the interest rate rises, thereby increasing the cost of postponing tax liabilities.

6. Philosophers have stressed that economists may well overestimate these improvements in welfare. See, for example, Heath (2002). This point is well taken and should in principle be taken into account in our intergenerational welfare comparison calculation.

7. The case for normative economic analysis as a necessary complement to public choice or positive political economy analysis is made at length in Boadway (2002).

8. A complete treatment of equality of opportunity along these lines may be found in Roemer (1998). While he applies it to intragenerational transfers, the same principle could apply between generations.

9. This source of market failure in health care is carefully discussed in Cutler (2002).

10. Helliwell (1998) has pointed out that social capital and society's institutions are also passed on to future generations, complicating the issue of intergenerational equity even further.

11. Generational accounting was developed in the US by Auerbach, Gokhale and Kotlikoff (1991), and has been applied to a number of countries, including Canada. See Auerbach, Kotlikoff and Leibfritz (1999). Canadian applications are also found in Corak (1998) and Oreopoulos and Vaillancourt (1998).

12. Some of these comments are found in Helliwell (1998) and Osberg (1998).

13. Moreover, Mérette (2002) has argued convincingly that the anticipated aging of the population is unlikely to have the pessimistic consequences that are often suggested. He claims that aging will create incentives for human capital accumulation that will serve to accelerate the rate of growth, and will induce higher labour market participation that will overcome the adverse consequences of a smaller labour force.

Bibliography

Auerbach, A.J., J. Gokhale, and L.J. Kotlikoff. 1991. "Generational Accounts: A Meaningful Alternative to Deficit Accounting." In *Tax Policy and the Economy*, 5, ed. D. Bradford. Cambridge, MA: MIT Press, pp. 55-110.

Auerbach, A.J., L.J. Kotlikoff, and W. Leibfritz, eds. 1999. *Generational Accounting Around the World*. Chicago: University of Chicago Press.

Barro, R.J. 1974. "Are Government Bonds Net Wealth?" *Journal of Political Economy* 82:1095-117.

Bernheim, B.D., and K. Bagwell. 1988. "Is Everything Neutral?" *Journal of Political Economy* 96:308-38.

Boadway, R. 2002. "The Role of Public Choice Considerations in Normative Public Economics." In *Political Economy and Public Finance*, ed. S.L. Winer and H. Shibata. Cheltenham, UK: Edward Elgar.

Boadway, R., and M. Keen. 2000. "Redistribution." In *Handbook of Income Distribution*, ed. A.B. Atkinson and F. Bourguignon. Amsterdam: North-Holland, pp. 677-789.

Boadway, R., and D. Wildasin. 1994. "Taxation and Savings: A Survey." *Fiscal Studies* 15:19-63.

Corak, M., ed. 1998. *Government Finance and Generational Equity*. Ottawa: Statistics Canada and Human Resources Development Canada.

Cutler, D.M. 2002. "Health Care and the Public Sector." In *Handbook of Public Economics*, 4, ed. A.J. Auerebach and M. Feldstein. Amsterdam: North-Holland.

Heath, J. 2002. "Should Productivity Growth be a Social Priority?" In *Review of Economic Performance and Social Progress*, 2, ed. A. Sharpe, K. Banting and F. St-Hilaire. Montreal and Ottawa: Institute for Research on Public Policy and Centre for the Study of Living Standards.

Helliwell, J.F. 1998. "What Will We Be Leaving You?" In *Government Finance and Generational Equity*, ed. M. Corak. Ottawa: Statistics Canada and Human Resources Development Canada, pp.141-47.

Kotlikoff, L.J. 1984. "Taxation and Savings: A Neoclassical Perspective." *Journal of Economic Literature* 22:1576-629.

Mérette, M. 2002. "The Bright Side: A Positive View on the Economics of Aging." *Choices* 8, no. 1:2-28.

Oreopoulos, P. 1999. "Canada: On the Road to Fiscal Balance." In *Generational Accounting Around the World*, ed. A.J. Auerbach, L.J. Kotlikoff and W. Leibfritz. Chicago: University of Chicago Press, pp. 199-217.

Oreopoulos, P., and F. Vaillancourt. 1998. *Taxes, Transfers, and Generations in Canada: Who Gains and Who Loses from the Demographic Transition*. Commentary no. 107. Toronto: C.D. Howe Institute.

Osberg, L. 1998. "Meaning and Measurement in Intergenerational Equity." In *Government Finance and Generational Equity*, ed. M. Corak. Ottawa: Statistics Canada and Human Resources Development Canada, pp. 131-39.

Rawls, J. 1971. *A Theory of Justice*. Cambridge, MA: Harvard University Press.

Roemer, J. 1998. *Equality of Opportunity*. Cambridge, MA: Harvard University Press.

Sen, A.K. 1985. *Commodities and Capabilities*. Cambridge, MA: Harvard University Press.

what do we get for public indebtedness?

Jeremy Rudin

I would summarize Robin Boadway's paper as follows: incurring debt is one government policy that can effect an intergenerational transfer, but it is not the only policy that can do that. Accordingly, to give policy advice about public debt one has to both assess how government policy is creating intergenerational transfers and evaluate those transfers against normative criteria for judging intergenerational transfers. One therefore needs to consider not only debt policy, but also all policies that can effect transfers across generations.

Not only do I agree with this conclusion, I find it almost inescapable. It is, however, a conclusion from which I would very much like to escape. If I could, then I would be able to provide policy advice based on the economically optimal level (or path) of debt. I would not be forced to weigh the negative impact that today's fiscal retrenchment has on the current generation to the benefit of one or more future generations (or the positive impact that today's fiscal expansion has on the current generation, to the detriment of one or more future generations).

Unfortunately, Robin's conclusion implies that this intergenerational transfer cannot be ignored, as it is the essence of a change in debt policy. As a result, there is no more an optimal level of government debt than there is an optimal degree of progressivity of the tax system, or an optimal ratio of government expenditure to gross domestic product (GDP), or an optimal fiscal equalization program.

But as a person whose job it is to give policy advice, I really would like to escape from Robin's conclusion, so let me try a few ways to wriggle out of it. As Robin points out, one potential avenue of escape is Ricardian equivalence, or at least the version of it set out in Barro's famous 1974 paper, which essentially ignores the impact of distortionary taxation. If Ricardian equivalence does hold, then changing the debt path does not change any real outcomes, including the intergenerational distribution of incomes. This would allow us to ignore intergenerational distribution in evaluating debt policy, though only because debt policy is irrelevant. As a result, even in this case, there is no optimal level (or path) of government debt: if the government's debt has no real effects, it does not matter what value the debt takes.

Another way to try to escape from Robin's conclusion would be to keep the Barro-style dynastic preferences, but to add significant tax distortions. In this case, as in the first, society has the preferences of an infinitely-lived representative agent, so debt policy does not affect intergenerational transfers. But with distortionary taxation the timing of taxes will have real effects. Under fairly general conditions there is indeed an optimal long-run level of debt, and it is negative, that is, the government should build up enough assets to generate enough revenue to eliminate taxation.

In such a world, negative government debt would not only be the optimal policy, it would be the actual policy, as it is what society would want. But since we never see real-world governments even thinking about eliminating taxation by building up assets, we can conclude that society does not have the requisite preferences, in which case, this policy is not optimal.

For completeness, I should mention a third approach to establishing an optimal debt level independent of intergenerational considerations that was proposed by Aiyigari and McGrattan (1998). In their work, they assume that households are subject to idiosyncratic shocks to their income but cannot buy insurance against prolonged spells of low income. They then show how the existence of net (not just gross) government debt can partially compensate for this inability to insure. While theirs is a very inventive paper, it eliminates the intergenerational transfer issue by simply assuming it away. Moreover, a number of intuitively appealing enrichments of the model overturn their result that optimal net government debt is positive (James and Karam 2001).

Even if we give up on the idea that there is some generally applicable way to analyze debt policy without having to evaluate intergenerational transfers, perhaps Robin overestimates the difficulty of such an evaluation: maybe in some special cases it won't be so hard. What we are looking for are circumstances, albeit possibly temporary, under which specific changes in debt policy would leave all generations better off. In such cases, it would not be necessary to take a view on the trade-off between generations. Reducing debt would constitute a Pareto improvement across generations.

One such special case arises if the economy is dynamically inefficient. Robin dismisses this possibility almost out of hand, and rightly so in my view. But perhaps it is just our training as economists that makes us believe no free lunch is ever possible. A more open-minded assessment would test empirically to see if some of the conditions needed for dynamic efficiency obtain or not (Abel et al. 1989).

We might also turn the dynamically inefficient case on its head, and look for particular circumstances in which fiscal retrenchment would actually benefit the current generation. Since retrenchment presumably would also benefit future generations, this would be a case in which all generations were better off and no intergenerational trade-off is required. Consider one case in which such a happy outcome might occur. Suppose an open economy has a large net foreign debt. Suppose further that its government debt is on a sufficiently explosive path that foreign investors are demanding a substantial risk premium if they are to hold such debt. And suppose yet further that the risk premium on government debt finds its way into the cost of private borrowing as well.

In that case, a sufficiently large fiscal retrenchment may eliminate the risk premium and provide enough benefit to current citizens to fully offset the loss that retrenchment undoubtedly causes them. This makes retrenchment "win-win" for all generations, although important *intra*generational distribution issues still might have to be dealt with. This example was inspired by Canada's experience during the Mexican peso crisis, although I would not go so far as to insist that it applies perfectly.

Inspired by the same period, Robin goes through a similar exercise, but arrives at the opposite conclusion. He argues at the end of his paper that the size of the Canadian fiscal retrenchment in the mid-1990s may have caused such long-term damage to government institutions that it offset the gain such a retrenchment would normally have implied for future generations.

How can Robin and I get such opposite results? In my "win-win" version of the episode, the fiscal retrenchment can improve the material standard of living of all generations. Consistent with the rest of his paper, Robin's "lose-lose" version appears to be based on a (much) broader view of well-being. In particular, Robin's well-being concept is something that can be affected by government institutions beyond the impact of those institutions on the material standard of living. It is therefore possible that both of our results could obtain at the same time. I am going to argue later that implementing this broader view (as interesting as it is) is impractical, so I will have to say I cannot assess Robin's conclusion.

Having failed to come up with anything other than very special and temporary exceptions to Robin's conclusion that debt-policy advice rests on an assessment of intergenerational trade-offs, let me turn to his analysis of how we might put his central recommendation – that we account thoroughly for the intergenerational implications of all government policies – into practice.

I agree very strongly that if we are to make any serious progress in this area, we should pay more attention either to explicit generational accounting or to something very much like it. Note that it is also possible to use overlapping generations (OLG) models either instead of or alongside generational accounts. OLG models allow the researcher to consider behavioural responses to government policies, though at the cost of reducing the amount of detail that can be considered. The choice of which technique to use would presumably depend on the issues an analyst wanted to consider.

For example, one common intergenerational concern is that baby boomers (like myself) will retire both relatively rich and with a greater ability to tax future workers than future workers will have to tax us. This is partly because of retired boomers' political clout, there are lots of us, and partly because retirees do not have labour income that future workers can tax. On the other hand, we wealthy future retirees may end up demanding a lot of personal services from a relatively small group of workers, and that group's wages would presumably rise as a result. Thus, future workers may be more able to tax retirees, at least implicitly, than we might think. To put it another way, 30 years from now may be a great time to be a teenager with a lawnmower.[1] This is the sort of complication that an OLG model could address but that generational accounts, which are only accounting, cannot. Of course, a researcher with a lot of time on his or her hands might generate behavioural responses using an OLG model and then plug those into a more detailed set of generational accounts.

One conclusion that follows from Robin's logic is that we need to consider each current and future generation separately. After all, if we care about the transfer from "later" to "now," we may also care about the transfer from "much later" to simply "later." This is implicit in our concern about the potential impact of population aging. So I agree with Robin that the once-common practice in generational accounting of lumping all future generations into an undifferentiated mass should be replaced by establishing separate accounts for all generations, although, of course, the problem does have to be truncated at some point.

Robin goes on to sketch out the formidable information requirements of the sort of exercise that he is recommending. The task that he describes would fall somewhere on the interval between "extremely daunting" and "completely impossible." Indeed, there is a sense in which even Robin's very scary list underestimates the difficulty of the task.

Robin, quite rightly, wants us to consider "the intergenerational impact of the government's long-term budgetary stance." But governments typically do not have long-term budgetary policies. Even a government that did want to have a long-term policy would be wasting its time, because it would have no way of committing itself or future administrations to that policy. This fact causes non-trivial problems in the sort of exercise Robin wants us to undertake.

For example, at the moment, elderly benefits in Canada are indexed to the rate of inflation, rather than to wage growth. If there is no labour productivity growth, then wages and prices will grow at about the same rate, and the income of those people who receive elderly benefits relative to the income of workers will not change over time. If, however, there is strong labour productivity growth then wages will rise faster than prices, and the relative income of those people who receive elderly benefits will tend to fall continuously.

Is it reasonable to suppose that strict price indexation would be maintained forever in that case? If the government had a long-term fiscal policy, it might well be to maintain price indexation only if the relative income of the low-income elderly did not drop below some particular level. Such a policy would have a very different intergenerational impact than strict price indexation. Unfortunately (for researchers at least), knowing the current policy does not tell us what the long-term policy is or would be.

This sort of problem also gets in the way of assessing how government policy affects intergenerational risk-sharing. We can at least try to analyze how a permanent regime of price-indexing stacks up in terms of intergenerational risk-sharing and then compare it to a permanent regime of wage-indexing. But there is no way to make either regime permanent, no reason to believe that either would be dynamically consistent, and no evidence of stability in the choice of regime.

As is often the case in economics, progress will be bought at the price of simplification. One item in Robin's *desiderata* that I think we can do without is a measure of well-being, if that means anything beyond real income or real consumption. While we cannot escape having to predict the real incomes of future generations, I see little to be gained in trying to project their well-being more broadly.

One reason is that the only guide we have about how real income translates into well-being is the experience of individuals in the economy. However, when an individual's income rises, he or she gains utility not only from the increase in absolute living standard, but also from the increase in his or her income relative to others. When an entire generation's income rises, they do not, they cannot, all enjoy an increase in relative income on average.[2] While we can see the problem, we do not know how to correct for it.

The other reason for avoiding measures of well-being is that many factors that doubtless affect it are not captured in the consumption bundle. To take an extreme example, almost everyone in the Washington, DC area feels much better now than when a murderous sniper was on the loose. It is hard enough to try to predict what will happen to real income; predicting what will happen to psychic income defies our current abilities.

Another way to simplify the problem, one I favour, is to use what we might call an axiomatic approach. This would involve positing some simple properties one might like intergenerational policy to have, and then seeing how current and projected policies stack up.

One advantage is that sufficiently simple axioms would be less information-ally demanding than the public finance principles that Robin sets out. However, the axiomatic approach has some other advantages as well. If the axioms really are simple enough, they make it much easier to communicate the reasoning and results of the analysis. After all, if you simply want to form your own view on public policy, your own preferences are all that matter. But if you want to influence public policy decisions, you have to be able to persuade others, and one thing that might help would be a simple explanation of the values or principles you are applying. Moreover, I suspect that many people have preferences about the policies that determine economic outcomes that are not simply derived from the outcomes themselves (or the expected values of the outcomes). As economists, we tend to ignore preferences about policies in favour of preferences about outcomes, though that may only be because we know how to model preferences about outcomes.

An example of an axiom that would have some appeal in the current Canadian context at least is the following: fiscal policy should not require future generations to experience an increase in tax rates in order to maintain the current level of public services. This is the reasoning (more or less) that animated the work of Scarth and Jackson, among others.[3] This single axiom would not identify a unique long-term fiscal policy, but it would rule some policies out. The work that would be involved to decide when such exclusions should be made is nonetheless extremely challenging, as many people at this conference can attest. One of a number of things that would have to be struggled with is the meaning of "current level of public services" in areas such as health care.

Another issue that would have to be dealt with is how to handle uncertainty. Perhaps we could look for policies that reduce the probability of raising taxes on, or cutting services to, future generations below some threshold. Adding additional axioms, if we can think of any, might further narrow the set of desirable policies.

I would like to conclude by noting how impressed I was with Robin's paper. If you are like me, you may have read the comments without reading the paper, thinking this would save you time. Let me encourage you to read the paper carefully; you will see how deep it is. If you are looking for a shortcut to appreciating the depth of thought, start by reading the title and then the conclusion. Robin asks in the title, "What do we get for public indebtedness?" His conclusion has a Zen-like depth and subtlety: there is no "we."

Notes

The views expressed are those of the author and do not reflect those of the Department of Finance.

1. This succinct summary of the issue is due to Cliff Halliwell.

2. For a formal treatment see Ok and Kockensen (2000).

3. Why "more or less"? In Scarth and Jackson's work, the axiom is more accurately stated as: fiscal policy should allow future generations a higher level of public services, without an increase in tax rates, if those generations face a decline in average living standards due to changing demographics. See Scarth and Jackson (1997).

Bibliography

Abel, A., N.G. Mankiw, L. Summers, and R. Zeckhauser. 1989. "Assessing Dynamic Efficiency: Theory and Evidence." *Review of Economic Studies* 56:1-19.

Aiyagari, R., and E.R. McGrattan. 1998. "The Optimum Quantity of Debt." *Journal of Monetary Economics* 42:447-69.

Barro, R. 1974. "Are Government Bonds Net Wealth?" *Journal of Political Economy* 82:1095-117.

James, S., and P. Karam. 2001. "The Role of Government Debt in a World of Incomplete Financial Markets." Department of Finance Working Paper no. 2001-01. Ottawa: Department of Finance.

Ok, E., and L. Kockesen. 2000. "Negatively Interdependent Preferences." *Social Choice and Welfare* 17:533-58.

Scarth, W., and H. Jackson. 1997. "The Target Debt-to-GDP Ratio: How Big Should It be? And How Quickly Should We Approach It?" In *Fiscal Targets and Economic Growth*, ed. T. Courchene and T. Wilson. Kingston: The John Deutsch Institute for the Study of Economic Policy, Queen's University, pp. 271-95.

4

does the debt matter?

David Johnson

Introduction

What should Canada do about government deficits and debts over the next 10 years? Answering this question requires that we understand how public deficits and debts affect the Canadian economy. The traditional answer is that deficits "crowd out" that is, reduce, the accumulation of new physical capital and net foreign assets of Canadians. When government deficits are large, Canadians can save by holding newly-issued government debt, which means they may reduce their savings in other forms, whether new physical capital or net foreign assets. If government deficits have this effect, then a larger government deficit means that Canada's capital stock could be lower than it would be otherwise. It is much more likely, as I will show, that the more important effect of government deficits in Canada is that Canadian net debts to foreigners are larger than they would otherwise be. In either case, the country suffers a substantial economic cost as a result of the decision to finance government spending with a deficit. This is the traditional reason to be concerned about government deficits.

The nontraditional answer, which is actually quite an old answer, is known as *Ricardian equivalence* (or RE), after David Ricardo (1772-1823), the great English economist who first proposed it. Ricardian equivalence was given its modern revival by Harvard University's Robert Barro (see Barro 1974). In the nontraditional RE world, it does not matter whether government spending is financed with a deficit or by taxes. The effects of a given course of real government spending now and in the future are the same no matter how that spending is financed. There is no crowding out. There is no reduction in the physical capital stock. There is no reduction in the net claims of Canadians on foreigners or the net claims of foreigners on Canadians. The choice between financing a given amount of government expenditure with debt or with taxes simply does not matter. This is a radical conclusion. A larger government debt does not matter. If we still wanted to have this conference, we would have to discuss only the optimal size of the government sector. Fortunately for the conference organizers and participants, although there is a logic to Ricardian equivalence that cannot be faulted, and although the idea itself has had some influence on government financial policy in the last 25 years, there are both theoretical and empirical grounds for believing that RE does not hold and that therefore the choice between tax finance and deficit finance did have and will continue to have important consequences for the Canadian economy.

Because RE does not hold for Canada, the deficits that Canadian governments ran over the last quarter of the twentieth century did impose large costs on the Canadian economy. I calculate these costs as ranging between 3 and 10 percent of gross domestic product (GDP). Of course, the fact that deficits were costly does not necessarily mean that running them must have been a bad policy choice. If future real incomes had been expected to grow rapidly in the last 25 years and then did so, possibly because lots of capital formation was taking place, then it may well have made sense to borrow from foreigners and consume against these higher expected future incomes as the capital formation took place. But, in fact, the large government deficits incurred in Canada between 1975 and 1996 did *not* coincide with a period of exceptionally rapid capital formation. It therefore seems unlikely that the public debt and increased foreign debt accumulated in the last quarter of the twentieth century reflected reasonable expectations of higher future incomes from this source.

Borrowing may also make sense if for some reason today's production and income are temporarily low. As households, we often borrow when we regard our current income as being temporarily low. As a nation we might reasonably decide to do the same. Governments might do some of that international borrowing on our behalf. But a "temporary" reduction in income can hardly explain why our governments ran deficits over two full decades. I conclude that the deficits incurred from 1975 to 1996 *did* reduce the future consumption opportunities of Canadians and that it is important to measure that cost.

How do I apply this reasoning to future debt policy? In my view, there is no compelling reason to expect the exceptionally rapid growth in real incomes in the first two decades of the new millennium that would justify a great deal of borrowing by governments in the next five years. If our governments did choose to return to the strategy of running large deficits, it is very likely that would reduce the future consumption opportunities of Canadians. Calculations that I make in the final section of the paper suggest that an increase in the ratio of government debt to GDP would not be a wise policy choice for the next decade. We continue to be constrained by the accumulation of past debts.

The paper proceeds in several stages. The next section elaborates the intuition of crowding-out in a "closed economy," one that has no economic interactions with other countries. In the real world, outside North Korea, perhaps, there are not any truly closed economies. But the closed-economy model provides a useful base case. The third section looks at the evidence for a connection between government deficits and consumption spending, which is the closed-economy test for whether or not Ricardian equivalence holds. Section four introduces a foreign sector into the discussion and the following section looks at evidence for the correlation between government deficits and current account deficits. This correlation is the open-economy test for whether or not Ricardian equivalence holds. I read the evidence as being against the validity of Ricardian equivalence. Section six describes what would happen if a "debt fairy" visited Canada and eliminated all the debt accumulated by our governments in the 1975-96 period: the effect would be an increase in gross national product (GNP) of between 3 and 10 percent. Section seven provides a brief summing-up on the RE issue. The final section tries to answer the question posed by this conference: What level of public debt should we aim for in Canada? In my view, we should aim for a slightly lower public debt than we have now. In this sense, the debt war continues.

Government Debt in a Closed Economy

Let's begin by thinking for a moment about a "closed" economy, one in which there is no trade with or borrowing from or lending to the outside world. This obviously is not true of Canada but it does help fix some ideas. The fundamental macroeconomic equation in a closed economy, familiar to all first-year economics students, is $Y = C + I + G$. This equation means that Y, national income and/or national output, the two are equal, is equal to consumption (C), plus investment (I), plus government spending (G). National output, Y, is the total value of newly-produced goods and services. Since the act of producing output is what gives people their incomes, whether in the form of wages or profits, the total output produced in a country is also the total income earned in a country. In the short run, if people decide to buy less than is produced, the economy may contract as goods go without buyers. In this paper I am less concerned with short-term macroeconomic fluctuations of this sort than with longer-run considerations, so I will ignore such contractions and look only at an economy that operates at full employment. When I look at the data, I use five-year averages so as to represent full employment years.[1]

$Y = C + I + G$ says that there are three things that can happen to newly-produced goods and services. They can be consumed; they can be invested (used to create new physical capital), or they can be purchased by the government. With output always at full employment, if one of these three activities is to be increased, either or both of the other two must decline. For instance, if people decide to consume a higher proportion of current output, either investment, I, or government spending, G, or some combination of the two must decline as a proportion of output. Recall the central problem in this paper and in the conference: What is the effect of the government's decision to finance *a given amount of public spending* by running a deficit rather than by raising taxes? In the context of this question it is only reasonable to assume that, G, government spending on goods and services, remains fixed. How the "crowding-out" of private investment might take place begins to become clear. If deficit spending is going to crowd-out private investment, then in a closed economy it has to do so by somehow inducing consumers to consume more.

Why might a government deficit increase consumer spending? That they will cause people to spend more is often the very rationale for deficits. Give people a tax break, argue the proponents of stimulative tax cuts, and they will spend more. Since this argument is so familiar in politics and the press, perhaps the better question is: Why should we suppose that deficit spending would *not* induce people to consume more? After all, if people get a tax break, won't they spend at least part of it? This is where Ricardo (and later Barro) come in. Like most economists, Ricardo believed that people are forward-looking. They make plans. If so, then they might "see through" the deficit spending. Suppose people have at least a rough idea both of what their future income is going to be and of how they would like to spend it. They know that if the government borrows money now in order to encourage them to spend, it will have to tax them more later in order to pay back what it has borrowed. Their lifetime income is therefore largely unaffected by the government's decision to run a deficit now. So why, they might ask themselves, should they change the way they want to consume now? If they do take that view, their response to the tax cut and the increased deficit is clear: they will not increase their consumption as a result of any tax cut the government provides but will instead save the extra disposable income to pay for the taxes in the future. But if their consumption does not change, that is if they do save all of the tax cut, then in the $Y = C + I + G$ equation, C remains constant. And recall that G, government spending on goods and services, is also constant by assumption. But with both C and G constant, investment (I) must be constant, too. Crowding-out does not take place.

Whether you think crowding-out will happen therefore depends in part on whether you think people do take the long view of their lives and plan consumption over their lifetime in this way. They clearly do, at least to a certain extent: many Canadians do save for retirement. So economists, in thinking of ways in which RE may *not* hold, have tended to focus on factors that may force people off their planned consumption paths and cause them to consume most or even all of the tax cut. The behaviour of two specific types of households has been emphasized.

The first type of household would die before the government repays its debt and does not care that the repayment and servicing of debt may change the real consumption opportunities of its descendants (if it has any). In fact, although economists have spent some time studying the bequest motives of individual households, decisive research results on this question have proved elusive. There is therefore little guidance from this direction on whether RE holds.

The second type of household that would spend the whole tax cut is a "liquidity-constrained" (LC) household. LC households expect to earn a higher income in the future but cannot borrow against that future income. LC households tend to be young. These households would like to borrow against their future labour income to consume now. But loans that use future labour income as collateral are usually hard to get. It is very hard for lenders to identify which potential borrowers will not repay. Such loan markets simply do not function.[2] Most household loans of significant size, car loans and mortgages, therefore require physical collateral.

Most of us have been liquidity constrained at one time or another in our lives. If an LC household receives a tax cut now, it is optimal for that household to spend all the tax cut now, increasing its consumption by the full amount of the cut. If LC households form a substantial part of society, then a tax cut will increase aggregate consumption and Ricardian equivalence does not hold. A great deal of aggregate and individual evidence, briefly discussed in the next section, suggests that in fact a substantial fraction of households are liquidity constrained.

The Evidence on RE and Liquidity Constraints Relating to Consumption Decisions

Since Barro (1974) reintroduced and emphasized the idea of Ricardian equivalence, a large literature testing its validity has emerged. Unfortunately, this is one case where economists live up to their reputation of always disagreeing. Thus, in his survey of this literature, Seater writes: "despite its nearly certain invalidity as a literal description of the role of public debt in the economy,

Ricardian equivalence holds as a close approximation" (1993, 143). While in his survey, Bernheim writes that "the Ricardian paradigm should be dismissed on theoretical grounds, as well as on the basis of indirect behavioural evidence. Much of the existing macroeconomic evidence, although weak, also supports the view that deficits have real effects" (1989, 71). Rather than recite these and other surveys, I review the evidence most pertinent to the Canadian situation.[3]

In a closed economy, as we have seen, higher government deficits may crowd out private investment by inducing people to consume more. One way of testing for Ricardian equivalence is therefore to see if an increase in government debt is associated with a rise in consumption. Estimating statistical relationships between consumption and various measures of income and wealth has a long history in macroeconomics. However, using these relationships to test for RE has proved very difficult. The thought-experiment presented in the previous section did only one thing: it shifted the government from tax to debt finance in isolation. In reality, an isolated change like that almost never takes place. Rather, simultaneous changes in income, wealth, expected future income, government spending, expected government spending and the stock of government bonds held by households are going on all the time. In a complex world, sorting out the single effect required to establish the validity or nonvalidity of RE does not seem possible. Cardia (1997) showed this problem very clearly. She created datasets using four artificial economies. In one of her economies, RE was valid, in three others it was not. After running a government deficit in each of the four economies to generate data series on the key variables in question, she then estimated the conventional relationships between consumption, income, wealth and household holdings of government and foreign assets. Even in this artificial world she was unable to confirm statistically which economy was the RE economy. Ordinary variations in income, and human and financial wealth simply swamped the variation in the stock of government debt. Conclusion? If it is hard to draw definitive inferences about the RE in artificial economies, it will be even more difficult in real-world economies.

That has not stopped people from trying, however. In a study of 19 countries, including Canada, Evans (1993) found that government bonds were net wealth: in other words, people did not fully take into account that new government bonds imply higher future taxes, but instead treated the government's decision to bond-finance its expenditures as representing a net increase in their lifetime income. On the other hand, Evans and Hasan (1994) (the same Evans!) looked at the Canadian data in greater detail and concluded that government bonds are *not* net wealth: people do *not* treat the wealth they hold in government bonds as a real addition to their wealth but instead evidently understand that its existence imposes future obligations on them. As a result, they do not increase their consumption in the same way as they would if there were no such obligation. This mix of results seems to confirm Cardia's basic point: direct decisive results on the validity of RE using the consumption function approach are not possible.

Several other studies of Canadian consumption behaviour provide substantial indirect evidence against RE. Both Macklem (1993) and Catiou (2002) estimate long-run relationships between consumption and wealth, using very careful definitions of wealth in both its "human capital" (i.e., current and future earning-power) and physical- and financial-capital forms. Although, strictly speaking, neither Macklem nor Catiou can decisively distinguish the RE and non-RE cases, a key result in both studies is that when long-run relationships between consumption and very carefully specified measures of wealth are estimated, the relationships estimated in both studies find a substantial role for current dis-posable income in the determination of consumption. This suggests strongly that liquidity constraints are important in Canada. Other studies by Wirtjanto (1996), Ostergaard, Sorensen and Yosha (2002) and Bacchetta and Gerlach (1997) also find that liquidity constraints play an important role in Canadian consumption decisions. Finally, Bernheim (1988) looks at data averaged over 12-year periods in a panel of countries (including Canada) and finds a rela-tionship between increases in consumption and government deficits.

I conclude that the better-quality estimates of consumption behaviour sug-gest that liquidity constraints are important in Canada and that, contrary to what Ricardian equivalence would predict, there is substantial evidence that government bonds are net wealth and do affect consumption decisions.[4]

The Effects of Increased Government Debt in an Open Economy

Of course, Canada is not a closed economy. On the contrary, it is one of the world's most open economies: goods, services, capital and to a lesser extent labour flow freely between it and many other economies. How does the effect of government debt change when we consider an economy in which trading with, borrowing from and lending to foreigners is possible? The most obvious change is in the basic macroeconomic equation, which now becomes $Y = C + I + G + (X - M)$, where Y, C, I and G are as before but X is our exports of goods and services and M our imports of goods and services. The difference between the two, $(X - M)$, is our net exports and the equation now says that we can now do four things with our output: consume it, invest it, have the government buy it, or sell it to people in other countries. If we sell more to foreigners than we buy from them, then our output will exceed $C + I + G$ (our own domestic use of this output), while if the reverse is true, our use of output, $C + I + G$, will exceed our production of output, Y. It is easy to understand how we could produce more output than we use. But how can we use more output than we produce? The answer is: by importing more than we export.

How does this new possible source and use of goods and services change our thinking about crowding-out and the possible effect of government deficits? Suppose, as before, that the government decides to finance a given level of public spending, G, by issuing debt rather than raising taxes. In a closed economy, if debt finance causes people to consume more, that is, causes C to rise, then, with G constant by assumption, investment (I) has to fall: the output that goes into greater consumption has to come from somewhere and in a closed economy the only other place it can come from is I, investment.

But in an open economy, that is no longer the case. If G is constant and the increase in government debt causes people to want to consume more, there are now two possibilities: either investment can fall (as before) or people can consume more *foreign* output. We assume, as in the closed-economy case, that domestic output is always at full employment and therefore cannot be increased. But the domestic *use* of resources can increase beyond what is produced at home. Canadians can now buy the extra goods we want from foreigners. Buying more from foreigners without selling any more to them means that X stays constant but M rises. Our trade surplus (X – M) will fall. Or if our trade surplus was negative to begin with, that is, we were running a "trade deficit," then that trade deficit will rise. The customary reference in the literature is to the "twin deficits" problem. If the government increases its fiscal deficit, and if people respond in a non-Ricardian way by increasing their consumption, then the result will be a trade deficit, or a greater trade deficit, if the country was already running a deficit. Thus, all else being equal, a correlation between fiscal deficits and trade deficits can be taken as evidence that Ricardian equivalence does not hold.

An important question remains, however. If domestic investment is unchanged, how is that investment financed? The government cannot be lending to domestic investors, since it is operating with a deficit and borrowing itself. Domestic consumers have increased their consumption as a result of the government's deficit, which means they have reduced their saving. In the closed economy, as we have seen, people's decision to save less/consume more is what forced domestic investment to decline. But in the open economy investment need not decline. If not, how does the investment get financed? In an open economy Canadians who need loans can borrow from foreigners. Thus, a second consequence of the government's running a deficit is that domestic investors may have to raise funds in other countries. This increases the foreign debts of Canadians. (Running a greater trade deficit may also have increased Canadians' foreign debts if they financed increased imports with foreign loans.)

In a closed economy in which Ricardian equivalence did not hold, the cost of government debt was reduced investment. In an open economy in which RE does not hold, investment is maintained but it is financed by foreign borrowing. Any increase in consumption associated with the increased government deficit is financed by foreign borrowing. But there is no free lunch. The cost of such foreign borrowing is the interest to be paid to foreigners in the future. Part of the future output of Canada must now be shared with foreigners. Borrowing today does allow access to more resources than the borrowing country is currently producing, but it requires that at some time in the future the borrowing country produces more resources than it uses. This must occur so that the interest on foreign debt is paid. There are times when that is a sensible trade-off. If a young country with a small population has many more good investment opportunities (sometimes because of its natural resources) than it can finance with its own savings, then borrowing to undertake them may be very wise. But if a mature country borrows merely to increase its current consumption beyond its productive capacity, that may not be so wise. Over the past century and a half, Canada has been one of the largest borrowers in international financial markets. We have typically spent more domestically than we have produced ourselves. That was not necessarily a bad thing. Foreign borrowing allowed us to build up the country and its wealth at a time when the resources we ourselves were generating would not have been adequate to the task. But there is always the possibility that even a very good thing can be carried too far.

Whether or not the foreign borrowing that government deficits cause is wise, the symptom they produce is a deterioration in the trade balance, as the borrowing country uses more goods and services than it produces. Afterwards there is a continuing flow of interest payments as a result of the foreign loans. Both the trade balance and net interest payments are part of the "current account" of a country's international balance of payments (as opposed to the "capital account," which, among other capital transactions, records loans when they are taken out or paid back). If Ricardian equivalence does not hold, both the trade balance and interest flows will turn toward negative values as a country's government borrows. A useful test of whether RE does or does not hold is therefore to ask whether an increase in the government's deficit led to an increase in the current account deficit. Are the government deficit and the current account deficit twins?

The Canadian Evidence on Twin Deficits

The conclusion of the last section was that in a small, open economy investment is unlikely to fall significantly when the government deficit is increased.

Thus, most of any increase in consumption associated with an increase in the government deficit will be financed by borrowing from foreigners. As a result, the main cost of today's government deficit is the future service and repayment of the increase in foreign debts caused by that government deficit. An increase in government deficits should be associated with an increase in current account deficits. This seems a strong and very intuitive result, and much effort was expended looking for it during the 1980s when the Reagan administration's policies seemed to create a large buildup of both US government debt and US international debt. The Canadian version of this phenomenon was also studied intensively. Unfortunately, as in the case of the simple consumption relationships, the most common methodology (looking for correlations in short-run data) yields results that are difficult to interpret. Amirkhalkhali et al. (1996) obtain no consistent results linking the budget deficit to the current account deficit in Canada, while studies of the US data in the short run yield a wide variety of results. Examples of US studies include Darrat (1988), Abell (1990) and Enders and Lee (1990).

On the other hand, relationships estimated with more structure over longer time horizons do yield more conclusive and more useful results. Normandin (1999) concluded that in Canada a budget deficit of $1 leads to an increase in the current account deficit of between 19 and 67 cents. Bernheim (1988) found that a budget deficit increased the current account deficit by approximately 30 cents per dollar of budget deficit. Finally, in a series of studies investigating the interaction between the accumulation of government debt, foreign debt and consumption (Johnson 1986a, b, 1994), I showed that treating government bonds as net wealth is more consistent with Canadian consumption behaviour than excluding government bonds from measures of net wealth. In other words, Ricardian equivalence does not hold. In this framework, a government deficit indirectly leads to a current account deficit. My various papers on this subject also found a role for liquidity constraints.[5] In my view, therefore, studies that either use a more structured model of consumption or focus on the long-run rather than short-run effects of budget deficits provide convincing evidence that Ricardian equivalence does not hold. My reading of the RE literature accords with Bernheim's (1989) summary statement: "the Ricardian paradigm should be dismissed on theoretical grounds, as well as on the basis of indirect behavioural evidence." There are strong theoretical reasons and good quality empirical evidence that reject Ricardian equivalence.

How are we to interpret descriptive data on government debts and current account deficits in Canada from 1962 to 2001 when RE does not hold? Tables 1 and 2 present such data. Table 2 makes a simple point, the source of Canadian deficits after 1977 was primarily federal. Only in the period from 1992–96 were provincial deficits large as a share of GNP. In both table 1 and table 2, the data are presented as shares of GNP, averaged over five-year periods to focus on longer-run, full-employment relationships. In both tables the key variable, the current account deficit, appears in the right-hand column. Although this deficit was relatively large both from 1972 to 1981 and from 1987 to 1996, these periods are in fact quite different. A very clear boom in private investment, particularly non-housing investment, occurs from 1977 to 1981. The current account deficit from 1977 to 1981 therefore appears to be a "good" current account deficit, that is, a deficit associated with the smoothing of consumption based on an antici-pated increase in future production as more capital was installed in Canada. In the next five years, 1982–86, there is both a sharp decline in the current account deficit and a sharp decline in investment activity. But when the current account deficit grows again from 1987 to 1996 there is no corresponding increase in investment activity. This brief look at the data suggests that while fluctuations in private-sector investment do, as predicted by theory, explain some of the fluctuations in the current account deficit, they do not provide a complete explanation. Because public sector capital formation declines throughout the period, the large government deficits after 1977 are not associated with instal-lation of new physical capital by the government sector.

As we have seen, when the government deficit increases in a small, open economy and Ricardian equivalence does *not* hold, an increase in consumption will be associated with an increase in the current account deficit. This looks quite consistent with the data in tables 1 and 2. The period 1977–96 is charac-terized both by large government deficits and by an increase in the share of consumption in GNP. As table 1 shows, the share of government spending on goods and services also rises slightly. If RE held, households should be ignoring government deficits and paying much more attention to the increase in the share of government spending as a measure of the current and expected real use of resources by the public sector. The increase in government spending, if per-ceived as permanent, should *reduce* consumption in most models where Ricardian equivalence holds. Instead, both consumption and the current account deficit *increase* when the government deficit increases.

Figure 1 graphs the association between government deficits and current account deficits, which looks quite strong, particularly after 1976. The turn-around in both deficits after 1996 is very striking. Governments in Canada moved from a deficit of 6 percent of GNP over the years 1992–96 to a surplus of 1.5 percent of GNP in 1997-2001. The largest swing was at the federal level, but the provinces also returned to surplus. At the same time, the current account moved from a deficit of 2 percent of GNP to a surplus of 0.6 percent of GNP. Moreover, the current account surplus turned positive in this period even

Table 1

The Uses of GNP in Canada, Five-Year Averages, 1962-2001 (percentages)

Period	Consumption	Investment	Of Which: Nonhousing	Government	Of Which: Capital	Net Exports	Current Account Deficit
1962–66	60.9	19.7	12.7	20.9	4.7	0.3	2.3
1967–71	57.7	18.8	12.5	24.0	4.4	1.3	1.4
1972–76	55.2	21.0	12.9	25.0	3.7	0	3.1
1977–81	55.4	21.3	14.2	25.3	3.1	0.7	3.5
1982–86	56.6	17.9	12.8	26.0	3.0	2.9	1.0
1987–91	58.2	19.4	12.5	25.5	2.9	0.3	3.7
1992–96	60.1	16.2	10.8	25.9	2.8	1.7	2.0
1997–01	58.8	18.5	13.2	21.9	2.4	3.6	-0.6

Source: Cansim II: Table 380017.

Table 2

Table 2: Canada's Government Deficits, Five-Year Averages, 1962-2001 (percent of GNP)

Period	Government Deficit: All Sectors	Federal	Provincial	Local	CPP/QPP	Current Account Deficit
1962–66	-1.9	0.7	-1.8	-0.6	—	2.3
1967–71	-2.5	0.3	-1.3	-0.1	-1.3	1.4
1972–76	-0.9	1.0	-0.8	0	-1.1	3.1
1977–81	2.2	3.8	-0.4	-0.2	-1.0	3.5
1982–86	6.0	5.9	1.1	-0.2	-0.8	1.0
1987–91	4.5	4.4	0.9	-0.5	-0.3	3.7
1992–96	6.0	4.3	2.1	-0.5	0.1	2.0
1997–01	-1.5	-0.6	-0.3	-0.4	-0.2	-0.6

Source: Cansim II, Table 380002. All governments V647166, federal government V647208, provincial governments V647243, local governments V647275, Canada Pension Plan V647302, Quebec Pension Plan, V647310. Cansim II, Table 3760001, V113713.

Figure 1

The Twin Deficits in Canada, 1961–2001

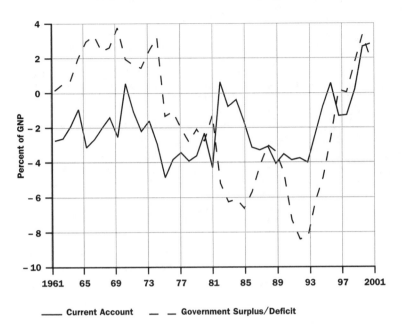

Percent of GNP

1961 65 69 73 77 81 85 89 93 97 2001

——— Current Account — — Government Surplus/Deficit

as private sector physical investment activity recovered sharply. As a share of GNP, consumption declined very markedly as tax finance was substituted for debt finance. All of these events are more consistent with a world in which Ricardian equivalence does not hold than one in which it does.

Table 3 presents some data on Canada's foreign indebtedness. The first column shows net foreign debt as a percent of GNP, averaged over five-year periods. Net foreign debt peaked in 1996, immediately after the long period of government deficits ended. The relationship between foreign debt and government deficits is shown in figure 2. It has the pattern you would expect to find when large government deficits crowd out the accumulation of foreign assets or when nonresidents buy the government's bonds directly. The middle column of table 3 shows how the liabilities of the government sector held directly by nonresidents rose rapidly from 1977 to 1996. Government deficits were partly financed with bonds sold directly to nonresidents while Canadians maintained or even increased their consumption. The third column of table 3 shows how the large increase in international debts led to a higher proportion of Canadian output being used to service this debt.[6] Finally as government deficits turn to surpluses, the process reverses itself from 1997 to 2001. Foreign indebtedness falls and the proportion of GDP used to service foreign debt falls. The current account surplus begins to repay foreign debts.

Table 3

Canada's Foreign Debts, Five-Year Averages, 1962–2001
(percent of GNP)

Period	Net Foreign Debt of All Canadians	Government Liabilities Held by Nonresidents	GDP-GNP Net Investment Income Earned by Foreigners
1962–66	40.0	9.1	1.73
1967–71	35.4	9.5	1.48
1972–76	30.0	7.7	1.80
1977–81	36.3	9.0	3.36
1982–86	37.3	12.2	3.40
1987–91	39.2	20.1	3.33
1992–96	43.3	30.5	3.38
1997–01	26.5	24.0	2.23

Source: Cansim II, Table 3760037, Table 3760040, Table 3800030.

Taken as a whole, the data in tables 1, 2 and 3 and figures 1 and 2 suggest very strongly that over the last four decades Canadian government deficits did lead to larger current account deficits. This increased the proportion of Canadian production that was used to service foreign debts and that is the most important cost of the government deficits in Canada.

A "Debt Fairy" Comes to Canada

What might Canada have looked like had its governments not run large deficits for the two decades following 1975? In a 1994 paper, the American economists Laurence Ball and Gregory Mankiw imagined that a debt fairy visited the United States and was able to instantly transform the existing stock of government debt into an increase in the physical capital stock. In the exercise described below, I imagine that the same debt fairy visits Canada in 1997 and replaces the increase in government liabilities issued from 1975 to 1996 with foreign assets held by Canadian residents. In the face of considerable uncertainty about how to measure the increase in government liabilities over this period, I perform the experiment twice.

Table 4 presents a very broad measure of government-sector liabilities from the system of national accounts. Total liabilities of all governments increased from $114.2 billion at the end of 1975 to $1,147.9 billion at the end of 1996, an increase of $1,033.7 billion. Canada's net international debts at the end of 1996 were $311.4 billion. In 1997, $27.7 billion was spent by Canadians to service their net foreign debts. If the debt fairy replaced all of the increase in the liabilities of

Figure 2

Net Foreign Debt and Government Deficits, 1961–2001
(percent of GNP)

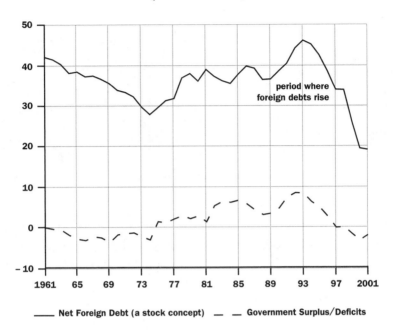

___ Net Foreign Debt (a stock concept)   _ _ Government Surplus/Deficits

the government sector with foreign assets, then Canada's net international debts of $311.4 billion in 1996 would have become net international assets of $722.3 billion. Using simple proportionality, Canada's debt service of $27.7 billion would have become net foreign investment earnings of $64.2 billion, a turn-around that would have increased Canada's 1997 GNP by 10.4 percent. In this extreme case, all of the increase in government liabilities become foreign assets when the debt fairy visits. However, the estimates discussed above of the increase in the current account deficit per dollar of budget deficit incurred were not one-for-one; rather, they ranged between 30 and 50 percent.[7] If a one-dollar increase in the budget deficit led to only a 50-cent increase in the current account deficit, the debt-fairy visit would still see Canada's net foreign indebtedness transformed into net foreign assets, although our GNP would now exceed our GDP by 2 per-cent rather than 7 percent. Rather than spending more time on variants of this calculation, table 5 undertakes similar calculations with a different measure of the increase in government liabilities. Table 5 records only marketable debt issued by governments. These are bonds and bills issued by governments and not held by the Canada Pension Plan, the Quebec Pension Plan or the Bank of Canada. The increase in this form of government debt from 1975 to 1996 is $665.1 billion,

Table 4

Government Liabilities by Issuer and Holder, 1975 and 1996
($ billions)

	1975		1996	
	Domestic	**Foreign**	**Domestic**	**Foreign**
Federal Total Liabilities	57.9	0.7	522.1	120.1
Provinces Total Liabilities	30.4	5.9	330.5	120.3
Municipal Total Liabilities	16.6	2.7	48.7	6.2

Sources: Cansim II, Tables 3780004, 3760040: V34441, V236443, V34517, V236450, V34550, V236457.

quite a bit less than the increase in total liabilities considered in table 4. Of that $665.1 billion, $236.2 billion is purchased directly by nonresidents. If the debt fairy transforms all of the increase in the marketable debts of governments into net foreign assets of Canadians in 1997, then net foreign assets swing from about minus $300 billion to about plus $300 billion and GNP rises by 7 percent. If only one-half of the increase in marketable debt were transformed into additional foreign assets, then net foreign debts would be about zero and GDP and GNP would be quite similar. This amounts to a 3 percent increase in GNP in 1997.

Summing up their results for the debt fairy's visit to the United States, Ball and Mankiw (1995) concluded that, in the end, the effects of the debt had not been very large. In the same way, in the Canadian case even a very large change in the stock of international debts makes quite a small change in the flow of resources used to service that debt or in the incomes earned from those assets, while the estimates of the increase in GNP that would have occurred had governments not incurred the large deficits from 1975 to 1996 range from 3 to 10 percentage points. As Ball and Mankiw (ibid.) note, three percentage points of GNP is about two years of normal GNP growth, not a huge amount. On the other hand, even very small percentages of a very large absolute number can be important and it is best not to forget that GNP, even Canadian GNP, is a large absolute number. It may therefore be more helpful to consider the effects on a per capita basis. In 1997, moving GNP to equality with GDP (a modest estimate of the effects of the debt-fairy visit) raises per capita incomes by $909. For a family of four, this is $3,636, or $303 per month, which most Canadians would probably regard as a substantial amount of money. Moreover, it is a conservative estimate of the costs of deficits to Canadians.

Table 5

Marketable Government Liabilities by Issuer and Holder, 1975 and 1996 ($ billions)

	1975		1996	
	Domestic	**Foreign**	**Domestic**	**Foreign**
Federal Total	28.5	0.9	313.6	120.1
Provinces	11.8	6.6	131.1	120.3
Municipal	15.4	2.7	39.9	6.0

Sources: Cansim II, Tables 3780004, 3760040.

A Summing-Up on RE and the Effects of Government Deficits

There is a clear link between national savings and the current account deficit. If the use of resources by Canadians exceeds their income, then foreign borrowing must make up the difference. Having access to foreign capital can be very useful. During investment booms, foreign borrowing allows the installation of new capital without a reduction in consumption. However, if government deficits lead to consumption booms, then the increase in consumption also generates an increase in foreign borrowing, one that must be repaid without an increase in production. This occurs when Ricardian equivalence does not hold and government deficits therefore crowd out the accumulation of foreign assets by Canadians. The long period of government deficits from 1975 to 1996 was associated with current account deficits. Reasonable estimates suggest that if Canada's governments had not run deficits over this period, in 1997 Canadians' incomes would have been between 3 and 10 percent higher. Canada would have had less foreign indebtedness and would have devoted less of its national output to paying interest on its foreign debts. In fact, it seems very likely that without the large government deficits of the 1980s and early 1990s, Canadians would have been net holders of foreign assets today and would be earning a substantial income from those assets. This is the most important cost of our two decades of deficits.

What to Do in the Next Ten Years about Debt and Deficits?

The question asked at this conference is "Is the debt war over?" This question can be interpreted in a variety of ways: Should Canadian governments continue to run surpluses and lower the ratio of national debt to GDP rapidly? Should they run balanced budgets and allow growth to reduce the debt-to-GDP ratio? Or should we return to deficits? In this last section, I try to understand why conference participants had some difficulty both answering these questions and identifying reasons from their particular choices.

In this paper, I have tried to identify the cost of previous deficits with some precision. I can therefore state that for every dollar of government surpluses over the next decade, it seems likely that Canada's net foreign assets will rise by between 30 and 50 cents. Over time, this will increase the resources available to Canadians. We will pay less interest on foreign debts or perhaps even earn interest on foreign assets. However, this calculation of the costs of deficits still does not lead to a clear answer to the question: What is the appropriate target for the ratio of government debt to GDP? A rather weak answer is to point out that there is some evidence that Canadians in a global economy wish to acquire more net foreign assets. A policy of continued government surpluses would aid in achieving that goal. But can any stronger statement be made?

I am willing to be a little bolder. I believe there is a consensus in Canadian society and (in all similar countries) that the public sector plays an important role in society. Justice, transport, the environment, defence are all public goods requiring resources for their provision. I also observe a consensus in favour of equality of opportunity, equality of access for medical care (at least for catastrophic care and likely far more), and some public provision of care for the elderly, the disabled and the temporarily unemployed. It is this kind of social spending that in fact dominates government provision of goods and services. In the G7 countries an average of 35 percent of GDP passes through the government sector, either as outlays or as revenue (*Fiscal Reference Tables*, Department of Finance, October 2002). The smallest government sector is in the United States (30 percent of GDP) and the largest is in France (48 percent of GDP). Canada lies in the middle. A tax system must exist to support this level of government activity. Any tax system must receive general support in order to function well. To give that support, taxpayers must believe they are receiving value for the taxes paid, that taxes are being used to create the goods and services associated with the public consensus. If governments are to manage about 35 percent of the economy, then in the long run about 35 percent of GDP must be raised as taxes. I will take as a "fact" that in Canada, 35 percent is the tax share of GDP Canadians will support.

From the 1960s to the early 1990s, the proportion of tax revenue used to service government debts steadily increased in Canada, from about 10 percent to about 20 percent of revenue. If 20 percent of tax revenue services public debt, there is a perception, which is at least partly true, that taxes are being raised primarily to service existing debt rather than to operate the public institutions that citizens want to see work effectively. As more and more of the revenue base services the debt, the actual provision of government goods and services falls and there is less and less support for the tax system. If the fiscal situation is unstable, then in the logical extreme, the possibility exists that taxes are raised *only* to service past government debts, and there are no public services. There would be no support for such a fiscal system. This did not occur in Canada in the 1980s and 1990s, but it was the underlying threat. It is to the credit of Finance Minister Paul Martin that he recognized that such a situation was possible and was able to convince Canadians that short-term pain was necessary to restore the country to a fiscal system in which stability and broad public support were possible. I conclude from the experience of the 1990s that when 20 percent of revenue is used to service debt, the proportion of debt service is too high to create general support for the kind of public sector that Canadians want.

How does this comment help us understand the large variation in the conference participants' targets for the debt-to-GDP ratio? It can be used to "back out" a prudent target for the debt-to-GDP ratio. Table 6 presents a simplistic calculation of various "steady-state" or target debt-to-GDP ratios. The government is assumed to divert 35 percent of GDP through both its revenue and expenditure streams. Each row of table 6 is an assumption about the acceptable percentage of that 35 percent that can be used to service debt. Each column of table 6 represents a nominal interest rate – nominal interest rates being what determines the interest payments that pass through the government's books. The nine values in the cells of the table are the steady-state ratios of government debt to GDP that occur at that nominal interest rate and that percentage of government spending used as interest to service the debt. The inflation component of the nominal interest rate would, in this setting, allow the government to run a nominal deficit equal to the stock of debt multiplied by the rate of inflation so that the ratio of debt-to-GDP remained the same. Readers need to use their own judgement as to the split of the nominal interest rates in the table between real and nominal components. It is the large variation in feasible or target debt-to-GDP ratios that is so striking to me. I think this variation is part of the reason for the wide variation in our answers to the question: What is an appropriate target ratio of debt-to-GDP? In my mind, the target ratio of debt-to-GDP allows the government to operate the desired public sector with a tax system that is generally supported. But reasonable people will have quite different opinions on both the row and column values. Small variations in judgement about the long-term equilibrium nominal interest rate will generate large variations in the target debt-to-GDP ratio. Small variations in perception of the maximum percentage of government revenue that can safely be diverted to debt service will generate large variations in the ratio of debt-to-GDP.

Table 6

Illustrative Calculations of a Steady-State Debt-to-GDP Ratio Consistent with Public Support of the Tax System

Assumed Debt Service as	Nominal Interest Rate Assumption		
a Percent of Revenues	2%	4%	6%
10%	175.0	87.50	58.33
15%	262.5	131.25	87.50
20%	350.0	175.00	116.66

Source: The calculations assume that 35 percent of GDP is diverted through the government sector. The column is the percentage of that revenue used to pay interest on the debt. The row is the nominal interest rate paid on government debt. The nine cells in the centre of the table are the debt-to-GDP ratios in steady state for the values in the associated row and column.

What do these calculations imply for policy over the next decade? The gross debt of all Canadian governments peaked in 1995 at 99.9 percent of GDP and has since dropped rapidly to 83.2 percent of GDP in 2001. Interest payments are now about 15 percent of the total revenues of all governments. This change took place with considerable agonizing about the consensus on the role of government in society and in the context of five years of relatively strong economic growth. A similar change, from an all-government debt-to-GDP ratio of 80 percent to a debt-to-GDP ratio of 60 percent over the next 5 to 10 years would leave the debt-to-GDP ratio below the debt-to-GDP ratio associated with all reasonable values of both the nominal interest rate and the percentage of tax revenue devoted to debt service. This is a very prudent strategy. My own personal beliefs lean to being sure that debt-to-GDP ratio is low enough so that we can be sure that the tax system receives strong public support. To ensure this situation comes to pass, it would be better to err on the side of caution than to push the envelope of a prudent debt-to-GDP ratio. A debt-to-GDP ratio of 60 percent would be very prudent. As a prudent person, this is a target level I would recommend. Such a target would free up the resources from the tax stream to carry out the tasks that Canadians want to see their governments perform. There is still work to be done to achieve this lower target for the ratio of government debt-to-GDP.

Notes

1. Using the full-employment case to present my arguments in the second section and fourth sections does NOT mean that I believe there was full employment in each and every year from 1961 to 2001. It does mean that I believe that large government deficits in Canada cannot be explained by a very prolonged period of less than full employment that persisted from 1976 to 1996.

2. Markets for student loans require government intervention to function. Lines of credit and credit card debt have limits set far below lifetime ability to repay. Neither removes liquidity constraints.

3. Other surveys are found in Bernheim (1987), Barro (1989), Leiderman and Blejer (1988), part of Ball and Mankiw (1995) and Elmendorf and Mankiw (1999). As mentioned in the introduction, in this section, I look at studies of "the consumption function," which are often used to test closed-economy predictions about crowding-out. Because Canada is not a closed economy, the two sections that follow look at both the theory and evidence of government deficits in the open economy. There is a third approach to testing the validity of the RE. Some researchers have looked for short-run effects of budget deficits on interest rates and exchange rates. The better work in the area tries to distinguish between the effect of expected and unexpected components of deficits on asset prices. This work is included in the surveys cited above. There are no decisive results.

4. In one further Canadian study of note, Mukhopadhyay (1994) takes the novel approach (for economists) of asking a random sample of consumer-taxpayers in Halifax if they pay attention to government deficits and government debt in making consumption-savings decisions. The answer was "no," which leads Mukhopadhyay to reject the validity of RE. Although economists often discount studies where such direct questions are asked, Mukhopadhyay's exercise provides us with a fascinating result.

5. It must be noted that Chen and Haug (1993), in a study similar to Normandin, do not find a relationship between the level of the government debt and the level of foreign debts.

6. I recognize that, with more inflation in the period from 1977 to 1992, there is an overstatement of debt service: part of nominal interest payments are in fact repayments of principal. However, a second peak in debt service at 3.38 percent of output occurs after inflation falls substantially in the period from 1992–97. This larger debt service is clearly associated with higher foreign debts.

7. It seems likely that the increased government deficits do crowd out some private capital formation as well. If private physical capital earns the same return as on foreign assets, the calculations will be similar.

Bibliography

Abell, J.D. 1990. "Twin Deficits During the 1980s: An Empirical Investigation." *Journal of Macroeconomics* 12:81-96.

Amirkhalkhali, S., A.A. Dar and S. Amirkhalkhali. 1996. "On the Dynamics of the Interrelationships between Fiscal Deficits and Some Important Macroeconomic Aggregates in Canada." *Canadian Journal of Economics* 29:S176-S180.

Bacchetta, P., and S. Gerlach. 1997. "Consumption and Credit Constraints: International Evidence." *Journal of Monetary Economics* 40:207-38.

Ball, L., and N.G. Mankiw. 1995. "What Do Budget Deficits Do?" In *Budget Deficits and Debt: Issues and Options*. A symposium sponsored by the Federal Reserve Bank of Kansas City.

Barro, R.J. 1974. "Are Government Bonds Net Wealth?" *Journal of Political Economy* 82:1095-117.

———. 1989. "The Ricardian Approach to Budget Deficits." *Journal of Economic Perspectives* 3:37-54.

Bernheim, B.D. 1987. "Ricardian Equivalence: An Evaluation of Theory and Evidence." In *NBER Macroeconomics Annual 1987*, ed. S. Fischer. Cambridge, MA: MIT Press.

———. 1988. "Budget Deficits and the Balance of Trade." In *Tax Policy and the Economy 2*, ed. L.H. Summers. Cambridge, MA: MIT Press.

———. 1989. "A Neoclassical Perspective on Budget Deficits." *Journal of Economic Perspectives* 3:55-72.

Cardia, E. 1997. "Replicating Ricardian Equivalence Tests with Simulated Series." *American Economic Review* 87:65-79.

Catiou, E. 2002. "Using Various Wealth Models to Explain Consumption in Canada: 1961-2001." Masters of Business Economics Major Research Paper. Waterloo, ON: Wilfrid Laurier University.

Chen, B., and A. Haug. 1993. "The Twin Deficits Hypothesis: Empirical Evidence for Canada." York University. Unpublished paper.

Darrat, A.F. 1988. "Structural Federal Deficits and Interest Rates: Some Causality and Cp-Integration Tests." *Southern Economic Journal* 56:752-59.

Elmendorf, D.W., and N.G. Mankiw. 1999. "Government Debt." In *Handbook of Macroeconomics*, ed. M. Woodford. Amsterdam: North-Holland.

Enders, W., and B.S. Lee. 1990. "Current Account and Budget Deficits: Twins or Distant Cousins?" *Review of Economics and Statistics* 72:373-81.

Evans, P. 1993. "Consumers are not Ricardian: Evidence from Nineteen Countries." *Economic Inquiry* 31:534-48.

Evans, P., and I. Hasan. 1994. "Are Consumers Ricardian? Evidence for Canada." *Quarterly Reveiw of Economics and Finance* 43:25-40.

Johnson, D. 1986a. "Are Government Bonds Net Wealth? Intertemporal Optimization and the Government Budget Constraint." *Journal of Macroeconomics* 8:435-53.

———. 1986b. "Consumption, Permanent Income, and Financial Wealth in Canada: Empirical Evidence on the Intertemporal Approach to the Current Account." *Canadian Journal of Economics* 19:189-206.

————. 1994. "Ricardian Equivalence: Assessing the Evidence for Canada." In *Deficit Reduction: What Pain, What Gain?* ed. W.B.P. Robson and W.M. Scarth. Toronto: C.D. Howe Institute.

Leiderman, L., and M.I. Blejer. 1988. "Modeling and Testing Ricardian Equivalence: A Survey." *IMF Staff Papers* 35. New York: IMF, pp. 1-35.

Macklem, R.T. 1994. *Wealth, Disposable Income and Consumption: Some Evidence for Canada.* Bank of Canada Technical Report no.71. Ottawa: Bank of Canada.

Mukhopadhyay, A.K. 1994. "Are Haligonians Ricardian? A Survey of Households' Savings Response to this Government's Budget Deficits." *Journal of Socio-Economics* 23:457-77.

Normandin, M. 1999. "Budget Deficit Persistence and the Twin Deficits Hypothesis." *Journal of International Economics* 49:171-93.

Ostergaard, C., B.E. Sorensen and O. Yosha. 2002. "Consumption and Aggregate Consumption: Evidence from U.S. States and Canadian Provinces." *Journal of Political Economy* 110:634-45.

Seater, J.J. 1993. "Ricardian Equivalence." *Journal of Economic Literature* 31:142-90.

Wirjanto, T.S. 1996. "An Empirical Investigation into the Permanent Income Hypothesis: Further Evidence from the Canadian Data." *Applied Economics* 28:1451-61.

does the debt matter?

Serge Coulombe

The Point

The question at issue in the Ricardian equivalence debate is whether a given path of public expenditure is best financed by raising taxes or issuing debt. To begin with, it is important to understand the "traditional view" regarding the economic effect of budget deficits. In fact, there are two traditional views of the consequences of postponing taxation. The first is Keynesian and deals with the short-run effect (at the business-cycle horizon) of budget deficits. The second is neoclassical and related to the long-run effect of postponing taxation in a growth model of capital accumulation.

The two traditional views provide a completely different diagnostic. In the short-run Keynesian world, postponing taxation stimulates the economy and creates wealth. Tax cuts fuel consumption and increases aggregate demand. Because the economy is not at full employment, the increase in aggregate demand generates its own saving and translates into higher capacity utilization, output and employment.

In the long-run neoclassical world, however, postponing taxation is bad: it "crowds out" saving, keeping it from going into capital accumulation. In general, financial markets direct private saving toward two ends: private investment and the financing of the government's budget deficit. Because the economy is at full employment, increasing budget deficits by cutting taxes permanently reduces living standards by reducing the supply of capital available to the economy. In the 1970s, these two alternative traditional views cohabited comfortably in a kind of neoclassical synthesis of Keynes: when the economy was not at full employment, the Keynesian view held; when it was at full employment, the neoclassical view prevailed.

Robert Barro's famous 1974 paper, "Are Government Bonds Net Wealth?" was, to say the least, a path-breaking departure in this time-honoured macro-economic debate. It succeeded in contradicting *both* traditional approaches. According to Barro, increasing public debt is exactly equivalent to raising taxes. Postponing taxation is therefore neutral. For intertemporally-maximizing, far-sighted agents, today's public debt just equals the present value of the future taxes required to pay it! So budget deficits are neither expansionary in the Keynesian way nor detrimental to capital accumulation as they are in neoclassical growth models. Government bonds are not net wealth.

In 1976, James Buchanan pointed out that Barro's analysis was "Ricardian" since it appears, without the math, in the writings of the great classical economist, David Ricardo (1772–1823). The alleged equivalence between debt financing and raising taxes therefore came to be known as *Ricardian equivalence* (RE).

Synthesizing Johnson's Synthesis

The great merit of David Johnson's pedagogical paper is that it focuses on the effect of government deficits in a small, open economy like Canada's. To synthesize his synthesis, let us consider the following well-known identity from national income accounting:

$$Y = C + I + G + NX = C + S + T$$

Y is national income. C is consumption, I investment, G government spending on goods and services, T government tax revenues and NX the trade balance, that is, the difference between exports and imports. The left-hand side of the equation is the overall demand for goods and services produced in the economy, which is made up of consumption demand, investment demand, demand from the government and demand from foreigners, while the right-hand side shows how these demands are financed by households: they spend on consumption directly themselves; they provide savings that can be used by investors, and they pay taxes that can be used by governments. National income accounting implies that the left-hand side equals the right-hand side. When changes in inventories are included in I, then simple arithmetic leads to the following basic relationship:

$$G - T = S - I - NX$$

The problem under study here is the substitution between taxes and debt for a given path of government expenditures. In a small, open economy, the domestic interest rate is determined abroad and it is convenient, for the sake of simplicity, to assume that investment is fixed. Consequently, both G and I are given in the experiment. Taking first differences (Δ) on both sides of the equation (and $\Delta G = \Delta I = 0$ since they are constant), we then get:

$$-\Delta T = \Delta S - \Delta NX \quad (1)$$

Postponing taxation by issuing debt ($-\Delta T$) either increases saving (ΔS), produces a trade deficit ($-\Delta NX$), or–and this is important for what I want to conclude about David Johnson's paper, *results in some combination of the two*. If we abstract from interest payments on net indebtedness, then the trade deficit, $-\Delta NX$, equals foreign borrowing, another term for which is "the capital account surplus." In effect, the increased debt is financed either domestically by increased saving or abroad by increased foreign borrowing, or, again, *by some combination of the two*. With RE,

$$-\Delta T = \Delta S \quad \text{and} \quad \Delta NX = 0$$

Johnson's paper shows that this RE prediction that ($-\Delta T$) and ($-\Delta NX$) should be independent appears to be rejected by Canadian data. Government deficits tend to coincide with current account deficits, a fact popularly known as the twin deficits problem. The rise in Canada's public debts between the mid-1970s and the mid-1990s may well account for the increase in its international indebtedness during the same period. Unlike in a closed economy, however, the negative long-run effect of debt financing is not on capital accumulation but on the difference between domestic and national product and income. With a rising public debt, a larger proportion of Canada's capital stock comes to be owned by foreigners. Our national income falls below our domestic product because we must send profits and interest to foreigners to service our borrowing from them. Because of this, Canadians are poorer. Johnson estimates the effect to be around 5 percent of national income.

The Other Side of the Story

I completely agree with Johnson's analysis. The pure RE proposition does appear to be rejected by Canadian data. But this should not be surprising because what Johnson is testing by looking at the relationship between public deficits and the current account is whether the RE proposition holds at 100 percent, whether, in the spirit of equation (1), $-\Delta T$ is *exactly* offset by ΔS.

Compared to the relative simplicity of economic models, the real world is extremely complex. No model applies perfectly to the real world. Conversely, no complex economic phenomenon could be fully explained by just one economic model. Only theoretical zealots claim that a model explains 100 percent of the real world. Johnson is not a theoretical zealot and he reports mixed results for empirical analyses regarding the RE proposition for Canada and various countries. For instance, according to Normandin (1999), a one-dollar increase in Canada's budget deficit generates an increase in the current account deficit of between 19 and 67 cents. In the spirit of equation (1), this means that the increase in $-\Delta T$ is matched between 33 and 81 percent by an increase in ΔS. Similarly, in a multi-country study, Bernheim (1988) estimated the effect of budget deficits on current account deficits to be around 30 percent, which implies that budget deficits would be about 70 percent offset by an increase in domestic net saving.

Johnson concludes his paper by saying that the link between budget deficits and current accounts follows from the fact that the RE proposition is not valid. He is certainly correct that the RE proposition is not verified at 100 percent. But according to the results he himself reports, it is verified at between 33 and 81 percent (Normandin) and at 70 percent (Bernheim 1988). If we believe these numbers, especially the higher-end estimates, we should conclude that RE is a very useful tool for understanding the evolution of such important macroeconomic variables as saving and consumption.

Consider an example. The evolution of the savings rate of Canadian households and unincorporated business over the period 1961–2002 is reported in figure 1. At first sight, the message emerging from this graph is frightening for the policy maker. Since the mid-1980s, Canadians have been getting poorer. In the early 1980s, the savings rate was above 15 percent. In recent years it is just above 4 percent! Put those numbers in a standard model of economic growth and such a sharp decrease in the Canadian savings rate will have a tremendous negative effect on the standard of living in the long run. What are the policy implications? We should stimulate saving in Canada.

Figure 2, however, provides another view of the behaviour of the Canadian savings rate. In the spirit of equation (1), the savings rate is coupled with the overall public sector surplus, with both being expressed as a ratio of gross domestic product (GDP). In constructing this graph, I used normalized data: when a series is above the zero line, that means it is above the average for the period and when it is below the line it is below the period average.

Figure 1

Private Savings Rate in Canada, 1961–2002

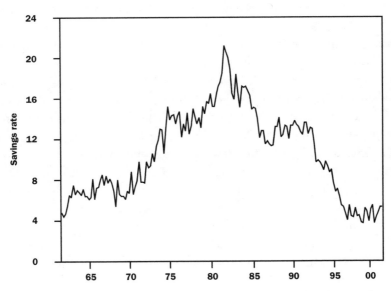

Question: Should we be concerned with the important decrease in the savings rate since the mid-1980s?

Figure 2

Canadian Private and Public Savings Rates

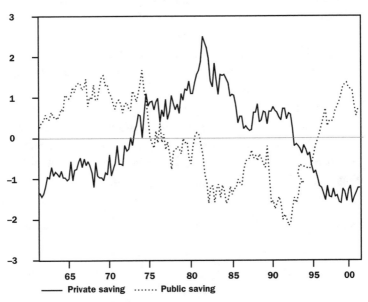

——— Private saving   ········ Public saving

Note: Normalized data – private saving from sector accounts – person and unincorporated buisnesses, CANSIM d 14915. Public saving is total government saving, CANSIM d 15236. Ratio-to-GDP CANSIM d 14915.

As is well known, public "saving" swung heavily into dis-saving, that is, budget deficits, between 1973 and 1996. If far-seeing Canadian households were taking future taxes into account, as in the RE world, private saving should have been above its average level during this period of high budget deficits (or low public saving). Conversely, the RE prediction is that the private saving line will be below the zero line when the public saving line is above it.

In fact, the fit between the RE prediction and the facts is striking. With the exception of the 1975–82 period, private saving and public saving *do* fall on opposite sides of the zero line. More importantly from a policy perspective, the RE prediction is very well corroborated in the post-1994 period: the swing from huge deficits to surpluses led to a decrease in household saving.

This is my bottom line. I fully agree with Johnson on his key point. Our budget deficits did force Canadians to borrow abroad and this is the best and simplest way to show why and how budget deficits are costly in an open economy. But I think RE remains a very useful tool in understanding the evolution of such an important macroeconomic variable as the savings rate. According to RE, policy makers should *not* worry about the decrease in the savings rate since 1992. Canadians do not have to save as much today as in the deficit era because they know that with the decrease in the debt-to-GDP ratio, they will have to pay less tax in the future. A lower savings rate is thus compatible with the "intertemporal budget constraint" of Canadians.

Before concluding, I would like to add an open-economy explanation for the fact that Ricardian equivalence is not fully verified for the Canadian economy. There are, of course, many reasons why RE does not hold fully in a closed economy. As discussed in Johnson's paper, the liquidity constraint is one of the most important. But in an open economy, labour mobility is a serious limitation on the validity of Ricardian equivalence. People could stay here when the government is becoming indebted and benefit from all the extra public services, but then leave the country when the debt comes due. Canadians who migrate to the United States do not have to pay their share of the federal debt. Again this implies that RE will not be fully verified because rational Canadians who anticipate migrating in the US might not be discounting future taxes.

A Ricardian Conversation with my Wife

I conclude by reporting a conversation held with my wife the Friday before I came to the conference on which this book is based. My wife is a non-economist working with economists and living with an economist. Consequently, she is usually interested in understanding how economists think and she sometimes enjoys discussing economics.

So at dinnertime, she told me:

"Serge, you didn't say anything about your conference in Montreal next weekend? I am surprised; usually you get so stressed before a conference."

I replied: "Oh, Lucie, I am just commenting on a paper."

She said: "How good is the paper?"

"I don't know. I didn't receive the paper yet."

"But, you should be nervous Serge, you don't know what to say?"

"Oh, it's simple. The paper is on Ricardian equivalence. If David Johnson, the author of the paper, argues that RE is verified, I will argue the reverse by looking at the current account. If he says that RE is not verified, I will argue the reverse by looking at the savings rate. In either case, I will say roughly the same thing. That is what is great with RE, you always have something to say."

Then she asked me: "Serge, what is Ricardian equivalence?" From the point of view of my own household budget management, I was not yet aware that I was about to make an important blunder.

I explained the concept to her carefully, though leaving aside from our dinner-table conversation such indigestible topics as the no-Ponzi game condition and the Euler equation. And I ended up with my interpretation of the decline in the Canadian savings rate in recent years. After a period of silence devoted, I thought, to the quiet appreciation of our *sushi* and white Bordeau, my wife said.

"That's a good one Serge. After all these years, finally I have learned something useful from one of your many conferences. You are going to Montreal next weekend. Tomorrow it's my time to have fun. As a *rational and far-sighted* Canadian, I will be going to Montreal tomorrow shopping at *Simons'* and *Les Ailes de la Mode* because of Paul Martin's great achievement. For, as I understand, the debt-to-GDP ratio continues to fall."

So this is my real bottom line. In this era of a declining debt-to-GDP ratio, RE is something that economists should not explain to their non-economist spouses. Rather, it is a secret that we should keep for us, and for our poor, long-suffering students.

Bibliography

Barro, R.J. 1974. "Are Government Bonds Net Wealth?" *Journal of Political Economy* 82:1095-117.

Bernheim, B.D. 1988. "Budget Deficits and the Balance of Trade." In *Tax Policy and the Economy* 2, ed. L.H. Summers. Cambridge, MA: MIT Press.

Buchanan, J.M. 1976. "Barro on the Ricardian Equivalence Theorem." *Journal of Political Economy* 84:337-42.

Normandin, M. 1999. "Budget Deficit Persistence and the Twin Deficits Hypothesis." *Journal of International Economics* 49:171-93.

5

what does the debt cost us?

Bev Dahlby

Introduction

Ten years ago, deficit reduction was a hot topic. Government policies concerning the deficit were fiercely debated. Parliamentary and legislative committees studied the issue, and many economists contributed to the public debate.[1] Gradually, the public mood shifted in favour of getting our federal and provincial fiscal houses in order. Over the past decade, Canadian governments' fiscal balances have swung from deficit to surplus, and the public debt has declined as a percentage of gross domestic product (GDP).

Now, the political winds seem to have changed. The emphasis is on increasing spending on health care, defence and income support programs for children. Since the Canadian public is seemingly unwilling to accept tax increases, Roy Romanow and others have suggested that we finance program enhancements by "spending the surplus."[2]

While our fiscal position has improved over the past 10 years, the same basic trade-off continues to apply: if higher spending is not matched by higher taxes, the burden of the public debt will be higher than it otherwise would be. But, what *is* the burden of the public debt? What do we gain by running budget surpluses and lowering our public debt ratio? Or, to turn the question around and use a fundamental term of economics, if enhanced expenditure programs come at the expense of a higher public debt ratio, what is the "opportunity cost" of these expenditure programs?

If we let the public debt rise, then over the long term taxes have to be higher so that we can pay the higher interest costs that result. Recent theoretical and empirical research suggests that a government's tax policy can affect the long-run growth rate of the economy. In particular, a higher tax rate reduces the incentive to save and invest.[3] Thus, the "true" burden of the public debt is a lower rate of investment and possibly a lower rate of economic growth. This paper focuses on that burden.

In the next section, I review a debate that erupted among economists in the late 1950s and 1960s over the existence and nature of the burden of the public debt. In that debate, a number of eminent economists challenged the prevailing Keynesian orthodoxy, which held that the public debt cannot impose a burden on future generations because "we owe it to ourselves." Reviewing this debate helps clarify key issues and assumptions concerning the nature of the burden of the public debt and points to what is now a widely (although not universally) accepted conclusion: that the public debt can impose a burden by reducing the stock of capital available in the future.

In the third section, I use a simple "endogenous growth" model, which is described in the appendix to this chapter, to explore the connections between the public debt, taxation, and the rate of economic growth. An increase in the public debt affects the growth rate of the economy through its effects on the investment rate. In a "closed" economy, where all public debt is held internally, the investment rate is equal to the net savings rate. The net savings rate, in turn, is equal to the private sector savings rate plus the public sector savings rate. If governments run deficits, the public-sector savings rate is negative. The larger the public-sector deficit ratio, the lower the net savings rate. An increase in the public *debt ratio* raises the interest payments the government must make and, if its program spending remains a constant percentage of GDP, the government's deficit ratio. If the private-sector savings rate remains constant, this increase in the deficit ratio crowds out private investment, lowering the rate of economic growth.

But the private-sector savings rate may not be constant. An increase in the public debt ratio can cause people to change their savings behaviour. In the model outlined in the appendix, an increase in the public debt has two offsetting effects on the private-sector savings rate. There is a *distortionary tax effect* – the higher tax rate that is required to finance interest payments on the additional debt reduces the net rate of return on saving, making savings less attractive. There is also a *Ricardian equivalence effect* – forward-looking individuals increase their current savings to pay for the future tax increase that is needed to finance a higher public debt. Thus, an increase in the public debt has an ambiguous effect on the private-sector savings rate. Overall, however, the net savings rate declines: the Ricardian equivalence effect exactly offsets the decline in public-sector savings rate, which means that the net savings rate declines because of the distortionary tax effect.

I use this simple model to calculate the impact of changes in the public debt on the rate of economic growth by choosing parameter values for the model that generate an equilibrium growth path and sustainable fiscal policy at the mid-1990s values of the Canadian debt-to-GDP ratio and ratio of government expenditure on goods and services to GDP. These calculations indicate that a doubling of the debt ratio leaves the private-sector savings rate virtually unaffected and causes only very modest declines in the investment rate and the growth rate.

On the other hand, even if an increase in the public debt has only a small effect on the long-term growth rate of an economy, it can have large cumulative impacts on aggregate output, and hence future living standards. I use the model to analyze the social cost of a marginal increase in the public debt, using the concept of the "marginal cost of public funds" (MCF). The MCF measures the cost of raising an additional dollar of revenue. The MCF usually exceeds one because a tax increase distorts private-sector decisions, leading to a less efficient allocation of resources and lower output. The MCF for funds that a government obtains by borrowing measures the marginal economic loss caused by the additional taxes that have to be levied in order to finance interest payments on an additional dollar of public debt. This MCF can be interpreted as the "hurdle benefit-cost ratio" that a debt-financed public project needs to meet in order to generate a net social gain. Alternatively, it can be interpreted as the social gain from lowering the public debt by one dollar.

Calculations using parameter values that reflect the public debt and program expenditure to GDP ratios for Canada in the mid-1990s and a range of econometric estimates of the responsiveness of savings to the after-tax rate of return on savings indicate that the MCF for debt financing is in the range of 1.06 to 1.27. (The higher values for the MCF arise when the savings are more responsive to the after-tax rate of return.) Even though the public debt has only a very small effect on the growth rate in this model, a public project financed by debt would have to have a benefit-cost ratio of 1.15 (using the base-case parameter values) in order to improve social welfare. Alternatively, debt-financed public expenditures should bring a return of 15 percent if they are to be considered worth the damage that financing them does to the economy. The model clearly suggests that there is a significant return from using "temporary" public-sector surpluses to pay down the public debt even when the growth-retarding effects of the public debt are relatively low. In other words, reducing the public debt by a dollar has a long-term payoff, through slightly higher rates of economic growth, in the range of $1.06 to $1.27. Many of the enhancements to expenditure programs on the "wishlists" of spending advocates would probably not have benefit-cost ratios in this range. From a cost-benefit perspective, therefore, paying down the public debt may be the best use of the federal surpluses. In the final section of the paper, I discuss some of the limitations of the model and directions for future research.

Is the Public Debt a Burden?

In the late 1950s and early 1960s, a major battle broke out among economists as four future Nobel laureates – James Buchanan, James Meade, Franco Modigliani and William Vickrey – challenged the prevailing Keynesian orthodoxy that the public debt does not impose a burden on future generations. Their contributions sparked a flurry of responses by the leading public finance economists of the day: Abba Lerner, Richard Musgrave, William Bowen, Carl Shoup, Tibor Scitovsky and E.J. Mishan.[4]

The main proponent of the Keynesian orthodoxy was Abba Lerner (1948), who argued that the public debt could not impose a burden on future generations because the "real" burden occurs when a government uses the resources that are financed by borrowing. When a government fights a war or builds a highway, it uses resources that could have been used by the private sector. According to the Keynesian orthodoxy, it is this reallocation of resources from the private to the public sector that constitutes the burden of the government expenditure, and this burden is independent of whether the expenditure is financed by taxation or borrowing. Because, in either case, the burden occurs at the time the resources are used by the public sector, it cannot be "transferred" to future generations. The Keynesian orthodoxy did acknowledge that interest payments on the public debt have to be financed by higher taxes on future generations, but pointed out that interest payments on the public debt also represent income for the future generation. Interest payments are merely a transfer from future taxpayers to future bondholders and do not represent a net loss to the future generation. In other, fewer words, a public debt does not constitute a burden because "we owe it to ourselves." According to the Keynesian orthodoxy, the method of financing public expenditure, taxation or borrowing, should be determined by macroeconomic considerations, namely, how big a deficit or surplus is required to keep the economy at full employment with a low rate of inflation.

Buchanan (1958) is generally credited with launching the assault on the Keynesian orthodoxy. A key element of his argument was the distinction between coercive and voluntary payments. Taxes are coercive payments. The element of coercion means the taxpayer is worse off for having to make the payment.

Otherwise, coercion would not be necessary. On the other hand, borrowing by government is based on the voluntary agreement of individuals to purchase government debt in exchange for claims on future resources. By definition, the current generation's voluntary purchase of the debt cannot make it worse off. Thus, the burden of government spending financed by debt must be borne by future generations.

How is this burden shifted to the future generation? In attempting to clarify the Buchanan position, Bowen, Davis and Kopf argued that:

> the issuance of government bonds permits the generations alive at the time the public project is undertaken [Generation I] to be compensated in the future for their initial sacrifice. Generation I merely makes a loan of its reduced consumption, and the real reduction of consumption is borne by the generation(s) alive at the time this loan is extinguished. Consequently, even though the real private consumption of the community as a whole need not be altered by the growth of the public debt, it is still possible for the distribution of the community's private consumption *between generations* to depend on whether or not public projects are debt-financed [italics in the original]. (1960, 703)

The Bowen et al. thesis is that the public debt is a burden because it is a claim on the resources of future generations. Some orthodox Keynesians challenged this thesis by arguing that the public debt might be constantly rolled over and never repaid. Future generations do not bear a burden because the debt is never "extinguished." Some even suggested that the interest payments on the debt could be infinitely postponed by further borrowing. Obviously, if government debt is a "Pyramid scheme," then the Bowen et al. mechanism never comes into play.

The grounds of the debate then shifted to the effect that the method of government finance has on the resources available to future generations. As Modigliani succinctly noted:

> the way we use today's resources can affect in three major ways the output that will result from tomorrow's labor input: (i) by affecting the natural resources available to the future; (ii) by improving technological knowledge; and (iii) by affecting the stock of man-made means of production, or capital, available to future generations. Hence government expenditure, and the way it is financed, *can* affect the economy in the future if it affects any of the above three items [italics in the original]. (1961, 736)

Vickrey provided a very concise description of the way in which the method of financing the government expenditures affects the stock of capital available to future generations. He noted that:

> if we assume a "public debt illusion" under which individuals pay no attention to their share in the liability represented by the public debt in determining how much of their income they will spend, we can expect consumer demand to be higher when the project is debt-financed than when it is tax-financed; ... the increased demand for borrowed funds represented by the debt financing must be allowed to tighten the money market ... drive interest rates up and generally increase the difficulties of financing to the point where private investment is curtailed sufficiently to remove inflationary pressure[5] ... The shifting of the burden to the future that is produced by debt financing is then essentially the shifting of resources out of private investment and into consumption that is induced by the change in the method of financing. (1961, 133)

A formal model of the burden of the public debt caused by the "crowding out" of private investment was provided by Modigliani (1961). His model is portrayed in figure 1. Individuals want to hold a certain amount of wealth based on their disposable incomes. Initially, there is no public debt, and therefore aggregate wealth is equal to the private stock of capital K. At time t_0, the government temporarily increases government spending on goods and services by dG (perhaps to fight a war) and it finances this increase in spending by issuing bonds equal to B. Government borrowing crowds out private investment in the manner described by Vickrey, and the capital stock declines to K_1. The reduction in the capital stock, $K_0 - K_1$, is equal to B. This decline in the capital stock is permanent because individuals treat the bonds as part of their wealth, and $B + K_1 = K_0$. Aggregate output and consumption are lower in every subsequent year. Future generations bear the burden of the public debt because they have a smaller capital stock, leading to lower output, lower wages and lower consumption.

The burden of the public debt can be measured by the reduction in annual output that occurs because of the reduction in the capital stock. The reduction in output from a one-dollar reduction in the capital stock is the marginal product of capital, r, which will also be equal to the rate of return on government bonds because investors will require the same pre-tax rate of return on private capital and government debt (ignoring for simplicity any differences in their risk characteristics). Therefore, the annual loss of output from an additional dollar of

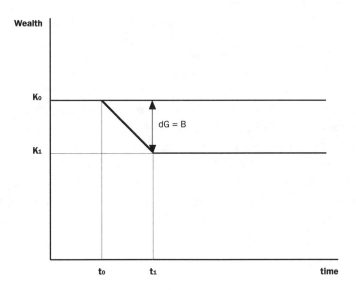

Figure 1

The Effect of Public Debt in the Modigliani (1961) Model

public debt is r. Since this annual output is lost forever, the present value of the lost output from one dollar of debt, calculated using the market interest rate, is equal to one dollar.[6] In other words, in the Modigliani model, the annual interest payment on the public debt measures the annual lost output caused by the public debt, and the value of the public debt measures the present value of current and future lost output.

Most of the "heavy hitters" in this debate were highly critical of the Keynesian orthodoxy, and it might be supposed that their side won. In fact, the Keynesian orthodoxy is no longer prevalent among economists, although it still has its adherents.[7] The view that the "public debt is a burden" emerged from the debate as a generally accepted proposition among academic economists until it was in turn challenged in the 1970s with the revival of the Ricardian equivalence view by Barro (1974). Johnson (this volume) discusses the issues concerning the Ricardian equivalence at length in his paper, so I will not discuss them here.

Before going on to the next section, which uses a simple model to examine the burden of the public financed by distortionary taxation in a growing economy, let me make three remarks about the burden of the public debt.

First, most economists agree that governments should incur deficits and increase their debt during a downturn in the economy. Governments should not try to balance their budget each year, but over the business cycle, running deficits during periods of slow economic growth and high unemployment and running surpluses during economic upturns. This means that, averaged over the business cycle, a government's debt level should remain roughly constant.[8]

Second, even if the public debt imposes a burden, incurring deficits and increasing the public debt is appropriate in some circumstances, especially if a government faces a large, non-recurring expenditure. For example, Cooley and Ohanian (1997) have argued that the British government's decision to finance a good part of its World War II expenditures with high taxes, especially on capital income, generated slower economic growth in the postwar period than would have been the case under a policy that smoothed the movement of tax rates by relying more on debt.

Third, as stressed in the paper by Robin Boadway in this volume, running large deficits that impose a burden on future generations can in some circumstances improve intergenerational equity and may therefore be Pareto-efficient.[9] The fact that the public debt lowers the welfare of future generations is not on its own evidence of economic inefficiency. However, as with any income transfer program financed by distortionary taxation, it is important to calculate the trade-off rate: just how much do future generations have to pay for the gains obtained by the current generation?

Public Debt, Distortionary Taxation and Economic Growth

The 1960s' debate about the burden of the public debt ignored the disincentive effects of the taxes that are required to finance the public debt. In the 1950s and 1960s, most academic economists thought that the distortionary effects of taxes were relatively small and that the most important impact of taxation occurred through individuals' responses to the reduction in their net income or wealth. Over the last 30 years, however, a host of theoretical and econometric studies has refined our understanding of the nature and magnitude of the resource allocation distortions caused by taxes. Today, any analysis of the burden of the public debt must incorporate the distortionary effects of the taxes that have to be imposed to finance the public debt.

The 1960s' debate also largely ignored the linkage between the public debt, government deficits, interest rates and the rate of economic growth. The models that economists used to analyze the burden of the public debt were essentially static models, that is, they looked at the effects at a given time, in an economy of a given size, even though borrowing is an inherently dynamic phenomenon. A dollar borrowed today requires interest payments in the future, and the taxes levied to finance those interest payments may affect savings and investment decisions. This in turn may affect the rate of economic growth and future levels of output.

Nor in the 1960s did the government sector's intertemporal budget constraint, the limitations on its ability to borrow, play a major role in the debate.

Today, a government's intertemporal budget constraint is central to any informed analysis of the public debt.[10] This constraint implies that the size of the public debt that a government can sustain, given its tax and program expenditure levels, depends on the rate of interest on the debt and the rate of economic growth. A lower rate of growth means either that taxes have to be raised or program expenditures cut if a government is to maintain its debt ratio. But the rate of economic growth may, in turn, be affected by the level of taxation that is required to finance the public debt.

In the appendix, I describe a simple version of what economists call an "endogenous growth model." An endogenous growth model is one in which the rate of growth is determined in the model, instead of being simply assumed, as is the case in many models (such as the Modigliani model discussed in the previous section). Readers familiar with the mathematics of simple models of economic growth will want to read the appendix. In the rest of this section, I try to provide an intuitive explanation of how, in this admittedly simple model, the size of the public debt, the level of distortionary taxation and the rate of economic growth are all linked to one another.

In this model, the growth rate of the economy is proportional to the share of investment in overall economic activity. In other words, an economy that devotes a higher percentage of GDP to investment will grow at a faster rate. The linkage between the investment rate and the growth rate of the economy, for which there is abundant empirical evidence, is the key feature of this model. The model assumes that the economy is closed, that it has no economic interaction with other countries. This means both that the investment rate is equal to the society's net savings rate (since there is no other source of savings) and that all public debt is held internally (since there are no foreigners available to buy any of it). The economy's net savings rate is the difference between the private-sector savings rate and the public-sector's deficit ratio. The net savings rate therefore declines if an increase in the public-sector deficit is not matched by an increase in the private-sector saving rate.

An increase in the public debt affects the growth rate of the economy through its effects on the public-sector deficit ratio and through it on the private-sector savings rate. Holding tax and expenditure rates constant, an increase in the public debt ratio will increase the deficit-to-GDP ratio. The reason is that a higher debt means higher debt interest payments for the government. The increase in the public-sector deficit reduces the net savings rate and the investment rate if the private-sector savings rate remains constant. In effect, the deficit crowds out the private investment rate, leading to a decline in the growth rate.

However, an increase in the public debt ratio may cause people to change their savings behaviour. In the model outlined in the appendix, an increase in the public debt has two offsetting effects on private savings. The first is a *distortionary tax effect* that arises because higher tax rates are required to finance interest payments on the additional debt. (The model assumes that the ratio of program spending to GDP is held constant.) The higher tax rate reduces the net rate of return on saving, making savings less attractive. The distortionary tax effect will be larger the more sensitive the savings rate is to changes in the after-tax rate of return on savings. In the calculations presented below, I use a range of values for the interest sensitivity of savings based on econometric studies. The second effect of the public debt on savings is a *Ricardian equivalence effect.* In this model, individuals are forward-looking, and they anticipate that a higher public debt means higher future tax rates. They therefore respond to a higher public debt by increasing their savings rate in order to pay for the future tax increases required to finance the public debt.

Thus, an increase in the public debt has an ambiguous effect on the private-sector savings rate. Even so, the model predicts that an increase in the public debt will reduce the investment rate, and with it the growth rate. This is because the increase in private-sector savings caused by the Ricardian equivalence effect *exactly* offsets the increase in the deficit ratio. Therefore, the net savings rate declines by an amount equal to the distortionary tax effect when the public debt increases. The magnitude of the distortionary tax effect ultimately determines the decline in the investment rate and the growth rate of the economy.

I use this simple model to calculate the impact of changes in the public debt on the rate of economic growth. I have calibrated the model to reflect the public debt and program expenditure ratios for Canada in the mid-1990s. During that period, the ratio of government spending on goods and services to GDP was 0.26 and the debt ratio for all levels of government was 0.83. (See Johnson, this volume, tables 3 and 7.) I assume that if the debt ratio was stabilized at 0.83, the long-term growth rate for the economy would be 1.5 percent. In the base-case scenario I use parameter values for the interest sensitivity of savings that fall in the middle of the range of values from econometric studies of savings behaviour.

With these values entered in it, the model predicts that the private-sector savings rate would be virtually unchanged even if the debt ratio increased from 0 to 150 percent, that is, even if the public debt rose from nothing to one and a half times GDP. The reason is that the Ricardian equivalence effect would almost exactly offset the distortionary tax effect. Given the resulting constancy of the private-sector savings rate, the investment rate would decline as the deficit ratio increased. Consequently, the growth rate also declines, although the predicted decline in the growth rate is very modest. For example, the model predicts that doubling the debt ratio, from 50 percent of GDP to 100 percent, would reduce the investment rate by 0.8 percentage points and the growth rate by just under one-tenth of a percentage point. Overall, the private-sector savings rate is virtually unaffected by increases in the debt ratio, and there are only very modest declines in the investment rate and the growth rate even when the debt ratio doubles.

While a further tenth of a percentage point reduction in the growth rate may seem like a small effect, it represents a 1.5 percent reduction in the present value of future output or approximately $15 billion in 2002. Thus, *even very small changes in the long-term growth rate of an economy can have large cumulative impacts on aggregate output, and hence future living standards.*

As stressed in the introduction, the opportunity cost of enhancing programs by running a smaller surplus or larger deficit is the value of the future output foregone because the public debt will be higher and the rate of economic growth lower. To quantify this opportunity cost I make use of the concept of the "marginal cost of public funds" – the economic loss that is caused by raising an additional dollar of revenue. The marginal cost of public funds is usually greater than one because tax rate increases lead to tax avoidance and evasion responses that shrink the government's tax base.[11] The shrinkage of the tax base reflects the loss of economic efficiency caused by the distortion in the allocation of resources in the economy. In other words, the less tax revenues rise in response to a tax rate increase (because tax avoidance and evasion shrink the tax base) the higher the MCF. One important aspect of the distortions caused by taxation may be the shrinkage of the tax base over time because of a reduction in the rate of economic growth. One could interpret the Modigliani model, described earlier, as indicating that the MCF from debt is one because in that model taxes are assumed to be nondistortionary. In our model, the MCF from debt is greater than one because the debt is financed by distortionary taxes.

The MCF for any funds the government obtains by borrowing is the marginal economic loss caused by the additional taxes that have to be levied in order to finance an additional dollar of public debt. This MCF can be interpreted as the "hurdle benefit-cost ratio" that a debt-financed public project needs to get over in order to generate a net social gain.

The MCF from debt financing depends on two factors. One is the responsiveness of the present value of the government's net revenue stream (revenues minus program expenditures) when there is an increase in the tax rate. If the distortionary tax effect is strong and individuals' savings decline when tax rates increase, then a larger tax increase will be required to increase government's net revenue stream to finance a given debt increase and the MCF will be higher. Therefore, the marginal social cost of public borrowing will be higher. On the other hand, if the private savings rate is relatively unresponsive to a tax-rate increase, tax revenues will increase almost in proportion to the tax-rate increase because the impact on the growth rate of the economy will be small. In that case, the MCF for debt financing will be close to one because the "excess burden," or lost output, from higher taxes will be low.

The other factor that affects the MCF is the reduction in the present value of the goods and services provided by the public sector. In this model, government expenditures are a constant proportion of GDP. A slower rate of economic growth, caused by a tax-rate increase, means that the level of public services will be lower than it otherwise would be. The calculations reported here indicate that the reduction in the level of public services caused by slower economic growth is an important aspect of the marginal social loss from a higher public debt.

Again using parameter values that reflect Canadian public debt and program expenditures in the mid-1990s and adopting "base-case" values for the sensitivity of savings to the after-tax rate of return, I calculate that the MCF for debt financing is 1.15. This means that an additional dollar of public debt imposes a social cost, in terms of reduced future output, that is equivalent to $1.15. As noted above, the computation of the MCF depends on the sensitivity of savings to the after-tax rate of return. Within a "reasonable" range of values for the interest sensitivity parameters, the calculated MCF for debt financing is in the $1.06 to $1.27 range. (The higher values for the MCF arise when the savings are more responsive to the after-tax rate of return.) Thus, even though the public debt has only a very small effect on the growth rate in this model, a public project financed by debt would have to have a benefit-cost ratio of 1.15 (using the base-case parameter values) in order to improve social welfare. Another way to look at it is that the project would have to have a 15 percent rate of return.

Reversing the logic for a moment, if increasing the debt costs 15 cents on the dollar at the margin, the government can save 15 cents on the dollar at the margin by reducing the debt. The model clearly suggests that there is a significant return from using "temporary" public-sector surpluses to pay down the public debt even when the growth-retarding effects of the public debt are relatively low. In other words, reducing the public debt by a dollar has a long-term payoff, through lower taxes and slightly higher rates of economic growth, that is, in the $1.06 to $1.27 range. This also represents the opportunity cost of projects "financed out of the surplus." I suspect that many of the program enhancements that are promoted by the spending advocates would have lower benefit-cost ratios than this. From a cost-benefit perspective, paying down the public debt may be the best use of the federal surpluses.

Conclusion

To summarize this paper's innovation, I have used a simple "endogenous growth" model to illustrate the interrelationships between the public debt, distortionary taxation and economic growth. This model has been used to calculate the social loss from increasing the public debt by one dollar, a loss that arises because higher taxes are required to finance the interest payments required by an additional dollar of debt. Higher taxes reduce the growth rate of the economy by lowering the savings and investment rate. Although the predicted reduction in the growth rate appears to be quite modest – doubling the debt ratio from 50 percent of GDP to 100 percent only reduces the growth rate by about a tenth of a percentage point – this represents a significant social loss because of the cumulative foregone public and private consumption. An additional dollar of debt imposes a social cost of $1.15 with the base-case parameter values that reflect the Canadian fiscal situation of the mid-1990s. Of course, the relationship works in reverse if we run a higher surplus and reduce public debt by a dollar. There is a social gain of $1.15 if we pay down the public debt by $1.00. Thus, there is a substantial gain from running surpluses that bring down the public debt and there is thus a significant "opportunity cost" if we "spend the surplus" to enhance program spending.

The model has the merit of providing a simple, intuitive framework for analyzing the impact of the public debt on the rate of economic growth. However, the model's simplicity also imposes a number of limitations. One of the most important is that the model only incorporates the aggregate tax rate, and it treats all taxes as if they taxed the return to financial and human capital. In practice, the tax mix may be more important than the level of taxation in determining the rate of economic growth, with taxes on the return to savings having a bigger impact on the growth rate than consumption taxes. It clearly would be very useful to incorporate a wider range of tax instruments in the model. It should be noted, however, that even if payroll and consumption taxes do not affect the rate of economic growth, they could affect the level of economic activity insofar as they reduce people's incentive to supply labour. These "level effects" are also a burden of the public debt. It would be very useful to extend the model to include a wider range of tax instruments and to include both the growth and the level effects of higher taxes in measuring the burden of the public debt.

Second, the model represents a closed economy with no foreign-held debt. Many countries borrow abroad, either directly or indirectly, in order to finance a public sector deficit. A higher public debt can impose a burden on the economy either by increasing the interest rate that foreigners require in order to finance the debt or by putting downward pressure on the exchange rate. Van der Ploeg (1996) and Turnovsky (1997) have developed open-economy endogenous growth models with foreign borrowing. In these models, a higher level of foreign indebtedness increases the interest rate charged by foreign lenders. An increase in the public debt increases foreign indebtedness, as discussed in David Johnson's paper in this volume, and the higher interest rate reduces investment and the rate of economic growth. Thus, the predicted effects of an increase in debt are similar, in qualitative terms, in open and closed endogenous growth models, though it would be interesting to have an analysis of the relative costs of public debt in open and closed economies.

A third limitation of the model is that it assumes that private sector savings behaviour is based on identical, forward-looking, infinitely-lived individuals, and this gives rise to the Ricardian equivalence effect in the savings response to an increase in the public debt. Although, like David Johnson, I doubt the empirical importance of Ricardian equivalence, I have adopted it in this model for two reasons. First, it greatly simplifies the modeling of savings behaviour and aggregate social welfare. Second, as Elmendorf and Mankiw (1999) note, Ricardian equivalence provides a useful benchmark, or a "natural starting point," in constructing a model of government debt. In the current context, it shows how a single departure from the conditions for strict Ricardian equivalence, in this case the use of distortionary taxes, will affect the results of the model. My model suggests that under strict Ricardian equivalence, distortionary taxes do not push the growth rate very far from its equilibrium value, but that even so they have a significant effect on the MCF from debt financing. It obviously would be useful to study the effects of the public debt on economic growth in models that do not assume Ricardian equivalence behaviour. Some steps have been made in this direction by Saint-Paul (1992), van der Ploeg (1996), and Scarth (this volume), but in these models taxes are nondistortionary. Incorporating public debt, financed by distortionary taxes, in a non-Ricardian endogenous growth model would be a very useful direction for future research.

Notes

I would like to thank Ergete Ferede, Tiff Macklem, Max Nikitin, Chris Ragan, Todd Smith and Bill Watson for their comments on an earlier draft of this paper.

1. See, for example, Dahlby (1994a). Many of the contributors to this volume also contributed papers to Robson and Scarth (1994).

2. This despite an opinion poll, conducted by the *National Post* in October 2002, in which only 14 percent of respondents said they would be willing to accept higher taxes for increased spending on health care.

3. See Ahn and Hemmings (2000) and Myles (2000) for surveys of the literature on taxation and economic growth.

4. Most of the papers in this debate are contained in Ferguson (1964). The debate was largely confined to the question of whether a public debt could impose a burden on future generations in a *closed* economy where there is no trade or capital flow with other countries. Even the orthodox Keynesians acknowledged that foreign borrowing, an external public debt, could impose a burden on future generations.

5. It is interesting to note that with his assumption of "public debt illusion" Vickrey explicitly assumed Ricardian equivalence does not hold.

6. The present value of r dollars per year forever, when the interest rate is r, is r/r = 1.

7. See, for example, Bellan (1986). Eisner (1987, 294) still argued in the 1980s that in a closed economy "the public debt would be irrelevant, except for distributional effects" if it could be financed by lump-sum (i.e., nondistortionary) taxes.

8. But see William Scarth's chapter in this volume for some dissenting views.

9. In this context, a policy is Pareto-efficient if it is not possible to find any other policy that makes future generations better off without making the current generation worse off, and vice versa.

10. See, for example, Kneebone and Chung's analysis, in this volume, of the growth of the public debt based on governments' intertemporal budget constraints.

11. See Dahlby (forthcoming) for a survey of the concept and measurement of the MCF.

appendix[1]

Let total output at time t be equal to:

$$Y_t = AK_t \quad (1)$$

where K_t is the accumulated factor of production (physical and human capital) and A is the constant rate of return on this input. We will restrict our attention to the balanced growth path for this economy, where total output is growing at a constant rate γ. The capital stock is also growing at the constant rate γ because it is assumed that there is no technological change and that A is a constant. This implies that the annual rate of net investment is $I_t = \gamma K_t$. Substituting back into (1), we obtain:

$$\gamma = Ai \quad (2)$$

where i is the investment rate, I/Y. In other words, the growth rate is proportional to the investment rate in the economy. Total output will grow at a faster rate the higher the return on capital and the greater the proportion of total output that is devoted to investment. This simple relationship between the growth rate of the economy and the investment rate is the key feature of this simple endogenous growth model, and there is considerable empirical evidence indicating that countries with higher investment rates also have higher growth rates (see, e.g., McGrattan 1998; Durlauf and Quah 1999).

The economy is assumed to be closed, so that the investment rate will be equal to the private-sector savings rate minus the public sector's deficit rate. The public-sector deficit is equal to the rate of increase in the public debt B_t where:

$$B_t = G_t + AB_t - \tau (Y_t + AB_t) \quad (3)$$

The first term on the right-hand side of (3) is the government's program spending, G_t, and the second term is its interest payments on the public debt. The third term is the government's tax revenues from a tax levied at the rate τ on income from production and interest payments on the public debt. Along the balanced growth path, the public sector's debt ratio, $b = B/Y$, its program expenditure ratio, $g = G/Y$, and the tax rate, τ, remain constant and the deficit ratio is equal to γb where:

$$\gamma b = (1 - \tau)Ab + g - \tau \quad (4)$$

This intertemporal budget constraint can also be written as:

$$\tau - g = [(1 - \tau)A - \gamma]b = \theta b \quad (5)$$

The government's primary surplus ratio, which is the left-hand side of (5), has to equal the equilibrium debt ratio multiplied by the difference between the after-tax rate of return on capital and the growth rate of the economy if the debt ratio is to remain constant. A condition for dynamic stability is that the after-tax rate of interest $(1-\tau)A$ has to exceed the rate of economic growth, γ. The intertemporal budget constraint implies that the present value of the government's current and future primary surpluses must equal its public debt. Note that this implies that a government with a constant debt ratio in an economy that is growing at the rate γ will be running a deficit equal to γb percent of output.

The investment rate will be equal to $i = s - \gamma b$, where s represents the private sector's savings ratio, S/Y. Figure A1 shows how the equilibrium growth rate is determined in this simple endogenous growth model. The private-sector savings rate s is based on individuals' savings decisions given A, g, b, and τ. If the debt ratio is b_0, the deficit ratio will increase as the growth rate increases, and the investment rate will decline. Therefore, along the balanced growth path, the investment rate will be i_0, and equilibrium growth rate will be γ_0.

An increase in the public debt ratio affects the economic growth rate through its effect on the deficit ratio and through its effect on the private sector savings rate. Figure A1 shows that an increase in the debt ratio from b_0 to b_1, holding the private-sector savings rate constant, will reduce the investment rate by increasing the deficit rate, and the equilibrium growth rate will decline from γ_0 to γ_1. It can

The Effect on the Growth Rate of an Increase in the Debt Ratio with a Constant Private-Sector Saving Rate

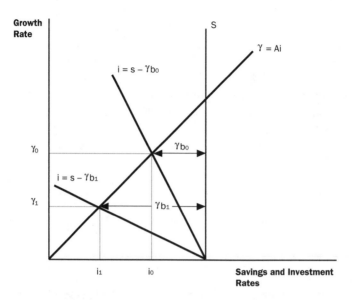

be shown that, holding the private-sector savings rate constant, the elasticity of the growth rate with respect to the debt ratio is equal to $-\gamma b/s$, which is the deficit ratio divided by the private-sector savings rate. In other words, if the government is initially maintaining a constant debt ratio with a deficit ratio equal to 1 percent of GDP and if the private-sector savings rate is 10 percent, then a 20-percent increase in the debt ratio will reduce the growth rate by 2 percent.

To determine the effect of the public debt on the growth rate via changes to the private-sector savings rate, individuals' preferences over current and future consumption have to be specified. In this model, a fairly general form of the utility function is used to model individuals' savings decisions. The key parameters in the utility function are the elasticity of substitution between consumption at different points in time, $\sigma > 0$, and the individuals' rate of time preference, $\rho > 0$, which is the discount rate that individuals use to calculate the current value of future utility.[2] The model assumes identical, infinitely-lived individuals, so that the model can be viewed as testing the extent to which Ricardian equivalence holds when the government uses distortionary taxes to finance its expenditures. With the optimal consumption plan, a representative individual wants consumption to grow at a rate $\gamma = \sigma[(1 - \tau)A - \rho]$. In other words, the desired growth rate of consumption is proportional to the difference between the after-tax rate of return on savings and the individual's rate of time preference. This is the behavioural relationship that underlies the individual's savings behaviour and determines the equilibrium growth rate.

For given values of g and b, the equilibrium τ is determined by the government's intertemporal budget constraint in (5), and the model can be solved for the equilibrium savings rate:

$$s = \sigma\left[\frac{1 + Ab}{A}\right]\left[\frac{(1 - g - pb)A - \rho}{1 + (1 - \sigma)Ab}\right] \quad (6)$$

This expression for the private-sector savings rate is quite complex, and an increase in the debt ratio (holding g constant) can either increase or decrease the savings rate. The reason for this ambiguity is that an increase in b has both a distortionary tax effect and a Ricardian equivalence effect, and these effects push the savings rate in opposite directions. The distortionary tax effect arises because of the higher tax rate that is required to finance additional debt. This reduces the net rate of return on saving, making savings less attractive. However, an increase in b also represents an increase in future taxes, and this prompts an individual to increase his or her savings rate to pay for the future tax increases: the Ricardian equivalence effect. This forward-looking response arises from our assumption that the economy is composed of infinitely-lived individuals.

We can also solve the model for the equilibrium growth rate:

$$\gamma = \sigma\left[\frac{(1 - g - pb)A - \rho}{1 + (1 - \sigma)Ab}\right] \quad (7)$$

An increase in b (holding g constant) reduces the equilibrium growth rate, assuming that the condition for dynamic stability is satisfied. The reason why γ declines when b increases, even though an increase in b has an ambiguous effect on the private-sector savings rate, can be explained as follows: recall that the change in the growth rate is proportional to the change in the investment rate, which in turn depends on the difference between the change in the private-sector savings rate and the increase in the deficit ratio. The Ricardian equivalence effect from the private-sector savings response completely offsets the increase in the deficit rate. Therefore, the total net savings rate declines by the distortionary tax effect, leading to declines in the investment rate and the equilibrium growth rate.

The model can be used to predict the effect of changes in the debt ratio on s, i, and γ. I have calibrated the model so that it produces a balanced growth path for an economy with the public debt and program expenditure ratios for Canada in the mid-1990s. During that period, the ratio of government spending on goods and services to GDP was 0.26 and the debt ratio for all levels of government was 0.83. (See Johnson, tables 3 and 7 in this volume.) I assume that if the debt ratio was stabilized at 0.83, the long-term growth rate for the economy would be 1.5 percent. I assume the rate of time preference, ρ, to be 0.02 and the intertemporal elasticity of substitution, σ, to be 0.25, which is in the middle of the range of values based on econometric studies of savings behaviour.[3] Given b = 0.83, g = 0.26, γ = 0.015, ρ = 0.02, and σ = 0.25, the remaining parameter value, A, can be calculated from (7) as 0.117. Given these parameter values, the model predicts that the consumption ratio would be 0.61 and the investment ratio would be 0.13 which are very close to their average values in the 1992–96 period, 0.601 and 0.162 respectively.

Figure A2 shows that the private-sector savings rate would remain almost constant as the debt ratio increases from 0 to 1.5 because the Ricardian equivalence effect almost exactly offsets the distortionary tax effect. Given the constancy of the private-sector savings rate, the investment rate would decline as the debt and deficit ratios increase. Consequently, the growth rate also declines, but the decline in the growth rate is very modest. For example, the model predicts that doubling the debt ratio, from 50 percent of GDP to 100 percent, would reduce the investment rate by 0.8 percentage points and reduce the growth rate by just under a tenth of a percentage point. Computations using other values of the key parameters (e.g., σ = 0.4 and A = 0.082 and σ = 0.10 and A = 0.278) yield the same qualitative prediction: *the private-sector savings rate is virtually unaffected by increases in the debt ratio, and there are only very modest declines in the investment rate and the growth rate when the debt ratio doubles.*

Figure A2

The Effect of an Increase in the Debt Ratio on the Savings, Investment and Growth Rates

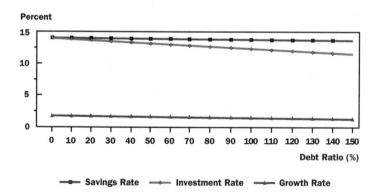

This is a very simple model, and it would not be wise to draw the general conclusion that the public debt has very little impact on an economy's economic growth rate. Still, the model suggests that if the private-sector savings rate is relatively constant, then the impact of increases in the public debt on the growth rate will be minimal. The model also suggests that if Ricardian equivalence does *not* hold (for reasons that are discussed in David Johnson's paper), then the impact of the public debt on the growth rate might be much more significant. Some "back-of-the-envelope" calculations indicate that in the absence of the Ricardian equivalence effect, the decline in the growth rate would be twice as large, that is, doubling the debt ratio, from 50 percent of GDP to 100 percent, would reduce the growth rate by two-tenths of a percentage point. While a further tenth of a percentage point reduction in the growth rate may seem like a small effect, it represents a 1.5 percent reduction in the present value of future output or approximately $15 billion in 2000. *Thus, even very small changes in the long-term growth rate of an economy can have large cumulative impacts on aggregate output, and hence future living standards.*

There have been a couple of recent econometric studies of the effect of the public debt on economic growth. Lin and Sosin (2001) found that the foreign debt ratio of African countries had a negative effect on their growth rates over the 1970–92 period, but an insignificant effect on the growth rates of developed and less-developed countries in other regions. Pattillo, Poirson and Ricci (2002) found that a doubling of the debt ratio reduced the growth rate by between 0.5 and one percentage point in their study of the growth of 93 developing countries over the 1969–98 period, representing an output loss of approximately 7.5 to 15 percent of GDP. Obviously, more econometric studies of the effects of foreign and domestic public debt on economic growth would be very useful.

Moreover, as stressed at the outset, there is a trade-off between higher spending financed out of the surplus and a higher public debt. To determine the opportunity cost of enhancing programs by running a smaller surplus or larger deficit, we need to know the social cost of a *marginal* increase in the public debt, not the total or average burden of the public debt. In this and many other situations, it is the marginal cost of public funds – the cost to society in raising an additional dollar of revenue – that is relevant in making fiscal decisions. The marginal cost of public funds is usually greater than one because tax-rate increases lead to tax avoidance and evasion responses that shrink the government's tax base. The shrinkage of the tax base reflects the loss of economic efficiency caused by the distortion in the allocation of resources in economy. In other words, the less tax revenues rise in response to a tax-rate increase (because tax avoidance and evasion shrink the tax base) the higher the MCF. One important aspect of the distortions caused by taxation may be the shrinkage of the tax base over time because of a reduction in the rate of economic growth. In this appendix, I briefly describe a measure of the MCF for debt financing. The details are contained in Dahlby (2002).

The government's intertemporal budget constraint, given in (5), implies that if the debt is increased by a dollar, the present value of the government's net revenue stream (taxes minus program expenditures) also has to increase by a dollar in order to finance it. Therefore, the MCF for debt financing can be defined as the present value of the current and future reduction in individuals' welfare when the government increases the present value of its net revenue stream (PVNR) by one dollar through a tax-rate increase.[4] In Dahlby (2002), the following formula for the MCF for debt financing is derived:

$$\text{MCF} = \left[1 + \sigma\beta\{\frac{c}{g}\}^{\frac{1-\sigma}{\sigma}}\right]\left(\frac{1 + Ab}{1 + Ab - \sigma Ab}\right) \quad (8)$$

where β is a parameter which measures the relative valuation of publicly-provided goods and services, and c is the ratio of the consumption of private goods to output. This formula indicates that the MCF from debt financing has two components. The component in round brackets is the inverse of the elasticity of the PVNR with respect to the tax rate. The lower the elasticity of the PVNR, the greater the distortionary effect of a tax increase, and the higher the MCF for debt financing. This component of the MCF will be higher the higher the ratio of interest payments on the public debt to total output, Ab, and the greater the intertemporal elasticity of the substitution because this makes the tax base more sensitive to tax-rate increases.

The other component in square brackets is the social loss caused by the reduction in the level of publicly-provided goods and services. In this model, government program expenditures are a constant proportion of GDP. A slower rate of economic growth, caused by a tax-rate increase, means that the level of public services is lower than it otherwise would be. Computations indicate that this component of the MCF may be larger than the revenue elasticity component.

This MCF can be interpreted as the "hurdle benefit-cost ratio" that a debt-financed public project needs in order to generate a net social gain. Equation (8) indicates that the MCF is greater than one and increasing in b, holding the (c/g) ratio constant. Finally, note that as s approaches zero, the MCF approaches one because taxes do not distort individuals' savings decisions when the intertemporal elasticity of substitution is zero. One could interpret the Modigliani model as indicating that the MCF from debt is one because in that model taxes are assumed to be nondistortionary.

Using the parameter values (discussed above) that replicate a balanced growth path at the mid-1990s debt level, the computed value of the MCF for debt is 1.15.[5] This value for the MCF is somewhat lower than the MCF of 1.4 for a general federal personal income tax-rate increase computed by Dahlby (1994b) using a static model of the economy where only labour income is taxed. However, that study incorporated the progressivity of the personal income tax system in the computation of the MCF and that is largely responsible for the higher MCF calculated in that study. Figure A3 shows that the MCF increases as the debt ratio increases, but that the rate of increase is very modest, in line with the predicted impact of the debt ratio on the growth rate in this model. With parameter values that reflect a more responsive savings rate to changes in the net rate of return on savings ($\sigma = 0.4$, A = 0.082, $\beta = 0.19$), the MCF is equal to 1.27. In the low savings response case, with parameter values of s = 0.10, A = 0.278, and $\beta = 0.00006$, the MCF is equal to 1.06.

Figure A3

The Effect of an Increase in the Debt Ratio on the MCF from Debt Financing

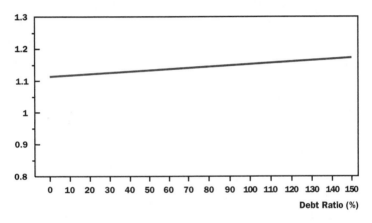

While it would be desirable to have a more highly refined dynamic model to compute the MCF, it is worth noting that even in this model, in which debt has only a very small effect on growth, a public project financed by debt would need a benefit-cost ratio of 1.15 in order to improve social welfare. In other words, the benefits of the project would not have to merely exceed its costs, they would have to exceed them by 15 percent. While there are clearly projects (fighting wars or repairing damage to social infrastructure from severe storms) that would satisfy this hurdle benefit-cost ratio, it sets a relatively high standard and would probably make a large number of debt-financed projects non-viable. Alternatively, the 1.15 value for the MCF can be viewed as indicating the return that our governments can achieve from increasing their primary surpluses and reducing our public debt by one dollar. The model clearly suggests that there is a significant return from using "temporary" public sector surpluses to pay down the public debt even when the growth-retarding effects of the public debt are relatively low.

Notes

1. For a detailed description of the model see Dahlby (2002).

2. See Dahlby (2002) for a specific functional form of the utility function.

3. Hall (1998) obtained an estimate of 0.1 for s for the United States. Patterson and Pesaran (1992) obtained an estimate of 0.4 for the United Kingdom.

4. See Liu (2002) has shown that when the cost of government programs is affected by the tax rate, the most appropriate way of defining the MCF is the welfare loss in raising an additional dollar of net revenues.

5. These calculations are based on a value of b = 0.0375. This is the value of b that is required in this model to make g = 0.26, the optimal program expenditure ratio at the mid-1990s debt level.

Bibliography

Ahn, S., and P. Hemmings. 2000. "Policy Influences on Economic Growth in OECD Countries: An Evaluation of the Evidence." OECD Economics Department Working Papers. Paris: OECD.

Barro, R. 1974. "Are Government Bonds Net Wealth?" *Journal of Political Economy* 82: 1095-117.

Bellan, R. 1986. *The Unnecessary Evil*. Toronto: McClelland & Stewart.

Bleaney, M., N. Gemmell, and R. Kneller. 2001. "Testing the Endogenous Growth Model: Public Expenditure, Taxation, and Growth over the Long-Run." *Canadian Journal of Economics* 34:36-57.

Bowen, W.G., R.G. Davis, and D.H. Kopf. 1960. "The Public Debt: A Burden on Future Generations?" *American Economic Review* 50:701-06.

Buchanan, J.M. 1958. *Public Principles of Public Debt*. Homewood, IL: Richard D. Irwin.

Cooley, T., and L. Ohanian. 1997. "Postwar British Economic Growth and the Legacy of Keynes." *Journal of Political Economy* 105, no. 3:439-72.

Dahlby, B. 1994a. *Canada's Deficit-Debt Problem: Why the Sceptics Are Wrong*. Calgary: Canada West Foundation.

———. 1994b. "The Distortionary Effect of Rising Taxes." In *Deficit Reduction: What Pain, What Gain?* ed. W.B.P. Robson and W.M. Scarth. Toronto: C.D. Howe Institute, pp. 44-72.

———. 2002. "Calculating the Burden of the Public Debt in an Endogenous Growth Model." Working Paper. Edmonton: Department of Economics, University of Alberta.

———. (forthcoming) "Using the Marginal Cost of Public Funds to Evaluate Public Expenditure Programs." In *Public Expenditure Evaluation: A Toolkit for Evaluators and Policy Makers*, sponsored by the World Bank and the Swiss Development Cooperation Agency.

Durlaf, S., and D. Quah. 1999. "The New Empirics of Economic Growth." In *Handbook of Marcroeconomics*, 1A, ed. J.B. Taylor and M. Woolford. Amsterdam: Elsevier.

Eisner, R. 1987. "The Burden of the Public Debt." In *The New Palgrave: A Dictionary of Economics*, 1, ed. J. Eatwell, M. Milgate and P. Newman. London: McMillan Press, pp. 294-96.

Elmendorf, D., and G. Mankiw. 1999. "Government Debt." In *Handbook of Macroeconomics*, 1A, ed. J.B. Taylor and M. Woodford. Amsterdam: Elsevier.

Ferguson, J.M. 1964. *Public Debt and Future Generations*. Chapel Hill, NC: The University of North Carolina Press.

Hall, R.E. 1988. "Intertemporal Substitution in Consumption." *Journal of Political Economy* 96:339-57.

Lerner, A.P. 1948. "The Burden of the National Debt." In *Income, Employment, and Public Policy: Essays in Honor of Alvin H. Hansen*, ed. L.A. Metzler. New York: W.W. Norton, pp. 255-75.

Lin, S., and K. Sosin. 2001. "Foreign Debt and Economic Growth." *Economics of Transition* 9, no. 3:635-55.

Liu, L. 2002. "The Marginal Cost of Funds: Incorporating Public Sector Inputs." Working Paper no. 0203. Austin, TX: Private Enterprise Research Center, Texas A&M University.

McGrattan, E.R. 1998. "A Defense of AK Growth Models." *Federal Reserve Bank of Minneapolis Quarterly Review* 22, no. 4:13-27.

Modigliani, F. 1961. "Long-Run Implications of Alternative Fiscal Policies and the Burden of the National Debt." *Economic Journal* 71:730-55.

Myles, G. 2000. "Taxation and Economic Growth." *Fiscal Studies* 21:141-68.

Patterson, K.D., and B. Pesaran. 1992. "The Intertemporal Elasticity of Substitution in the United States and the United Kingdom." *Review of Economics and Statistics* 74:573-84.

Pattillo, C., H. Poirson, and L. Ricci. 2002. "External Debt and Growth." Research Department Working Paper no. WP/02/69. New York: International Monetary Fund.

Robson, W.B.P., and W.M. Scarth. 1994. *Deficit Reduction: What Pain, What Gain?* Toronto: C.D. Howe Institute.

Saint-Paul, G. 1992. "Fiscal Policy in an Endogenous Growth Model." *Quarterly Journal of Economics* (November):1243-59.

Turnovsky, S. 1997. "Equilibrium Growth in a Small Economy Facing an Imperfect World Capital Market." *Review of Development Economics* 1, no. 1:1-22.

van der Ploeg, F. 1996. "Budgetary Policies, Foreign Indebtedness, the Stock Market, and Economic Growth." *Oxford Economic Papers* 48:382-96.

Vickrey, W. 1961. "The Burden of the Public Debt: Comment." *American Economic Review* 51:132-37.

what does the debt cost us?

Tiff Macklem

Bev Dahlby's paper does what good economic analysis of public policy issues should do. It takes on an important and well-defined policy question and explores the issue within a sound and relevant framework. The question it asks is: What is the burden of government debt? In other words, what is the economic cost of government debt to the economy and by implication to its citizens? Though straightforward, this question is by no means simple.

The framework Dahlby uses is a textbook "endogenous growth" model, that is, one in which the economy's growth rate is determined within the model, with the added feature that government policies can affect the growth rate of economic activity. The model is based on optimizing behaviour on the part of households, so that outcomes reflect the best that households can do to maximize their own self-interest given the cards they have been dealt by the government.

Previous work examining the burden of government debt in Canada has used more traditional "exogenous growth" models in which government policies can permanently affect the level of economic activity, but not the long-run growth rate (see, e.g., Macklem, Rose and Tetlow 1994; James 1994). Hence, Dahlby's re-examination of the issue using newer endogenous growth models is a welcome addition to the literature on this important subject.

My discussion addresses three questions: first, why does government debt impose a burden in Dahlby's model? Second, should we take this simple textbook model seriously? And, finally, are the quantitative predictions of the model plausible?

Why Does Government Debt Impose a Burden in this Model?

This is a simple model. The economy is closed so all investment must be financed by domestic savings. Investment is the engine of growth in the model. Output is proportional to capital; hence, more investment means more capital and this translates into more output.

Households in this model look forward and plan ahead. They realize that higher public debt requires higher future taxes to repay the debt plus any interest. So when the government runs a deficit, households buy the government bonds and save the interest they receive on the bonds in order to pay the higher taxes in the future. If taxes were *nondistortionary*, the interest income on the government debt would just cover the higher taxes, and public debt would have no effect on savings, investment or output. In other words, the debt would have no burden because increased private savings would just offset lower public savings, so total savings, which equals total investment, would be unchanged. This is the *Ricardian effect*.

The problem is that taxes *are* distortionary. Specifically, taxes in the model are levied on income. Income can be divided into savings and consumption, so taxing income imposes a tax on both saving and consuming. Taxing savings reduces the return to savings so households will save less. With lower saving, there is less investment and hence less capital and less output. This is the *distortionary tax effect*. Because investment is the engine of growth in the model, the effect on output is a growth effect.

What Dahlby shows is that an increase in government debt in his model has almost no *net* effect on private saving because the Ricardian effect pushing private saving up is just offset by the distortionary tax effect pushing private saving down. Total saving therefore falls by the increase in the government deficit. This lowers the rate of investment and hence the rate of output growth.

Should We Take this Simple Textbook Model Seriously?

It depends.

As an example illustrating how simple it is to offset the Ricardian effect, the answer is "yes." The Ricardian effect is controversial; the fact that we pay income taxes is not. But even allowing for a full Ricardian effect, the reality that taxes are distortionary imposes a burden from debt.

However, as a model of the channels through which government debt imposes a burden on the economy, the model is clearly inadequate. One measure of this is that in Dahlby's model an intelligent government can avoid much of the burden of government debt by simply replacing the income tax with a consumption tax (or, equivalently, combining complete tax sheltering of saving with an income tax). Because it would not tax saving and hence investment and capital, a consumption tax would not affect the growth rate of output in the model. The consumption tax would lower the level of consumption, but the much more harmful growth effect would disappear. Of course, if it was that easy to avoid much of the burden of government debt, governments presumably would have already done so.

The reality is that there are several other channels through which government debt imposes a burden, and these are not easily circumvented. The Ricardian effect itself breaks down if current generations do not take sufficient account of the effects of higher government debt levels on future generations, either because liquidity or borrowing constraints prevent this or because they put their own welfare above that of future generations.

Distortionary tax effects influence economic outcomes through other channels, such as the work disincentive effects of income taxes.

Government debt also creates uncertainty. There is a difference between taxes today and taxes tomorrow. Taxes today are known. The incidence and timing of future taxes are not known. What kind of tax will be imposed? Income tax, consumption tax, payroll tax, capital tax, inflation tax? And when? These different taxes affect different players in the economy very differently. In extreme circumstances, there is also uncertainty about whether the government will make good on its commitment to repay or even service the debt. These various types of uncertainty show up in risk premiums, not only on government debt but also on private debt denominated in the domestic currency. These risk premiums increase the burden of debt both directly by increasing the cost of servicing it and indirectly, and more importantly, by raising the cost of capital and thereby discouraging investment.

Dahlby's model provides for the full Ricardian effect, a single distortionary tax effect and no uncertainty effect. Changing the model to include impediments to the Ricardian effect, adding more margins and taxes to the distortionary tax effect and factoring in uncertainty would all increase the burden of government debt.

A number of other types of extensions to the model could also be considered to make it more relevant to the Canadian economy. Dahlby discusses several of these in the conclusion. The most obvious would be to extend the closed-economy model to address the reality that Canada is an open economy that relies heavily on international trade to sell its products abroad and to buy investment and consumer goods. Another would be to model the capital accumulation process more carefully by distinguishing between human capital and physical capital, and to add labour input into production with an endogenous labour supply decision.

These extensions would enrich the model and change the results, but unlike the first set of extensions mentioned above, which would add more channels through which government debt has real effects, the implications of these extensions for the burden of government debt are ambiguous. On the one hand, adding sectors, including labour inputs and introducing trade, particularly in conjunction with a broader set of taxes, would provide more margins for taxes to impose distortions. On the other hand, giving households a richer set of choices and separating the savings and investment decisions by allowing foreign investment would provide households with more ways to avoid the most distortionary effects of taxes.

Are the Model's Quantitative Predictions Plausible?

Perhaps surprisingly given the model's simplicity, the answer is "yes."

The quantitative effect of government debt on the growth rate of the economy is very small. Using Dahlby's baseline calibration, the rather extreme experiment of reducing the debt-to-gross domestic product (GDP) ratio from 80 percent to zero, would raise the economy's growth rate by only 0.17 percentage points: from 1.5 percent to 1.67 percent. However, even very small growth rate effects, when sustained over long periods of time, can cumulate to big level effects. To see how, consider the implications of increasing the growth rate from 1.5 percent to 1.67 percent. After 10 years consumption would be 2 percent higher. After 20 years it would be 5 percent higher and after 30 years it would be 8 percent higher. Very small growth effects may take a while to cumulate, but their implications for levels are not at all small. This explains why, despite these very small growth-rate effects, the cost-benefit ratio Dahlby calculates for a debt-financed project to improve the welfare of households is as high as 1.15.

How do Dahlby's estimates of the burden of government debt compare to other estimates for Canada? Two studies I am very familiar with are one by myself, with David Rose and Robert Tetlow, and another by Steven James, both published in the 1994 C. D. Howe Institute volume *Deficit Reduction: What Pain, What Gain?* Both these models are exogenous growth models, so there are level effects from the debt, but no growth effects. Both models are also considerably richer than Dahlby's in that they consider a range of channels through which debt can affect economic activity. Nonetheless, if we define the "long run" as about 30 years, the long-run level effects of government debt in these models are of the same order of magnitude as Dahlby's growth effects. In Macklem, Rose and Tetlow, lowering the debt-to-GDP ratio from 80 percent to zero raises the long-run level of consumption by 7.4 percent. In James, the comparable statistic is 9 percent. Both these results are remarkably close to the 8 percent level effect in Dahlby's endogenous growth model after 30 years.

To conclude, this paper demonstrates that allowing for growth effects is a very interesting extension to the literature assessing the burden of government debt. In this respect the paper is successful.

The model only serves the role of an example, however. A more serious assessment of the burden of government debt demands several extensions along the lines suggested both here and by Dahlby himself.

From a policy perspective, a complete analysis of this issue also requires some consideration of the transition costs associated with reducing government debt. Measuring the burden of government debt tells us the long-run benefit of having a lower debt. To assess the desirability of actually lowering the debt-to-GDP ratio, we also need to know how costly it will be to get there from here. We should all hope that in future work Bev Dahlby will extend his analysis to address these issues.

.

Note

1. The views in this discussion are my own. No responsibility for them should be attributed to the Bank of Canada. I am grateful to Nooman Rebei for his assistance.

Bibliography

James, S. 1994. "Debt Reduction with Distorting Taxes and Incomplete Ricardianism: A Computable Dynamic General Equilibrium Analysis." In *Deficit Reduction: What Pain, What Gain?* ed. W.B.P. Robson and W.M. Scarth. Toronto: C.D. Howe Institute, pp. 279-319.

Macklem, T., D. Rose, and R. Tetlow. 1994. "Government Debt and Deficits in Canada: A Macro Simulation Analysis." In *Deficit Reduction: What Pain, What Gain?* ed. W.B.P. Robson and W.M. Scarth. Toronto: C.D. Howe Institute, pp. 231-72.

Robson, W.B.P., and W.M. Scarth, eds. 1994. *Deficit Reduction: What Pain, What Gain?* Policy Study no. 23. Toronto: C.D. Howe Institute.

6

what should we do about the debt?

William Scarth

Economists usually consider government policy from three perspectives: evaluating its effect on economic *efficiency*, *equity* and macroeconomic *stability*. In this paper, I try to outline how following this tradition can help us determine an "optimal" target for the government debt-to-gross domestic product (GDP) ratio. (The reasons for the quotation marks around "optimal" will become clear later.) As it turns out, considerations of efficiency and stability do not lead to any very precise target for the debt-to-GDP ratio. But considerations of equity do. While I conclude that a target value in the 20–25 percent range for the federal government (or in the 50 percent range for the federal and provincial governments taken together) can be defended, I emphasize that reaching this conclusion requires a definition of equity that some may regard as arbitrary. Thus, my main purpose here is to lay out the issues in an orderly fashion so that readers can attach their own weights to the various considerations that impinge on the government's debt decision and then reach their own views of what that decision should be.

The rest of the paper is organized as follows. Efficiency considerations are discussed in the next section, equity considerations in the following three sections, and macroeconomic stability in the sixth section, with concluding remarks in the final section. Several technical details are explained in the appendix.

Government Debt and Economic Efficiency

From a microeconomic perspective, the question of the optimal level of public debt raises efficiency issues. Does a high level of debt raise or lower the level of distortions that pull the economy away from its "first-best," most efficient allocation of resources? Economists distinguish first-best, which should really be called "best" allocations, from the "second-best" allocations that governments typically settle for when they accept political or other constraints on their policies, or when they simply have to accept some degree of market failure. Typically there have been two general views in this regard.

The first general view of the optimal debt problem assumes that in the absence of government, "markets would work," that is, there would be no economic distortions except that "public goods" – goods that no private agents have an incentive to provide, such as national defence, city streets or public lighting – would not be provided. When combined with the proposition that all taxes create economic inefficiency by distorting economic behaviour, this view leads to the suggestion that debt policy be used to circumvent the distortions associated with taxation. In their recent graduate text, Ljungqvist and Sargent adopt this view, and in a section entitled "Should all taxes be zero?" they answer "yes" (2000, 347-48). The policy-design problem then involves determining the optimal pattern of budget surpluses that must be incurred during the transition to that long-run equilibrium. Eventually, instead of annual interest payment obligations, the government builds up enough net claims on private agents, that is, financial assets, to generate annual interest receipts sufficient to finance its ongoing expenditures on public goods without levying any taxes. In effect, the optimal debt ratio is negative: the government becomes a major holder of assets and lives off the interest these assets pay. In fact, Ljungqvist and Sargent calculate that the optimal debt ratio is at least negative 300 percent:[1] in other words, governments should hold net assets that sum to *at least* three times the annual GDP. In Canada's case, the 2002 GDP was $1.14 trillion, so our governments' net worth should be at least $3.42 trillion. As their 2002 net worth was roughly –$0.86 trillion (counting just traditional debt), they clearly have some way to go to meet this objective.

In fact, Turnovsky (2000, 443) has shown that the proposition that the optimal debt ratio is negative hinges on the assumption that governments cannot levy consumption taxes. If they can, and in the real world they obviously do, the optimal level of saving can be secured with positive taxation, and the optimal level of government debt can easily be positive. The most reasonable conclusion, which government officials seem to have made already, albeit probably for other reasons, is that this "complete markets" approach does not support negative public debt after all.

The second general view of the optimal debt problem assumes that, quite apart from public goods problems, the economy usually does involve distortions. The most commonly cited second-best problem is an imperfection in capital markets. Because individuals cannot offer complete collateral when borrowing against expected future wage income, they cannot smooth consumption over their lifetimes as completely as they could if none of their wealth was in the form of human capital. Instead, they have to do without in years when their incomes are low. Given this market imperfection, there is a role for the state – acting, in effect, as these individuals' agent – to do their borrowing for them. It borrows and finances the higher current consumption that they favour (say when they are young), and then they pay down the debt later in life when their earnings are higher. So long as "liquidity-constrained" individuals keep coming along, this view justifies the existence of a positive level of public debt in the "steady state" (that is, on a permanent basis).

A similar line of argument (pursued by Ljungqvist and Sargent in another chapter of their text, 2000) is that, given the "moral hazard" and "adverse selection" problems that are inherent in the provision of private insurance, people self-insure by accumulating "too large" a stock of assets. When they can't buy the insurance they want, they protect themselves by saving more than they'd really like to. This outcome involves too much capital accumulation, a problem that the government can lessen either by taxing capital's earnings so as to discourage investment (Aiyagari 1995) or by running a deficit and building up public debt that crowds out private capital formation (Aiyagari and McGrattan 1998).

Unfortunately, it is difficult for economists to test formally which of these two views of government debt applies in the real world. Thus, economists have not done the hard calculations that would tell us just how big a debt is justified. In most instances, policy advisors simply align themselves with one view or the other on the basis of their own impression of the likely importance of each set of underlying assumptions. Those to the right of the political spectrum usually cite studies illustrating the large "excess burden" associated with taxation and assume that other market distortions are not likely to be this large. Those to the left of the political spectrum focus on the liquidity constraints that many households face and assume that the associated market distortions are likely to be bigger than the efficiency costs of taxation. Still, the empirical cupboard is not entirely bare. A couple of recent studies have explicitly compared these two views within one, internally consistent, framework.

Aiyagari and McGrattan (1998) calculate the optimal debt ratio by constructing a general equilibrium model of the US economy that takes into account both distortionary taxation and incomplete insurance markets, and then calibrating it to parameter values consistent with known empirical regularities. Using the numerical version of the model to compare the relative importance of the two competing effects, they arrive at two important findings. First, the optimal debt ratio is 66 percent, so that, with Canada's consolidated federal plus provincial debt ratio running at about 75 percent today, the analysis does not support a major amount of further debt reduction at this time. Second, they find that the losses incurred when society chooses a debt ratio very different from 66 percent are extremely small. This is because targeting a lower debt ratio involves both a benefit and a cost. On the one hand, taxes can be lowered, which reduces distortions. On the other hand, with decreased ability to borrow through the government, individuals are more liquidity-constrained, so their ability to smooth consumption in the face of shocks is reduced, which means they are worse off. According to Aiyagari and McGrattan's simulations, these two effects almost exactly cancel. Even substantial departures from the optimum debt ratio therefore appear to carry little net cost.

Several reactions to these findings are possible. One is to point out some of the limitations of the study and to call for more research before the policy issue is decided. Aiyagari and McGrattan examine a closed economy and calibrate it for the United States, which makes their model less interesting for Canadians, who live in a very open economy. Also, they only consider one form of taxation and one type of market failure. We know that when similar analyses have examined the benefits of disinflation, the answer has depended on which of several other taxes is raised to allow the government to make up the revenue lost when it no longer receives the inflation tax.[2] This same sensitivity testing has not yet been provided in the optimal debt literature. A similar concern can be raised on the other side of the ledger. According to the "imperfect information" approach to economics, incomplete borrowing is not the only market imperfection that might affect government borrowing. Asymmetric information leads to involuntary unemployment as well. If the Aiyagari and McGrattan analysis could be extended to include additional sources of tax-induced distortions such as unemployment, we might well find that a lower debt ratio would be deemed optimal. For example, a now-standard approach to interpreting unemployment is to acknowledge that, with an incomplete ability to monitor worker effort, firms have to offer higher wages to induce higher productivity. High taxes (which are necessary to cover the interest payments associated with high government debt) pull down after-tax wages and, therefore, productivity. When firms restore productivity by raising pre-tax wages, they cannot afford to hire as many workers, and the equilibrium level of unemployment rises. The net result is that high government debt can lead to higher structural unemployment.

In fact, James and Karam (2001) have recently provided sensitivity testing that confirms these conjectures. They make two important adjustments to the Aiyagari and McGrattan model. First, they specify that government spending is more useful than in the original model (by assuming that public programs are a better substitute for private consumption than Aiyagari and McGrattan assumed). As a result, the cost of high government debt rises: the crowding-out of program spending by interest payments is all the more hurtful. Second, they model a small, open economy in which individuals can smooth consumption by borrowing from or lending to the rest of the world. The economy is less "over-capitalized" as a result, so the benefit of high government debt is smaller. Given these changes, it is not surprising that the optimal debt ratio is no longer 66 percent. Indeed, it drops to –200 percent: as in the pure "markets work" model, the government should become a net creditor and live off its interest earnings.

James and Karam's changes to the Aiyagari-McGrattan model also increase the cost of departing from the optimal debt ratio. For example, reducing the debt from 65 percent to 15 percent now results in an increase in welfare of one-third of 1 percent, instead of a decline in welfare of six one-hundredths of 1 percent. That may be a bigger difference, but it is still not a big difference. Although sensitivity testing has dramatic effects on the "point estimate" of the optimal debt ratio, it supports the proposition that even very large changes in government debt do not have a big effect on overall social welfare. In sum, although it is not yet well developed, this literature does not provide a strong case for any particular debt ratio. For all intents and purposes, the efficiency approach to the debt question says that little is lost if we adopt some other criterion, such as considerations of fairness, to decide the debt issue.

Equity Considerations

According to the equity approach to government debt, we should aim for the level of debt that is most consistent with our view of intergenerational fairness. In this view, government debt is an instrument that society can use to smooth the burden of major structural shocks across generations.

The classic application of this approach involves the Great Depression and World War II. There was such hardship during the 15 years from 1930 to 1945 that most Canadians appeared to be comfortable with the federal government allowing its debt ratio to rise from about 50 percent in 1930 to about 110 percent in 1945. To most people, it probably seemed fair that some of the burden of these difficult times be spread to future generations, who as a result of the debt experienced living standards that were lower than they would have been because the public debt had to be serviced and ultimately paid off. In addition, the war endowed future generations with a precious asset, freedom, as well as a debt.

From the mid-1940s to the mid-1970s, the federal debt ratio was reduced to about 25 percent. This happened for two reasons. First, the government ran a series of budget surpluses, so that year over year the debt declined in absolute (i.e., dollar) terms. Second, we enjoyed a period during which the economy's average growth rate exceeded the interest rate that the government had to pay on the debt. When this happens, and the non-interest part of the government's budget is balanced, the numerator of the debt ratio (i.e., the debt) grows more slowly than the denominator (i.e., GDP), which means the ratio falls. Canadians appeared to approve of this gradual working back down of the debt ratio, perhaps because they implicitly understood that this was necessary if the government was to be well-positioned to run it back up again should another major negative shock hit.

Between the mid-1970s and the mid-1990s the federal government did run up the debt ratio again – by almost 50 percentage points. In retrospect, most Canadians have difficulty identifying the major shock that might have justified this development. Some point to the oil crisis of the 1970s, but since Canada is approximately self-sufficient in energy, this was a crisis mainly for central Canada. The drop in the growth rate of productivity that took place around the time of OPEC-I is another candidate. Unfortunately, we still do not know what caused this slowdown. Nor is there any real basis for confidence that we are now entering a period of sustained higher productivity growth. Looking at much longer periods of data, it now seems that the 1950s and 1960s were the abnormal period: the mid-1970s to mid-1990s were fairly normal in terms of productivity growth rates. They seemed depressed only in view of the abnormally high growth rates observed in the 25 years that preceded them. But if all that happened to productivity post-1973 was a return to economic normality, there was no justification, not *ex post*, at least, for running up debt as a compensation for temporary difficulties. A final consideration is that we had tough recessions in the early 1980s and the early 1990s, and these events could have justified some load-spreading. But this consideration can justify only *temporary* increases in the debt ratio that should have been removed by the mid-1990s. By the early 1990s, therefore, many Canadians had reached the conclusion that the debt ratio had to be brought back down, both because there now appeared to be little justification for having run it up in the previous 20 years and because we needed to be ready for an occasion when deficit budgets would be appropriate.

One final consideration is suggested by recent history. A federal debt ratio of about 75 percent (or a consolidated federal-provincial debt ratio of about 100 percent) seems to be about as high as prudence allows. They exceed New Zealand's debt ratio when foreign lenders stopped buying that country's debt entirely. Moreover, the bond rating agencies downgraded Canadian government debt when we reached this level of indebtedness in the mid-1990s.

I suggest the following reaction to this history on the part of Canadian policy makers; they should approach the debt issue by answering the following three questions:

1. What is the maximum debt ratio that can be sustained without significant costs being imposed by lenders demanding a costly risk premium?
2. What is the next "bad" development to hit Canada likely to be, and by how much do we expect this development to reduce living standards – albeit not necessarily in absolute terms but compared to what they would otherwise grow to?
3. Can debt reduction be used to counteract this coming threat to living standards?

In earlier work, Harriet Jackson of Finance Canada and I pursued just such an approach (see Scarth and Jackson 1998). We started from the proposition that our postwar high in government indebtedness (a federal debt ratio of about 75 percent (or a consolidated federal-provincial debt ratio of about 100 percent) is about as high as we should go. Next, we identified the retirement of the baby-boom generation as the next major socio-economic shock awaiting Canada. The big disparity in the size of the baby-boom cohort and the post-baby-boom generation can be interpreted as another of the legacies of the depression and the war. We then built a simple intergenerational model to examine the effects of the increased old-age dependency ratio that is expected by the demographers. Finally, we asked the model how much the mid-1990s debt ratio would have to be decreased if the country were to avoid the reduction in living standards that would otherwise accompany this demographic change. Note that the reduction in question is not in absolute living standards as they are today but in living standards as they would have been without the demographic shift. Our answer was that the debt ratio needed to be reduced by 50 percentage points. We concluded that intergenerational equity required a federal government debt ratio roughly equal to Canada's postwar low (between 20 and 25 percent), and therefore a consolidated (federal plus provincial) debt-ratio target of about 50 percent.

The reasoning that drove this conclusion can be clarified by reference to figures 1 and 2 (overleaf), which show the time path of per capita consumption. Without the aging of the baby boom, our model predicts that per capita consumption would continue along the dashed line in figure 1. With population aging, however, the time path follows the solid line: living standards decline because a high proportion of the population will be dependent on a much smaller group of workers. With labour being the relatively scarce factor of production when the baby boomers are retired, wages will rise, so those in the post-baby-boom generation can be better off, and simulations verify the likelihood of this possibility (see Scarth 2002). But since capital will be a relatively abundant factor of production, its return will likely fall, and since retired individuals depend heavily on interest income, the baby boomers themselves will be less well off than they would have been without this disparity in cohort sizes. Simulations indicate that this reduction in living standards for the baby boomers will dominate any improvement in the economic well-being of the following generation, so, overall, living standards will decline.

Figure 2 indicates what happens to this measure of average living standards with government debt reduction and no aging of the population. If no debt reduction were undertaken (and with no population aging), per capita consumption would follow the dashed line in figure 2. But with debt reduction, there is short-term pain and long-term gain, as illustrated by the solid line in figure 2. The reason is that, in the short term, programs must be cut and/or taxes must be increased to eliminate the deficit. But, after a period of surplus budgets, a lower level of debt remains, and new room in the government's budget is created by the reduction in interest payment obligations. This new room permits more generous programs and/or lower taxes. It is not just that debt reduction makes it possible for governments to provide more with lower taxes. When citizens save more (by having their governments stop *dis*-saving) the level of the nation's foreign indebtedness falls. This development allows domestic citizens to keep a bigger share of the GDP for domestic consumption (instead of having to use it for making interest payments to foreigners).

We used our algebraic model to answer the following geometric question: How much debt reduction is needed to ensure that distance CD in figure 2 equals distance AB in figure 1? The strategy is to have no change in living standards since there will be one "good" development cancelling off one "bad" one. The good development is that living standards will be pushed up by debt reduction, the bad development that they will be pushed down by the increase in the old-age dependency ratio. How much debt reduction, we wanted to know, would just offset the reduction in living standards caused by the increase in the old-age dependency ratio?

Our answer was, as I have indicated, a reduction of about 50 percent from the high levels of the 1990s, which means that by the end of 2002 about half the debt-reduction job had been done. Of course, it is possible to embrace the intergenerational equity criterion for selecting a debt-ratio target without accepting either our numerical estimates or our presumption that the exogenous growth theory we used is a suitable basis for the analysis. ("Exogenous

Figure 1
Time Path of Per-Capita Consumption

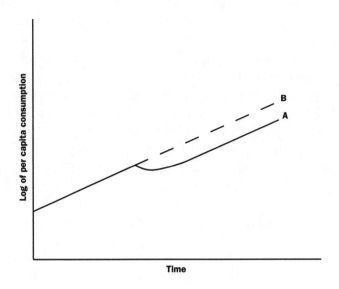

Figure 2
Time Path of Per-Capita Consumption

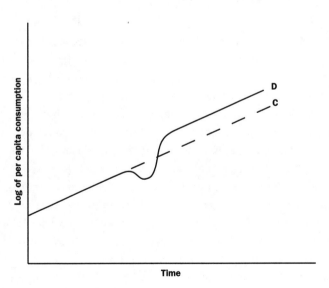

growth" means the growth rate is set by factors that do not emerge from our model: we simply take the rate as given.) For one thing, as Jack Mintz argued at this conference, the costs of the aging population may be larger than we assumed, and if so, an even lower debt-ratio target would be appropriate. For another, the analysis could be redone in an endogenous growth setting, by exploring the effects that both population aging and lower debt have on the growth rate itself. Referring back to figures 1 and 2, population aging and debt reduction may result in the solid lines having slopes that are different from that of the dashed line in each figure. Population aging might flatten the growth path (that is, slow growth down) while debt reduction might steepen the path (by speeding growth up). If so, policy makers would need to know how much debt reduction is needed to keep the growth path of living standards unaffected in a world in which the growth rate itself does indeed respond to both debt reduction and population aging.

In fact, in a recent paper I have considered the aging population half of this package (see Scarth 2002). The details of the model economy I use are explained in the appendix of that paper. Here I simply note the main features of the analysis and discuss the results. My model economy has two sectors: the manufacturing sector, which produces both consumption goods and physical capital, and the education sector, which produces human capital. Both forms of capital are employed in the manufacturing sector, while only human capital plays a role in the production of knowledge. Manufacturing firms hire factors with a view to maximizing profits, and households make all their decisions – allocating their holdings of wealth across the two forms of capital, choosing the proportion of their time to work, and deciding how much to save each period – with a view to maximizing lifetime utility. Generations overlap, that is, when today's young people are old, their children are young, with each individual facing the same life expectancy and the same retirement age.

I use this model to illustrate the effects on the rate of economic growth of a one-time reduction in the retirement age that raises the old-age dependency ratio by the amount demographers expect the aging of Canada's baby boomers to do. In fact, I find no discernable effect on the growth rate, since competing effects tend to cancel each other out. At the individual level, there are growth-rate-increasing developments. For example, individuals know they will spend more time in retirement, so they save more, and more physical capital is accumulated. However, there is also a reduction in aggregate human capital, since more individuals are retired and this development retards growth. The simulations indicate that these competing effects on the growth rate almost exactly cancel out. This means that no debt reduction whatsoever is required to insulate the growth rate of living standards from the higher old-age dependency ratio.

In writing the present paper, I have extended this analysis to allow for debt reduction. The specific changes are explained in part I of the appendix. In keeping with the current situation facing our federal authorities, I have examined the government lowering the debt ratio from an initial value of 50 percent to 25 percent. This policy (with its accompanying reduction in the tax rate) raises the equilibrium annual growth rate above its initial value of 2.5 percent by 4/100 of one percentage point. The intuition is straightforward: debt reduction permits lower taxes, and a lower tax rate results in a higher after-tax return on saving. With this increased incentive to save, more capital is accumulated, and this pushes up the growth rate. But is the estimated magnitude of this response a "significant" effect? Because the growth is permanently higher, the extra income accrues year after year into the future, so how much people value it depends on how they feel about future income, and that depends on interest rates and tax rates. Using plausible values for these variables, a reasonable guess is that living standards would be about two and a quarter percent higher.[3] This estimate suggests that debt reduction may be about twice as effective for raising living standards, compared to what Harriet Jackson and I derived from our simpler analysis that abstracted from a growth rate effect.

Overall, how should the sensitivity tests that have been discussed in the last four paragraphs affect our interpretation of our application of the intergenerational equity criterion for defining a debt-ratio target? Some analysts, including Jack Mintz in this volume, have accepted the exogenous growth specification, but have argued that the costs of the aging population may be larger than we considered. This line of argument leads to a recommendation for a lower debt-ratio target. The endogenous growth analysis that I have reported here supports the earlier work in that it suggests that debt reduction is an effective tool for raising average living standards. A reduction in the debt ratio raises the growth rate by an amount that is roughly equivalent to the one-time upward shift in the level of the per-capita consumption growth path that has been estimated in the simpler exogenous growth models. But, in another sense, my endogenous growth rate analysis does not support my earlier work with Harriet Jackson, since it indicates that a higher old-age dependency ratio brings no significant reduction in the growth rate of living standards. This finding implies that less debt reduction (that is, a higher debt-ratio target) is called for. Thus, by simplifying and ignoring endogenous growth, Harriet Jackson and I introduced a bias in our analysis that works in the opposite direction than does the possibility that we may have underestimated the costs of population aging. It is possible that our omissions may cancel each other out. (In this case, two wrongs may make a right.) If so, our original conclusion that a federal debt-ratio target of between 20 and 25 percent of GDP and an overall debt-ratio target of about

50 percent remains appealing. Unfortunately, much more detailed analysis (that is beyond the scope of this paper) is needed to pursue this possibility. But if, as a very rough approximation, we assume that our separately estimated one-time level and growth-rate effects on living standards can simply be added together, and if we assume that the depressing effect of the aging population will be double what we have estimated, then no revision in the estimated target debt ratio is called for. Of course, a fuller analysis of the transitional dynamics in an endogenous growth-rate setting may not support the simple adding together of the two separately estimated effects on living standards. But it is also the case that many (such as Mérette 2002) argue that the negative effect of the aging population on living standards may be less, not more, than what Harriet Jackson and I have estimated. In the end, therefore, our earlier estimate for a target debt ratio seems a reasonable compromise in the light of existing controversy.

Who Receives the Benefits of Debt Reduction?

Other things being equal, debt reduction gives the government new room in its annual budget, since the authorities have smaller interest payments to make each year. Who benefits from this new room in the budget depends on what the government does with it. In our 1998 analysis, Harriet Jackson and I assumed that the government increases the level of a general transfer payment that goes to all individuals and has no incentive effects. To allow for interesting *within*-generation equity considerations, our analysis involved what Mankiw (2000) later called for: two groups of households. One is forward-looking, and since it faces no borrowing constraints beyond the simple proposition that its net worth not be negative, its spending decisions are based on its future lifetime wealth, not its current income. The other group of households is impatient, consuming all its current income each period. In effect, it is liquidity-constrained and lives "hand-to-mouth."

Now suppose that instead of increasing general transfer payments the government cuts the tax on capital. What happens? It depends on which group you belong to. Because the forward-looking group derives a significant portion of its income from capital, which is now less heavily taxed, these households' living standards rise. This result supports those who argue that the government should use its fiscal dividend to make the economy more internationally tax-competitive rather than spend it raising transfer payments. But sceptics fear that things may work out less favourably for the liquidity-constrained households. Living standards for this group improve only if wages rise significantly. The intuition behind this uncertainty is straightforward. On the one hand, the hand-to-mouth group loses because (like the other group) its receipt of transfer payments is less than in the base case. On the other hand, this group gains because the tax cut brings a "trickle-down" benefit. With lower interest rates, there is more capital for labour to work with, and so everyone's wage income is higher. It turns out that, in our standard model at least, this trickle-down benefit must be the dominant consideration. This is because the tax on capital has incentive effects, while a general transfer payment does not. By using the fiscal dividend to partially eliminate a measure that restricts the overall size of GDP, as the capital tax does, there is more material welfare available. A similar increase in the size of the overall "economic pie" does not emerge with an increase in transfer payments. Further, since the capital tax cut makes it possible for the pre-tax rate of return on capital to fall, labour's relative price must rise. Thus, hand-to-mouth households, which depend so heavily on labour income, must be better off.

Of course, other comparisons can lead to different conclusions. Suppose the government is choosing between using the fiscal dividend to cut the tax on capital and using it to cut an employee payroll tax. This comparison involves two measures that both have incentive effects. In a more general model involving structural unemployment, a lower payroll tax leads to lower unemployment. With increased labour to work with, capital is more productive. It is then possible for there to be more goods produced, even if the quantity of capital operating within the country is reduced by the tax on capital. As explained in Scarth (2003, 255-56) hand-to-mouth households are likely to be better off if it is the payroll tax, not the tax on capital, that is cut. But, our federal government has chosen to increase, not decrease, payroll taxes (to keep the public pension system financially viable with the aging population). Given this fact, I consider the initial comparison (between a cut in the tax on capital and an increase in transfer payments) as the more relevant discussion of alternatives for the fiscal dividend. As a result, I conclude that even the liquidity-constrained households do better if the fiscal dividend is *not* used for making general transfer payments more generous. This is an important conclusion, since it is necessary to support the case for debt reduction with the fiscal dividend earmarked for corporate tax cuts. After all, if the case for debt reduction is based on *inter*generational *equity* it hardly makes sense to opt for a policy package that could be undesirable on *within*-generation equity grounds.

The analysis of the previous paragraph is reassuring for lower-income individuals, since it indicates that they benefit from debt reduction even when the fiscal dividend is used in a way that appears to ignore them. But it must be remembered that, so far, I have summarized a before-and-after analysis of what economists call "full-equilibrium" effects and I have said nothing about what happens to living standards during the transition between a period of high debt to one involving low debt. Some studies, such as Macklem, Rose and Tetlow (1994) have calculated the present value of both the consumption losses incurred during the belt-tightening period and the consumption gains enjoyed later on, and have concluded that the gains exceed the losses, so debt reduction passes the present-value test. It may be more difficult to support this conclusion when the analysis is applied to lower-income households, however.

Suppose the government initiates debt reduction by cutting transfer payments, and then gradually restores them as new room in the budget gradually appears. In this case, consumption on the part of liquidity-constrained individuals displays a time path that is identical to the government's fiscal dividend. Part II of the appendix uses the basic government accounting identities to calculate the present value of this series of changes, which turns out to be a weighted average of the initial undesirable effect and the eventual desirable effect. The weights in the average are the speed of adjustment to the full equilibrium (the economy's growth rate), and the discount rate used in social decisions. The faster the economy gets to the new equilibrium, the less important are the short-run undesirable effects, so (appropriately) the summary calculation puts less weight on these short-run developments and more weight on the long-run desirable effect. On the other hand, the less people care about the future compared to the present (the bigger is the discount rate), the more the future is ignored, so the bigger is the weight given to the undesirable short-run effect in the summary calculation. By consulting the appendix the reader can verify that setting the social discount rate equal to the after-tax interest rate makes this present value zero. In this case, debt reduction does not pass (or fail) the present-value test. But it is not clear how much emphasis should be given to this finding. After all, the patient segment of the population discounts the future less heavily (has a smaller discount rate than the economy's interest rate) while the hand-to-mouth group pays less attention to the future (has a discount rate that is higher than the rate of interest). If the discount rate in the overall present value calculation is set equal to the rate of time preference of the forward-looking segment of the population, debt reduction is supported. But if the discount rate is set equal to the rate of time preference of the liquidity-constrained group, debt reduction is not supported. Because there is no good reason to use the time preference rate for one group (the one that faces no borrowing constraints) to assess the worth of debt reduction for the other (lower-income) group, we conclude that the case for debt reduction, if ultimately it must be based on equity considerations, may be less complete than is often assumed.

A Capital-Budgeting Approach to Government Debt

Another equity-based argument that is sometimes made is that a government should issue debt only when it acquires capital that generates a rate of return equal to that earned on private capital. One virtue of this rule is that it ensures the government always has assets to balance its debts. Another is that it directs our attention to public investments (e.g., in health and education) that have the highest payoffs. But the problem with this approach is that it makes it very difficult for the government to use debt policy as a mechanism for effecting transfers across generations. In the model used in this paper, this difficulty can be illustrated by deriving the effects on per capita consumption that follow from a reduction in the debt ratio in which the fiscal dividend is used to raise government spending (instead of increasing transfer payments or cutting corporate taxes). Assume that government spending is on investment goods that are just as productive as the capital that is accumulated via private investment spending. As explained in part II of the appendix, the result is that living standards of both the forward-looking and the liquidity-constrained groups are completely unaffected by debt reduction. Again, the intuition is straightforward. Government debt brings both desirable and undesirable effects. The undesirable effect is that it "crowds out" privately-financed capital accumulation. The desirable effect is that it makes possible publicly-financed capital accumulation that is of equal value. But the two effects exactly cancel. The outcome observed earlier, in which the government used borrowing to finance an increase in the consumption of liquidity-constrained households who could not borrow, does not take place: there is no overall increase in consumption. Investment spending of one kind is replaced with investment spending of another kind. The point of this analysis is not to claim that there is no difference between (say) public investment in health or education and private investment in physical capital. Instead, it is intended to show that *if* there is no such difference (and this is the underlying rationale behind the capital-budgeting approach to the government) debt reduction loses its ability to redistribute across generations.

This analysis makes clear that using debt reduction to effect redistribution across generations is based on the assumption that the government does *not* use its fiscal dividend to finance increased spending on investment goods that are just as valuable as privately-financed capital. In sum, the capital-budgeting approach removes the underlying (intergenerational) rationale for debt reduction.

Government Debt and Macroeconomic Stability

In addition to the efficiency and equity criteria for assessing government initiatives, economists also usually evaluate public policy from the vantage point of macroeconomic stability. Are the built-in stability features of the economy increased or decreased by our public debt policy? When applying this criterion to the debt question, two propositions are usually stressed.

The first is that a high debt ratio disturbs the bond-rating agencies. The resulting cost may be fairly small if all that happens is that the country must pay a risk premium on its international debt-service costs, thus reducing the living standards of its citizens to some extent. Or the cost may be large if financial capital flees the country and interest rates escalate to very high levels in an exchange-rate crisis. We assume that Canada is not facing a scenario anything like this, so that considerations of this sort are second-order.

The second nexus between debt and macro stability concerns whether the debt ratio should be allowed to vary over the business cycle – whatever long-run average value for the ratio has been decided upon. One of the central lessons of the Great Depression was that adjusting annual spending and taxation with a view to maintaining a fixed budget-balance target "come hell or high water" increases output volatility: spending has to be cut and taxes raised as the economy slows down, which is exactly the time you do not want that to happen. The Keynesian message was that it is better to help balance the economy by balancing the budget over the time horizon of one full business cycle, not over an arbitrary shorter period such as one year. Thus, for at least a half-century following the depression, it was assumed that a rigid annually balanced budget approach was "obviously" to be avoided. But the Keynesian message has been increasingly ignored in recent years. As the "hell or high water" quotation indicates, our federal government has reverted to annual budget-balance targets with only a fairly small contingency fund to permit departures from a more rigid regime. Adoption of the "Growth and Stability Pact" in Europe has had a similar effect. As *The Economist* magazine has editorialized:

> as the euro area faces the possibility of its first recession … the stability pact must not only preclude any fiscal easing but even trammel the operation of fiscal "automatic stabilizers." That could mean that these countries are required to increase taxes or cut public spending even as their economies slow. That smacks of 1930s-style self-flagellation (25 August 2001, 13).

Are *The Economist's* editorial writers correct or are they simply in the thrall of a hopelessly outdated Keynesianism? Is it, or is it not, appropriate for the government to allow cyclical variation in its debt ratio by running deficits during recessions and surpluses during booms?

In a paper written in 1999, the C. D. Howe Institute's William Robson and I tried to remind people that there is a long literature assessing the usefulness of Keynesian-style "built-in stabilizers." For example, 30 years ago, Helliwell and Gorbet (1971) and Smyth (1974) showed that these mechanisms can serve as *de*-stabilizers. Running a deficit budget during a downturn may well decrease the size of that initial recession. But over time the government debt must be worked back down, so the overall speed of adjustment of the economy is reduced. The initial recession is smaller, but the recovery takes longer.

In a paper written in 2002, Jean-Paul Lam and I investigated whether this (undesirable) "increased persistence" property of the Keynesian debt policy is bigger or smaller than the (desirable) decreased impact-effect property, when that regime is compared to the rigid regime in a setting that respects the requirements of the modern approach to business-cycle theory.[4] We concluded that in many cases the rigid regime delivers output volatility that is not appreciably larger than occurs in the Keynesian regime. Amano, Coletti and Macklem (1999, 28, 42) report a similar result.

One of the reasons for this perhaps surprising result is that monetary policy changes with the fiscal regime. The goal of monetary policy – maintaining zero expected future inflation – does not change. But the central bank's "response function" is derived within the model, and it *does* depend on changes in the rest of the model, including a shift in the fiscal regime. It turns out to be optimal for the central bank to raise the interest rate whenever expected future output is rising, even when the economy is recovering from a recession. But the magnitude of this response is less when the rigid regime is in place. It seems that the central bank can afford to be less aggressive when the fiscal authority has adopted the regime that has a more stabilizing effect on long-term expectations. So the bank pays more attention to the short-run output considerations that makers of fiscal policy in effect are ignoring. Considering this work and the related analysis of Amano, Coletti and Macklem (1999), I conclude that short-run output volatility is increased only to a very limited extent when a fairly rigid target for the annual budget deficit is adopted.

Conclusions

In this paper I have evaluated alternative levels of government debt in terms of their effect on economic efficiency, equity and macroeconomic stability. For some of these criteria, the available literature does not deliver any specific policy advice. In particular, studies focusing on efficiency indicate that virtually any debt ratio is as good, or not, as any other. Similarly, research on macro stability issues suggests that surprisingly little is lost if the annual deficit-ratio target does not vary over the business cycle. These somewhat negative findings imply that the chosen target for the debt ratio must be based primarily on its consistency with society's equity objectives, and particularly its objectives for intergenerational equity. This is not an altogether comforting conclusion for an economist to make, since my profession's expertise traditionally has been thought to concern efficiency and macroeconomic stability, not equity.

Nevertheless, the intergenerational equity approach that is implied involves letting the debt ratio rise when the nation faces major events – such as World War II or unique demographic events such as population aging – that can reasonably be expected to lower living standards. Government debt is a tool that allows society to spread the burden of such events across several generations. But if society is to follow this approach, it must work the debt ratio back down after each of the *limited number* of such major events. Only by doing so can governments employ this consumption-smoothing policy on an ongoing basis without putting their long-run credibility at risk. If there is a long-run upward trend to the debt ratio, we eventually reach a state when individuals refuse to purchase more debt. This outcome has two effects. It limits further government initiatives, and it raises interest rates generally, so that our ability to accumulate capital is reduced and the growth in general living standards compromised. At the present time, with the impending aging of the baby boomers, this consumption-smoothing strategy calls for working the federal debt ratio down to the 20–25 percent range (and the consolidated federal and provincial debt ratio down to the 45–50 percent range) within the next 10 years.

Such a target can only be approximate, however, the benefits of debt reduction depend on how the resulting fiscal dividend is used, and on whether debt reduction and population aging lead to permanent effects on the economy's growth *rate*. Here I have relied on specific models to try to illustrate the sensitivity of the results to these issues. Several conclusions, some encouraging and some discouraging, have emerged. On the encouraging side, the analysis involving "hand-to-mouth" consumers who own no capital suggests that the benefits of debt reduction do "trickle down" to these households, even when the fiscal dividend is devoted entirely to cutting taxes on capital. On the discouraging side, for these hand-to-mouth households, we have found that the present value of the short-term pain of debt reduction exceeds the present value of this long-term gain.

I hope that, with these dimensions of the debate a little clearer, readers are in a position to attach their own weights to the various issues, and to reach their own decision concerning the "optimal" debt-ratio target. Some readers may wish to attach weight to society's "revealed preference" that is inherent in past political outcomes. The postwar low for the federal government's debt ratio (achieved in the early 1970s) was in the 20–25 percent range. This is the very target that has emerged from the analysis in this paper.

appendix

This appendix contains two parts. The first cannot be read independently of Scarth (2002); it outlines the changes in the endogenous growth model analyzed in that paper that are necessary to allow for debt (and this analysis is referred to in the third section of this paper). The second outlines the model that lies behind the following two sections of this paper.

Part I

The government budget constraint in Scarth (2002) is changed to

$$(n + z)b = g - t \ (dK/Y) + r^*b,$$

where $r^* = r(1 - t)$, and g, t, r, n, z, d, K and Y denote, respectively, the ratio of program spending to GDP, the ratio of taxes to GDP, the interest rate, the productivity growth rate, the population growth rate, the depreciation rate of capital, the stock of physical capital, and GDP. Given this different specification of the government accounts, the calibration had to be altered somewhat. The result reported in the text (which is representative of several simulations involving alternative parameter sets) involves the following assumptions: net return on capital: 6 percent, depreciation rate of capital: 4 percent, initial productivity growth rate: 2.5 percent, population growth rate: 0.5 percent, physical capital's share of output in the manufacturing sector: 33 percent, rate of time preference:

2.9 percent, tax rate on incomes earned in the manufacturing sector: 18.67 percent, initial debt ratio: 50 percent, life expectancy: 50 years after commencing work, and no retirement. These assumptions imply that the ratios of consumption, investment and program spending to GDP are 65 percent, 20 percent and 15 percent.

Part II

The full-equilibrium version of the model discussed in the fourth and fifth sections is given by the following relationships:

$$r + d = aylk \quad (1)$$

$$r^* = r(1 - t) \quad (2)$$

$$g + q + (r^* - n - z)b = trk + s(1 - a)y \quad (3)$$

$$-(r^* - n - z)v = y - (r^* + d)k - g - c - e \quad (4)$$

$$e = (1 - j)[(1 - s)(1 - a)y + q] \quad (5)$$

$$(r^* - m - n)c = (p + z)(p + m)(v + b) \quad (6)$$

All variables are defined on a per-unit-of-effective-labour basis (and n is the exogenous growth rate in labour productivity). The notation is: c: consumption spending on the part of the forward-looking households, e: expenditure on the part of the liquidity-constrained households, j: proportion of households who are not liquidity constrained, v: that portion of the domestically employed capital (k) that is domestically owned, s: tax on labour income, t: tax on capital's net-of-depreciation returns, q: level of transfer payments made to all citizens, g: government spending on goods, b: government debt, k: capital, d: depreciation rate, a: capital's exponent in the Cobb-Douglas production function, $y = Ak^a$.

A detailed explanation of each equation is available in Scarth and Jackson (1998); a brief sketch of the model's structure is given here.

Labour supply is exogenous and there is full employment. Capital is hired so that its marginal product equals its rental cost (equation (1)), and the after-tax rate of return is fixed by perfect international capital mobility (equation (2)). Equation (3) is the government budget identity and equation (4) indicates that net exports just pay for the net interest payment obligations to foreigners.

Equations (5) and (6) are the consumption functions; the liquidity-constrained individuals set expenditures equal to their income (equation (5)) and the forward-looking planners follow the consumption function derived in Blanchard (1985), (equation (6)).

To support the conclusions in the fourth section, we derive how c and e are affected by a cut in t that is financed by a cut in q (with b held constant). To support the conclusions in the fifth section, we derive how c and e are affected by a cut in b that is used to raise g, with $g = \Delta k_2 + (n - r^*)k_2$, $k = k_1 + k_2$, and with v involving just k_1.

The present-value test for debt reduction (referred to in section four) can be explained as follows. The government's fiscal dividend is denoted by DIV. In each period, the deficit-to-GDP ratio equals $g - t + r^* b$, and in full equilibrium it equals $((n + z)b)$. These relationships imply that the initial effect of a reduction in spending of one unit on the fiscal dividend is $\Delta DIV_1 = 1$, and that the eventual effect on the fiscal dividend is $\Delta DIV_2 = -(r^* - n - z)/(n + z)$. As explained in Scarth (1996, 241-42), the present value of these changes equals $[1/r^*(r^* + n + z)] [(n + z)\Delta DIV_2 + i\Delta DIV_1]$, if i is the social discount rate. The reader can verify that $i = r^*$ makes this present value zero.

Notes

Without implication, I wish to thank the participants at the conference (in particular Robin Boadway, Chris Ragan, David Johnson, Tiff Macklem, and Jeremy Rudin) and Cheng Chang and Bill Watson for helpful comments.

1. In absolute value, the optimal debt ratio is equal to the ratio of the government's program spending (defined as a proportion of GDP) to the difference between the interest rate the government receives on its claims and the GDP growth rate (so long as the interest rate exceeds the growth rate). Since a low value for the program spending ratio is 15 percent and a high value for the net interest rate is 5 percent, the optimal debt ratio is at least negative 300 percent, according to this "complete markets" view.

2. For example, Cooley and Hansen (1991) show that disinflation has a positive net benefit when consumption taxes are used to fill this void, but a negative net benefit if capital taxes are relied upon.

3. One way to approach this question is to note that if consumption grows at rate n, and if i denotes the discount rate, the present value of that perpetual stream of consumption is $1/(i - n)$. This present value is $1/(0.0445-0.025)$ initially (with the discount rate equalling the average of the after-tax interest rate and the households' rate of time preference in the baseline calibration outlined in the appendix). With debt reduction of 25 percentage points it rises by 2.2 percent to $1/(0.0445-0.02541)$. Given the estimates of the benefits that accompany this amount of debt reduction that are available in the exogenous growth literature (an increase in living standards of between 1.7 percent and 3.2 percent; see Robson and Scarth (1994, 29-32, 38)), this growth-*rate* effect should be interpreted as significant.

4. We used a "new neoclassical synthesis" model which combines the simplified aggregative structure of more traditional studies with explicit underpinnings based on intertemporal optimization. The synthesis model involves four components: (i) an expectational demand function, based on the Ramsey (1928) theory of consumption (with total spending depending on the real interest rate, expected future output, and the expected change in government spending), (ii) an expectations-augmented aggregate supply relationship of the sort described in Calvo (1983) or McCallum (1994), (iii) the central bank's interest rate-setting relationship (which is derived by minimizing expected future inflation), and (iv) the government budget constraint.

Bibliography

Aiyagari, S. 1995. "Optimal Capital Income Taxation with Incomplete Markets and Borrowing Constraints." *Journal of Political Economy* 103:1158-75.

Aiyagari, S., and E. McGrattan. 1998. "The Optimum Quantity of Debt." *Journal of Monetary Economics* 42:447-69.

Amano, R., D. Coletti and T. Macklem. 1999. "Monetary Rules when Economic Behaviour Changes." Working Paper no. 99-8. Ottawa: Bank of Canada.

Barro, R., and X. Sala-i-Martin. 1995. *Economic Growth.* New York: McGraw-Hill.

Blanchard, O. 1985. "Debt, Deficits, and Finite Horizons." *Journal of Political Economy* 93:223-47.

Calvo, G. 1983. "Staggered Contracts in a Utility-Maximizing Framework." *Journal of Monetary Economics* 12:383-98.

Cooley, T., and G. Hansen. 1991. "The Welfare Cost of Moderate Inflation." *Journal of Money, Credit and Banking* 23:483-503.

Helliwell, J.F., and F. Gorbet. 1971. "Assessing the Dynamic Efficiency of Automatic Stabilizers." *Journal of Political Economy* 79:826-45.

James, S., and P. Karam. 2001. "The Role of Government Debt in a World of Incomplete Financial Markets." Working Paper no. 2001-01. Ottawa: Finance Canada.

Lam, J.-P., and W. Scarth. 2002. "Alternative Public Spending Rules and Output Volatility." Working Paper no. 2002-37. Ottawa: Bank of Canada.

Lucas, R. 1988. "On the Mechanics of Development Planning." *Journal of Monetary Economics* 22:3-42.

Ljungqvist, L., and T. Sargent. 2000. *Recursive Macroeconomic Theory.* Cambridge, MA: MIT Press.

Macklem, T., D. Rose and R. Tetlow. 1994. "Government Debt and Deficits in Canada: A Macro Simulation Analysis." In *Deficit Reduction: What Pain, What Gain?* ed. W. Robson and W. Scarth. Policy Study no. 23. Toronto: C.D. Howe Institute.

Mankiw, N.G. 2000. "The Savers-Spenders Theory of Fiscal Policy." *American Economic Review, Papers and Proceedings* 90:120-25.

McCallum, B. 1994. "A Semi-Classical Model of Price Level Adjustment." *Carnegie-Rochester Conference Series on Public Policy* 41:251-84.

Mérette, M. 2002. "The Bright Side: A Positive View on the Economics of Aging." *Choices* 8, no. 1.

Ramsey, F. 1928. "A Mathematical Theory of Saving." *Economic Journal* 38:543-59.

Robson, W., and W. Scarth. 1994. "Debating Deficit Reduction: Economic Perspectives and Policy Choices." In *Deficit Reduction: What Pain, What Gain?* ed. W. Robson and W. Scarth. Policy Study no. 23. Toronto: C.D. Howe Institute.

————. 1999. *Accident-Proof Budgeting: Debt-Reduction Payoffs, Fiscal Credibility, and Economic Stabilization.* Commentary no. 129. Toronto: C.D. Howe Institute.

Scarth, W. 1996. *Macroeconomics: An Introduction to Advanced Methods,* 2d ed. Toronto: Dryden Press.

————. 2002. "Population Aging, Productivity and Growth in Living Standards." In *Review of Economic Performance and Social Progress: Towards a Social Understanding of*

Productivity, ed. A. Sharpe, F. St-Hilaire and K. Banting. Montreal: Centre for the Study of Living Standards and Institute for Research on Public Policy, pp. 145-56.

————. 2003. *Economics: The Essentials*, 3d ed. Toronto: Thomson/Nelson.

Scarth, W., and H. Jackson. 1998. "The Target Debt-to-GDP Ratio: How Big Should It Be? And How Quickly Should We Approach It?" In *Fiscal Targets and Economic Growth*, ed. T. Courchene and T. Wilson. Kingston: The John Deutsch Institute for the Study of Economic Policy, Queen's University.

Smyth, D.J. 1974. "Built-in Flexibility of Taxation and Stability in a Simple Dynamic IS-LM Model." *Public Finance* 29:111-13.

Turnovsky, S. 2000. *Methods of Macroeconomic Dynamics*, 2d ed. Cambridge, MA: MIT Press.

the target debt ratio:
a balance-sheet view

François Vaillancourt

These brief comments are divided into two parts. First, I react to some aspects of William Scarth's paper. Then I present some evidence from a balance-sheet perspective, one Scarth scarcely touches upon.

Reactions to the Scarth Paper

Efficiency. Scarth first reports the intriguing finding (by Ljungqvist and Sargent 2000) that tax revenues should be entirely replaced by interest payments that former taxpayers would make to a government whose debt would equal –300 percent of gross domestic product (GDP). In other words, the government would accumulate assets equal to 300 percent of GDP and then live off the interest. He then turns to the view (Aiyagari and McGrattan 1998) that because of imperfect markets, individuals accumulate too many assets so the state should increase their welfare by borrowing. Finally, he reports on simulation results that yield an optimal debt-to-GDP ratio ranging between –200 to +66 percent.

Scarth is correct in saying that this literature "does not provide a strong case for any particular debt ratio," but one would have liked him to indicate what credence, if any, should be given to models that argue for no taxation and negative debt. Moreover, even if one believes that on balance people do overaccumulate assets, something which is not clear given that they may be animated by a "conditional bequest" motive (i.e., "If I end up not to need it all, my utility will be enhanced by bequeathing it"), how does one match an overall public debt to the specific behaviour of various individuals? Improvements to imperfect financial markets, whether through reverse mortgages or more varied types of annuities, might well yield better results by making it more possible for people to get closer to their preferred level of savings.

Equity. Scarth first argues that "we should select the level of debt that is most consistent with our view of intergenerational fairness," taking into account the maximum debt ratio acceptable to lenders, the shocks that affect living standards and the use of debt reduction to reduce such shocks. He then examines who benefits from debt reduction, distinguishing between, on the one hand, forward-looking individuals who save and, on the other, people who live hand-to-mouth and do not save. He notes, finally, that linking debt to the acquisition of assets constrains intergenerational transfers.

Scarth illustrates his first point, about intergenerational equity, by reviewing recent Canadian experience with debt. The federal debt increased between 1925 and 1945 from 45 percent to 110 percent of GDP. It then fell to 25 percent in 1975, rose to almost 75 percent in 1995 and has since declined. What is interesting is that in explaining this roller-coaster ride Scarth puts on the same footing: a true exogenous shock (World War II), a policy shock generated by ignorance (the Great Depression) and a policy shock (in the 1970s) that was the choice of a government that may have been blinded by future oil revenues but was not constrained by either war or ignorance. In my view, his approach to this problem is incorrect: not all types of shock impose the same reimbursement requirements on a given generation (more on this later).

Scarth's second concern, which is an intragenerational question, is to ask why some individuals are "liquidity-constrained," that is, must live from hand to mouth. If it is by choice – they are "born-to-shop" types – then it is not clear why society should be concerned more by their circumstances than by those of the savers Scarth describes. If it is not by choice, then the appropriate policy response may be some kind of transfer payment, perhaps with a requirement for financial training, but there is no reason why the cost of such a payment should be passed on to future generations.

Scarth's third point, on how allowing governments to use debt finance only when they are acquiring assets would constrain intergenerational transfers, is particularly important. Such constraints are a good idea. Why would we want one generation of voters to have the right to make intergenerational transfers of debt when experience shows that, at least in Canada and the United States, such transfers are often made to finance current consumption? Our revealed debt preferences have certainly taken us a long way from Rawls' suggestion that each generation should put aside some real capital for the next. Rawls does not specify the exact amount of capital, though he suggests that what one would see as a fair claim on one's parents should guide a generation in deciding what to leave to its descendants (Rawls 1972). I note that this prescription applies to both private and public capital accumulation.

Macroeconomic stability. On this question, Scarth argues that issues revolving around access to financial markets are not relevant. I agree. He then turns to the short-term and long-term aspects of trying to smooth economic activity, arguing that changes in monetary policies resulting from changes in borrowing are such that even a very rigid deficit constraint (of the Herbert Hoover or *Treaty of Maastricht* type) does not have much impact on the short-run volatility of the GDP. In making this conclusion, however, he leaves aside the relevance of zero deficit constraints for public policy purposes, a result of neglecting the balance sheet aspect of debt, to which I now turn.

Good Debt, Bad Debt and Canada's Balance Sheet

Leaving aside transfers of resources from abroad, in a given period a society can only consume what it produces during that period or what it accumulated during a previous period. Taxation is one means by which, in a given period, a government can acquire the real resources it needs to finance the consumption of publicly provided goods and services; it does not create claims by taxpayers on resources in future periods. Public borrowing also allows the government to acquire resources in a given period but, unlike taxation, it does create claims by lenders on the resources available to future generations. The question thus is: When if at all should one allow living, voting adults to create claims on non-voting children, both born and unborn? The answer is that it is not possible to calculate an optimal debt-to-GDP ratio without taking into account what the long-term debt is used for. A 50 percent debt ratio when the debt was incurred to acquire productive assets, such as roads and ports that allow for more efficient internal/international trade or universities that allow the production of a better-skilled labour force is more appropriate than a 25 percent ratio incurred to finance current consumption, such as unduly generous transfer payments to individuals or a high public-sector wage bill due to either (or both) excess public employment or excess wage rates. I use the term "more appropriate" since it allows the matching, if done properly, of the lifespan of the assets and of the length of the debt. If long-lived assets are financed with long-term debt, each generation pays for what it uses, a result not achieved with zero deficit constraints, which require current generations to pay the full cost of investments that may produce benefits long into the future.

Table 1 shows information on the balance sheet of the three levels of government in Canada for six years, from 1961, the first year for which we have

Table 1

Public Sector Balance Sheet, Canada, Selected Years, 1961–2001 (percent of GDP)

Year	Assets	Liabilities	Net Worth
All Governments			
1961	108.0	79.9	28.1
1971	114.0	73.9	40.0
1981	101.4	71.5	29.9
1991	93.8	115.6	−21.9
1996	90.6	132.4	−41.8
2001	90.0	110.1	−20.2
Federal Government			
1961	51.4	52.6	−1.2
1971	40.4	41.0	−0.6
1981	21.9	37.7	−15.8
1991	15.5	67.5	−52.0
1996	14.6	76.5	−61.9
2001	16.3	58.1	−41.9
Provincial Governments			
1961	32.4	14.6	17.7
1971	41.3	20.6	20.7
1981	47.0	26.1	20.9
1991	46.3	41.3	5.0
1996	45.0	49.3	−4.3
2001	44.0	47.0	−3.0
Local (Municipal and School Boards) Governments			
1961	24.3	12.7	11.5
1971	26.0	12.4	13.7
1981	24.5	7.7	16.9
1991	23.7	6.9	16.9
1996	24.6	6.5	18.1
2001	23.4	5.0	18.4

Source: See appendix, table A1.

data, until 2001, the last year for which we have data. These data are not perfect; for example, they do not include as assets the value of Crown lands. They are of good quality overall, however. What is shown is that from 1971 onwards the federal government incurred debt without a corresponding increase in assets, that the provinces resisted this kind of behaviour until 1981 before finally imitating the federal government, and that local governments actually improved their net worth position from 1961 to 2001. (Table A1 in the appendix reproduces this table in dollar terms rather than as a percent of GDP.)

Table 1 suggests that the debt does not pose the same problem for each level of government. The debt is not an issue at all for the local level of government and only a minor one for the provincial level of government. Furthermore, if one consolidates these two levels, which is reasonable, given that municipalities, one of the two kinds of local government, have no constitutional status but are creatures of the provinces, then the entire subnational sector in Canada does not have a debt problem. The good financial health of local governments may be due to a combination of their expenditure responsibilities (they do little in the way of transfers to individuals), of their revenue sources (property taxes, a highly visible revenue source given its collection as an annual amount) and of the borrowing approval mechanism (which requires referendums in some provinces and provincial oversight in all). As for provinces, they saw their financial situation deteriorate in the 1980s, a period when federal transfers were being reduced by legal unilateral changes in the financing rules for Established Program Financing (see Vaillancourt 2000). The February 2003 Health Accord once again raises the provinces' dependence on federal transfers, thus increasing their vulnerability to outside fiscal shocks.

In sum, it was only the federal government that imposed a heavy net debt burden on future generations in the 1975–95 period. As Scarth points out, why this was done is unclear. There was no war or threat of war and no Great Depression. The most plausible explanation seems to be reluctance to adapt to a new and more demanding economic environment with higher world energy prices. But whatever the cause, we are left with a legacy of a $450 billion negative net worth. Fairness requires that, as much as possible, this be paid back by those who chose to have debt-funded public services provided, either because they benefited directly from them (by consuming health services, for instance) or indirectly (if they helped educate their children or funded transfers for the poor). In brief, the policy should be to "make the baby boomers pay." One can think of various ways to achieve this.

One approach would be to increase taxes over and above what is required to provide the normal level of public goods and services and to use the excess for debt reduction. In doing so, however, one would want to use targeted taxes. One possibility is an age-specific tax applicable to individuals who benefited from the unfunded spending and were the relevant electorate. Thus, an individual aged 45 in 2002, who had been 18, the minimum voting age, in 1975, would be fully responsible for a surtax of, say, 10 percent of personal income tax, while anyone aged 35 would only be responsible for 50 percent of the amount since they reached voting age in 1985, halfway through the deficit-generating period. Given the small likelihood that such a tax would be adopted, an alternative would be to tax the returns of registered pension assets (both employer pension plans and registered retirement savings plans, RRSPs) on the assumption that the accumulation of these assets was facilitated by the deficits of the federal government. Levied at a rate of, say, 25 percent on interest, dividends and realized capital gains, such a tax would reduce the value of these savings but would have no impact on current personal income.

Another approach is to leave the tax burden unchanged but to ration services to the profligate generation. In that case, the amount of federal financing for health care to older individuals (those over 50, say) would be rationed and provinces could either raise their own taxes and charge age-specific user fees or allow for the private provision of such services to this generation. A public facing rationing may in fact prefer private provision, but people made subject to private provision would have to finance it with their own resources.

In practice, of course, we are unlikely to see any attempt to erase the negative net worth that was built up from 1975 to 1995 and we thus risk facing a major spending problem when the retirement of the baby boomers hits around 2010 (see Oreopoulos and Vaillancourt 1998).

Conclusion

William Scarth's paper is an interesting and clear exposition of a macro perspective on an optimal debt-to-GDP ratio for Canada. But in my view, the fact that he does not take account of the overall balance sheet of our governments, and in particular of the federal government, means that his recommendation of a 25/50 (federal/total) debt-to-GDP ratio is not well founded. If you believe, as I do, that debt should be incurred only to ensure a smoothing over time of the costs of acquiring real capital, then the current situation requires that for the foreseeable future the federal government run surpluses in order to redress its balance sheet. Only when this is done should taxes be reduced, new spending initiated or tax room transferred to the provinces so that they can spend on priority items in their areas of responsibility – a policy that is preferable to the re-conditionalizing of federal grants.

appendix

Table A1

Public Sector Balance Sheet, Canada, Selected years, 1961–2001, Current $ (000,000)

Year	Assets	Liabilities	Net Worth
All Governments			
1961	44,565	32,972	11,593
1971	112,405	72,933	39,472
1981	366,394	258,243	108,151
1991	644,265	794,388	150,123
1996	760,234	1,111,268	−351,304
2001	976,448	1,195,255	−218,807
Federal Government			
1961	21,208	21,686	−478
1971	39,827	40,441	−614
1981	79,267	136,206	−56,939
1991	106,602	463,734	357,132
1996	122,597	642,242	−519,645
2001	176,805	630,985	−454,180
Provincial Governments			
1961	13,346	6,038	7,308
1971	40,714	20,285	20,429
1981	169,971	94,393	75,578
1991	318,097	283,575	34,522
1996	377,938	414,071	−36,133
2001	477,583	510,021	−32,438
Local (Municipal and School Boards) Governments			
1961	10,011	5,248	4,763
1971	25,681	12,207	13,474
1981	88,533	27,644	60,889
1991	162,867	47,079	115,788
1996	206,493	54,955	151,538
2001	253,494	54,147	199,347

Source: Cansim, matrices 378-0004, 384-0013,
380-0016 et 075-0009.

Bibliography

Aiyagari, S., and E. McGrattan. 1998. "The Optimum Quantity of Debt." *Journal of Monetary Economics* 42:447-69.

Ljungqvist, L., and T. Sargent. 2000. *Recursive Macroeconomic Theory*. Cambridge, MA: MIT Press.

Oreopoulos, P., and F. Vaillancourt. 1998. *Taxes, Transfers and Generations in Canada: Who Gains and Who Loses from the Demographic Transition*. Commentary no. 107. Toronto: C.D. Howe Institute.

Rawls, J. 1972. *A Theory of Justice*. Oxford: Clarendon Press

Vaillancourt, F. 2000. « Les transferts fédéraux-provinciaux au Canada, 1947-1998: évolution et évaluation. » In *Les défis de la gouvernance à l'aube du XXIe siècle*, ed. A. Downs and G. Paquet. Montreal: Actes du Congrès 1999, ASDEQ, pp. 191-212.

7

how should we manage the debt?

David Bolder and Clifton Lee-Sing

Introduction

Managing government debt is a complicated business. Two factors in particular make it a surprisingly difficult problem: uncertainty and time. Substantial uncertainty arises because future interest rates, economic output, government financial requirements, inflation and the state of the business cycle are unknown. We may have some idea of the range of possible future outcomes for these variables, but determining which specific set of events will occur is virtually impossible. Time is important because a government is, at least in principle, an infinitely-lived organization. Debt managers cannot merely focus on a one- or two-year decision-making horizon. They have to look well into the future. Moreover, there is a strong "path dependency" in the debt-management problem: outcomes in a given period depend strongly on outcomes in previous periods.

To aid in resolving these thorny issues, recourse is generally made to mathematical models. In conjunction with a number of assumptions, these simplifications of reality assist in making sense of the otherwise overwhelming complexity of the problem. Debt models certainly are not a panacea, but a tool that assists in the process. Rather than discuss the various challenges of the modelling process, a discussion that would become very technical very quickly, this paper focuses on the nature of the questions that need to be addressed. It is therefore something of a prerequisite to the debt-modelling literature, with a particular focus on the

Figure 1

International Debt-Management Objectives

Canada	Our debt-management objective is to raise stable, low-cost funding for the government and to maintain a well-functioning market for government securities.
United Kingdom	To meet the annual remit set by Treasury ministers for the sale and purchase of gilts [British Government bonds], with high regard to long-term cost minimization taking account of risk.
United States	Borrow what is necessary to meet the monetary needs of the government; minimize the cost of the federal government's borrowing activities; [and] provide mechanisms for participation by a wide range of investors in Treasury debt financing.
Japan	Our debt-management strategy focuses on two priorities. First, to ensure smooth and stable financing through JGBs [Japanese Government bonds]. Second, to curb financing costs over many years, thus alleviating the burden on taxpayers.
Australia	The principal objective of the Australian Office of Financial Management is for Commonwealth debt to be raised, managed and retired at the lowest possible long-term cost, consistent with an acceptable degree of risk exposure.
France	The aim of government debt and Treasury management is to ensure that the government is able to meet its financial liabilities under all circumstances ... This core mission must be pursued in the interest of the taxpayer, i.e., at the lowest possible cost and in compliance with the highest standards of security.
New Zealand	The objective ... is to maximize the long-term economic return on the government's financial assets and debt in the context of the government's fiscal strategy, particularly its aversion to risk. That objective requires ... balance [of] the likely risks incurred in minimizing cost.
Sweden	The Swedish National Debt Office ... manages central government debt and borrowing at the lowest possible cost, taking into account risk.

Canadian situation. We readily concede that describing which questions have to be asked is easier than actually answering them.

A natural starting point for the discussion is to look at the various annual publications of government debt managers to see how they characterize their objectives. Most countries delegate debt management to the finance ministry, the central bank, a separate debt-management agency, or some combination of these three institutions. In a review of the relevant institutions' debt-management publications, whose highlights are described in figure 1, the same themes turn up with surprising frequency.

Although the exact wording varies from country to country the general message is quite similar across nations. If we were to try to summarize the goals of the various countries' debt-management authorities in a generic mission statement, something like the following might do:

Our debt-management objective is to raise stable, low-cost funding for the government and to maintain a well-functioning market for government securities.

Although only Canada and the United States explicitly mention the importance of government debt markets in their official statements of their goals for debt management, all sovereign debt managers are interested in seeing to the proper functioning of such markets. We will see that well-functioning government debt markets have important indirect implications for the cost-effectiveness of debt strategy.

Our goal in this paper is to try to explain exactly what this generic message means. We will refer to cost concerns as "cost-effectiveness" and use the term "prudence" to summarize the idea of stability or risk limitation. Clearly, no government would desire unstable, high-cost funding combined with poorly-functioning government securities' markets. In that sense, this statement of a debt manager's objectives is not immediately useful. But by expanding on it we hope to put it into a strategic and operational context, and in so doing introduce the reader to the challenges and realities of government debt management. To accomplish this, we will discuss what cost-effectiveness, prudence and well-functioning government securities markets mean. At the same time, we will address other important aspects of government debt management.

Cost-Effectiveness

The first order of business is to explain what is meant by cost-effectiveness. Governments, which in the literature on debt management are customarily known as "sovereigns," issue debt to finance budgetary deficits and to refinance previous borrowing. If a sovereign always ran a balanced budget, there would be no government debt and no need for government debt management. In reality, however, governments do at least occasionally run budgetary deficits, especially during recessions, when they often try to use government spending or tax cuts to provide fiscal stimulus, and over time these deficits give rise to a government debt portfolio. Figure 2 shows the recent evolution of Canadian, American and Organisation for Economic Co-operation and Development (OECD) average budget deficits as a percentage of gross domestic product (GDP). Most developed countries have debt portfolios in excess of 30 percent of their GDP. Table 1 and figure 3 provide a brief summary of two key central government debt statistics for a selection of countries.

The bottom line is that many governments, including Canada, have sizable debt portfolios that require careful management. Each year the government

Figure 2

Central Government Deficit or Surplus as Percentage of GDP

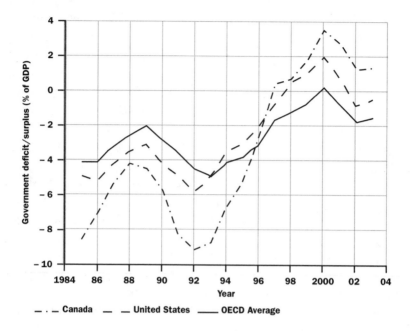

- - · - Canada   - - - United States   ——— OECD Average

must borrow enough to both cover its current budget deficit and refinance maturing debt. The sum of these two elements is the government's "annual borrowing requirement."[1]

When debts are large, the cost of servicing debt makes up an important part of the government's annual expenditures. Clearly, the government would like these debt-service charges to be as small as possible. In its simplest interpretation, cost-effectiveness therefore means minimizing the debt-service charges associated with the government debt portfolio.

At this point, it is important to draw a distinction between those elements of a government's debt portfolio that debt managers control and those they do not. The overall debt of a government consists of two key components: *non-market debt* and *market debt*. The debt manager only controls market debt. Market debt is comprised of financial claims that are distributed, through financial markets, to investors. Non-market debt is internal debt of the government, which typically consists of accounts payable, accrued liabilities and public sector pension liabilities. Although non-market debt is important our focus will be on market debt because this is the part of a government's debt portfolio over which a debt manager exercises control. As of 31 March 2001 approximately 70 percent of the Canadian government's debt portfolio was market debt while the

Table 1

Central Government Debt

Country	Central Government Market Debt	
	(%) of GDP	US$ billions
Canada	40	301.1
France	42	631.4
Germany	30	655.3
United States	31	3,395.5
United Kingdom	37	593.7
Australia	12	46.4
Sweden	60	137.2
Japan	81	4,320.9

Figure 3

Central Government Net Financial Liabilities

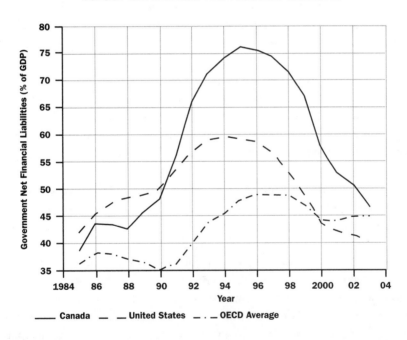

remaining 30 percent consisted of non-market debt. The distinction between market and non-market debt and the vagaries of international debt statistics reporting account for the slight differences in the values reported in table 1 and figure 3.

To discuss cost-effectiveness in more depth, we need to introduce the concept of a *financing strategy*. A financing strategy is a rule that describes how much of each available debt instrument a given sovereign will issue. In principle, the set of available instruments could be quite small. For example, a simple financing strategy might involve a sovereign borrowing exclusively with six-month treasury bills. While such a strategy does offer simplicity, it requires that the government refinance its entire debt portfolio every six months. Because government debt portfolios are typically quite large, this could be a problem. There might not be enough investor demand for six-month treasury bills to meet the government's annual borrowing requirements.

To avoid this problem, most sovereigns use a number of different debt instruments to meet their annual financing needs. Debt managers attempt to issue a broad enough range of instruments to appeal to a wide variety of different investors. In this way, the government can reduce its reliance on a small number of investors and provides itself with a form of diversification. Of course, the downside of diversification is the greater complexity of managing a larger array of different financing vehicles. While most sovereigns use enough debt instruments to diversify their investor base, they limit the number of alternative instruments to avoid the costs of an overly diverse portfolio. In the following paragraphs, we briefly review the primary debt instruments used by sovereign borrowers.

The two most common sovereign debt instruments are *treasury bills* and *coupon bonds*. A treasury bill is a *pure-discount bond*. In other words, it is issued at a discount, say $95, and matures at its face value of $100. The interest rate is a function of the size of the discount. (In this case, with continuous compounding and one-year maturity, the implicit interest rate is approximately 5.1 percent.) Pure-discount bonds typically are not issued beyond one or two years. There are two reasons for this. First, as the term increases the proceeds of the issue become quite small. For instance, with a 6 percent implicit yield, a 10-year pure-discount bond provides only about $55 for every $100 of face value. This is not terribly efficient from a practical perspective. Second, investors often are concerned about the credit exposure associated with purchasing long-term bonds that make no interim payment until the final maturity date.[2]

To answer this concern, governments also issue bonds that make fixed interest payments on an annual or semi-annual basis. These are termed *nominal coupon bonds*. The coupon, which describes the size of the periodic interest payment, is chosen to ensure that these instruments are typically issued close to their face value, which avoids the discount problem associated with treasury bills. In fact, there are facilities in the coupon-bond market to disaggregate the coupon and principal payments of an individual bond and sell them separately. In effect, this *strip market* allows investors to purchase synthetically created long-term treasury bills. Moreover, an investor can reaggregate the coupon and principal payments back into the original bond, a practice known as *reconstitution*.[3]

One of the drawbacks of coupon bonds is their exposure to inflation. Greater-than-anticipated inflation over the life of a given coupon bond will erode the bond's value. In order to broaden their investor bases further, a number of sovereigns have introduced bonds with coupons linked to an inflation index such as the consumer price index (CPI). Each interest and principal payment is adjusted for inflation. If inflation is much higher than anticipated, then the payments associated with these bonds will be commensurately higher than anticipated. In this way these so-called *index-linked bonds* – in Canada they are known as *real return bonds* – offer protection against inflation.[4] They are generally popular with investors who have inflation-sensitive liabilities, such as non-indexed wages insured by disability coverage offered by insurance companies, that they wish to hedge with inflation-sensitive assets.

Who holds these instruments? While in the first instance the government sells them to financial institutions, a significant share ultimately finds its way into mutual funds held by retail investors. Moreover, a number of sovereigns, including Canada, have developed a wide variety of products marketed directly to retail investors. Instruments may be instantly redeemable, enjoy protection against increasing interest rates, or be essentially identical to a guaranteed investment certificate (GIC).[5]

The Canadian government offers two retail debt products: the Canada Savings Bond (CSB) and the Canada Premium Bond (CPB). The CSB provides a minimum guaranteed interest rate that will be increased if market conditions warrant. Moreover, a CSB can be redeemed, or exchanged, for cash, at any time. A CPB, by contrast, may only be redeemed once per year, on the anniversary date of the issue. A CPB also has a minimum guaranteed interest rate, but the interest payment is not adjusted upward in response to market conditions. A CPB does, however, typically carry a higher interest rate than a CSB.

So far our discussion has implicitly assumed that the financial instruments mentioned are all issued in the sovereign's domestic currency. In most developed countries, the government's domestic obligations are funded entirely in the domestic currency. This is certainly the case in Canada. Although the Canadian government does borrow in foreign currencies to raise funds for its foreign reserve portfolio, these funds are offset by reinvesting the proceeds in foreign-denominated assets. As a result, the Canadian government's annual financial requirement is not financed with foreign-denominated debt.

Some sovereigns do meet a proportion of their internal financing needs by borrowing in foreign currency. Issuing foreign debt can be costly for at least three reasons. First, domestic debt is typically somewhat cheaper than foreign debt because domestic investors are generally better informed about the government. To be fair, this factor can work in the opposite direction. Better-informed domestic investors may require a premium in the event of concerns about the credit quality of the sovereign although this effect may be tempered by the ability of a sovereign to monetize domestic debt. Second, there is the possibility of unfavourable foreign exchange movements. If the domestic currency depreciates relative to a foreign currency, the domestic-currency cost of servicing any debt held in that currency will increase. The effect can work in reverse, of course, but debt managers are usually more concerned with potential downsides. There are ways of hedging such currency risks, but given the scale of government borrowing, hedging can be difficult to accomplish or prohibitively expensive. Finally, while most domestic debt can be distributed in a relatively inexpensive auction, foreign borrowing usually is done by syndication, and that can be costly.[6]

Given these greater costs, why would a sovereign ever choose to borrow in a foreign currency? The primary reason is that its internal debt market may not be sufficiently large or developed to meet its borrowing needs. One useful way to think about this issue is to consider how corporations finance themselves. Corporate financial analysts customarily talk about a "hierarchy of financing options."[7] First, a company will use internally generated funds, followed by bank lending, then market-debt instruments, and finally equity. This order reflects the relative cost-effectiveness of these borrowing alternatives. With governments, the structure is conceptually similar. A government meets it domestic borrowing needs first with taxes, then with domestic borrowing, and finally with foreign borrowing, as necessary. Many undeveloped and emerging economies, for example, do not have well enough developed domestic capital markets to meet all their financing needs and are forced to use costly and potentially volatile foreign borrowing.

To summarize, a financing strategy involves choosing the amount of each of the instruments – treasury bills, nominal coupon bonds, index-linked bonds, retail debt products and foreign-denominated obligations – that a government will use to finance its annual borrowing requirement. Figure 4 outlines the structure of the Government of Canada's marketable debt portfolio as at 31 March 2002. In addition, table 2 provides a similar breakdown for the last decade. The data in figure 4 and table 2 clearly highlight the dominant role of treasury bills and nominal coupon bonds in Canada's federal debt portfolio.

Unfortunately, simply describing the set of financial instruments used by governments fails to address the potential intertemporal complexity in a financing strategy. A government can select a strategy that varies over time with the business cycle or with movements in the term structure of interest rates or in any of an almost infinite number of ways. More specifically, a government could elect to finance itself solely with three-month treasury bills or entirely

Figure 4
The Government of Canada's Debt Portfolio

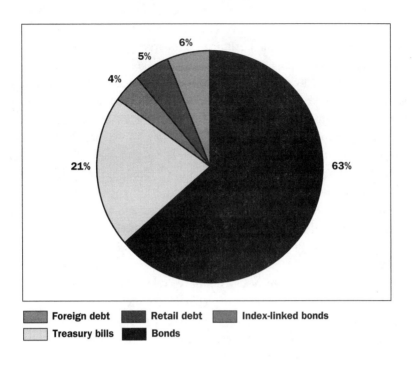

| Foreign debt | Retail debt | Index-linked bonds |
| Treasury bills | Bonds |

Table 2
Government of Canada Debt, 1992–2002 (percent of total)

Fiscal Year	Treasury Bills	Total Bonds	Retail Debt	Foreign Debt
1992-93	42.34	46.62	8.85	1.43
1993-94	40.10	49.13	7.46	2.58
1994-95	37.29	51.14	6.97	3.84
1995-96	35.37	53.76	6.56	3.58
1996-97	28.39	59.15	6.90	4.83
1997-98	24.03	62.91	6.48	5.80
1998-99	21.06	64.05	6.26	7.82
1999-00	21.88	64.25	5.94	7.15
2000-01	19.90	65.93	5.94	7.50
2001-02	21.42	66.96	5.47	6.15

Source: Canada. Department of Finance (2002).

with 30-year coupon bonds. Alternatively, it might issue one-year treasury bills if five-year market yields are above 4.5 percent, but 10-year coupon bonds otherwise. While almost anything is possible in theory, in practice changes from year to year tend to be small. Over a number of years, however, such small changes can add up. Indeed, table 2 shows a substantial change in the Canadian government's debt portfolio through the latter part of the 1990s. We will discuss the underlying rationale for this change in financing strategy a little later.

Because governments' financing needs tend to be large, rapid changes in their use of a given instrument can be difficult for market participants to absorb. This is a critical aspect of the government debt-management problem that private debt managers usually do not face. In a corporate setting, the borrower is usually assumed to be a price-taker in debt markets. A minimal issuance size may be required to create sufficient liquidity, but otherwise no single borrower has an impact on the price of a given kind of debt. For a government borrower, however, this is not the case. Government issuance can and does influence the price of debt. Insufficient issuance in a given sector will reduce the liquidity – that is, the ability to resell a position in a timely and inexpensive manner – of the instrument in question and generally lead to higher issuance costs. These higher costs are termed the *liquidity premium*. Excessive issuance in any given sector essentially creates a situation of oversupply. Higher issuance costs will be required to clear the market. The reason that this is not usually important in a corporate setting is that corporate borrowers cannot typically generate the great volume of issuance that is common for a sovereign borrower. One consequence of the dominant role played by the sovereign borrower is that government debt becomes the benchmark for all other debt issuance in the economy; this important issue is addressed in detail later in the paper.

How much to issue of each type of instrument described is only part of the problem a government debt manager faces. Once a decision has been made as to the proportion of nominal coupon bonds, for example, a secondary set of choices regarding the maturity structure of those bonds must also be made. Common maturities for coupon bonds are two, three, five, seven and ten years. A number of countries, including Canada, also issue 30-year coupon bonds, while some countries issue at the 20-year maturity. Treasury bills can also be issued at a variety of maturities; common choices include one, three, six and twelve months. Alternative maturity choices also apply to retail and index-linked debt.

Why does the maturity structure of the government debt portfolio matter? It matters because in most countries at most times the term structure of interest rates is upward-sloping, that is, short-term interest rates are generally lower than long-term interest rates. A variety of theories tries to explain this phenomenon. The most pervasive and appealing is that investors demand a premium for the uncertainty of moving further and further out the term structure. But whatever the underlying reason, the fact that interest rates do usually rise through the term structure has important implications for government debt management. Short-term debt will have a lower expected cost, long-term debt a higher expected cost. Note the use of "expected": in this context it means this is what we observe on average. The term structure of interest rates is not always upward sloping: there may be times when long-term debt is actually less expensive than short-term debt. Still, the usual pattern is that short rates will be lower than long rates and short-term debt cheaper than long-term debt. That does not mean governments will always prefer short-term debt, however. Lower cost may be offset by higher risk, as we shall see in a moment.

In sum, in order to finance the government's debt in a low-cost manner, the government debt manager needs to carefully consider the amount of issuance in a wide range of instruments including treasury bills, nominal coupon bonds, index-linked bonds, retail-debt products and foreign-denominated debt. Moreover, once the proportion of issuance in each of these instruments is determined, important decisions must be made about the terms to maturity of these debt offerings. Different choices of instrument and maturity structure will have different implications for the cost-effectiveness of the government debt program.

Prudence

At first glance, cost might seem to be the only relevant dimension of the debt-management problem. After all, the lower the debt-service cost to the government, the more money will be available to pay down the debt, reduce taxes, or spend on government programs. While that is true, another aspect of the problem needs to be considered: prudence, the second goal highlighted by our selection of debt managers' mission statements. Prudence requires focusing on the stability of debt-service cost. A prudent debt structure is one that is robust to negative future macroeconomic outcomes such as volatile interest-rate conditions and extended recessions.

What does "robust" mean in this context? Imagine two financing strategies. The first has a low expected cost in some states of the world, but high expected costs in other states of the world. The second has medium costs across all future states of the world. Which is the superior strategy? The answer is not obvious. It depends on the relative probability of the various states of the world and on the government's attitude toward risk. This relates back to the problem of uncertainty. Because future states of the world – interest rates, borrowing requirements, inflation and the path of the business cycle – are not known, it is important to consider the variability of future debt-service cost outcomes.

The short end of the term structure of interest rates typically exhibits substantially more variability than the long end. In other words, three-month interest rates generally jump around more than 10-year interest rates. As a result, financing strategies that favour substantial amounts of short-term debt will produce greater volatility in the cost of debt than strategies that focus on the longer end of the market. On the other hand, shorter-term debt is usually cheaper. So there is a fundamental trade-off between expected debt-service cost and debt-service cost variability. To put it more simply, there is a trade-off between cost and risk. A debt manager can reduce risk by adopting financing strategies with a greater proportion of long-term debt, but this comes at a greater expected cost.

We can think of the debt manager's problem as being the inverse of that faced by the typical investor. Investors cannot arbitrarily increase their expected return without a commensurate increase in risk. Corporate equities usually offer high expected payoffs but, unlike safer financial instruments, may involve negative returns or even bankruptcy in a number of possible future states of the world. Debt managers are in a similar situation in that they cannot engage in low-risk borrowing with low expected costs. This is one of the fundamental facts of debt-management life.

In addition to facing the higher risk implied by the volatility of short-term rates, financing strategies that focus on short-term assets require more frequent refinancing. The shorter the maturity of the debt, the more often it must be refinanced and the greater the exposure to negative macroeconomic outcomes. This is typically termed *refinancing risk* or *rollover risk*. Were a government to issue only three-month treasury bills to meet its borrowing requirements, it would have to refinance its entire portfolio four times a year. That is a dramatic exposure to negative market conditions. Conversely, a financing strategy involving only 10-year nominal coupon bonds would involve refinancing only about one-tenth of the portfolio each year. There is a trade-off, however, because while 10-year bonds are less risky they are usually more costly than three-month treasury bills. Even so, governments typically do not issue all their debt at the short end of the term structure. During negative macroeconomic outcomes, the higher debt-servicing costs of a short-term dominated financing strategy could lead to a drastic deterioration in the government's financial position.

A number of real-world examples highlight this fact. The Asian crisis of 1998, while properly speaking a banking crisis, was aggravated by the debt-management practices of a number of the sovereigns involved. In particular, these debt managers faced substantial difficulties in refinancing short-term domestic and foreign-denominated debt. Malaysia, Thailand and the Philippines all experienced an increase in foreign-indebtedness of more than 20 percentage points relative to GDP over the period 1996–98, and they were starting from foreign-debt-to-GDP ratios ranging from 41 percent to 60 percent.

The current situation in Latin America, whether in Brazil, Argentina or Chile, is similar in some respects.[8] As of 2001, Brazil, Argentina, and Chile have foreign-debt-to-GDP ratios of approximately 41, 52 and 57 percent respectively, thereby exposing these nations to sizable increases in overall indebtedness in the event of even a moderate depreciation of their currency.

But why, it might be asked, do governments care about risk at all? Unlike private firms, governments hardly ever fail. Why should they worry about the ups and downs of their debt-service costs? When their debts are small compared to GDP maybe they shouldn't. As the debt burden rises, however, debt-service charges become an important element of the government's expenditures. Under extreme market conditions, a risky financing strategy can cause a deterioration of a country's fiscal position and maybe even push the government into a deficit position. The subsequent reduction in fiscal credibility associated with increasing deficits will generally require higher debt yields to encourage continued investment.[9] These higher debt costs only exacerbate the government's budgetary position. In short, getting debt-management wrong can have serious consequences in a crisis.

The discussion can be made more concrete by considering the Canadian situation. As table 2 showed, from the mid-1990s on the Canadian government increased the proportion of long-term debt in its portfolio so as to achieve greater cost stability. This increased use of fixed-rate debt, which essentially involved refinancing a proportion of treasury bills as longer-term coupon bonds, provides a greater level of protection against unexpected increases in interest rates. In other words, it provides a measure of protection against refinancing risk. As we have seen, under stable macroeconomic conditions a greater emphasis on short-term debt could result in lower debt costs. When the macroeconomic environment is less stable, however, these short-term financing strategies often result in higher debt charges. Canadian debt managers evidently decided that moving to an increased proportion of fixed-rate debt was a prudent course of action. Although this decision was also consistent with the strategy adopted by other sovereign borrowers, both market participants and credit-rating agencies had expressed concern about Canada's relatively high proportion of short-term funding. In the February 2003 budget, however, the Canadian government announced that the target for the fixed-rate share of the debt will be reduced over the next five years. This decision was made as a consequence of a strengthening, over the past five years, of Canada's economic and fiscal position. The federal debt has fallen to its lowest level, relative to GDP, in almost 20 years. The consequence of the debt reduction has been to provide greater financial stability, reduce sensitivity to external events, and to assist in restoring Canada's triple-A credit rating. The stable macroeconomic conditions experienced in

Figure 5
An Aside: Issues in Debt Modelling

Understanding and accurately characterizing the trade-off between debt-servicing cost and debt-service cost volatility is a key element in debt management. As we have seen, government debt managers aim for a debt structure that is reasonably robust to a variety of economic conditions, including more extreme events, at the lowest possible cost. This desire is complicated by the wide range of possible instruments, their attendant maturity structures, uncertainty regarding future economic outcomes, and the time dimension. Because of this complexity, mathematical models are an essential tool of the sovereign debt manager. These admittedly abstract representations of reality are critical in making sense of the rather bewildering range of financing strategies facing the government. Not surprisingly, debt modelling is a rather involved undertaking. Although a detailed discussion of how it is done is beyond the scope of this paper, it may be worth briefly addressing some key modelling issues insofar as they highlight the challenges faced by the sovereign debt manager.*

The models that are used seek to describe the future dynamics of key macroeconomic variables such as interest rates, output, government financial requirements, inflation, and the business cycle. They also permit comparison of various financing strategies on the basis of their cost and riskiness. In essence, they compare the statistical distribution of debt-service charges for a number of alternative financing strategies across a range of future macroeconomic outcomes.

Government debt managers are particularly concerned with the risk associated with extreme events. It is during such extreme events – like the Asian, the Mexican and the Russian debt crises – that short-term dominated financing strategies can prove dangerous. If a government has to refinance large amounts of debt when interest rates are spiking, the consequent increase in its debt-service charges can have a lasting negative impact on its financial position. A key purpose of debt-modelling is therefore to consider how a given financing strategy performs under a variety of extreme market conditions. In the end, a combination of model output, operational knowledge, and experience allows the debt manager to make decisions on an annual financing strategy. Almost as important as the nuts and bolts of these models are the explicit consideration of model assumptions, extreme market conditions, and the sensitivity of the results to different choices of model.

Note: *See Bolder (2001b, 2002a, b), Hörngren (1999), Batley (2002), OECD (2002), Holmlund (1999), and Holmlund and Lindberg (2002) for more detailed discussion of debt-management modelling issues.

recent years allow for a greater emphasis on short-term debt and are expected to result in lower debt costs while maintaining a prudent debt structure.

Well-Functioning Markets

The final question we want to address is why governments care about the impact on the market of implementing their financing strategies. Why, as we have seen, do debt managers typically focus on maintaining a well-functioning market for government securities? There are three main reasons. First, a well-functioning market contributes to an efficient overall debt market and thereby facilitates the allocation of capital in the economy. Second, and perhaps most importantly from a debt manager's perspective, a well-functioning market contributes to lower borrowing costs for the government. Finally, government securities can assist in the effective transmission of monetary policy. We address each of these issues in turn.

Market participants generally view a liquid and active government securities market as the essential foundation of an efficient domestic debt market. Given their risk-free nature and coverage across a wide maturity range, government treasury bills and bonds act as pricing benchmarks for other fixed-income securities, including Crown corporation, government agency, provincial, municipal and corporate debt issues. For the same reasons, the returns on various government securities constitute a yield curve that is the reference for interest rates in the broader fixed-income market. Ultimately, this is because government yield curves generally factor-in market expectations better than yield curves fitted from instruments whose returns include an unknown component of credit risk.

Because governments loom so large in debt markets, government bonds and treasury bills are widely used as cash-management tools or held as the basic elements in fixed-income portfolios. Government securities are used by financial intermediaries as the primary form of collateral in short-term financing transactions and by pension funds and insurance companies as long-term credit-free instruments. They are also often used as hedging vehicles in cross-currency and interest-rate swaps as well as in loan syndication. By maintaining a diverse, liquid and efficient market for government securities, sovereign borrowers facilitate a variety of financial transactions that support the efficient movement of capital that is essential for a country's economic growth.

Another reason why governments focus on the market for government securities is to aid in the efficiency of monetary policy. The Bank of Canada, through its influence on the amount of settlement balances in the economy, can determine the level of the overnight interest rate. (Settlement balances are deposits held by private financial institutions at the Bank of Canada in order to settle the daily clearing of payments.) Changes in the overnight rate contribute to changes in longer-term interest rates, and this, in turn, affects aggregate demand through changes in spending that, over time, impact both production and employment. Ultimately, these changes feed into the economy's price level. This sequence of events is termed the "transmission mechanism" of monetary policy.[10] Strictly speaking, government securities markets are not required for the implementation of monetary policy. The existence of a banking sector would be enough. On the other hand, well-functioning government securities markets do increase the timeliness and efficiency of the process. The existence of a deep and liquid government securities markets engenders strong domestic fixed-income markets and this contributes to a more robust monetary transmission mechanism.

The third and final reason for focusing on a well-functioning market is that it contributes to lower borrowing costs for the government. By maintaining the

Figure 6

Government Issuance Size and Bid-Offer Spread

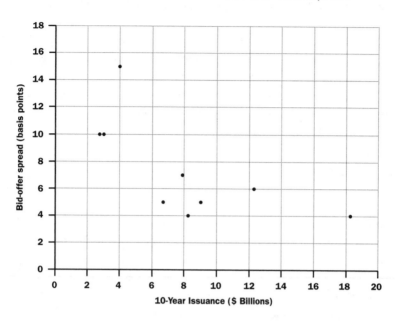

liquidity and integrity of markets, governments ensure that investors can rapidly execute large transactions without having a significant impact on price. In illiquid markets, even the execution of small orders can heavily influence the price, making transactions expensive. Indeed, this is often viewed as a transaction cost. In the absence of liquidity, distributors of government securities will pass on these liquidity-related transaction costs to the government during securities auctions. To mitigate this problem, as mentioned earlier, many national governments follow a passive-issuance strategy that involves the regular issuance of securities in a few selected maturity sectors and in relatively large sizes. That is, large issuance of relatively homogenous securities characterized by standardized coupon-payment and maturity dates help promote narrower "bid-offer spreads." This spread, which is the difference between what sellers want for a security and what demanders are bidding for it, embodies the transaction costs associated with the purchase of a security and is a common measure of liquidity.[11] Figure 6 illustrates a negative relationship between bid-offer spread and total issuance for a selection of 10-year bonds issued by nine sovereigns. In brief, investors evidently prefer the liquidity associated with fewer, larger debt issues at specific maturities to a situation with a larger number of small debt maturities. Furthermore, they are willing to accept a lower yield in exchange for this additional liquidity.

Because markets evolve constantly, maintaining liquidity is a dynamic problem. In the late 1990s, budgetary surpluses in many industrialized countries contributed to a decline in government financial requirements and debt levels. Sovereign borrowers were faced with falling or even negative net debt issuance, that is, they ran surpluses and retired debt. In general, of course, this is a positive development, but it has led to a change in the structure of global fixed-income markets. Consider the market for Canadian government securities. Before 1995, the domestic fixed-income market was dominated by the deficit-financing needs of the Canadian federal and provincial governments. The consequence of this large and growing government presence in fixed-income markets was a crowding-out of private-sector issuers. Since 1997, however, both levels of government have begun to run surpluses. This has contributed to a material reduction in the overall level of government financing activity and an increase in domestic activity by corporate borrowers.

How exactly did this happen? Lower financing requirements, combined with the federal government's move to increase prudence by raising the fixed-rate portion of its debt, significantly reduced the stock of treasury bills (thus demonstrating the interplay between cost, prudence and well-functioning of debt markets). The decline in the treasury-bill stock spurred growth in other money market instruments, which can be considered a "crowding-in" of the private sector. The market adjustment process, which was quite smooth, was facilitated by a sharp increase in other forms of short-term paper, including asset-backed securities. On the bond side, there has been a steady increase in corporate bond issuance (see figures 7 and 8). Government bonds, however, continue to dominate trading activity.

The Canadian domestic market has not seen the same development of government bond surrogates as has occurred in the United States, where the markets for agency debt, swaps and even high-grade corporate debt are now large and well developed. The stock of American marketable treasury debt, for example, is about one-third of agency, mortgage-related and municipal debt. In Canada, by contrast, marketable government debt is about twice the size of the debt issued by Canadian federal Crown corporations, municipalities and financial corporations. Moreover, the relatively small number of federal Crown corporations that borrow with the full faith and credit of the Canadian government have relatively small operations. As such, their bond issues are not as liquid as Government of Canada bonds. Similarly, the domestic swap market, while active, is not yet the deep and liquid investment alternative and pricing benchmark it has become in other countries. This implies that the Canadian government has a continuing role to play as the benchmark borrower in the Canadian fixed-income market.

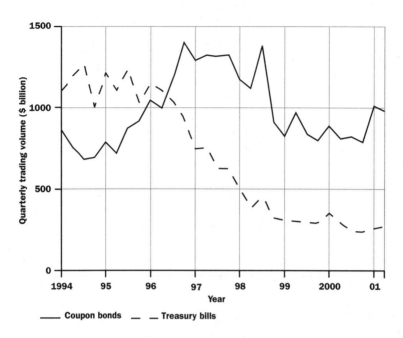

Figure 7
Quarterly Trading Volume

Coupon bonds — — Treasury bills

In Australia, New Zealand and several European countries, the debate on the role of the government as the benchmark borrower is further along than it is in Canada. With a crowding-in of pricing substitutes, the pricing benchmark may increasingly carry some credit risk. Opinions are mixed on whether this will affect financial markets adversely. Another consideration in the debate is whether governments should maintain a minimum level of gross issuance so as to maintain a presence in financial markets and thus avoid the cost of rebuilding a government bond market should the need to borrow arise again at some time in the future.

This rapid improvement in government financial positions has also created a number of difficulties in maintaining well-functioning markets for government securities. The trend to lower levels of issuance has contributed to reduced liquidity, while because of recent consolidations among banks, dealers and institutional investors the overall number of market participants has fallen. In the early 1990s, very rapid growth in the government securities markets encouraged the entry of more players. The greater competition that resulted led to narrower bid-offer spreads and improved price transparency, but the lower revenues this implies have subsequently caused the exit of a number of players from the fixed-income market, which has caused liquidity to decline. Figure 9

Figure 8

Net New Issuance of Debt Securities

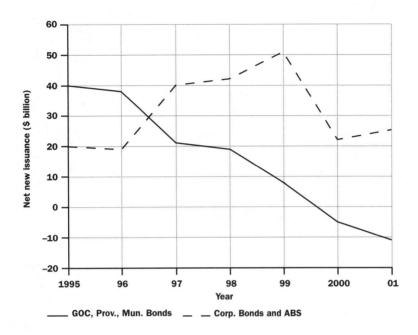

demonstrates the trend toward consolidation among Government of Canada securities dealers.

What can a sovereign debt manager do about these changes? In light of the shift in Canada's financial position, a large number of initiatives have been taken to manage a continued reduction in market debt and to support both primary and secondary Government of Canada securities markets.[12] In the primary market, treasury-bill and bond programs have been structured with a focus on maintaining liquidity at key benchmark maturities. The idea is that the greater the outstanding volume of a given fixed-income security, the easier it is to buy or sell a position in that instrument and, consequently, the greater is its liquidity. For treasury bills, the issuance cycle has evolved a number of times through the 1990s to allow larger amounts to be offered during less frequent auctions. In particular, issues are reopened to build common-date maturities to larger sizes. For instance, a one-year treasury bill may be issued at 52 weeks and then again at 50 weeks, both with the same maturity date of 20 March 2004. Then, six months later, the six-month treasury bill will be auctioned, also with a 20 March 2004 maturity date, thus increasing the effective supply of this instrument. For bonds, the government moved in the 1990s to regularize issuance into benchmark securities as key reference points on the yield curve (at two, five, ten

Figure 9

Bond Dealer Concentration and Market Share

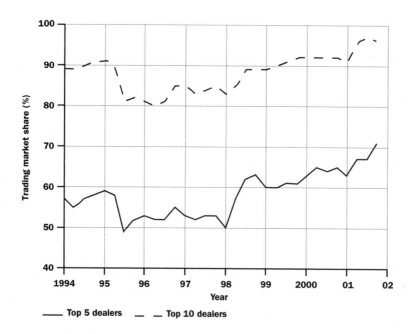

and thirty years). These programs and initiatives have also been reviewed periodically to explicitly consider the preferences of market participants.

To enhance the liquidity of new-bond issuance, a bond buy-back program was initiated in the late 1990s. Bond buy-back or repurchase programs have also been established in the United States and all major European economies except Germany. The program supports the size of the new-bond issue market by allowing the government to buy back less liquid, older bonds from market participants. These repurchases are financed through the issuance of current benchmark bonds. Ultimately, they permit market participants to sell illiquid bonds back to the government, which may in turn issue greater amounts of new securities. Simply put, these buy-backs permit the overall size of the auction to be maintained in a period of declining net issuance. The heightened liquidity associated with the buy-back initiative contributes to lower financing costs for the government.

To enhance liquidity in the secondary market, the government also agreed to remove the ceiling on the reconstitution of bonds. This means that when there are two Government of Canada securities with matching maturity dates, market participants are able to move supply from one bond to the other, thereby creating a larger amount of a given bond than was originally issued. Consider the following example with two bonds sharing a 1 June 2004 maturity date with outstanding amounts of $1 and $2 billion respectively. Market participants may strip the first bond and, through reconstitution, create up to $3 billion of bonds outstanding in the second bond.[13] Why would this be helpful? Occasionally, due to market factors, certain bonds come into very high demand and consequently become more expensive and less liquid: if a bond is in high demand, but short supply, market participants who hold these securities will be reluctant to sell them. The reconstitution alternative provides a mechanism for market participants to add supply and thereby enhance liquidity. It is expected that the greatest benefit of this initiative will be in cases where smaller, less liquid securities share the same maturity date as benchmark securities, in which case additional supply of the benchmark security can be created.

More recently, the government introduced a buy-back program on a switch basis whereby market participants would exchange an older, less liquid bond for a new benchmark bond. A switch is a trade of older, less liquid bonds for new, liquid bonds. The trading price is determined by the relative value of the two securities involved. Essentially, this is another form of buy-back program that does not involve the exchange of cash for securities, but rather the exchange of illiquid for liquid securities. Overall, through the gradual scaling-up of the bond buy-back programs, the government has been able to maintain the level of gross issuance at a relatively constant level. The buy-back program has been useful in mitigating the reduced liquidity and higher issuance costs that otherwise would be associated with falling issuance.

Another important aspect of maintaining well-functioning markets involves putting rules in place that ensure appropriate behaviour by all participants. To this end, to help with the secondary market, the government has worked with the Investment Dealers Association of Canada to establish a set of guidelines for secondary market activity which will promote public confidence in the integrity of the market and enhance liquidity, transparency and the maintenance of active trading in those markets. In addition, the government has supported the development of alternative trading systems, including electronic trading, in order to improve the price transparency of Government of Canada securities and other fixed-income securities in a way that is fair for dealers, brokers and investors. Dealers and brokers play an important intermediary role in distributing government securities. They also "make markets" in government securities. This market-making role is critical in the continued provision of liquidity to government security markets. A fair playing-field ensures the integrity of this system.

Debt managers have a variety of tools at their disposal to aid in enhancing the liquidity and ensuring the effective organization of government securities markets. As we have argued, the smooth functioning of these markets contributes to a more effective transmission mechanism for monetary policy and facilitates the efficient allocation of capital in economy. As a consequence, debt-management practice provides a public good to society in general. Happily, the provision of this public good also contributes to lower financing costs for the government. Thus, an important role of the government debt manager involves ensuring a well-functioning government securities markets.

Conclusion

In this paper, we have discussed the objectives of the sovereign debt manager: to select a cost-effective and prudent financing strategy that is consistent with well-functioning government securities markets. We showed that the term structure and variability of interest rates create a fundamental tension between debt-service cost and volatility: short-term debt instruments may carry lower interest rates at any point in time, but carrying large amounts of short-term debt leaves a government vulnerable to spikes in interest rates when it has to refinance its debt, as, with short-term debt, it would have to do frequently. This highlights the need of the sovereign debt manager to balance short- and long-term debt instruments in the government's debt portfolio. Along the way, we also outlined a number of other factors that make the debt-management problem both interesting and challenging. This discussion underscored the need to use mathematical models to aid in the creation of clear, informed policy. Finally, in describing the importance of well-functioning government debt markets, we emphasized the importance of debt-management decisions for the allocation of resources in the economy, the cost of debt issuance and the transmission of monetary policy.

What we have not done, however, is present a blueprint for the management of government debt. Our goal was neither to explain what the government should do in a specific circumstance nor to provide a generally optimal policy solution. Instead, this work represents an introduction to debt management. Armed with this background, the interested reader should be comfortable proceeding to a more detailed technical discussion of these issues.

Notes

This paper reflects the views of the authors and no responsibility for these views should be attributed to the World Bank, the Department of Finance Canada or the Bank of Canada.

1. Note, of course, that if the government's budgetary position is in surplus then this should lead to a corresponding decrease in the size of its debt portfolio.

2. A detailed discussion of the Canadian treasury-bill and nominal bond markets is found in Branion (1995) and Boisvert and Harvey (1998).

3. For more on the Canadian strip market see Whittingham (1997) and Bolder (1998). Deacon and Derry (1998) is an excellent general reference on index-linked securities.

4. For more on the Canadian real-return bond market see Coté et al. (1996).

5. These features may also be substantially more complex. In Sweden, for example, lottery bonds are marketed to retail investors. As their name implies, the payment structure on these bonds is determined through a lottery. Generally speaking, however, retail debt instruments account for only a small proportion of most governments' overall debt portfolio.

6. Syndication involves selling bonds to a consortium of investment banks for a guaranteed price plus commissions. The investment banks, which ultimately bear the risk in the transaction in return for their fees, then sell these assets to their investor base.

7. This is "Myers pecking-order theory" and, while the asymmetric information-based arguments behind it do not directly apply to governments, they do face a similar hierarchy.

8. For more on these issues see World Bank (1999) and Feltenstein and Iwata (2002).

9. This is particularly true in a small, open economy such as Canada's in which a substantial amount of debt is held by foreign-based investors.

10. For more on the transmission mechanism, see Clinton and Engert (2000), Engert and Selody (1998) and Thiessen (1995).

11. In particular, one sells securities at the bid price and can purchase them at the offer price. The offer price, however, exceeds the bid price: the larger the spread between these prices, the greater the cost of a simultaneous purchase and resale of a given security. The bid-offer spread therefore represents the transaction costs and profit of the dealer, who is on the other side of the transaction.

12. A comprehensive discussion of the Canadian government's initiatives in this area is found in Harvey (1999). Similar initiatives have been undertaken in other countries.

13. In practice, this can be done in a multitude of different ways.

Bibliography

Batley, R. 2002. "A Long Run View to Optimal Debt Issuance Strategy." Unclassified Internal UK Debt Management Office Document.

Boisvert, S., and N. Harvey. 1998. "The Declining Supply of Treasury Bills and the Canadian Money Market." *Bank of Canada Review.*

Bolder, D.J. 1998. "Easing Restrictions on the Stripping and Reconstitution of Government of Canada Bonds." Working Paper no. 98-8. Ottawa: Bank of Canada.

———. 2001. "Affine Term-Structure Models: Theory and Implementation." Working Paper no. 2001-15. Ottawa: Bank of Canada.

———. 2002a. "A Proposed Stochastic Simulation Framework for the Government of Canada's Debt Strategy Problem." Working Paper. Ottawa: Bank of Canada.

———. 2002b. "Towards a More Complete Debt Strategy Simulation Framework." Working Paper no. 2002-13. Ottawa: Bank of Canada.

Branion, A. 1995. "The Government of Canada Bond Market Since 1980." *Bank of Canada Review.*

Canada. Department of Finance. 2002. *Debt Management Report 2001–2002.* Ottawa: Department of Finance.

Clinton, K., and W. Engert. 2000. "Conference Summary: Money, Monetary Policy, and Transmission Mechanisms." *Bank of Canada Review.*

Coté, A., J. Jacob, J. Nelmes and M. Whittingham. 1996. "Inflation Expectations and Real Return Bonds." *Bank of Canada Review.*

Deacon, M., and A. Derry. 1998. *Inflation-Index Securities.* New York: Prentice Hall.

Engert, W., and J. Selody. 1998. "Uncertainty and Multiple Paradigms of the Transmission Mechanism." Working Paper no. 98-7. Ottawa: Bank of Canada.

Feltenstein, A., and S. Iwata. 2002. "Why Is it So Hard to Finance Budget Deficits? Problems of Developing Countries." IMF Working Paper no. 02-95. New York: International Monetary Fund.

Harvey, N. 1999. "Recent Initiatives in the Canadian Market for Government of Canada Securities." *Bank of Canada Review.*

Holmlund, A. 1999. *The Debt Office's Model for Analyzing Duration Choice for the Swedish Kronor Debt.* Riksgälds Kontoret: The Swedish National Debt Office.

Holmlund, A., and S. Lindberg. 2002. *The SNDO's Simulation Model for Government Debt Analysis* (Preliminary Draft). Riksgälds Kontoret: The Swedish National Debt Office.

Hörngren, L. 1999. *Methods for Analyzing the Structure of the Central Government Debt.* Riksgälds Kontoret: The Swedish National Debt Office.

Myers, S.C. 1984. "The Capital Structure Puzzle." *The Journal of Finance* 39, no. 3.

Organisation for Economic Co-operation and Development (OECD). 2002. "Trends and Structural Changes." Discussion Paper. Paris: OECD.

Thiessen, G. 1995. "Uncertainty and the Transmission of Monetary Policy in Canada." *Bank of Canada Review.*

Whittingham, M. 1997. "The Canadian Market for Zero-Coupon Bonds." *Bank of Canada Review.*

World Bank. 1999. "Does Debt Management Matter? Yes." Discussion Paper. New York: The World Bank.

how should we manage the debt?

Huntley Schaller

This nice, well-organized, well-written paper provides a good introduction to the government debt-management issue. It also presents some interesting time series data. Because the paper is so clear there is little need for me to repeat or explain its main points. Instead, let me make two very brief comments and then say something slightly more detailed about crowding-out.

The first brief comment is that we must never forget that Canada has a federal structure in which provinces play a large role. In terms of public spending, the provinces are the federal government's equal. The paper looks at a number of issues, including deficit-to-gross domestic product (GDP) ratios, debt-to-GDP ratios, comparisons over time and across countries, the objective of prudence, and the objective of well-functioning markets. In several instances it might be argued that provincial government debt would have a slightly different effect from federal debt, but provincial debt very likely would have an effect and the paper would therefore have benefited by taking more explicit account of what has been happening to provincial debts. For example, some of the discussion at this conference has focused on what might be a desirable debt-to-GDP ratio for Canada. In terms of effects on capital markets and the economy, it would be much more natural to consider the combined federal and provincial debt-to-GDP ratio in thinking about such a target.

The second brief comment is that the idea that, in government debt management, there is a trade-off between the cost of borrowing and its risk is an interesting one. When households make choices about what assets to hold in their investment portfolios, standard theory suggests that the covariance of returns across assets is central in their thinking: they want to know to what extent the returns of different assets move in unison or in separate rhythms. They do not want to be caught holding all their eggs in identical baskets. Bolder and Lee-Sing do not address this issue explicitly, but in the context of government debt management, the relevant concept is the covariance of debt-service costs. A natural question is: The covariance of debt-service costs with what? Potential candidates might be the government's net revenue, some measure of the business cycle (such as aggregate output or unemployment), or the intertemporal marginal rate of substitution (that is, people's varying valuation of present versus future consumption). The last is the concept that features prominently in standard asset-pricing models.

To understand why covariances are relevant, consider a simple example. Suppose debt-service costs from a particular type of government debt tend to go up at the same time government revenue goes down. Then the government will be faced with higher costs at the very time it has less revenue to pay these costs. The debt-management implications of this kind of negative covariance of debt-service costs and government revenue could obviously be quite important.

Crowding-Out

Bolder and Lee-Sing provide what amounts to an interesting variation on the standard story of crowding-out. In their way of seeing things, crowding out of investment can take place even in a small, open economy, even if the world interest rate does not change. To my mind, that is an interesting idea.

The standard crowding-out story is that an increase in the government's debt causes interest rates to rise. The government's decision to "dis-save" reduces overall national savings, which increases the difference between the supply of savings and the demand for them on the part of people who would like to borrow them and invest in newly-produced capital. This larger gap between supply and demand increases interest rates and "crowds out" interest-sensitive components of aggregate demand, such as investment.

Crowding-out has potentially important implications. The capital stock, which represents the accumulation over time of past investment, affects the standard of living. More capital implies higher potential output and therefore a higher average income, so if government deficits do crowd out investment, the result can be a lower level of per capita output. In some "endogenous growth" models, that is, models that try to explain the growth rate, rather than simply take it as a given, the capital stock affects not just the level of output but also the *growth rate* of productivity, which in the long run is the most important determinant of the standard of living. Although these models imply a potentially even greater impact of crowding-out, I will not dwell further on these issues, since another paper at the conference describes them in considerable detail. Similarly, the possibility that an increase in the budget deficit will induce an offsetting increase in private savings, known in the literature as *Ricardian equivalence*, is dealt with at length in David Johnson's paper, so I will not mention it further, except to note, as Johnson argues, that the evidence is not consistent with full Ricardian equivalence.

Although, in theory at least, crowding-out can be very important, the strength of the interest-rate effect on investment is a matter of some controversy empirically. Quite a few studies find only a slight effect, while still others find virtually no effect or even (though these studies show up only rarely in professional journals) a positive effect. As long as investment is at least somewhat responsive to the real interest rate, however, there will be a change in the equilibrium quantity of investment. How to measure the percentage response of the capital stock to a percentage change in the interest rate is a longstanding problem in economics. The main difficulty is that the many influences that impinge on investment decisions may mask the effects of interest rates. In my own recent work (Schaller 2002), I propose two solutions to this "identification problem." First, I use techniques that focus on the long run, so that one set of other influences – demand shocks – matter less. Second, I look at a small, open economy (specifically, Canada), which in theory should have access to virtually as much capital as it wants at the going world rate of interest. Using this approach, I find that the effect of the interest rate on investment is strongly negative: increases in the interest rate give rise to large reductions in investment, much larger in fact than in a big economy like the United States.

So far we have been talking only about a closed economy. In an open economy, it is not so clear that an increase in the budget deficit will lead to a change in the quantity of investment. In an open economy, if we have more public and private uses of savings than we have savings, we can borrow abroad. The possibility of foreign borrowing in effect relaxes the closed-economy constraint that investment must equal national savings. In analyzing a small, open economy, we usually think of the interest rate as being determined by conditions in international capital markets. Since Canada is a relatively small player in world capital markets, our savings and investment decisions are usually believed to have a negligible influence on the world interest rate. Thus, an increase in our budget deficit will not affect the interest rate that Canadian firms must pay and therefore will not lead to any reduction in investment. Government deficits will lead to greater reliance on foreign borrowing, which may have negative consequences for the economy, but there should be no harmful effect on Canadian investment.

If we are to believe that changes in Canada's budget deficit have no effect on the world interest rate, we therefore have to find some other reason why the deficit might affect investment. Bolder and Lee-Sing mention the problem of "asymmetric information," which refers to the fact that lenders know less about the people they are lending money to than the borrowers themselves do. That fact of life can lead to a "financing hierarchy," in which borrowers face a continuum that runs from more favourable to less favourable borrowing terms as they move from lenders who know relatively more about them to those who know less. In this view, if larger Canadian government deficits force private Canadian borrowers into offshore capital markets, such borrowers will face a higher interest rate *even though the underlying world interest rate has not changed.* To repeat, world interest rates remain where they were, but because private Canadian borrowers must now deal with lenders who know less and less about them they face higher and higher interest rates. Combine this with the interest sensitivity of domestic investment that, my own work suggests, is greater than is usually thought and the crowding-out caused by government deficits could be substantial even in the open-economy case.

In sum, there are two potential channels for crowding out: (a) the conventional channel, in which an increase in the budget deficit leads to an increase in the observed interest rate and therefore a decrease in investment; and (b) the financing hierarchy channel, in which an increase in the budget deficit implies a reduction in national savings, which leads to a decrease in investment without a corresponding increase in the observed interest rate.

Were either or both channels important in recent decades in Canada? Casual empiricism suggests they may well have been. Canada certainly saw high interest rates during the years of high budget deficits. Moreover, concerns have frequently been expressed both about lower Canadian investment and lower Canadian productivity growth than in other countries, particularly the US. Lower productivity growth is a potential side-effect of lower investment. More careful empirical study would be required to determine if there is really evidence of these phenomena and whether they are, in fact, linked to these two crowding-out channels.

Bolder and Lee-Sing implicitly suggest a test of the financing hierarchy channel, namely an examination of whether there is a negative correlation between private securities issues and government securities issues, as suggested by the partial evidence in figure 8 of their paper. (An important caveat is that we would also need to look at other potential sources of corporate finance beyond those shown in their figure 8, such as bank loans.) A second type of test would be similar to that proposed by Feldstein and Horioka (1980). Specifically, it might be possible to test whether Canadian investment is positively correlated with Canadian savings using time series data. Similarly, if one divides national savings into private savings and government savings (where government savings is the negative of the budget deficit), does government saving have a positive effect on investment?

Bibliography

Feldstein, M., and C. Horioka. 1980. "Domestic Saving and International Capital Flows." *Economic Journal 90* (June): 314-29.

Schaller, H. 2002. "Estimating the Long-Run User Cost Elasticity." Department of Economics Working Paper no. 02-31. Cambridge, MA: Massachusetts Institute of Technology.

8

do we need fiscal rules?

Don Drummond

Introduction

There are many excellent articles examining the experience of various countries and subnational governments with fiscal rules (Boothe and Reid 1998; Geist 1997/98; Kennedy and Robbins 2001; Kopits 2001; Millar 1997; Parker and Major 2002). This note briefly summarizes the major findings of these studies in order to provide context for the question this paper addresses: Should Canada's federal government establish fiscal rules and, if so, what should their nature be?

What Are Fiscal Rules?

A fiscal rule is a statutory or constitutional restriction on a government's policy options. The rule can be focused on the budgetary balance, debt, spending or taxation. In theory, discretionary policy can achieve the same outcomes as fiscal rules. And in practice, there are many fiscal success stories that did not depend on rules. One of the more recent is the turnaround in the Canadian federal budget over the four-year period, 1993–94 to 1997–98 from a deficit of 5.3 percent of the gross domestic product (GDP) to a surplus. Whether rules were in place or not, after the early 1990s all Canadian provinces made considerable progress in reducing their deficits. And for several of the provinces that now do have rules, much of the progress was made before the rules were implemented. Therefore, on both theoretical and practical grounds we can state that fiscal rules are not a requirement for fiscal discipline. But can they be helpful?

The idea behind fiscal rules is that present or future governments may be unwilling or unable to implement a sound fiscal policy without external pressure. More precisely, the notion is that the framework for fiscal policy needs to be depoliticized in order to prevent a bias toward deficits. This bias may arise if politicians apply an unduly short time horizon to their policy considerations – one that does not extend far past the next election, for instance. For developing countries and for nations with spotty fiscal records, rules can enhance confidence and lower the risk premium on the cost of capital. Rules can also be a useful communications device. If they are sufficiently transparent and simple, they can galvanize public and market support for the government's fiscal objectives. They can also exert a useful external pressure on legislators contemplating new spending programs.

A potential disadvantage of rules is that they can compromise the fiscal authorities' ability to apply counter-cyclical measures, as currently seems to be the case in Europe, where several euro-using countries have run up against the *Maastricht Treaty's* rule that deficits not exceed 3 percent of GDP. This limitation on counter-cyclical policy is less of an issue with subnational orders of government because they tend to place less emphasis on the demand-management side of fiscal policy, perhaps due to the substantial leakages that take place from most local economies. Not surprisingly, it is at the subnational level that rules are most prevalent. All but two American states have rules requiring a balanced budget. Ten Canadian provinces and territories also have fiscal rules. The only ones that do not are Prince Edward Island and Newfoundland.

Fiscal rules could also dampen longer-term growth prospects. The growth-enhancing effects of investment in certain forms of public infrastructure may mean that it would be socially equitable to run deficits so as to push the financing costs of these investments forward onto the people who will share in their benefits. A fiscal rule that prohibited deficit spending could prevent such expenditures from being made: if they had to be financed entirely through tax revenues, the current generation might rationally conclude that the benefits it would enjoy as a result of the expenditure were considerably less than the total cost of the project, which it nevertheless was being asked to finance.

The most common fiscal rule is a restriction on the budget balance. The limitations this imposes on counter-cyclical policy and the difficulty of hitting precise budget targets as the economy moves through cycles are often addressed by applying a multi-year framework, requiring that budgets balance over a full economic cycle. In addition to budget-balancing requirements, the European

Union's *Maastricht Treaty,* most American states and a few Canadian provinces and territories apply targets or limits to governments' total debt.

To address the problems of targeting variables that are beyond the close control of the policy authorities, some jurisdictions have instead targeted their expenditures or the structures and rates of their taxation, which *are* relatively easy to control. At the federal level, the Mulroney government introduced a *Spending Control Act* in 1991. In theory at least, it had an attractive design: any spending in excess of the target could be offset by cutting spending below the target over the following two years. Moreover, expenditures related to emergencies and to strongly cyclical programs such as employment insurance were exempt. The Mulroney government's experience taught at least one useful lesson: in the end, the legislation was so complex that it failed to pass the communications test. Actual expenditures were quickly driven well below the initial targets. Rather than revising the targets down, the incoming Liberals simply allowed the legislation to lapse. Few Canadians noticed.

Upon first coming into office in late 1993, the Liberal government studied fiscal rules carefully. It soon decided, however, that in reducing the deficit, strong language and strong action would be more powerful than legislation. The internal debate on whether to set debt targets lasted longer. In the end the practical obstacles proved too substantial. For instance, every substantial revision to GDP quelled the appetite for any rule that had the size of the economy in the denominator. Because of worries that a debt rule would cause policy to be too pro-cyclical most people who favoured a rule preferred a multi-year framework. But then that ran up against the lesson of the *Spending Control Act*: it was feared that the rules being studied would quickly fail any public communications test. Above all, the lack of widely supported specific debt objectives doomed such exercises, and still does.

What Features Contribute to the Success of Fiscal Rules?

The evidence on whether fiscal rules in general have been helpful in establishing fiscal discipline is spotty. History offers few examples, particularly at the national level, where countries have changed fiscal policies because of rules. The real tests are likely to come in future, particularly if global economic growth remains weak. As noted, several countries are running afoul of the European Union's fiscal rules. Portugal exceeded the 3 percent of GDP deficit ceiling in 2001, France exceeded the limit last year and Germany is also in danger of being offside. Initially, there was much more debate about how the rules should be changed than about what these countries need to do to stay on side. The debate to change the rules is not over. Most of the major European economies are suffering from weak growth and concerned about compounding the situation through a pro-cyclical fiscal tightening. As of early March 2003, there is debate about either suspending the fiscal rules in light of the economic and fiscal threat from the situation in Iraq, or at least applying them with discretion. At the same time, some fiscal actions are being implemented. Portugal first established some one-time measures to raise revenues and then tightened growth in the public-sector wage bill. A proposal is being debated in Germany to eliminate a number of tax concessions in the interest of raising revenues. France continues to struggle with the implications of the rules. Rather than focusing on the actions required, countries seem to be seeking extra time to comply and are engaging in a vigorous debate over the underlying economic assumptions in the hope of minimizing any *ex ante* calculations of the excess deficit. Meanwhile, closer to home, there was considerable debate in early 2002 on just how much Ontario would have to cut spending in order to respect both its balanced-budget legislation and its *Taxpayer Protection Act*. Instead, the Ontario government decided to alter the legislation so that legislated tax cuts could be postponed.

History does not offer us hard and fast examples on what does and does not work. However, certain features do seem to bolster the chances of success. A list of desirable features, albeit with some internal inconsistencies discussed below, includes the following. In sum, fiscal rules should be:

- backed by firm political leadership
- strict
- accompanied by transparent accounting and budget procedures
- based upon generally accepted fiscal objectives
- simple and easy to communicate
- based on actual, not forecast outcomes
- based on budget balances, not spending or revenues
- difficult to amend (with constitutional authority generally being more convincing in this regard than statutory)
- enforced by an external party with substantial penalties (whether financial or political)
- sufficiently flexible to accommodate legitimate emergencies or anomalies.

This list points to two fascinating dynamic characteristics of fiscal rules. First, they require firm political leadership. But the firmer the leadership, the less the rules are needed. Former Finance Minister Paul Martin's bold declaration that the Liberal Party's fiscal targets would be hit "come hell or high water" was probably more powerful a commitment than specific fiscal rules would have been.

Second, there is a natural evolution to rules. They typically start out being quite strict and straightforward. That gives them a real communications punch that politicians, the public and markets can rally around. Concerns then mount over their pro-cyclical nature and possible effects in dampening growth. To address these concerns, the rules become both more flexible and more complex. Eventually, they lose their communications punch and fade from attention. Readers who are not already tired of this movie should watch the European Union debate over the coming year.

Would Fiscal Rules Help the Federal Government?

As I have argued, in the 1990s, Ottawa's vividly expressed determination to eliminate the deficit bound the government to the fiscal cause as powerfully as constitutional or statutory rules could have. And since eliminating the deficit in 1997–98, the federal government has maintained a strong verbal commitment to balancing the budget – a commitment that, as we all know, it has kept. The fiscal year 2002–03 will mark Ottawa's sixth consecutive budget surplus. The "no-deficits" pledge could, of course, be enshrined in legislation or even in the constitution, even if there are obvious difficulties in making constitutional amendments in Canada. However, I would argue that doing so would not address the principal fiscal issues of the day. In addition to the problem of budgetary balance, the critical issues in this first decade of the twenty-first century are the public debt burden, the tax burden and the growth and com-position of spending. Unfortunately, the groundwork for fiscal rules on these issues has not yet been done.

The debt-to-GDP ratio has fallen from 67.5 percent in 1995–96 to 46.5 per-cent in 2001–02. While such progress is commendable, the ratio is only back to where it was in the mid-1980s, just before the fiscal situation fell apart. In the late 1960s, when the federal government last ran a string of budget balances or surpluses, the debt-to-GDP ratio was under 30 percent. Similarly, despite some progress, the overall Canadian tax burden remains high, both by historical stan-dards and compared to that in the United States. In particular, we have very high marginal tax rates on personal income and a heavy reliance on growth-impairing taxes on capital. The 18 February 2003 budget addressed the capital tax, but allocated additional spending to many areas rather than applying a more general attack on the tax and debt burdens.

Laying down clear, simple rules for the budget balance would have no effect on this wider range of fiscal issues. Unfortunately, the government is in no posi-tion at this time to specify rules for debt, taxation or spending that would be generally accepted. In part, this reflects its steadfast refusal to provide a longer-term context for fiscal policy. It was only with great reluctance that it was finally persuaded to extend the fiscal framework to five years. But, as other papers in this volume have shown, most important questions about government debt are intergenerational in nature. A five-year framework simply does not permit an evaluation of these important debt-burden issues, particularly in light of the fact that the real surge of baby-boomer retirees does not start until after 2011. The absence of a longer-term framework also weakens the ability to examine what tax and spending structures would be optimal for economic and social objectives.

To be fair, it is not just the government that is ill-prepared to face the critical fiscal issues of our time. Beyond preaching the need to eliminate the deficit, the economics profession has not offered very clear views on where fiscal policy should be headed (James and Karam 2000–01; Scarth and Jackson 1998). It seems obvious, however, that any fiscal rule that is contemplated must address not only the budgetary balance, but also the debt burden. Canadians should not feel comfortable at a 46.5 percent debt-to-GDP level. A debt that high presents serious economic, fiscal and political-economy challenges that will have to be grappled with. Consider that for every revenue dollar sent to Ottawa this year, 20 cents will be allocated to paying the interest on this debt. In other words, one out of every five dollars Ottawa collects is used, not to address the current and future needs of Canadians, nor to bring the tax burden down, but to pay for past consumption. By comparison, when the federal government last ran balanced budgets, in the 1960s, only 11 cents of every revenue dollar was used for public debt charges.

It is true that the public debt does not present an immediate problem; debt is like icebergs in that respect. In fact, the debt-to-GDP ratio is likely to fall further over the next few years, but we need to be concerned about the pressures that will come later, as demographic change takes hold. Given the potential seriousness of the problem, there has been relatively little debate in the economics profession on what the "optimal" debt burden should be, nor on the desired path for getting to that optimum. Further, that "optimal" burden should presumably be sensitive to the split between the government's consumption, on the one hand, and its investment, on the other. There are also tricky issues with targeting a variable, such as the ratio of debt to GDP, which the government cannot control directly: for instance, small errors in projecting the path of nominal GDP could require profound fiscal corrections. As well, GDP can be revised substantially, again requiring large fiscal corrections which may not be appropriate for current economic circumstances.

Purely for illustrative purposes, appendix tables A1 and A2 show the 18 February 2003 fiscal forecast (2002–03 to 2004–05) along with two longer-term scenarios. Under both long-term extrapolations, revenue growth is projected at 4.5 percent per year, on par with nominal GDP growth. In extrapolation 1, the budget is balanced each year on a planning basis (that is, after subtracting the contingency reserve and economic prudence), leaving program spending to be the residual. In contrast, in extrapolation 2, program spending is held constant in real per capita terms, with the underlying budget balance becoming the residual. The two extrapolations give quite different results.

Figure 1 plots the future debt-to-GDP ratio for extrapolation 1, under which the federal government maintains balanced budgets. From the current level of 46.5 percent, the ratio declines to 38.4 percent in 2005–06, 29.5 percent in 2011–12 and 23.6 percent in 2016–17. By that time, public debt charges would be absorbing 10 cents of every revenue dollar, as in the 1960s. Is this pace of progress in reducing the debt burden satisfactory? If not, then larger budgetary surpluses must be run. This scenario provides scope to increase program spending faster than GDP, allowing many current and future spending pressures to be addressed. But should we be concerned that no further progress is made in cutting the tax burden? And if so, what is the appropriate trade-off between tax cuts, spending increases and debt reduction?

Figure 1

Future Debt-to-GDP Ratio

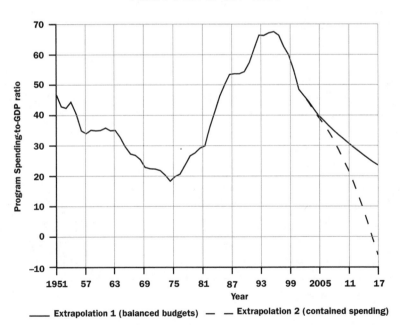

Note: From 1993-94, fiscal data are on a full accrual basis, as per the 18 February 2003 budget. As Finance Canada has not yet provided a full set of revised data, prior data are on the previous modified accrual system of accounts. Last year plotted: 2016–17. Forecast by TD Economics as at March 2003.

A number of economists and business associations have advocated guidelines for the growth in program spending. In part, this is a reaction to the 8.3 percent increase in federal spending in 2000–01 and the 9.4 percent increase projected in the December 2001 budget for 2001–02. As it turned out, departments had trouble getting money out the door quite that fast, so program spending increased by "only" 4.9 percent in 2001–02 (there were as well accounting changes). Restraining the growth of program spending to the sum of population growth and inflation is the most common recommendation (Chamber of Commerce and others) and it is therefore embodied in extrapolation 2. This would see spending rise just under 3 percent per year. Because productivity increases in the economy would not be reflected in higher government spending, the program spending-to-GDP ratio would be steadily driven down. Figure 2 shows that under this scenario, the program spending-to-GDP ratio would be 9.6 percent in 2016–17, its lowest level, by a considerable margin, in the postwar era. With revenues the same as in extrapolation 1, the federal government would be in a net asset position by 2016–17. That is an impressive performance in eliminating debt, but in fact how well thought-out are such spending guidelines? Many proposed spending rules seem to be driven more from an instinctive reaction that "spending is bad." Little consideration is usually given to what is driving the spending. Is it reasonable that productivity gains would never be used to increase the public provision of goods and services? And surely the nature of spending should matter. Growth-enhancing infrastructure outlays presumably warrant a stronger public spending track than increases in consumption-related activities.

Just a few years ago, there was tremendous pressure on all Canadian governments to cut taxes. And almost all governments delivered to some extent, cutting marginal personal and corporate income tax rates. While few people, including the governments in question, saw the tax cuts that were put in place as the end of the process, the cries for tax cuts have certainly been dampened recently. The 30 September 2002 Speech from the Throne and the 18 February 2003 budget leave the impression that the federal government thinks its tax-cutting obligations have been fulfilled. Yet there are still important outstanding issues in the tax system. While Canada remains in its customary position in the middle of the Organisation for Economic Co-operation and Development (OECD) pack in terms of our overall tax burden, we still have a considerably higher burden than the United States. A good part of the difference has been required because of the extra burden of public debt charges, although the US debt burden is rapidly rising and will soon exceed Canada's. And relative to many other countries, we still rely heavily on taxing income, savings and capital. A positive move in the 18 February 2003 budget was to phase-out the

Figure 2
Program Spending-to-GDP Ratio

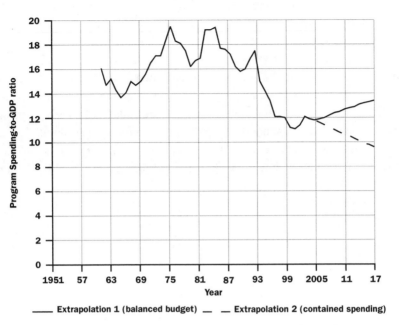

_____ Extrapolation 1 (balanced budget) __ __ Extrapolation 2 (contained spending)

Note: From 1993-94, fiscal data are on a full accrual basis, as per the 18 February 2003 budget. As Finance Canada has not yet provided a full set of revised data, prior data are on the previous modified accrual system of accounts.

federal capital tax. Hopefully, the provinces still levying capital taxes will follow suit. It would be nice, of course, to see the overall tax burden come down. But if that is inconsistent with other fiscal objectives such as reducing the debt burden, then we should at least look at shifting the tax burden more toward consumption. Consumption taxes are less of a drag on economic growth than taxes on income, savings and capital.

Conclusion: Time for Economists to Lay the Groundwork

Since balancing the budget in 1997–98, the Canadian federal government has been conducting fiscal policy without a strong anchor. There is a clear determination to balance the budget. But beyond that, little consideration has been given to critical issues such as the appropriate debt burden, the ideal growth rate and structure of spending, or the fairest and most efficient level and composition of the tax burden. Legislating a budgetary balance requirement would do precious little to address these broader considerations. Unfortunately, it is premature to contemplate fiscal rules concerning the future path of the public debt. As we have seen, one of the features of successful regimes is that the rules are generally accepted. So far, the intellectual groundwork on debt rules has not yet been laid in Canada. If it is to be laid, economists must step forward and take spades in hand.

If the federal government is unwilling to publish longer-term fiscal projections and highlight the challenges they imply, then others should step into the void. Economists should develop views on where the fiscal situation in Canada should be headed – not just as represented by the budget balance, but through all the major fiscal components. If general agreement can be achieved, then the government may well be persuaded to incorporate economists' views into fiscal planning. That may or may not eventually lead to legislated fiscal rules. But a firm fiscal plan would be a powerful start.

Bibliography

Boothe, P., and B. Reid. 1998. "Credibility, Flexibility and Risk: Designing Balanced-Budget Rules." *Policy Options* 19 (January/February):16-19.

Geist, M. 1997/98. "Balanced Budget Legislation: An Assessment of the Recent Canadian Experience." *Ottawa Law Review* 29.

James, S., and P. Karam. 2000/01. "The Role of Government Debt in a World of Incomplete Financial Markets." Working Paper. Ottawa: Department of Finance.

Kennedy, S., and J. Robbins. 2001. "The Role of Fiscal Risks in Determining Fiscal Performance." Working Paper no. 2001-16. Ottawa: Department of Finance.

Kopits, G. 2001. "Fiscal Rules: Useful Policy Framework or Unnecessary Ornament?" IMF Working Paper. New York: International Monetary Fund.

Millar, J. 1997. "The Effects of Budget Rules on Fiscal Performance and Macroeconomic Stabilization." Working Paper no. 97-15. Ottawa: Bank of Canada.

Parker, G., and T. Major. 2002. "Feeling the Strain." *Financial Times*, 12 July.

Scarth, W., and H. Jackson. 1998. "The Target Debt-to-GDP Ratio: How Big Should It Be and How Quickly Should We Approach It?" In *Fiscal Targets and Economic Growth*, ed. T.J. Courchene and T.A. Wilson. Kingston: John Deutsch Institute for the Study of Economic Policy, Queen's University.

Table A1

Canadian Federal Government Fiscal Position: Balanced Budgets
(billions of dollars unless otherwise indicated)

Fiscal Years (1 April - 31 March)	1998-99	1999-00	2000-01	February 2003 Budget					Extrapolation 1**	
				01-02	02-03	03-04	04-05	05-06	11-12	16-17
Budgetary Revenues	156.0	165.7	182.3	171.7	178.7	184.7	192.9	201.6	262.5	327.1
% change	2.6	6.2	10.0	-5.8	4.1	3.4	4.4	4.5	4.5	4.5
Program Spending	110.0	109.4	118.5	124.3	138.6	143.0	149.6	157.5	220.5	287.1
% change	2.9	-0.5	8.3	4.9	11.5	3.2	4.6	5.3	5.7	5.2
Public Debt Charges	42.9	43.1	43.6	39.3	37.2	37.6	38.4	38.1	35.0	33.0
% change	1.2	0.5	1.2	-9.9	-5.3	1.1	2.1	-0.8	-1.4	0.0
Underlying Budget Balance	3.1	13.2	20.2	8.2	3.0	4.0	5.0	6.0	7.0	7.0
Contingency Reserve	—	—	—	—	3.0	3.0	3.0	3.0	3.0	3.0
Economic Prudence*	—	—	—	—	—	1.0	2.0	3.0	4.0	4.0
TOTAL	—	—	—	—	3.0	4.0	5.0	6.0	7.0	7.0
Planning Surplus/Deficit (-)	3.1	13.2	20.2	8.2	0.0	0.0	0.0	0.0	0.0	0.0
Federal Debt (Accumulated Deficit)										
Contingency Reserve Spent	549.4	536.2	516.0	507.7	507.7	507.7	507.7	507.7	507.7	507.7
Revenues/GDP	17.0	16.9	17.1	15.7	15.6	15.4	15.2	15.2	15.2	15.2
Program Spending/GDP	12.0	11.2	11.1	11.4	12.1	11.9	11.8	11.9	12.8	13.4
Public Debt Charges/Debt (t-1)	7.8	7.8	8.1	7.6	7.3	7.4	7.6	7.5	6.9	6.5

Table A1 (Continued)
Canadian Federal Government Fiscal Position: Balanced Budgets
(billions of dollars unless otherwise indicated)

Fiscal Years (1 April - 31 March)	1998-99	99-00	2000-01	01-02	02-03	03-04	04-05	05-06	11-12	16-17
					February 2003 Budget				Extrapolation 1**	
Federal Debt (Accumulated Deficit)/GDP										
Contingency Reserve Spent	60.0	54.7	48.5	46.5	44.5	42.2	40.1	38.4	29.5	23.6
Contingency Reserve-to-Debt Paydown	60.0	54.7	48.5	46.5	44.2	41.7	39.4	37.5	27.7	21.6

Notes:

* Contingency reserve and economic prudence are included in the budget projections to cover unanticipated risks.
Because of space limitations, only selected years shown.

** As per the budget, the forecast assumes that the contingency reserve and economic prudence are used, and will not go toward debt reduction.
Forecast by TD Economics as at February 2003; Source: Federal government, Statistics Canada, TD Economics.

Table A2
Canadian Federal Government Fiscal Position: Contained Spending
(billions of dollars unless otherwise indicated)

Fiscal Years (1 April - 31 March)	1998-99	99-00	2000-01	01-02	February 2003 Budget 02-03	03-04	04-05	05-06	Extrapolation 2** 11-12	16-17
Budgetary Revenues	156.0	165.7	182.3	171.7	178.7	184.7	192.9	201.6	262.5	327.1
% change	2.6	6.2	10.0	-5.8	4.1	3.4	4.4	4.5	4.5	4.5
Program Spending	110.0	109.4	118.5	124.3	138.6	143.0	149.6	153.6	180.3	206.0
% change	2.9	-0.5	8.3	4.9	11.5	3.2	4.6	2.7	2.7	2.7
Public Debt Charges	42.9	43.1	43.6	39.3	37.2	37.6	38.4	38.1	26.7	1.8
% change	1.2	0.5	1.2	-9.9	-5.3	1.1	2.1	-0.8	-10.4	-77.6
Underlying Budget Balance	3.1	13.2	20.2	8.2	3.0	4.0	5.0	9.9	55.5	119.3
Contingency Reserve	–	–	–	–	3.0	3.0	3.0	3.0	3.0	3.0
Economic Prudence*	–	–	–	–	–	1.0	2.0	3.0	4.0	4.0
TOTAL	–	–	–	–	3.0	4.0	5.0	6.0	7.0	7.0
Planning Surplus/Deficit (–)	3.1	13.2	20.2	8.2	0.0	0.0	0.0	3.9	48.5	112.3
Federal Debt (Accumulated Deficit) Contingency Reserve Spent	549.4	536.2	516.0	507.7	507.7	507.7	507.7	503.8	339.0	-84.1
Revenues/GDP	17.0	16.9	17.1	15.7	15.6	15.4	15.2	15.2	15.2	15.2
Program Spending/GDP	12.0	11.2	11.1	11.4	12.1	11.9	11.8	11.6	10.5	9.6
Public Debt Charges/Debt (t–1)	7.8	7.8	8.1	7.6	7.3	7.4	7.6	7.5	6.9	6.5

Table A2 (Continued)
Canadian Federal Government Fiscal Position: Contained Spending
(billions of dollars unless otherwise indicated)

| Fiscal Years (1 April - 31 March) | 1998-99 | 99-00 | 2000-01 | February 2003 Budget | | | | | Extrapolation 2** | |
				01-02	02-03	03-04	04-05	05-06	11-12	16-17
Federal Debt (Accumulated Deficit)										
Contingency Reserve Spent	60.0	54.7	48.5	46.5	44.5	42.2	40.1	38.1	19.7	-3.9
Contingency Reserve-to-Debt Paydown	60.0	54.7	48.5	46.5	44.2	41.7	39.4	37.2	17.9	-6.0

Notes:

* Contingency reserve and economic prudence are included in the budget projections to cover unanticipated risks.
Because of space limitations, only selected years shown.

** As per the budget, the forecast assumes that the contingency reserve and economic prudence are used, and will not go toward debt reduction.

Forecast by TD Economics as at February 2003; Source: Federal government, Statistics Canada, TD Economics.

do we need fiscal rules?
some evidence from western Canada

Paul Boothe

Introduction

Although some people's memories are already dimming, it is only a decade ago that Canada's federal and provincial governments were facing up to the long-neglected chore of eliminating unprecedented deficits. The legacy of those deficits – in the form of large government debts and attendant annual debt-service payments – is still with us. With a number of provinces again entering the deficit danger zone, it is useful to look at how we dealt with government deficits in the early 1990s in order to see what worked and what did not. One of the key questions regarding that period is the role that fiscal rules played in helping to eliminate deficits. Based on his experience at the very centre of federal deficit elimination efforts, Don Drummond gives us an insider's view of fiscal rules. Here I would like to summarize what I learned from the Drummond paper, bring some provincial evidence to bear on the issue of fiscal rules, based on my own experience in the Alberta and Saskatchewan governments, and then conclude with a brief look at an upcoming issue.

Evidence from Federal Deficit Elimination

The academic literature on fiscal rules is large and growing and Drummond cites some recent work in the area. Overall, the evidence seems to suggest that while fiscal rules may be helpful in eliminating existing deficits or preventing new ones, rules are not really necessary. As Drummond emphasizes, the successful elimination of Canada's federal deficit in the mid-1990s provides a case in point. Even so, most Canadian provinces have adopted fiscal rules of various sorts.

Drummond argues, correctly in my view, that if such rules are to contribute significantly to deficit elimination efforts, they should have a number of characteristics. Above all, they must enjoy the support of the government that must live under them and the voters that put it in power. Beyond that, rules should be simple, strict, hard to amend and easy to communicate, both to spending departments and the public. Finally, adherence to fiscal rules should be easy to measure, and the benchmark against which they are measured should be the actual objective – for example, the realized budget balance – not forecasted outcomes.

When fiscal objectives include both deficit prevention and debt reduction, rules need to ensure that the government runs a surplus on average. This combination of objectives means that a target surplus with some flexibility can serve a dual role. Unexpected (or at least, unbudgeted) revenues or expenditures can be absorbed by the flexible surplus, while over time balances that are positive on average bring debts down. This is exactly what has happened at both the federal level and in Alberta.

A related issue is the role for counter-cyclical fiscal policy. Although one usually thinks of activist measures when contemplating counter-cyclical policy, it is important to understand that the bulk of any counter-cyclical fiscal impulse normally comes from the automatic stabilizers. Governments that undertake nonautomatic (i.e., "activist" or "discretionary") counter-cyclical policy are invariably too late to have the desired effect (see Boothe and Petchey 1996). A good example is provided by the Canada Infrastructure Works Program. Conceived by the federal government in 1993 to combat the recession of the early 1990s, the partnership agreements were signed in 1994 and work began in 1995. By 1995, the Canadian economy had returned to trend output. The bulk of the spending was planned to occur between 1995 and 1997, long after the recession it was intended to counter had ended.

Drummond also warns us that care should be taken in constructing the target measure for use with a fiscal rule. For example, deficit-to-GDP and debt-to-GDP ratios will vary both because of changes in deficits and debts (the true targets) and because of variation in gross domestic product (GDP). The key point is that using GDP as the denominator adds additional volatility to the measure and makes the fiscal rule more complicated. From this standpoint, it may well be that because of its relative stability population is the best variable to use to scale the fiscal measure of interest.

Evidence from Provincial Deficit Elimination

My own experience with reducing deficits is based on work with the Alberta and Saskatchewan governments during their deficit elimination programs of the 1990s. Alberta and Saskatchewan are interesting case studies because Alberta relied heavily on a fiscal rule to help eliminate its deficit while Saskatchewan did not (Boothe and Reid 2001). The New Democratic Party government of Saskatchewan simply made a political commitment that it would balance its budget within its first mandate. Alberta put its commitment into legislation with four annual deficit targets ending with deficit elimination. Given that Saskatchewan eliminated its deficit and reduced its debt without the benefit of a fiscal rule, why was the fiscal rule important in Alberta?

In my view, the main role of fiscal rules is to serve as a tool to help political leaders resist demands for increased spending. Working in a finance department, one quickly realizes that even after you eliminate spending requests of questionable value, there are always more worthy projects than there is money available to finance them. Thus, a key use of fiscal rules is to allow fiscal managers to draw the line on spending requests coming from Cabinet colleagues or the public. For example, early in the deficit elimination process in Alberta, ministry officials were shocked when Treasury Board told them that special warrants were no longer permitted and they would have to find the funding to cover unexpected forest-fire suppression costs within their ministry budget.

A second important role for fiscal rules is to help build up the credibility of fiscal managers, even if this benefit is only realized over time as the public eventually comes to realize that the government is indeed keeping to its fiscal rules. The importance of credibility is hard to overestimate: a large academic literature shows that credibility on the part of fiscal managers reduces the cost of meeting fiscal goals (see Boothe and Reid 1998). In part, this helps explain why complex fiscal rules usually fail. If they are too complicated to be understood by the public, they cannot contribute to the credibility of fiscal managers and thus lower the cost of achieving fiscal goals as time goes on.

The main benefit of Alberta's fiscal rule was the help it provided in dealing with revenue volatility. Simple measures of revenue volatility show Alberta's revenues to be almost twice as volatile as those of the next most volatile province, largely as a result of the volatility of energy revenues. The fiscal rule currently in place in Alberta is specifically designed to deal with revenue volatility by specifying that three-quarters of revenue windfalls must be allocated to debt reduction. Further, a revenue cushion of 2.5 percent must be maintained to prevent in-year volatility from resulting in deficits.

Thus, while Saskatchewan's experience suggests that fiscal rules are not necessary to eliminate or prevent a deficit, they may be helpful in particular circumstances. For its part, Alberta's experience suggests that one area in which fiscal rules can be helpful is in dealing with extreme revenue volatility. The relative stability of federal revenues may help explain why the federal government was successful in eliminating its deficit without the help of an explicit fiscal rule.

Looking Ahead

One of the important changes on the horizon for federal and provincial fiscal managers is the current movement toward accrual accounting for public sector capital. Briefly, this means that the cost of building public roads, buildings and other infrastructure will be removed from the government's operating budget and replaced by the calculated depreciation of the public capital stock. In jurisdictions that are enlarging their capital stock, purchasing a dollar of new capital will increase budgeted expenses only by its current depreciation, say five cents. The new incentives for politicians created by this accounting change are obvious and possibly dangerous.

This change in accounting standards also means that traditional notions of deficits will need to be revised and new fiscal rules will have to be developed along with them. For example, traditional measures of deficits may have to be replaced by notions of "changes in net debt." With the concept of expenditure changing to exclude capital spending, the traditional notion of a deficit becomes less useful. Relevant debt measures will have to be defined and medium-term targets set in order for fiscal rules to operate and fiscal performance to be measured.

In his own closing remarks, Drummond argues that with deficits eliminated in most Canadian jurisdictions, economists need to lead the debate around a new fiscal framework focused on growth. He has done a good job of laying out what he believes are the essential elements of that framework. In my view, part of that debate should focus on whether fiscal rules will contribute to achieving our fiscal goals in the future.

Note

1. The views expressed in this paper are my own and should not be attributed to any other individual or institution.

Bibliography

Boothe, P., and B. Reid. 1998. "Fiscal Prudence and Federal Budgeting in the Medium Term." In *Fiscal Targets and Economic Growth*, ed. T. J. Courchene and T. A. Wilson. Kingston: John Deutsch Institute for the Study of Economic Policy, Queen's University.

———, eds. 2001. *Deficit Reduction in the Far West: The Great Experiment*. Edmonton: University of Alberta Press.

Boothe, P., and J. Petchey. 1996. "Assigning Responsibility for Regional Stabilization: Evidence from Canada and Australia." In *Reforming Fiscal Federalism for Global Competition*, ed. P. Boothe. Edmonton: University of Alberta Press.

what is the real issue in the debt debate?

Lars Osberg

Is there a debate about public debt in Canada – and if there is, why should anyone care about it?

Ten years ago, the context for discussion of public debt in Canada was an economy in which federal and provincial governments were still running substantial deficits, despite the fact that public debt had recently risen rapidly to fractions of GDP that had not been seen in half a century. In addition, with high unemployment and a recent growth experience that contrasted very unfavourably with the United States, Canadians had ample reason for dissatisfaction with their real economic outcomes. Debate on the issue of public deficits and debts was therefore fierce, with frequent expressions of a sense of crisis, many adverse comparisons with other nations and a broad awareness of the importance of the government debt issue for Canadian society.

In contrast, in 2002–03, the federal government, like most provinces, was running a financial surplus, and economic growth was strong. The debt-to-gross-domestic product (GDP)[1] ratio was, as a consequence, dropping like a stone. Canadians were adjusting to the prevalence of newspaper stories about the superior job-creation record of the Canadian labour market, as growth in the US slipped below that in Canada. With dramatic speed, both federal and state governments in the US had shifted from large surpluses to large structural deficits. In broader international comparisons, Canada's low and falling debt-to-GDP ratio compared favourably with other Organisation for Economic Co-operation and Development (OECD) countries, and Canada was the only G7 country to have a budgetary surplus in 2002 and to project another surplus for 2003.

With so much good news about, it was perhaps not surprising that the debt-deficit issue slipped off the media agenda and ranked relatively low in polling estimates of the policy concerns of Canadians. So why should there be a debate? What exactly is the problem?

One problem is that we do not have a clear objective for the ultimate level of the debt-to-GDP ratio and there is little evidence of agreement on how far Canadians want it to decline. Certainly there is little consensus among professional economists about the appropriate level of the public debt or the size and nature of its social costs and benefits. A second problem, which interacts with the first, is that it remains unclear exactly why "we" should care or why "we" might have a common opinion. "Efficiency" arguments do not produce a clear guide and "equity" arguments depend crucially on personal values, which are bound to differ. In the controversy over the implications of the public debt, there has been a tendency to interpret the debt issue in terms of intergenerational equity, but I will argue that such an emphasis is fundamentally misplaced. In practice, the debate on deficits and debts has had the subtext of continuing disagreements over the size of government and the appropriate degree of redistribution by the state. Until this is recognized explicitly, we are unlikely to make much progress.

What is the Optimal Size of the Debt?

As Don Drummond's calculations in this volume illustrate, the current policy settings of the federal government imply a continuing and rapid decline in the debt-to-GDP ratio. Although the recent string of surpluses has brought a useful reduction in debt principal, the main action is in the denominator, not the numerator of the debt-to-GDP ratio (the total stock of nominal debt is only declining slightly, but nominal GDP is currently rising at about 6 percent annually).[2] The question Drummond poses is: "How low should we go? What is the optimal level of the debt-to-GDP ratio?" He sees this as a challenge to the Canadian economics profession: surely economics should have something useful to say about the "fiscal anchor" of government and when one should stop the process of debt reduction.

In an informal poll at the final session of the conference, participants were asked to specify their own estimate of the optimal long-run debt-to-GDP ratio of all levels of government and the appropriate time frame for Canada to get there. At the time, the combined debt-to-GDP ratio of federal and provincial governments was slightly over 70 percent, and all respondents thought some reduction was desirable.[3] None of the 20 respondents was willing to suggest an optimal ratio less than 20 percent or greater than 50 percent. However, the two most frequently specified ranges (by 30 percent of respondents in each case) were right at the edges of this band: 20 to 25 percent and 46 to 50 percent. Although other responses were spread in between, and the average response was almost exactly in the middle of the range (35.7 percent), that average clearly masks a significant divergence of opinion.

To some readers, the 20 percent to 50 percent range may seem like quite a dispersion of expert opinion. In fact, it represents a considerable compression of the range of published estimates cited by Scarth in his paper in this volume. These range from +60 percent to −300 percent.[4] His own preference is for a debt ratio in the 20 to 25 percent range, largely because that would correspond to the approximate levels of the mid-1970s. However, Scarth does not make strong claims for this particular ratio and he emphasizes that departures from the optimal debt ratio do not appear to have large efficiency costs. Furthermore, he regards deviations from the optimal range, both over the business cycle and for longer periods, as desirable, and he argues for a policy of "letting the debt ratio rise when we face major events that are expected to lower living standards."

As a "fiscal anchor" for government budgets, this may seem to many people to be somewhat elastic, and the low cost of divergences from the optimum ratio that Scarth notes may prompt some readers to conclude that it does not matter much. However, Scarth does also get at the issues that sit behind the debate on government debt. He recognizes that debt may finance government spending on productive capital, so that estimates of the efficiency impacts of such debt depend heavily on one's own opinions about the relative productivity of government or private sector investment expenditure. As well, Scarth argues that the chosen target for the debt ratio "must be based primarily on its consistency with our equity objectives" and he distinguishes between the distributional implications of tax cuts or spending increases as alternatives to debt reduction. As he notes, "liquidity-constrained (i.e., poorer) households may do better if the tax cut use for the fiscal dividend is rejected." In this, he comes close to recognizing that disagreements over the appropriate role, size and income distributional impact of government have been the subtext for the debate on deficits and debts in Canada.

In an accounting sense, it is the *difference* between government revenue and expenditure, and not the *level* of either, that affects the deficit and the debt. In principle, one could solve "the debt problem" either at high levels of public expenditure accompanied by high taxes or at low levels of expenditure and taxation. In principle, the level of public expenditure is also analytically distinct from the redistributional impact of that expenditure: the same level of expenditure can give rise to many different patterns of redistribution, while a given redistribution can be achieved at many different levels of expenditure. In practice, however, in Canada the issue of debts and deficits has become intertwined with broader, and more ideological, debates about the appropriate role and size of government. In practice, expenditure cuts have been crucial in producing the recent surpluses of Canadian governments, and tax cuts have followed, so deficit elimination, debt repayment and a reduction of distributional equity and the role of government in Canadian society have coincided.

Intergenerational Equity is a Misleading Focus

Of course, any mention of the term "equity" presupposes some conception of "equity among whom." In the papers presented at this conference, the primary focus was on "intergenerational equity," and with the exception of Scarth's paper, generations were thought of in terms of a "representative agent," so issues of "intragenerational equity" (i.e., equity between the rich and the poor of any given generation) were almost entirely ignored.

I would argue that this emphasis is profoundly misplaced. Over time it is the real assets of a nation's residents that will determine their aggregate productive potential and consequently the economic well-being of different generations. But *government debt is a financial instrument*. Financial instruments are inherently an asset to some people (in this case, the holders of government bonds) but a liability to others (in this case, taxpayers). Hence, like any other financial instrument, bonds serve to redistribute income (i.e., potential consumption) among the Canadians who are alive at any given point in time. If more bonds are in existence at some future time, more of that period's potential consumption will be transferred from taxpayers to bondholders, which means that *intra*generational distribution, and the equity implications of that redistribution, are central to the debt debate.

If one uses the term "generation" to mean "the set of all Canadians alive at any particular time" the issue of the "intragenerational distribution of income" is the distribution of income among the different persons who are alive at a particular time, while the issue of the "intergenerational distribution of income" is the distribution of aggregate income among people who are alive at different times. Since no generation can compel the labour supply of another generation living at a different time, no generation can directly determine the aggregate income of future generations. But each generation *can* determine the potential income of future generations by leaving an aggregate bequest of productive resources. In this sense, the crucial issue in the "intergenerational distribution of income" is the time path of the aggregate stock of productive resources, which one should interpret broadly to include human, environmental and social capital, as well as physical capital in machinery, equipment and structures.[5] At any point in time, Canadian society has a particular potential aggregate income, as implied by Canada's aggregate stocks of capital and labour. The intragenerational distribution of that aggregate income is determined by the distribution of labour incomes, by public policy decisions on transfer payments and tax burdens, and by the set of legal claims to property income (including bonds).

In this view, financial claims have the twofold character of being an asset to their holder and a liability to their issuer. Domestically held government debt is an asset to the bondholder and a liability to the taxpayer, both of whom are living Canadian members of the same "generation." It follows that we cannot get very far in understanding the debt problem if we assume there is only one type of agent, because taxpayers and bondholders are then the same "representative agent." As Dahlby notes in his paper, if there is a single representative agent, "everyone holds the same amount of the public debt and everyone in the economy would be better off if the government repudiated the public debt." In a representative agent model with only one type of agent, everyone owns debt, and everyone owes the taxes that pay the same debt. As a consequence, the public debt creates a "deadweight loss" for everyone since everyone's labour supply decisions are distorted by the taxation necessary to pay the debt.[6] However, nobody gets a net benefit since everyone is both a taxpayer and a bondholder. In this sort of economy, there is a pure Pareto improvement from debt repudiation, everybody benefits, and therefore there is no reason not to do it.[7]

Hence, government debt only comes into existence and poses an issue for society because of the heterogeneity of types of agents. The collective decision to issue public debt would make no sense if all individuals were to buy the same amount of it, since they might as well just pay that amount as taxes. Heterogeneity in initial wealth and/or time preference is needed if we are to explain why some people initially make the individual choice to buy bonds (and abstain from consumption) while others do not, preferring instead to consume more in the initial period and defer their tax burden to the future. However, given that there is a heterogeneity of wealth and time preferences, one of the social benefits of a market for public debt is that individuals are able to reallocate their potential consumption over time without risk of default.[8]

In order to finance a given level of government expenditure over time, governments have to decide, at the margin, whether to tax or borrow in the current period. Borrowing now means a greater government debt, which implies higher future tax rates than would otherwise have been the case, which means more intragenerational redistribution (from taxpayers to bondholders) among the people who will be alive at different times in the future. If higher future tax rates imply distortions in future labour supply or savings behaviour that reduce future output, this deadweight loss will be a cost in the aggregate output of future generations that should be counted as "intergenerational redistribution of income."[9] Of course, taxing now would also imply deadweight loss so the correct measure of the impact of debt financing on intergenerational distribution is the difference in the present value of the deadweight loss between taxing now and taxing later. The issue of "equity" in intergenerational distribution then depends, like the aggregate savings decision that determines the capital stock, on what one thinks the "fair" time path of aggregate consumption should be, and there is a large and profound literature on this point.

Intragenerational Redistribution is the Key Issue

Up to this point, the term generation has been used to mean "those Canadians alive at a given time." This usage is consistent with the discussion of national output, consumption and debt in many of the papers in this volume: e.g., those by Dahlby and Johnson. It is not the definition used by Boadway, however, who refers to a generation as "all those born at time t." Whichever definition is used, it is still true that a bond is an asset to its holder and a liability to its payer. But if we use "generation" in Boadway's sense of "birth cohort," then some of each birth cohort will own bonds, while others will not.[10] This inequality between people of the same age who have financial wealth and those who do not is an important determinant of "intragenerational distribution."

If all birth cohorts had the same proportion of bondholders and distribution of income and bond wealth, then there would be no net payments of bond interest between birth cohorts. The issue of "intergenerational distribution" (in Boadway's sense of "generation") that is posed by the government debt therefore depends on the extent to which birth cohorts differ in the proportion of bondholders and in their distributions of income and wealth. However, bondholders rather disappear from Boadway's paper. When he says "the essential feature of long-term debt financing is that it is essentially an intergenerational transfer," he does not mention that some members of *every* birth cohort will be receiving the payments that taxpayers are making.

If distribution between birth cohorts is the issue, then one must recognize that cohorts are linked within the family, both by inheritance and by *inter vivos* transfers. Within family lines, some families will pass bond portfolios to their descendants, while others will pass on only tax liabilities. Greater debt financing does imply a greater intergenerational (i.e., between birth cohorts) transfer of this type of financial instrument *within families*, (i.e., more assets for those who inherit bonds, larger future tax liabilities for those who do not), but the empirical issue is whether or not other transfers are unaffected. Although the Barro hypothesis of equal offsetting changes in other intra-family transfers is extreme, it is also extreme to argue that families do not regard government bonds and other assets as being any sort of substitute for one another in their bequest decisions. To the extent that families treat government debt as equivalent to other assets, the *form* of intergenerational transfers within families will be affected by greater issuance of public debt, but not the level.

Debt Reduction and the Size of Government

To this point, it could be argued that we have implicitly seen the public debt as being the result of a sequential decision process, in which the first decision to be made is the optimal level of public expenditure and the second decision is how much of that spending to finance by current taxation and how much to finance by future taxation (i.e., public debt). In this view, the level of spending and the financing decision are not logically linked. However, although this viewpoint is analytically appealing, and has been the favoured assumption in this volume, it is rather dissonant with the actual debate on public debt in Canada, which has had the size of government as a consistent subtext.

If debt financing and the level of public spending are linked, then in calculating the aggregate intergenerational impact of greater debt, one should include the impact of the associated government spending on future productive resources. Does public spending crowd out productive private-sector investment? Does public spending increase future productive resources, or does it all go to current consumption (evidence that "governments have spent beyond their means" as Robson puts it)?[11] It is at this stage that the debt debate begins to merge with the broader and more ideological public debate on the appropriate size and role of government.

Both Boadway and Robson advocate "generational accounting" without any real mention of the implications of its crucial assumption that all government expenditure should be allocated *at cost* to particular birth cohorts. To take a concrete example, if governments spend more on the maintenance or creation of physical infrastructure such as roads or bridges, or on human capital via spending on health, education or retraining, such expenditures add to the deficit and thereby increase the tax liabilities of future generations. Will the public capital stock and private human capital resulting from these expenditures also add to the incomes of future generations? In generational accounting the answer is assumed to be "no." All government expenditure is assumed to be consumption: the rate of return on all public-sector projects is implicitly set to zero.

This assumption that the public sector produces no value-added is really quite fundamental to "generational accounting." If public-sector expenditures on things like education are presumed to be unproductive, their dollar values can be allocated, as "consumption," to individuals in particular birth cohorts, and the dollar value of benefits to individuals is equal to the dollar value of costs to government. Individuals are, in this scenario, presumed to be indifferent between receiving a public service (e.g., an education) or a tax cut or a cash transfer of equal cost, so the net total of transfers and services received minus taxes paid can be calculated for each cohort. (The calculation is, of course, crucially contingent on the assumptions made about sharing within families and about the future incomes and taxes paid by each cohort.) The value of total expenditure will then correspond to the discounted dollar value of the taxation required to pay for such expenditures. In the accounting identity stressed by generational accountants, the "tax payments of the unborn" is the residual that balances the tax and expenditure sides of government accounts. However, if expenditures on services such as education yield greater dollar benefits to recipient individuals than their dollar cost to government (i.e., if the rate of return on human capital is positive), this fundamental accounting identity of "generational accounts" becomes meaningless.

Even if all public spending were unproductive, generational accounts are entirely dependent on the allocation of expenditure to cohorts, which is extremely sensitive to how transfers of resources within households are modelled. For example, are education or health services received by children benefits to them personally or to the head of the household to which they belong? Generational accountants usually assume there is zero shifting between generations either of tax burdens or transfer benefits. It may well be that burdens and benefits are not fully shifted, but this assumption that there is *no* linkage between generations, except through the public debt, is clearly extreme.

As Kotlikoff and Summers (1981) demonstrated long ago, in 1974 at best some 19 percent of total US wealth was the result of life-cycle savings. The remainder of the US capital stock was transferred within families as intergenerational bequests, and since then wealth inequality has increased considerably. The "generational accounts" perspective can only be rescued if it is argued that actual intergenerational transfers are all unintentional, arising only because of the uncertainty of lifetimes and the non-availability of annuities.[12]

In considering equity between different birth cohorts, we are focusing attention on a particular type of *group* equity. When there is much greater variation within groups than there is between groups, as there is, it might be considered misleading to organize one's data so as to suppress consideration of most of the inequality among individuals, and concentrate on the between-group differences that, empirically, constitute a relatively small component of aggregate inequality. Differences among individuals within birth cohorts are much larger in magnitude than differences between cohorts in average income. In fact, in the 1990s in Canada, as in other countries, over 90 percent of aggregate income inequality (as measured by the Theil index) can be ascribed to inequality among people of the same birth cohorts, and less than 10 percent to between-cohort differences in average equivalent money income (see Osberg 2003, 127).

The Costs of Deficit Reduction

As Boadway has pointed out elsewhere, much of what government actually does is redistributive, either in direct transfer payments or as "quasi-private services" such as education, health or welfare services. As he says, "these quasi-private services fulfil an important equity role in the economy; indeed they constitute perhaps the main instruments of redistribution available to governments" (Boadway and Flatters 1994, 28). However, as Kneebone and Chung's chapter in the current volume notes, it was the expenditure cuts between 1993 and 1997 that produced an increase of 3.8 percent in the federal government's primary balance, and set the stage for the dramatic declines in the debt-to-GDP ratio we have seen since then.[13]

In several recent federal budgets, it has been noted that "federal government spending, as percentage of GDP, is at its lowest level in 50 years," and that "the program spending to GDP ratio has declined significantly, from about 16 percent in 1993–94 to about 11 percent in 2000–01. This decline was largely attributable to the expenditure reduction initiatives announced in the 1995 budget aimed at eliminating the deficit" (Canada 2003). Although a one-time increase in health-care transfers to the provinces increases the ratio in 2002–03, the growth rate of federal expenditures is projected to be less than that of GDP, implying that federal government expenditure will continue to shrink as a percentage of Canada's economy. A small and forever declining role for the federal government in Canadian economic and social life means that the cuts in federal expenditures in the 1990s represent a permanent change in the size of the public sector, not a temporary belt-tightening. Although during the 1990s Canadians were encouraged to think of expenditure restraint in terms of the necessary sacrifices needed to solve a deficit problem, now that the deficit has been eliminated there is no intention to gradually restore expenditure to its historic share of GDP.

It should not be thought that reducing the size of the federal government has been a small achievement. Total federal program spending fluctuated between 15 and 16.2 percent of GDP from 1959–60 to 1989–90 but is forecast to be just

11.8 percent in 2004–2005. From 1951 to 1994, total federal spending was only once below 14 percent of GDP.[14] In 1948/49 total federal program spending (including transfers to the provinces) was 10.3 percent of GDP and in 1949/50 it was 11.5 percent.[15] Since the Second World War, these are the only two years in which federal spending was below its current level. Since1940–47 was dominated by the war effort, when federal expenditure was a much higher fraction of aggregate national output, one really has to go back to the 1930s to find a similar span of time in which federal government expenditure has been a comparable share of aggregate Canadian GDP.

As the federal budget of 2003 noted when one adds together all the different levels of government, the picture is, if anything, magnified:

> The rapid turnaround in Canada's financial position, as a percentage of GDP, is attributable in large part to a sharp reduction in program spending, that is, all expenditures less gross debt charges. Between 1992 and 2002, Canada's total government program spending as a share of GDP was reduced by 9.1 percentage points, a far greater reduction than in any other G7 country. As a result, Canada's program spending relative to GDP is now below the G7 average whereas in 1992 it was well above the G7 average. In fact, in 2002 Canada's program spending, as a percentage of GDP, was lower than in all other G7 countries except the USA. (Canada 2003, annex 4, p. 6)

It is clear that the debt crisis of the 1990s has been the occasion for a truly profound shift in the size of Canada's public sector – one that has been at least partially locked in by the tax cuts of the 2001 and subsequent budgets. One will look in vain for polling evidence that this long-term change is what most Canadians wanted, but it is what they have got, along with a reduction in the tax burden, particularly of upper income groups.[16]

Cuts of this magnitude mean that the "social wage" of public services for all citizens has fallen, but the pain of this is least keenly felt by those who have high market incomes with which to purchase private substitutes. When, for example, the public education system is starved of resources, affluent parents can afford to pay for private alternatives to public primary and secondary schools and they can also afford the increasing tuition charges of postsecondary education. The decline in quality of public education is, as a consequence, experienced primarily by those who cannot afford alternatives. Meanwhile, any disincentive effect of higher postsecondary tuition fees increases the relative scarcity of university graduates, and the private returns to postsecondary education of those who can afford to go. Debt reduction has been funded in part by decreased spending on education, which does have an intergenerational impact, but it differs qualitatively among family lines. The combination of a relatively better private education for the children of the affluent, greater scarcity value for their educational credentials and lower income tax rates on those higher earnings means greater individual incomes. But factory schooling for the masses, plus greater financial barriers to postsecondary education mean the less affluent have less chance of accessibility, and a greater private debt burden if they do persist in education.

Hence, in my view, the real issue in the debt debate is the implication for equity, within generations, of how we have chosen to deal with debt. The public policy choices on taxation and expenditure that will shape the evolution of the debt will certainly affect "intergenerational equity," in the sense of equality of opportunity, as well as "intragenerational equity," in the sense of equality of outcomes, but it is misleading in the extreme to portray the debt issue as a conflict between generations.

Notes

1. In 2001–02 the federal debt-to-GDP ratio was 46.5 percent, down nearly 20 percentage points from its peak in 1995–96. On a total government sector basis, between 1995 and 2002 Canada's debt-to-GDP ratio was reduced by 26.8 percentage points, the largest decline in the G7 (Canada 2003, ch. 8).

2. Third-quarter 2002 over third-quarter 2001 – see CANSIM II – variable V498918.

3. My own view is that there are large costs (both economic and political) when public finances become highly vulnerable to variations in interest rates, so my preference is for a continued decline in the debt-to-GDP ratio. I do not have strong opinions about the target debt-to-GDP ratio, but something like 40 percent (federal plus provincial) seems reasonable.

4. Note that an optimal debt ratio of –300 percent (i.e., a net asset position for government of three times GDP) means that the state would own much, if not all, of the nation's capital stock.

5. There is a substantial literature on the importance of human and social capital for long-term economic growth (see, e.g., Helliwell 2001). Public expenditure on education, training and health care clearly adds to the human capital stock, and in practice such spending dominates the program expenditure of governments. However, national income accounting conventions only count public sector investment in fixed capital and infrastructure as part of "capital formation." Hence, although Scarth is correct in his comment that "government spends a very small proportion of its funds on *what the national accounts refer to as* investment goods" (italics added), it is the omission of human capital from the national accounts that explains this.

Throughout the conference, there was continual slippage back and forth between the System of National Accounts conception that government spending (G) is government's consumptive use of resources (which does *not* include transfers between individuals) and the Public Accounts measures of public spending (which do include transfers).

6. "Deadweight loss" is a measure of the inefficiencies in a market system created by taxation, that is, the loss of consumer and producer surplus implied by the "wedge" that taxes impose between the prices that buyers pay and the revenue that sellers receive, in either product or labour markets. Theoretically, deadweight loss increases strongly as the tax rate rises, but there are substantial disagreements about how large it is in practice.

7. In a representative agent model, there is also no reason for the public debt to be issued in the first place. In Dahlby's model, it is just assumed that the economy starts with a government debt.

8. As the Bolder and Lee-Sing paper argues, in financial markets "market participants generally view a liquid and active government securities market as the essential foundation of an efficient domestic debt market." Hence, they argue that "debt-management practice provides a public good to the Canadian public." Of course, this argument that efficient financial markets depend on the sufficiently large availability of a risk-free debt instrument in a variety of terms is only an argument for a positive *gross* level of public debt. The *net* level of debt could be zero (or even negative) if government owned a sufficiently large stock of assets to offset its gross debt. Government ownership of the capital stock has not been much in fashion recently, indeed the trend to privatization runs the other way.

9. Hence, Bev Dahlby's model is asking the intergenerational question in the right way, by looking at the impact of higher debt/income ratios (D/Y) on the time path of aggregate income (e.g., because increased debt-to-GDP will reduce capital accumulation or distort labour supply). In the real world, management of the debt incurs a real resource cost, which should be added to the future deadweight loss of debt financing. Surprisingly, nobody mentioned the administrative costs of debt management at this conference.

10. If we are thinking in terms of the lifetime well-being of the individuals who belong to the same birth cohort, then one would have to count both the bonds they now hold and the present value of any bonds they might expect to acquire later by inheritance.

11. Public spending on physical capital, such as roads, is captured as investment in the national balance sheet but arguably most public spending, especially on education and health, assists in the production of human capital, which is individually owned and not counted as investment in the System of National Accounts. Whether or not government spending actually crowds out private investment clearly depends on whether the economy is presumed to be closed or open to capital imports at the going international rate of interest and whether it is at or below full employment.

12. This implies that the failure of capital markets to supply the option of annuities is truly colossal and that the elderly who die leaving the multi-million dollar estates that in fact comprise much of the capital stock must have had highly exaggerated ideas of their potential life span, and/or future spending. As well, it implies that inheritance taxation, even at a confiscatory rate, would have no impact on savings or labour supply behaviour, since all bequests are assumed to be unintentional.

13. Kneebone and Chung estimate the relative role of structural and cyclical expenditures on debt accumulation, but their Hodrick-Prescott filter methodology for estimating potential output is basically a moving average of actual output (in this case, with an unusual and arbitrary "smoothing constant"), which essentially assumes that the makers of macro policy can make no lasting errors. There is actually a lot of uncertainty about the level of "potential output" (even the Bank of Canada now presents the confidence bands surrounding its point estimates of potential output), so one needs to beware of "false precision." However, the more fundamental objection is that Kneebone and Chung are engaged in an accounting exercise, which ignores the impacts of interest rates on GDP growth, and the consequent impact of growth on tax revenues and program expenditures. For a simulation of the time path of the debt-to-GDP ratio which does take into account the general equilibrium effects of monetary policy in the 1988–93 period, see McCracken (1998), who concludes that the monetary policy regime change of 1988 was responsible for essentially all of the debt accumulation of the early 1990s.

14. In 1965–66, it was 13.7 percent of GDP.

15. All figures from Osberg (2001) updated from Canada (2003, ch. 8).

16. See Osberg (2001) for a detailed discussion and *www.ekos.com* for more recent updates.

Bibliography

Boadway, R., and F. Flatters. 1994. "Is the System in Crisis?" In *Future of Fiscal Federalism*, ed. K.G. Banting, D.H. Brown and T. Courchene. Kingston: School of Policy Studies, Institute of Intergovernmental Relations and John Deutsch Institute for the Study of Economic Policy, Queen's University, pp. 25-74.

Canada. Department of Finance Canada. 2003. *The Budget Plan 2003*. Ottawa: Department of Finance.

Helliwell, J., ed. 2001. *The Contribution of Human and Social Capital to Sustained Economic Growth and Well-Being*, International Symposium Report. Paris and Ottawa: Organisation for Economic Co-operation and Development and Human Resource Development Canada.

Kotlikoff, J., and L. Summers. 1981. "The Role of Intergenerational Transfers in Aggregate Capital Accumulation." *Journal of Political Economy* 89, no. 4:706-32.

McCracken, M. 1998. "Recent Canadian Monetary Policy: Deficit and Debt Implications." In *Hard Money, Hard Times*, ed. L. Osberg and P. Fortin. Toronto: James Lorimer Publishers, pp. 74-114.

Osberg, L. 2001. "Federal Expenditures in Canada: The Millennial Vision and its Tensions." In *The 2000 Federal Budget: Retrospect and Prospect*, ed. P. Hobson and T. Wilson. Kingston: John Deutsch Institute for the Study of Economics Policy, Queen's University.

———. 2003. "Long-Run Trends in Income Inequality in the USA, UK, Sweden, Germany and Canada - A Birth Cohort View." *Eastern Economic Journal* 29, no. 1:121-42.

Osberg, L., and P. Fortin, eds. 1998. *Hard Money, Hard Times*. Toronto: James Lorimer Publishers.

afterword

is the debt war over?
what have we learned?

Jack M. Mintz

In my review of these excellent papers, I want to go back to the original question before us: Is the debt war over? For reasons I will detail below, I believe we have not answered this question adequately. My own view is that, given the potential burden of taxes that could be imposed on the next generation of the working population by the demographic challenge posed by the retirement of the baby-boom cohort, the debt war is in fact far from over. I might be wrong. Unfortunately, no paper presented at this conference has addressed this problem in a serious way.

Should We Care about Public Debt?

One of the issues raised in several papers is whether we should care about public debt at all. One argument, based on so-called *Ricardian equivalence*, suggests that public debt does not affect the economy. If the government borrows today, it defers taxes owed by the existing population into the future. People anticipate these additional taxes in the future and therefore increase their own private savings to meet these future obligations. As a result, national savings, the sum of private and public savings, is unaffected by a buildup of public debt. Because total savings remain the same there is no change in the capital markets.

This view has always seemed extreme to me. People do not live forever. It is clear that they would view future taxes as burdens imposed on them. But if they don't, they will not increase their private savings fully in response to changes in public balances. The existing population might care about those of their heirs who will bear the burden, but, as suggested by Bernheim and Bagwell (1988), it is hard to believe that people would be altruistic about the tax obligations left to *all* members of the future generation. *A priori* reasoning aside, whether private savings respond dollar-for-dollar to every increase in public deficits can be resolved empirically. Adjusting for inflation, accrued capital gains, foreign borrowing and other factors influencing our measure of private savings rates, the evidence in favour of Ricardian equivalence is weak (see Bernheim 1989 and David Johnson's paper in this volume). Debt therefore does matter, and it could well reduce economic growth, as both Bev Dahlby and Bill Scarth argue in their papers.

Is There an Optimal Level of Public Debt?

If public debt does matter, then how much debt should governments issue? This is not an easy question for an economist to answer. In first-year economics courses, we teach students that people like to trade off current for future consumption, depending on the interest rate they face. When people borrow, they are able to consume more today, but at the sacrifice of reducing their consumption in the future since they have to pay back their debt obligations. The decision as to how much a person saves or borrows depends both on their current and future resources and on their preferences.

From society's perspective, the question is even more complex. When governments borrow to spend on existing public programs, they create burdens for future populations that have no ability to influence voting decisions made today. Unless current voters care sufficiently about the future, they may borrow too much and put an unfair burden on subsequent generations of taxpayers.

On the other hand, if current taxpayers are short-sighted about the costs of future taxes, they may also be short-sighted about the benefits of public investments made today that will bear fruit many years from now. As suggested in the early cost-benefit literature, debt-finance of public capital expenditures is appropriate if governments use a "social discount rate" for public investment that is less than the market interest rate (see Atkinson and Stiglitz 1980). If the social discount rate is zero, so that future generational consumption is weighted equally with current generational consumption, as some have argued it should be, then governments should be making substantial investments in public capital for future benefits. Public debt would be a perfectly reasonable way of financing such investments: if future generations receive at least part of the benefits, they can be asked to pay at least part of the costs.

There is no easy answer to the question: Is there an optimal amount of public debt? If today's citizens do not care about future burdens, the governments they elect will not care either and will borrow too much. On the other hand, if today's citizens are very altruistic, to the point even of caring about their heirs as much as they care about themselves, then government borrowing to finance public capital expenditures will be optimal. However, this second possibility depends on the same assumptions about thorough-going altruism that are needed to make Ricardian equivalence work, and such assumptions have generally been dismissed. It is therefore reasonable to conclude that democratically elected governments will have a tendency to borrow too much relative to what would be appropriate at an optimal "social" discount rate.

Debt and Government Expenditure

An important debate at the conference, as illustrated by the discussion of Bev Dahbly's paper, is whether public debt mainly funds current or future consumption. Proponents of public debt suggest that governments should fund assets that provide long-term benefits to society. Opponents of public debt argue that the economic costs of deferred taxation outweigh any benefits from debt finance. On this score, my view is that this conference, like others before it, failed to provide any helpful guidance for policy makers.

Theoretically, our tolerance for debt is greater if we believe governments are spending on public capital that yields returns greater than the market rate of interest (with the market rate evaluated at the pre-tax rate of return to capital if debt crowds out investments by businesses or the post-tax rate of return to capital if debt is drawn from personal savings). If the returns from public investments are not greater than those available in the private sector, then the money should be left in the private sector. There is a net loss to society from using it in the public sector.

While in our theoretical work economists understand these results and make policy conclusions based on them, empirically we have little to say. We do not know very much about what aspects of public expenditure are truly investments rather than consumption. Nor do we know, except in limited cases, the actual rates of return on government investments, so we have no way of comparing them to the returns on private-sector alternatives.

Two clear examples of government expenditure on "capital"-like activities that have a long life are spending on education and on physical infrastructure such as transportation and communication networks. The rate of return on infrastructure investments is sometimes quite high (as in the case of highways connecting major centres) but it may also be very low or even negative (as in the case of the Swan Hills treatment centre for toxic waste in Alberta) (Mintz 1995). Vaillancourt and Bordeau-Primeau (2002) have computed rates of return to education, and find that they are high for certain programs but low for others, even in some cases below market interest rates. Thus, some public capital expenditures, but by no means all, probably should be financed with debt.

Other public expenditures, on health care, for instance, provide what clearly are consumption services. The relief of pain and suffering is obviously important, but its benefit is immediate and not necessarily very long-lasting. Because many health-care expenditures help people who are already retired there may be no big payback in terms of future productivity (Mintz 2001). Other expenditures, such as income security, mainly provide current consumption for their beneficiaries although in some cases they may encourage greater labour force participation over time.

All this suggests that economists are simply unable to say whether the rate of return to government spending justifies as large a national debt as we now have. Hypothesizing is fine, but it would be far better if we had some real empirical estimates on which to base firmer conclusions. The literature on economic growth and government (Tanzi and Schuknecht 2000; Scully 1996; Branson and Knox Lovell 2001) suggests that the growth-maximizing size of government is no more than 30 percent of GDP. Beyond that level, governments arguably become inefficient, largely transferring income from one hand to the other and incurring economic costs in doing so without changing the distribution of income. At the moment, Canadian governments account for more than 30 percent of the economy, so as a general matter the long-run impact of public expenditure may not justify Canada's current indebtedness of almost $1.2 trillion (Robson 2001).

Foreign Indebtedness

If this conference had been held ten years ago, its focus would have been on foreign indebtedness. At that time, government borrowing had resulted in a substantial increase in both public and private net foreign debt, which together had reached 43 percent of gross domestic product (GDP) (see David Johnson's paper), one of the highest levels among industrialized countries. In contrast, Belgium and Italy, despite high government debt burdens, had much lower foreign indebtedness because of their high private savings rates. Foreign indebtedness raises the cost of capital for both governments and the private sector. Ten years ago interest rates were much higher in Canada than in the United States and the difference could not be explained by differences in inflation rates.

As David Johnson shows, however, Canada's foreign indebtedness has fallen sharply and is now at a low level. Foreign indebtedness is therefore of less concern today in determining the appropriate level of national public debt.

The Missing Paper: Demographics and Intergenerational Impacts

While this conference contains several excellent papers, I did not feel that any of them addressed the key concern today. Given the aging of Canada's population and its low fertility, will our existing level of national debt be a problem in the future? I believe this question is crucial in any analysis of debt today.

Several papers, including Robin Boadway's, did refer to the importance of debt in determining the gains and losses incurred by generations. Today's national debt benefits the current population to the extent that it finances consumption rather than investment. Future generations are benefited to the extent that public debt funds investments that bring high returns. However, the full burden of debt is imposed on future generations through higher taxes. If the current generation faces substantial risks or is poorer than future generations are likely to be, it can be argued on both efficiency and equity grounds that debt is an appropriate means of finance: future generations will be better able to absorb a higher tax burden than today's generation.

On the other hand, if generations are equally weighted in terms of their potential wealth, tax rates should be "smoothed" over time and across different generations. If today's generation faces very high levels of tax (because of a war, say), then it would be appropriate to use debt-finance to bring down current tax levels and raise them in the future, when they are more easily borne. From the point of view of efficiency, the economic cost of taxation increases exponentially with the tax rate. Spikes in tax rates therefore cause disproportionate efficiency losses, while evening-out taxes over time provides economic gains across generations. From the point of view of equity, keeping tax rates roughly similar across generations is appropriate if their real incomes are expected to be roughly similar. On the other hand, if one generation is expected to be richer than the other, then it could reasonably be made to face higher tax rates.

The sharp rise in national debt after the Great Depression and the Second World War seemed appropriate at that time since the working generation could not have afforded to fund public expenditures without facing crushingly high tax rates. The buildup of Canada's debt since 1975 is less excusable. No war or special shocks can explain why Canada's indebtedness increased so much, especially compared to that of other nations. The high levels of taxation that we face today – government revenues are running at about 42 percent of GDP – represent substantial payments by the current working generation for past fiscal errors. As Kneebone and Chung show in this volume, almost four-fifths of the buildup of debt at the federal and provincial levels is due to a structural mismatch between revenues and expenditures, cyclical and interest-rate spikes explain the small remainder of the debt buildup. Governments have simply overextended themselves.

The important question now is how today's tax levels might compare to those in the future. I was surprised that most of the papers either provided no empirical assessment or assumed tax rates would be constant across generations. Yet, in view of the demographic changes Canada now faces, it would be quite incorrect to assume that tax rates will remain constant over the next 40 years. Only Bill Robson's paper hinted at this problem with his analysis of how demographics impact Canada's total indebtedness.

The aging of Canada's population, a trend that is occurring in other industrialized nations, will have several impacts on public fiscal balances (see OECD 2001, and for health-care estimates, Robson 2001). According to the OECD, increases in pensions and public health-care costs and declines in tax revenues as increasing numbers of people retire will lead to a deterioration of Canada's fiscal position of fully 8 percent of GDP, even after netting out any savings from lower education and child-benefit costs due to low fertility.[1] Although Canadian governments are running positive balances at the moment, thus reducing both their debts and their future interest costs, the tendency to ramp up expenditures or to provide further tax cuts is leading many of them toward balanced budgets, not surpluses. If that continues to happen, an eight-point deterioration in the future fiscal position could cause Canada's revenue-GDP ratio to rise above 50 percent.

Calculations such as these depend crucially on how much incomes rise over time. In fact, over time businesses may not retire people as quickly although, with rising incomes, people might prefer greater leisure. Health-care costs may not rise as much if people are generally healthier, although if people live longer as a result, elderly benefits will become more costly. Clearly, the role of economists is to try to make sure we understand these issues better.

A reduction in the public debt over the next 15 years could help forestall some of these demographic impacts. For example, if public debt falls from the existing level of about 75 percent of GDP to 25 percent, public debt charges could decline by about five percentage points of GDP. With a reduction in debt, governments would be able to save interest expenses. Instead of using these savings to ramp up program expenditures, governments could afford further tax cuts. Tax levels could then be reduced by a similar amount to reductions in public debt charges, thereby smoothing out tax rates over time.

Given the demographic challenges facing us, this conference needed a paper that evaluated the potential tax burdens on future generations and compared them to what we pay today. Such a comparison would have helped us decide whether we need to reduce debt today in order to get a smoother level of taxes over time. It is not enough to discuss these issues theoretically. Real numbers are needed if we are, first, to understand current and future tax burdens and then to act on our understanding. On balance, given recent analyses of demographic effects provided by the OECD and others, I believe the debt war is far from over.

Note

1. The OECD estimates might be too high since they project that elderly benefits will rise with wages rather than inflation, which is the current Canadian policy. Further work is needed in refining the estimates developed so far by the OECD. Some work which has been done in this area has been piecemeal, only looking at one or two expenditure functions and tax revenues to assess demographic impacts. To do the job right, the whole government sector must be considered, which was the approach used by the OECD.

Bibliography

Atkinson, A.B., and J.E. Stiglitz. 1980. *Lectures in Public Economics*. London: MacMillan Press.

Bernheim, B.D. 1989. "A Neoclassical Perspective on Budget Deficits." *Journal of Economic Perspectives* 3:55-72.

Bernheim, B.D., and K. Bagwell. 1988. "Is Everything Neutral?" *Journal of Political Economy* 96:303-38.

Branson, J., and C.A. Knox Lovell. 2001. "A Growth Maximizing Tax Structure for New Zealand." *International Tax and Public Finance* 8, no. 2:129-46.

Mintz, J. 1995. "An Evaluation of the Joint Venture Agreement Establishing the Alberta Waste Management System." Toronto: University of Toronto. Unpublished manuscript.

———. 2001. *Most Favored Nation*. Toronto: C. D. Howe Institute.

Organisation for Economic Co-operation and Development (OECD). 2001. "Fiscal Implications of Ageing: Projections of Age-Related Spending." *OECD Economic Outlook* 69:145-67.

Robson, W. 2001. *Will the Baby Boomers Bust the Health Budget? Demographic Change and Health Care Financing Reform*. Commentary no. 148. Toronto: C. D. Howe Institute.

Scully, G.W. 1996. "Taxation and Economic Growth in New Zealand." Working Paper no. 14 (revised). In *Working Papers on Monitoring the Health of the Tax System*. Wellington, NZ: Inland Revenue.

Tanzi, V., and L. Schuknecht. 2000. *Public Spending in the 20th Century: A Global Perspective*. Cambridge: Cambridge University Press.

Vaillancourt, F., and S. Bordeau-Primeau. 2002. "The Returns to University Education in Canada, 1990 and 1995." In *Renovating the Ivory Tower: Canadian Universities and the Knowledge Economy*, ed. D. Laidler. Toronto: C. D. Howe Institute.

notes on contributors

Steve Ambler is a professor of economics at UQAM and the associate editor of *Canadian Public Policy*. Professor Ambler recently merited the Jean Monnet Fellowship at the European University Institute and is a former president of the Société canadienne de science économique. Among his many published works, he is the co-author of the forthcoming article in the *European Economic Review*, "International Transmission of the Business Cycle in a Multi-Sectoral Model."

Robin Boadway is the Sir Edward Peacock Professor of Economic Theory at Queen's University. He is co-editor of the *Journal of Public Economics* and the *German Economic Review*, and the editorial advisor for the *Canadian Tax Journal*. He serves on the executive of the International Seminar on Public Economics and the management board of the International Institute of Public Finance. His work is in the broad area of public sector economics, with special emphasis on tax-transfer policy, fiscal federalism and cost-benefit analysis.

When this paper was written, **David Bolder** was a principal researcher in the Financial Markets Department of the Bank of Canada. He is currently a Senior Financial Officer in the Treasury Department of the World Bank in Washington, DC. His responsibilities involve quantitative support of the World Bank's borrowing and asset-liability management activities. In 2001, he spent a six-month internship in the Risk Control Department of the European Bank for Reconstruction and Development (EBRD) in London, England. He holds a master's degree in mathematics from the University of Waterloo and an MBA from the University of British Columbia.

Paul Boothe is a professor of economics at the University of Alberta. He recently completed a two-year secondment as the deputy minister of finance and secretary to Treasury Board for the province of Saskatchewan. His current research interests include fiscal relations between governments and government budgeting and performance measurement. Professor Boothe is a fellow of the Institute for Public Economics and the C. D. Howe Institute.

Jennifer Chung is an economist who is currently working at the federal Department of Finance in the Federal-Provincial Relations Division. Her contribution to the volume was written while she was a graduate student at the University of Calgary.

Serge Coulombe is a full professor in the economics department at the University of Ottawa. He has also served as a special research advisor in the economic studies group of the federal Finance Department. He is known for a series of papers on Canadian regional growth, convergence and fiscal federalism, published in *Regional Studies*, the *Canadian Journal of Economics*, *Canadian Public Policy*, the *Canadian Journal of Regional Science*, the *Canadian Tax Journal* and the *Journal of Economic Studies*. Professor Coulombe is currently working on issues related to North-American economic integration and economic growth.

Bev Dahlby has been a professor in the Department of Economics at the University of Alberta since 1978. He has published extensively on tax policy, fiscal federalism and the economics of insurance. Professor Dahlby was a member of the Technical Committee on Business Taxation, which issued its report on reforming business taxation in April 1998. He has served as a policy advisor to the Alberta government, worked on tax reform projects at the Thailand Development Research Institute in Bangkok, and served as a technical advisor on an International Monetary Fund mission to Malawi. In August 2002, he was an Abe Greenbaum Visiting Fellow at the Australian Taxation Studies Program, University of New South Wales, in Sydney, Australia.

Don Drummond is senior vice-president and chief economist for the TD Bank Financial Group. During almost 23 years in the federal Department of Finance, Mr. Drummond held a series of progressively more senior positions in the areas of economic analysis and forecasting, fiscal policy and tax policy. As associate deputy minister, Mr. Drummond was responsible for economic analysis, fiscal policy, tax policy, social policy and federal-provincial relations. In particular, he coordinated the planning of the annual federal budgets. He now leads TD Economics' work in analyzing and forecasting economic performance in Canada and abroad.

David Johnson is a professor of economics at Wilfrid Laurier University. His areas of specialty are macroeconomics and international finance. His current work is in the field of educational evaluation, and includes studies of Canada's international debts, the influence of American interest rates on Canadian interest rates, and the determination of the Canada-US exchange rate. He has also written extensively on monetary policy in Canada and around the world, both on the goal of lower inflation and on the role of inflation targets. He is co-author of *Macroeconomics*, Second Canadian Edition (2002). Professor Johnson worked for two years at the Bank of Canada and one year at the National Bureau of Economic Research.

Ronald Kneebone is a professor of economics at the University of Calgary. His research interests lie mainly in the areas of macroeconomic aspects of public finances and fiscal federalism. He has published work on the problems of government budget financing with more than one level of government, on the history of government fiscal and monetary relations in Canada and on the characteristics of Canadian fiscal policy choices. He is co-author of *Principles of Economics*, with Gregory Mankiw, Ken McKenzie and Nick Rowe. In 1999, he and Ken McKenzie were awarded the Doug Purvis Memorial Prize for the best published work in public policy in Canada.

Clifton Lee-Sing is a financial economist in the domestic debt-management section within the federal Department of Finance. Mr. Lee-Sing works on the formulation of the federal government's debt strategy, provides policy advice on the structure of the debt and is involved with the pricing of government retail debt instruments.

Tiff Macklem is chief of the research department of the Bank of Canada. To support the formulation of monetary policy, he keeps the Bank fully informed about the significance of current economic developments and prospects in Canada. An aspect of his responsibility is to seek further understanding of the operation of the economy and the effects of monetary and fiscal policies. In 1984 he joined the Bank in the Department of Monetary and Financial Analysis, but left the next year to pursue a PhD in economics at the University of Western Ontario. He returned to the Bank and in 1993 was appointed assistant chief of the research department. He is currently on secondment to the Department of Finance Canada as the general director in the Financial Sector Policy Branch.

Jack M. Mintz is president and CEO of the C. D. Howe Institute. He is professor of taxation at the Joseph L. Rotman School of Management and co-director of the international tax program at the Institute of International Business, both at the University of Toronto. Dr. Mintz has published extensively in the fields of public economics and fiscal federalism. He serves on the board of governors of the National Tax Association in Washington, DC and is a research fellow of CESifo, Munich, Germany. He is the author of *Most Favored Nation: A Framework for Smart Economic Policy*, winner of the 2002 Purvis Prize for best book in economic policy.

Lars Osberg is McCulloch Professor of Economics at Dalhousie University. He received his PhD in economics from Yale University in 1975 and taught at the University of Western Ontario from 1974 to 1977 before moving to Dalhousie University. He has published numerous articles in academic journals and seven books, including *Unnecessary Debts*, co-edited with Pierre Fortin. In 1999-2000, he served as president of the Canadian Economics Association.

Christopher Ragan is an associate professor in the Department of Economics and an associate dean in the Faculty of Arts at McGill University. He has been teaching at McGill since 1989, when he completed his PhD in economics at MIT. He is the co-author with Richard Lipsey of a widely used introductory textbook, *Economics*, the latest edition of which is published in March, 2004. He also has many research papers on various matters of economic policy, including "Would Fixed Rates Make Markets More Flexible?" *Policy Options* (May 2001) and "Should We Expect Higher Growth From Lower Inflation?" *Canadian Business Economics* (August 2000). Professor Ragan's interests include inflation, monetary policy, exchange rates, and other aspects of macroeconomics and macroeconomic policy.

William B. P. Robson specializes in Canadian fiscal and monetary policy. He has an MA from the Norman Paterson School of International Affairs at Carleton University and has written extensively on government budgets, pension and health-care financing and on inflation and currency issues. His 1994 book, *The Great Canadian Disinflation* (co-authored with David Laidler) won the Canadian Economics Association's Doug Purvis Memorial Prize for excellence in writing on Canadian economic policy, and his 2001 commentary, *Will the Baby Boomers Bust the Health Budget? Demographic Changes and Health-Care*

Financing Reform, won the Policy Research Secretariat's Outstanding Research Contribution Award.

Jeremy Rudin is currently the general director of the economic and fiscal policy branch at Finance Canada. He joined the department in 1993, after teaching economics at the University of British Columbia and at Queen's University. While at UBC, he co-wrote (with Robert Hall and John Taylor) the textbook *Macroeconomics: The Canadian Economy.*

William Scarth is a professor of economics at McMaster University, where he has been awarded the President's Award for Best Teacher and the McMaster Student Union Lifetime Teaching Award. In addition to publishing many articles in academic journals in the areas of macroeconomics, labour economics, international trade and public finance, Professor Scarth has authored four textbooks. He has been active in Canadian policy debates as a research fellow at the C. D. Howe Institute since 1994. Professor Scarth's recent work looks at how globalization affects the scope for independent economic policy in small, open economies.

Huntley Schaller is a professor of economics at Carleton University. His research has focused primarily on macroeconomics and financial markets and has been published in a variety of academic journals, including the *American Economic Review,* the *Journal of Monetary Economics* and the *Canadian Journal of Economics.* He has presented papers at the World Congress of the Econometric Society and the American Economic Association, at Princeton, Columbia and H.E.C. (Paris and Montreal), and to the Board of Governors of the Federal Reserve System and the Bank of Canada. He is currently teaching at MIT.

François Vaillancourt holds a PhD from Queen's University and is a professor of economics and a research fellow at the Centre de recherche et développement en économique (CRDE) at the University of Montreal. He is also a fellow at the C. D. Howe Institute. He teaches, conducts research and has published extensively in the areas of public finance and the economics of language. He has conducted research and acted as a consultant for organizations such as the Canadian Tax Foundation, the Conseil de la langue française, the Department of Finance, the Economic Council of Canada, Statistics Canada and the World Bank.

Marc Van Audenrode is a full professor in the Department of Economics at Laval University in Quebec City and has served as head of the department since 1998. His research concerns the role of economic politics and institutions on the labour market. He has been involved in assessing labour market policies, such as the reform of employment insurance and social assistance. His assessments of the law on employment insurance have been accorded widespread recognition, and several of his publications are now regarded as major contributions to the field. His work with Pierre Fortin significantly influenced the recent reform of Canada's employment insurance scheme.

William Watson was born and raised in Montreal and educated at McGill and Yale. He has taught economics at McGill since 1977. From 1998–2002 he edited *Policy Options politiques*, the magazine of the IRPP, where he is currently a senior research fellow. He is also a research fellow at the C. D. Howe Institute in Toronto. Before that, while on a leave from McGill in 1997–98, he served for 21 months as editorial pages editor of the *Ottawa Citizen*.

MEMBER OF SCABRINI MEDIA

Quebec, Canada
2004